INTELLIGENCE
IN DEMOCRATIC TRANSITIONS

A COMPARATIVE ANALYSIS OF
PORTUGAL, GREECE, AND SPAIN

GEORGETOWN UNIVERSITY PRESS / WASHINGTON, DC

The publisher is not responsible for third-party websites or their content. URL links were active at time of publication.

Library of Congress Cataloging-in-Publication Data

Names: Tzamarelou, Sofia, author.
Title: Intelligence in democratic transitions : a comparative analysis of Portugal, Greece, and Spain / Sofia Tzamarelou.
Identifiers: LCCN 2023035490 (print) | LCCN 2023035491 (ebook) | ISBN 9781647124472 (hardcover) | ISBN 9781647124489 (paperback) | ISBN 9781647124496 (ebook)
Subjects: LCSH: Intelligence service—Portugal. | Intelligence service—Greece. | Intelligence service—Spain. | Democratization—Portugal. | Democratization—Greece. | Democratization—Spain. | Civil society—Portugal. | Civil society—Greece. | Civil society—Spain.
Classification: LCC JN8520.I57 T93 2024 (print) | LCC JN8520.I57 (ebook) | DDC 327.1246—dc23/eng/20230812
LC record available at https://lccn.loc.gov/2023035490
LC ebook record available at https://lccn.loc.gov/2023035491

∞ This paper meets the requirements of ANSI/NISO Z39.48-1992 (Permanence of Paper).

25 24   9 8 7 6 5 4 3 2 First printing

Printed in the United States of America

Cover design by James Keller
Interior design by BookComp, Inc.

CONTENTS

TABLES

PREFACE

The idea leading to this book started about a decade ago when I was doing my master's in intelligence studies in the United Kingdom. As a student, I realized quickly that emphasis is put on intelligence matters in the UK, United States, and Soviet Union both from a history and an intelligence perspective. Having a Greek background and having been exposed to history studies outside the UK, I wanted to offer a different angle that could contribute to the intelligence debate outside the Anglosphere. With intelligence-related events taking place throughout the past twenty-plus years, including 9/11, the war in Iraq, and the Edward Snowden revelations, intelligence reform has become a key component in political agendas throughout the world, and questions about intelligence democratization have become more prominent. At the top of the list of works on intelligence remain those related to the UK, the US, and the post-Soviet states, while the majority of the available analyses focus on isolated case studies.

This book is an effort to break the mold and focus on three understudied postauthoritarian case studies outside the Anglosphere and under the umbrella of intelligence democratization by way of a consistent comparative approach. As intelligence democratization is a process and not an end destination, the effort lies in measuring how close each state has come to intelligence democratization through specific security sector reform indicators and see if we could use them to measure other cases. It is the hope of this author that this book will contribute to the (academic) debate on intelligence democratization and stimulate students, practitioners, and other authors to expand their analyses to more underresearched cases, in the way that I was inspired by key figures in the academic intelligence world, including Peter Gill and my professors Philip H. J. Davies and Kristian Gustafson.

ACKNOWLEDGMENTS

To my professors Philip H. J. Davies and Kristian Gustafson for their thoughtful guidance and immeasurable patience and support in bringing this project to fruition.

ABBREVIATIONS

ADAE	Authority for Ensuring the Confidentiality of Communications
AOME	Agrupación Operativa de Misiones Especiales (Special Operations Group)
ASAE	Autoridade de Segurança Alimentar e Económica (Economic and Food Safety Authority)
ASALA	Armenian Secret Army for the Liberation of Armenia
BPS	Brigada Político-Social (Political-Social Brigade)
BE	Batallón Vasco Español (Basque Spanish Battalion)
CEMPL	Comissão de Extinção da PIDE-DGS, MP e LP (Commission for the Abolition of the Political Police, Portuguese Legion and Portuguese Youth)
CESIBE	Central-Servicio de Información Bis del Ejército (Central Information Service of the Army)
CESID	Centro Superior de Información de la Defensa (Superior Center for Defense Information)
CFSIRP	Conselho de Fiscalização do SIRP (Supervisory Board of the Information System of the Portuguese Republic)
CNI	Centro Nacional de Inteligencia (National Intelligence Center)
CSE	State Security Corps
DEDIDE	Departamento Especial de Información del Estado (Special Information Department of the State)
Dev Sol	Devrimci Sol (Revolutionary Left)
DGS	Direcção-Geral de Segurança (Directorate-General of Security)
DIKA	Διεύθυνση Κρατικής Ασφάλειας / Diéfthynsi Kkratikís Aasfáleias (Directorate of State Security)
DINFO	Military Intelligence Service in Portugal Divisão de Informações (Division of Intelligence)
DSE	Dimokratikós Stratós Elládas (Democratic Army of Greece)
EAN	Ellinikí Anti-Diktatorikí Neolaía (Greek Anti-Dictatorial Youth)
ELA	Epanastatikos Laikos Agonas (Revolutionary People's Struggle)

ELAS	Ellinikós Laïkos Apeleftherotikos Stratos (Greek People's Liberation Army)
11M	Madrid train bombings of May 2004
ELP	Exército de Libertação de Portugal (Liberation Army of Portugal)
ESA	Ellinikí Stratiotikí Astynomía (Hellenic Military Police)
ETA	Euskadi ta Askatasuna (Basque Homeland and Liberty)
EYP	Ethnikι Ypiresιa Pliroforion (National Intelligence Service)
FP-25	Forças Populares 25 de Abril (Popular Forces 25 April)
FSB	Federal Security Service of the Russian Federation
GAL	Grupos Antiterroristas de Liberación (Antiterrorist Liberation Groups)
GEETHA	Geniko Epiteleio Ethinkis Aminas (Hellenic National Defense General Staff)
GNR	Guarda Nacional Republicana (National Republican Guard)
GOE	Grupo de Operações Especiais (Special Operations Group)
IPCO	Investigatory Powers Commissioner's Office
KKE	Κομμουνιστικό Κόμμα Ελλάδας / Kommounistikó Kómma Elládas (Greek Communist Party)
KYP	Κεντρική Υπηρεσία Πληροφοριών / Kentrikí Ypiresía Pliroforión (Central Information Service)
KYPE	Κεντρική Υπηρεσία Πληροφοριών και Ερευνών / Kentrikí Ypiresía Pliroforión kai Erevnón (Central Information and Research Service)
MFA	Movimento das Forcas Armadas (Armed Forces Movement)
MPDJC	Movimento Pro-reintegracao dos Despedidos sem Justa Causa (Movement for the Reintegration of the Unfairly Dismissed)
OCN	Organización Contrasubversiva Nacional (National Countersubversive Organization)
ONS	Oficina Nacional de Seguridad (National Security Office)
PASOK	Panellínio Sosialistikó Kínima (Panhellenic Socialist Movement)
PCP	Portuguese Communist Party; Portuguese Criminal Police
PIC	Polícia de Investigação Criminal (Criminal Investigation Police)
PIDE	Polícia Internacional e de Defesa do Estado (International and State Defense Police)
PIM	Polícia de Informação Militar (Military Information Police)
PL	Legião Portuguesa (Portuguese Legion)
PNA	Portuguese National Archive
PRP-BR	Partido Revolucionário do Proletariado–Brigadas Revolucionárias (Revolutionary Party of the Proletariat–Revolutionary Brigades)
PSOE	Partido Socialista Obrero Españo (Spanish Socialist Workers Party)

PSP	Polícia de Segurança Pública (Public Security Police)
PVDE	Polícia de Vigilância e de Defesa do Estado (Surveillance and State Defense Police)
RIEAS	Research Institute for European and American Studies
SDCI	Serviço Director e Coordenador da Informação (Information Direction and Coordination Service)
SECED	Servicio Central de Documentación (Central Documentation Service)
SIAEM	Sección de Información del Alto Estado Mayor (Third Section of the Information Service of the Supreme High Command)
SIED	Serviço de Informações Estratégicas de Defesa (Strategic DefenceDefense Information Service)
SIEDM	Serviço de Informações Estratégicas de Defesa e Militares (Military and Defense Strategic Information Service)
SIFNE	Servicio de Informamción de la Frontera Noroeste de España (Information Service of the Northwest Frontier of Spain)
SIM	Servicio de Informamción de la Frontera Noroeste de España (Information Service of the Northwest Frontier of Spain)
SIM	Servicio de Investigación Militar (Military Information Service)
SIPM	Servicio de Información y Policía Militar (Military Police and Information Service)
SIRP	Sistema de Informações da República Portuguesa (Informations System of the Portuguese Republic)
SIS	Serviço de Informações de Segurança (Security Information Service)
SSI	Sistema de Segurança Interna (System of Internal Security)
SSR	Security Sector Reform
UCAT	Unidade de Coordenação Antiterrorismo (Counter-Terrorism Coordination Unit)
17N	Epanastatiki Organosi dekaefta Noemvri (Revolutionary Organization 17 November)
YAK	Ypiresía Amýnis Kérkyras (Corfu Defense Service)
YGAK	Ypiresía Genikís Asfaleías tou Kratous (National General Security Service)

OTHER

CIA	Central Intelligence Agency
EU	European Union
FBI	Federal Bureau of Investigation
IRA	Irish Republican Army

ISIS	Islamic State of Iraq and Syria
MI5	Military Intelligence, Section 5 / Security Service
MI6	Military Intelligence, Section 6 / Secret Intelligence Service
NATO	North Atlantic Treaty Organization
NGO	nongovernmental organization
OLAF	European Anti-Fraud Office
PIRA	Provisional Irish Republican Army
PKK	Partiya Karkerên Kurdistanê (Kurdistan Workers' Party)
PLO	Palestinian Liberation Organization
UN	United Nations

TIMELINE OF KEY DEVELOPMENTS

April 25, 1974	Portugal: Marcelo Caetano regime overthrown, and the DGS dissolved. Start of a period of "revolutionary transitional justice."
July 24, 1974	Greece: Collapse of the Greek military junta. Start of the period after the fall.
March 14, 1975	Portugal: The PIM is dissolved. The Portuguese Armed Forces take on all intelligence-related tasks.
July 28, 1975	Greece: Start of Greek junta trials.
November 20, 1975	Spain: Death of Gen. Francisco Franco.
July 1976	Spain: King Juan Carlos fires the Francoist prime minister, Carlos Arias Navarro, and replaces him with the democrat Adolfo Suárez.
July 14, 1977	Spain: The SECED and SIPG dissolved. CESID created, with a focus on defense matters.
October 15, 1977	Spain: Passing of Law 46/1977, the Spanish 1977 Amnesty Law, also known as "the pact of forgetting."
January 29, 1981	Spain: Failed coup attempt by members of the Guarda Civil and AOME under the command of Lt. Col. Antonio Tejero.
October 15, 1983	Spain: Secret creation of the GAL to fight the ETA.
September 5, 1984	Portugal: Legislation passed for the creation of SIRP, SIED, the SIM, and the SIS. Creation of an advisory technical commission and a supervisory independent oversight body.
1986	Portugal: The SIS becomes operational under the leadership of Dr. Ramiro Ladeiro Monteiro. Greece: The KYP is transformed into the EYP. Creation of advisory Intelligence Council.
1990	Portugal: PIDE and DGS archive transferred to the PNA.
May 5, 1997	Portugal: SIED merged with the SIM to create SIEDM, with Ambassador António Monteiro as director-general.

June 29, 2002	Greece: Capture of 17N.
May 6, 2002	Spain: Creation of the CNI. Judicial and parliamentary control extended over Spanish intelligence activities.
2004	Portugal: SIEDM becomes SIED. Spain: Madrid terrorist attacks occur, and reform follows.

Introduction

In an authoritarian regime, the country's intelligence services are among the principal instruments of repression. Establishing democratic control over intelligence services has become a key component of political reform for states that are transitioning from nondemocratic types of rule toward democratic forms of government. However, reforming the authoritarian agencies may be easier said than done. It does not happen automatically, and transitions may be incomplete.[1]

In countries transitioning to democracy, the need to deal with previously antidemocratic behavior on the part of state institutions pushes intelligence reform and democratization to the center of the political stage. In the 1970s three countries in Southern Europe moved from nondemocratic regimes to democratic ones within eighteen months of each other. These were Portugal, Greece, and Spain. This book will compare the varying levels of intelligence democratization in these three countries and make conclusions about what their histories can tell us about intelligence democratization more broadly.

When comparing the three intelligence services of the three case studies in question, it becomes evident that there is a stickiness to the authoritarian behaviors associated with the power of bureaucracies that impede progress and reform.[2] Intelligence organizations have access to information and are protected by secrecy, which enhances their power. If kept outside of proper control and oversight, they are incapable of changing themselves unless forced either by uprooting the old authority through an intensive "purging" process early on or through the experience of key events or "critical junctures" that can foster reform.[3] Portugal was faced with its own critical juncture—the Carnation Revolution in 1974, when Portuguese civil society played a fundamental role in regime change. Greece and Spain transitioned to democracy in a smoother way around that same time. In Greece the military junta resigned, while in Spain Franco's death ensured a smooth yet cosmetic transition. In the following chapters, we will see that critical junctures play a key role in reinforcing democratic transition. Key events that followed the fall of the dictatorship in each state, such as the 9/11 terrorist attacks in 2001 and the Madrid bombings in 2004, operated as critical junctures and facilitated (some) reform in Greece and Spain at that later point. One of the most interesting questions is, Why did the Portuguese, Greek, and Spanish intelligence services share different intelligence democratization outcomes when they all transitioned to democracy around the same time?

Indeed, we observe different levels and speeds of intelligence democratization across the three countries although they all transitioned to democracy around the same time. When comparing the three intelligence services of Portugal, Greece, and Spain, one notices that the three case studies present different levels of intelligence democratization, *mainly because of authoritarian legacies that acted as barriers to reform.* The Portuguese intelligence service emerges as the most democratized among the three because it uprooted authoritarian components early on through a process of lustration. It is important to note that although authoritarian legacies came up as the main reason that obstructed reform, there were others that contributed to progress (as well as acted as impediments). These included, among others, the role of civil society itself and the media as part of it, the willingness of policymakers to reform the intelligence services, and "critical junctures" that took place over the years. Indeed, the role of civil society in Portugal was fundamental as it did not only contribute to driving the Carnation Revolution but also facilitated and demanded the lustration process that followed the fall of the dictatorship.

As for source material, primary sources were used throughout the study, including governmental documents and legal statutes, such as draft laws, bills, and presidential decrees for each intelligence service in each country, along with "outside" primary source reporting, such as analysis reporting by the United States' Central Intelligence Agency (CIA). Primary source material was complemented by secondary source material from the limited number of established authors in each country who focus and specialize on intelligence as well as a wide range of historical accounts that provide context. Sources in English, Portuguese, Spanish, and Greek were examined.

Analyzing Portugal, Greece, and Spain is innovative as, save for the efforts of a select few authors, these case studies have often been overlooked in the intelligence literature.[4] On one hand, this is a testament to the nature of intelligence literature itself, which has typically been dominated by the research of Anglophone intelligence entities both before and after 9/11. External research, where it has been conducted, has often been focused on "target countries"—for example, on Soviet and post-Soviet intelligence systems rather than other, less high-profile states. As intelligence matters have become more prominent in the political and popular discourse, and intelligence studies itself has become a more respected pursuit, this has begun to change, with more and more studies focusing on the area of intelligence democratization.[5] However, analysis often revolves around events examined in isolation, rather than overall programs of reform. To that end, one of the objectives of this book is to fill the gap for some of the understudied countries within the intelligence democratization sphere, comparatively.

THE IMPORTANCE OF COMPARATIVE METHODS

Comparative politics is well established, but little systematic comparative work has been produced in intelligence studies despite the fact that comparative analysis is "one of the most powerful methodological tools available in the contemporary social science arsenal."[6] Indeed, if we were to examine a case in isolation, we would find ourselves in the pitfall of not being able to say with certainty whether that case is unique or not, nor would we be able to generalize hypotheses and outcomes—meaning that just because things are done a certain way in country A, it does not mean that the same happens in country B. In this way, comparative analysis provides a safety net from ethnocentrism.[7] Apart from operating as a protective tool, the comparative method can also serve the reader in a diagnostic capacity. Where quantitative set measures or variables that in sciences such as mathematics would be countable are absent or irrelevant, comparison can provide qualitative findings.[8] In brief, it has to do with looking at similar cases that present different outcomes and then asking what is driving them apart or looking at different cases with similar outcomes and trying to understand what brings them together.[9]

Comparative methods have both protective and diagnostic capacities.[10] Philip H. J. Davies and Kristian Gustafson back John Stuart Mill's argument that "taking two different cases with similar outcomes and seeking to understand what drives them together" is valuable.[11] As Glenn Hastedt notes, "the fundamental assumption of the comparative method is that true insight into the nature of political ideas, institutions, and processes is not possible if a subject is viewed in isolation from similar phenomena. Only by making comparisons one can come to appreciate what is a unique or a shared characteristic."[12] Comparative analysis, as opposed to studying a case in isolation, shows that supposed distinctive elements of the case study in question may not be unique at all.[13] The value of comparative methods also emerges when looking at the change of focus from predominant case studies, such as those of the United States and the United Kingdom, to intelligence organizations in other states, something that can prove that the intelligence system of a single country cannot be applied universally and helps overcome conventional wisdom. Comparative methods can establish cross cultural learning paradigms and are, indeed, an extremely powerful methodological tool.[14]

Another parameter that needs to be considered in order to understand the value of a comparative study of intelligence is change in the international system.

The emergence of a different, post–Cold War environment has raised questions about the importance and place of intelligence with regard to a country's foreign policy. The change or emergence of new threats has rendered intelligence reform a vital necessity for Western states. All three countries in this book's case studies applied different packages of reform within their intelligence services, especially after 9/11.[15] This is because critical junctures, such as 9/11, facilitated reforms that did not take place earlier. These critical junctures demonstrated that intelligence services should target different threats from the ones they had been focused on from the fall of their dictatorships until the events of 9/11 and the Madrid bombings.

Portugal, Greece, and Spain were picked for this book because they are all Southern European states. They are all relatively new democracies, as they all transitioned in the 1970s, and are currently all member states of the European Union (EU) and the North Atlantic Treaty Organization (NATO). The latter is a factor that is supposed to have helped them establish Western European intelligence standards.

INTELLIGENCE DEMOCRATIZATION IN PORTUGAL, GREECE, AND SPAIN

Before we dive into intelligence democratization across the three countries in question, it is important to give a brief definition of intelligence democratization.[16] Democratization is a process rather than an end destination and can be facilitated or impeded. Democratization is ultimately determined by "the complexity of reform itself; legacies of the authoritarian regime; resistance and reluctance to reform by intelligence services; lack of expertise by civilians; lack of support for intelligence culture among intelligence outsiders; corruption and organised crime . . . and the threat of overall democratic regress."[17] In the face of these challenges, "success" is said to only be made possible by "the willingness of political decision-makers to foster intelligence reform and achieve a balance between effectiveness and transparency; . . . foreign assistance; . . . increased cooperation and intelligence sharing; and the role of the civil society and media."[18] Timothy Edmunds views this as a three-step process, with standards and procedures for democratic civilian control and oversight coming first, followed by consolidation via laws and legal action, and last the development of a new intelligence culture that has removed any "systematic impurities."[19]

To be able to *measure* the levels of intelligence democratization for each case study, the author has utilized a chosen set of security sector reform (SSR) indicators that emerged organically in the available democratization, intelligence, and SSR literature. These will then be applied in a comparative way to be able to identify the variation in terms of intelligence democratization levels among the three countries. SSR has historically been criticized for its applicability to intelligence. However, we find that it can be utilized to measure levels of intelligence democratization. A definition is provided for each indicator in the following chapter. Key questions arise for the chosen indicators during and after the democratic transition:

- **Lustration:** Did each country go through a robust lustration process, and if so, when? What was the positive effect of lustration for each country?
- **Control and oversight:** Is there a legal basis for oversight? Is there sufficient control? Is there proper parliamentary oversight? Are there any other established forms and levels of (external) oversight, such as judiciary? Can we make observations about their applicability?
- **Recruitment:** Do the intelligence services hire based on merit and qualifications or on loyalty to the regime/government? If yes to the former, when did they start doing so? Are there uniformed personnel present within the civilian intelligence services?
- **Targeting:** Do the intelligence services target actual threats to national security (rather than threats to the regime), and, if yes, when did they start doing so? Do the intelligence services use any illegal methods to collect information? Is there a legal basis for oversight when it comes to targeting?
- **Civil society:** Are there civil society groups and a robust media presence that drive informal oversight? Are there established partnerships between universities and the intelligence services? Is there an open culture of intelligence? Is there a legal basis for informal oversight through, for instance, transparency laws?

The SSR indicators will be applied in a qualitative manner. This means that the analysis will not focus on the presence or absence of each of the indicators as the only way to measure levels of intelligence democratization but will also aim to examine those in a deep-dive way to make useful conclusions. For example, when looking at the SSR indicator civil society, it would not be enough to say that Portugal has an engaged civil society when it comes to intelligence matters and that Greece and Spain do not. We must investigate deeper questions, such as what does an "engaged" civil society mean? For instance, is there a robust media presence? Are there established partnerships between universities and the intelligence services? Using SSR indicators to measure intelligence democratization, paired with the comparative method, breaks new ground in our understanding of the levels of democratization in Portugal, Greece, and Spain and in showing how intelligence can be included within the wider SSR framework. This is the case even if further work is needed to reconcile the policy's overt push toward transparency when intelligence by nature and necessity remains an opaque area of activity.

Thinking about SSR as a framework, one wonders about the notions of democratization and intelligence democratization in particular. Since the nineteenth century, a wealth of literature has emerged discussing the definition of democracy and the process of democratization. Intelligence organizations have featured within such works on occasion, but focus has been put on these organizations as part of a state's institutions that act as hurdles to democratization. Taking it a step further, several authors have suggested that intelligence by nature is incompatible with democratic systems.[20] One of the most important points is that democratization is a *process* and not an end destination.[21] Therefore, it is not about reaching a complete status of intelligence democratization for each case study, if this were even at all possible. Rather, which case study has made more steps closer to intelligence democratization, and why?

For the first time, the author makes a comparative analysis on case studies outside the Anglosphere with regard to intelligence democratization. So far, any case studies have been examined in isolation without the use of SSR to systematically measure levels of intelligence democratization and while there is not a unified conceptual analysis across the discipline on these specific countries.

NOTES

1. Peter Gill and Lee Wilson, "Intelligence and Security Sector Reform in Indonesia," in *Intelligence Elsewhere: Spies and Espionage outside the Anglosphere*, ed. Philip H. J. Davies and Kristian Gustafson (Washington, DC: Georgetown University Press, 2013), 157.
2. Florina Cristiana Matei and Thomas Bruneau, "Intelligence Reform in New Democracies: Factors Supporting or Arresting Progress," *Democratization* 18, no. 3 (2011): 602–30.
3. Natalia Letki, "Lustration and Democratisation in East-Central Europe," *Europe-Asia Studies* 54, no. 4 (2002): 529–52. See also Eduardo E. Estévez, "Intelligence Community Reforms: The Case of Argentina," in Davies and Gustafson, *Intelligence Elsewhere*, and Peter Gill and Michael Andregg, eds., *Democratization of Intelligence* (Abingdon, UK: Routledge, 2017).
4. For efforts to shed light on intelligence culture in Portugal, see the work of Antonio Costa Pinto, including "The Legacy of the Authoritarian Past in Portugal's Democratisation, 1974–6," *Totalitarian Movements and Political Religions* 9, nos. 2–3 (2008): 265–91, and Antonio Costa Pinto, "Coping with the Double Legacy of Authoritarianism and Revolution in Portuguese Democracy," *South European Society and Politics* 15, no. 3 (2010): 395–412. For Greece, John Nomikos, including "Intelligence Studies in Greece: The Development of an Academic Discipline," *Journal of Mediterranean and Balkan Intelligence* 5, no. 1 (2015). For Spain, Antonio Díaz Fernández, including *Los servicios de intelligencia españoles: De la*

guerra civil hasta el 11-M [The Spanish intelligence services: From the civil war to 11-M] (Madrid: Alianzia Editorial, 2006).

5. Michael M. Andregg and Peter Gill, "Comparing the Democratization of Intelligence," *Intelligence and National Security* 29, no. 4 (2014): 487–97; Peter Gill, *Intelligence Governance and Democratisation: A Comparative Analysis of the Limits of Reform* (Abingdon, UK: Routledge, 2016); Matei and Bruneau, "Intelligence Reform in New Democracies," 602–30; Thomas C. Bruneau and Steven C. Boraz, *Reforming Intelligence: Obstacles to Democratic Control and Effectiveness* (Austin: University of Texas Press, 2011). See also F. C. Matei and C. Halladay, *The Conduct of Intelligence in Democracies: Processes, Practices, Cultures* (Boulder, CO: Lynne Reinner, 2019).

6. Angelo Codevilla, "Comparative Historical Experience of Doctrine and Organization," in *Intelligence Requirements for the 1980's: Analysis and Estimates*, ed. Roy Godson (Washington, DC: National Strategy Information Center, 1980), 11–36. See also, Kevin M. O'Connell, "Thinking about Intelligence Comparatively," *Brown Journal of World Affairs* 11, no. 1 (2004), and Davies and Gustafson, *Intelligence Elsewhere*.

7. Mattei Dogan and Dominique Pelassy, *How to Compare Nations: Strategies in Comparative Politics* (Chatham, NJ: Chatham House, 1984).

8. Davies and Gustafson, *Intelligence Elsewhere*, 5–6; Talcott Parsons, *The Structure of Social Action* (Glencoe, IL: Free Press, 1937).

9. Davies and Gustafson, *Intelligence Elsewhere*.

10. Davies and Gustafson, 4–6.

11. Davies and Gustafson, 5

12. Glenn Hastedt, "Towards the Comparative Study of Intelligence," *Conflict Quarterly* 55 (1991).

13. Davies and Gustafson, *Intelligence Elsewhere*, 4–6.

14. Roy Godson, ed., *Intelligence Requirements for the 1980's: Analysis and Estimates* (Washington, DC: National Strategy Information Center, 1980).

15. B. Guy Peters, *Comparative Politics: Theory and Methods* (London: Macmillan, 1998), chap. 2. See also Todd Landman and Edzia Carvalho, *Issues and Methods in Comparative Politics: An Introduction* (Abingdon, UK: Routledge, 2017), and Gary King, Robert O. Keohane, and Sidney Verba, *Designing Social Inquiry* (Princeton, NJ: Princeton University Press, 1994).

16. See chapter 1 for a detailed analysis on democratization and intelligence democratization.

17. Matei, and Bruneau, "Intelligence Reform in New Democracies," 607.

18. Matei, and Bruneau, 615.

19. Timothy Edmunds, "Intelligence Agencies and Democratisation," *Europe-Asia Studies* 60, no. 1 (2008): note 9. For a complete list of indicators of democratization, see also Alejandra Otamendi and Eduardo E. Estévez, "Intelligence Challenges in Latin America and Prospects for Reform: A Comparative Matrix on Democratic Governance" (paper, Fourth International LAVITS Symposium, "New Paradigms of Surveillance: Views from Latin America," Buenos Aires, 2017), https://lavits.org/wp-content/uploads/2017/08/P5_Otamendi_etal-1.pdf.

20. Gill and Wilson, "Intelligence and Security Sector Reform in Indonesia," 157–79.

21. Gill, *Intelligence Governance and Democratisation*.

THEORY AND HISTORY

1

A Theoretical Framework of Security Sector Reform and Intelligence

What is democratization, and what is intelligence democratization? What factors facilitate intelligence democratization, and why? There are several reasons why progress and reform might be supported or impeded when a state transitions to democracy and attempts to reform its intelligence community. Reform can be obstructed because of, among other reasons, reluctance from those on the inside to reform, the complexity of intelligence reform itself, lack of civilian expertise, and the persistence of authoritarian elements.[1] On the other hand, there are also many factors that can support the democratization of intelligence services. These include "the willingness of decision-makers to foster intelligence reform and achieve a balance between effectiveness and transparency; the role and influence of foreign assistance; increased cooperation and intelligence sharing; and the role of civil society and the media."[2]

In this book, it will become evident that although all of these reasons are important, the most fundamental is the persistence or removal of authoritarian elements within the intelligence community. Indeed, if authoritarian elements have not been completely and properly uprooted early on, it becomes increasingly difficult to truly reform the intelligence institutions. Lustration therefore is the first step toward reform and perhaps one that has not received enough conceptual attention when it comes to intelligence democratization. This chapter is about security sector reform (SSR) as the benchmarking system for evaluating the rate and level of democratization in states undergoing transition. As well as looking at SSR as the policy framework of the analysis and explaining why it has been chosen for this book, the chapter will also define the indicators used to measure intelligence democratization in Portugal, Greece, and Spain.

WHAT IS INTELLIGENCE DEMOCRATIZATION?

Before we dive into each case study, it is key to understand and define intelligence democratization in conjunction with the indicators that will be used to measure the levels of intelligence democratization. Although a wide range of academic discussions has centered on democratization throughout the years, intelligence democratization, especially in countries outside the Anglosphere, has been a significantly understudied area.

The downfall of the Soviet Union and the end of the Cold War from 1989 to 1991 enhanced significantly the debate on democratization, with prominent figures such as Francis Fukuyama leading the conversation. His 1992 work *The End of History and the Last Man* argued that liberal democracy probably constituted "the end point of mankind's ideological evolution" as well as the "final form of human government," given that it had overcome "hereditary monarchy, fascism, and communism."[3] Fukuyama's argument was in a sense confirmed when dictatorial regimes fell in rapid succession across Eastern Europe, Latin America, and Asia.[4] This flurry of new democracies significantly contributed to debates on what factors could help new democracies solidify, including enfranchisement, the rule of law, accountability, market economics, and legitimization.[5]

Legitimization of the new, democratic status quo is key. This is where the role of civil society is fundamental. Larry Diamond underlines "the process of achieving broad and deep legitimation," with the broad understanding that democracy is the optimum option.[6] Or, as Juan J. Linz and Alfred Stepan define it, first there is a transitional phase, "during which politics is fluid and democracy not assured," before the start of a consolidation phase, "when democracy becomes the only game in town."[7] They continue, saying that civil society "is the realm of organized social life that is open, voluntary, self-generating, at least partially self-supporting, autonomous from the state, and bound by a legal order or set of shared rules. It is distinct from 'society' in general in that it involves citizens acting collectively in a public sphere." The purpose of such cooperation is "to achieve collective goals, to make demands on the state . . . and to hold state officials accountable."[8] Such examples first came up in the 1980s and referred to nonstate actors such as Solidarity, which was challenging authoritarian rule in Poland.[9] Such movements have become key indicators when looking at the health of a democracy and democratic consolidation. As Jean Grugel states, "democracies are political systems comprising institutions that translate citizens' preferences into policy, have effective states that act to protect and deepen democratic rights, and count on a strong participatory and critical civil society."[10]

Citizens therefore should be able to "intervene" and hold public institutions to account, including intelligence organizations.[11] Mary Kaldor and Ivan Vejvoda argue that democracy is a process "that has to be continually reproduced, a way of regulating power relations in such a way as to maximize the opportunities for individuals to influence the conditions in which they live, to participate in and influence debates about the key decisions that affect society."[12] This is key because there are instances whereby states can appear to have all the democratic preconditions ticked off, when in reality they do not offer their citizens meaningful participation in the regulation, distribution, and use of power.

Democracy itself remains a contested concept and a process, with civil society being at the forefront because it can hold the government to account by applying and maintaining an influence on the national discourse. Citizens are thus able to both influence the decision-making process and legitimize the ruling system as a whole through free expressions of sentiment and the regular casting of votes. Throughout all of this, they, not the government, are protected by the intelligence services. Reaching such a consolidated outcome is not easy, however. Although "democracy requires that security and intelligence activities are subject to *control and oversight* in the interests of effectiveness, efficiency, legality, propriety and respect for human rights," the nature and operation of intelligence organizations make achieving overall "democratic control" very difficult.[13]

The main sticking point lies between the participation, openness, and transparency upheld in modern democracies and the secretive nature and specific functions of intelligence organizations. As one scholar pointed out, "expertise in surveillance, capacity to carry out covert operations, control of sensitive information, and functioning behind a veil of secrecy may serve to undermine democratic governance and the fundamental rights and liberties of citizens."[14] This notion is not limited to relatively new democracies struggling to overcome past examples of undemocratic behavior but also to so-called old democracies that have established intelligence cultures and rules on secrecy. In 1976, for example, Marcus Raskin posited that democratic control of US intelligence organizations had been subverted by the so-called national security state—an entity that had arisen during the Second World War and placed an overt amount of power in the hands of big businesses, the military, and the ruling executive.[15] These elements of the so-called dual state each operated according to a "para-legal structure," with their own administrative and self-justifying systems.[16] According to Thomas Bruneau and Steven Boraz, it was only through the setting of direction and the establishment of thorough oversight that this situation was rectified.[17] The first step "is civilian guidance to a nation's intelligence community with respect to its overall mission." The second, meanwhile, "identifies the processes a democratic government has in place to review all aspects of an intelligence community's organization, budget, personnel management, and legal framework for intelligence operations."[18] Bruneau and Boraz both argue that these components of democratic control can be achieved through the involvement of the executive and legislative branches and the intelligence organizations themselves—in addition to other "external" entities, such as the judiciary and, finally, civil society as a whole, including nongovernmental organizations (NGOs) and the media.

In both authoritarian and democratic regime types, including parliamentary systems, the executive plays a huge role in setting the direction of intelligence organizations. The key difference, however, is that in authoritarian types the primary function of any organization is often to help preserve the current regime and suppress any opposition.[19] Importantly, those setting the direction in modern democracies have often been elected in free and fair elections rather than having been appointed in an arbitrary manner. It is to this end that executive control on its own is claimed by some to be enough of an indication of democratization due to the way in which it helps prevent an organization going rogue or performing actions outside the government's knowledge and control. That is often why executive control of intelligence organizations is one of the first things that newly elected officials seek to achieve. As Miroslav Hadžic recounts of Western Balkan countries, "after the breakdown of the old regime in each of these countries, securing the legitimacy of the civilian authorities' supremacy in the security policy and security sector was on the top of the priority list." The next item on the agenda was to secure full subordination of the state apparatuses of force to the legitimate civilian authorities and leadership.[20] This was also the case in former Warsaw Pact countries such as Romania following the end of the Cold War, where "establishing sovereign national control over the domestic security apparatus and the loyalty of its personnel became major objectives of post-communist reform efforts."[21] Hans Born and Ian Leigh set out how this is often achieved by making organizations beholden to the democratic rule of law. The Canadian Security Intelligence Service Act of 1984, for example, specifically refers to the director of the service having "the control and management of the service" but "under the direction" of the minister.[22] In this kind of setup, the relevant intelligence service is accountable to an elected official, who is themself accountable to the general public.

The same is the case for Poland, where "the Prime Minister shall define the directions of the Agencies' activities by means of instructions," and in the Netherlands, where "the services and the coordinator exercise their duties in accordance with the law and subordination to the relevant Minister."[23] The main issue with relying purely on executive control is that while it is helpful for setting direction, it also runs the risk of the executive using the intelligence services for its own benefit. Such is the case now in Russia, where the domestic agency Federal Security Service of the Russian Federation (FSB) consequently "resembles the ruthless Mukhabarat, the secret police of the Arab world: devoted to the protection of authoritarian regimes, answering only to those in power, impenetrable, thoroughly corrupted, and unopposed to employing brutal methods against individuals and groups suspected of terrorism or dissent."[24] It is for this reason that several "transitional" countries such as Bosnia-Herzegovina have attempted to build safeguards into legislation governing the relationship between the executive and the national intelligence organization, the former being "expressly prevented" from assuming "in whole or in part the rights and responsibilities" of the director-general or the deputy director-general.[25] However, this still places the power to control information in the hands of a select few, reducing the ability of citizens to understand what actions may be performed in the name of their protection and safety.

This is particularly the case given the tendency of any government, democratic or not, to limit the amount of information disseminated to the public. As Abram Shulsky and Gary Schmitt posit, the fundamental liberal view of government and society in which "the free flow of information is the rule, and its classification is the exception" has rarely been the norm. Instead, "the more common tradition has been that of governmental secrecy, broken only when the government itself sees some advantage in disclosing information."[26] As evidence of this assertion, Shulsky and Schmitt cite the Ronald Reagan administration's revelation that the United States had intercepted Libyan communications indicating that they had coordinated an attack on a Berlin nightclub frequented by US service members. This revelation undermined US intelligence-collection capabilities but served to boost political support for air strikes against Libya.[27] A more recent and controversial example would perhaps be the George W. Bush administration's flawed indictment of Iraq's weapons program, which was made publicly by then secretary of state Colin Powell to the UN in 2003.[28] In both cases, the veil of secrecy surrounding what the US government knew and how it knew it was dropped in order to build support for a certain policy position. At no point was there general outrage among the American public that they did not already know this information. This is something that K. G. Robertson puts down to the fact that when it comes to foreign intelligence collection at least, the majority of citizens "are unlikely to see activities such as tasking, remote sensing, analysis, and dissemination as impinging on their interests." It is only when the collection process or *targeting* involves spying on one's own citizens that controversy usually arises and there are loud calls for transparency, openness, and regulation.[29] Methods of intelligence collection and targeting therefore are key in understanding if illegal means have been used, taking intelligence agencies away from democratic norms. The key questions that arise relate to who is rendered as the target for any intelligence-collection activities.

This is why "control" is often paired with "oversight" throughout available pieces of work on intelligence democratization. It is only through "superintendence" by outside entities that the power wielded by the executive is balanced and the key organizational, budgetary, personnel, and legal oversight mechanisms of an intelligence community are created.[30] This is critical for Born and Leigh because in any democracy "no area of state activity should be a 'no-go' for parliament, including the security and intelligence sector."[31] It is also a necessity for Bruce Berkowitz, who argues that it should be possible to hold each official accountable for their policy decisions in a timely fashion.[32] Certainly, legislative oversight of this sector is critical as it is key to granting organizations legitimacy and democratic accountability, without which it would be hard to ensure that they are "serving the state as a whole and protecting the constitution, rather than narrower political or sectional interests."[33]

Oversight is often the harder of the two components to achieve, however, as it is where the struggle between openness and secrecy is most pronounced. As Berkowitz surmises, "information is the engine that makes democracy work, while effectiveness of intelligence depends on restricting the flow of information."[34] The objective, therefore, when it comes to democratization is one of balance—balancing the potential harm to national security from the sharing of intelligence information against the requirements of the domestic political order for openness and transparency in governmental affairs.[35] As a result, for intelligence organizations to function within a democracy, there must be "a trade-off between diverging interests," something that must occur in a manner that is politically and legally sound.[36] Ideally this results in the oversight being performed through standing or special committees in order to "enact laws on intelligence, control and review intelligence agencies' activities, budgets, and personnel."[37] The UK's Intelligence and Security Committee is a good example of what form this oversight can take. The committee, "which is made up of nine cross-party Members of Parliament (MPs), reports directly to the prime minister, operates within what is known as the 'ring of secrecy,' and is privy to some of the most highly classified information within the United Kingdom's national intelligence machinery." It also produces an annual report on Britain's intelligence services for Parliament's benefit as well as conducts regular reviews and ad hoc reports.[38] L. K. Johnson, Hans Born, and Ian Leigh reference at least six other democratic countries that maintain similar oversight bodies, all with varying mandates but the majority appointed from the ranks of the legislature with appropriate levels of security vetting.[39] These kinds of committees can often lead the way in holding both the executive and intelligence organizations to account via legislative actions, such as the 1974 Hughes-Ryan Amendment. This prohibited funding for covert action by the CIA until the president made a case to the appropriate congressional committees "in a timely fashion" that such action was essential to the national security of the United States.[40]

Certainly, in addition to the UK and the US, oversight bodies have become the norm in many Western countries in recent years. They are thus important indicators of relative levels of democratization in any intelligence organization, but they are not themselves completely infallible. In recent years, for example, both K. G. Robertson and Peter Gill have come to strongly critique the way the system of declassification and oversight works in countries such as the United Kingdom, where the landmark 1994 Intelligence Services Act established an official form of oversight for the UK's intelligence services rather than the start of a period of increased openness motivated by "democratic logic."[41] B. Rittberger and K. H. Goetz believe that this kind of behavior is not just limited to the UK but is also displayed by almost all intelligence organizations when faced with pressure to be more transparent and accountable. More often than not, no more than symbolic reforms are undertaken to mitigate such requests, rendering any processes cosmetic.[42] As Michael Glennon states in reference to the Snowden revelations, another example of questionable targeting and collection practices, democratic control and oversight in the US intelligence community had somehow become "largely an illusion fostered by those institutions' pedigree, ritual, intelligibility, mystery, and superficial harmony with the network's ambitions. The courts, Congress, and even the presidency in reality impose little constraint. Judicial review is negligible; congressional oversight dysfunctional."[43]

Indeed, as one member of Congress allegedly told Peter Gill and Michael Andregg, "the House and Senate oversight committees were intended and designed to 'overlook' more than to oversee," with caution usually being exercised by members due to the fact that "when these guys [intelligence organizations] get mad, there are real consequences."[44] Even where robust oversight measures are put in place and those responsible have the courage to challenge and critique, huge resources are usually required to establish even simple facts. This is due to the use of tactics such as "burying," the objective of which is to overload committee members with so much irrelevant information that the relevant information becomes lost or ignored.[45] The drawn-out battle between the Senate's intelligence committee and the CIA over allegations of torture is just one example of how this can play out in even well-established democracies with oversight measures already in place.[46] It is important to note that these examples are also linked to collection practices as part of targeting.

This is one such reason why the judiciary is also cited as having an important role to play when it comes to both democratic control and oversight. It alone has the power to review and interpret the legal framework under which intelligence operations are conducted.[47] It also routinely considers requests for surveillance and collection so as to "ensure that agencies use their special powers according to the law, and protect citizens' rights from the agencies' intrusive collection and searches."[48] The Federal Court of Canada, for example, is the sole entity that can authorize a warrant allowing the Canadian Security and Intelligence Service (CSIS) to intercept telephone communications, the warrant only being issued as a result of a long and intensive decision-making process ending with the signature of the Canadian solicitor general and a review by the Federal Court.[49] The independent UK's Investigatory Powers Commissioner's Office (IPCO) plays a similar role: determining the legality, necessity, and proportionality of applications made by intelligence organizations and overseeing the implementation of legal guidance issued to them, such as the 2010 Consolidated Guidance on the Detention and Interviewing of Detainees Overseas, now called The Principles.[50] The main weakness of relying on judicial oversight is that its strength is dependent on the knowledge and independence of those involved. Indeed, in many postauthoritarian countries, the judiciary is often as tainted by its past activities as any other state institution, and questions remain about how trustworthy it really is in ensuring justice, at least in the immediate term.[51] Beyond this, judicial influence can also be extended inside intelligence organizations themselves "in the form of in-house counsels and inspectors general (IGs). In general, internal controls include not only counsels and IGs but also the IC's own professional ethos and institutional norms."[52] Accordingly, before external oversight even needs to be applied, these internal measures can review budgetary, personnel, and legal matters—even investigate citizen complaints where appropriate.

If democratic control and oversight can prove ineffective, therefore, what other indicators and measures can be relied upon to ensure democratization? In many countries, oversight does not start and end with the three branches of government. This is where we circle back to the importance of civil society as an oversight tool. In some cases, this can offer even more of a check on abuses of power than either the executive, the legislature, the parliament, or the judiciary. In reviewing the democratization of the Argentinian intelligence services, for example, Eduardo Estévez acknowledges the energy directed into debating and passing legislation to restructure the intelligence community in order to allow for the exercise of executive and legislative control and oversight. He also, however, emphasizes the role played by NGOs and the media in bringing to light incidents of misconduct and incompetence. This, together with the declassification of archival material, is what Estévez alleges to have had the greatest impact on intelligence democratization in the country, as opposed to "less than effective" oversight.[53] This reaffirms arguments made by Peter Gill on the central role that civil society plays in "fostering awareness and trust in a reformed intelligence structure" despite the risk that it may also become "captured by special interests, become 'uncivil,' violate human rights and weaken the rule of law."[54]

Where civil society has not yet had time to develop, the media has often stepped in and provided the kind of checks on unregulated power that formal control and oversight measures may have failed to achieve. In doing so, not only have they "kindled regular debates on the intelligence and security matters, but also forced the hand of decision-makers to undertake intelligence reform and exercise control and oversight more thoroughly."[55] This was especially the case in postcommunist Romania, where the influence of the media contributed to the reduction of the number of the state's intelligence organizations, an acceleration of the vetting of new recruits, screening and firing of former authoritarian officers, the opening up of archives, and the exposure of collaborators and agents.[56] Both the media and civil society's ability to perform these kind of functions increases when there is base-level openness on the part of intelligence organizations. This can be through limits on the amount of time that information can remain secret, cooperation with freedom of information requests, or engagement with outside actors in order to share knowledge and establish trust. In his review of Spanish intelligence culture, for example, Rubén Arcos highlights the Intelligence Culture Initiative of the Centro Nacional de Inteligencia (CNI; National Intelligence Center). This marked the start of a period of openness that linked universities and intelligence organizations for the first time and helped reduce the levels of "general mistrust and lack of knowledge concerning matters of intelligence amongst the service's stakeholders."[57] The same kind of engagement can also be performed with the media—as was attempted by the Mexican Homeland Security and Investigation Center (CISEN) in 2000—although the results should not always be expected to be positive.[58]

Lustration is another key catalyst that supports intelligence democratization. It is a method that is usually used by intelligence organizations themselves, which have it within their power to become compliant with democratic norms and values by agreeing to changes to their internal culture and composition. During the transitional phase, this entails some form of review of the organizations' employees so as to establish whether they are suitably fit to carry out duties in the new democratic environment.

Transparent *recruitment* processes should follow. Fair recruitment is a fundamental element that helps with democratization levels within an intelligence service. Maintaining the old guard or recruiting personnel based on connections rather than merit drives intelligence services away from democratic principles. Civil society can be a driving force for lustration too. Seva Gunitsky argues that democratization can take place only if a state has chosen to "reject authoritarianism" or any antidemocratic rule, whether as the result of "vertical" external influences, such as foreign invasion, or "horizontal" local linkages centered on an internal cataclysmic event, such as a revolution.[59] This is something that happened in one of the case studies, Portugal, where civil society played a key role in driving lustration.[60] Romania was the first of the postcommunist states to initiate a formal vetting of intelligence personnel, with the culling starting immediately after the security apparatus was subordinated to the defense ministry at the end of December 1989.[61] The process, which was completed by February 1990, "found 4,944 out of 15,312 personnel acceptable for re-employment in the new intelligence service. A further cut of 800 personnel that same month resulted in the re-employment of 4,144 (28 percent) of the ex-*Securitate* personnel in the new security intelligence service (SRI)."[62] Ideally, this process of lustration occurs very early on, but it is not unknown for it to occur several years into democratic rule. Such was the case in the Republic of North Macedonia, which introduced a lustration law only in 2008 to address past injustices and stop former collaborators from holding public employment. This entailed the creation of a dedicated Lustration Commission, which examined over twenty-nine thousand documents and indicted 140 individuals.[63] Although often admirable in their original aims, the downside of such commissions is that they can encourage a politicization of intelligence services, to the detriment of their overall effectiveness. The sudden decision of Argentinian president Cristina Fernández de Kirchner to purge the state intelligence service following the death of state prosecutor Alberto Nisman is one such murky example of the difficulties of building a truly democratic intelligence organization, particularly when the organization and different branches of government are engulfed in questionable activities.[64] It is interesting to note that despite these insightful pieces of work where there is so much emphasis put on authoritarian regimes arresting reform, there is no clear analysis of lustration as a process that can uproot these authoritarian elements, resulting in a robust control and oversight structure and an engaged civil society.

SSR AND ITS RELATIONSHIP WITH INTELLIGENCE

Many have gravitated toward two existing fields of study when considering the case of intelligence democratization. These are the fields of civil-military relations (CMR) and SSR. To be able to measure democratization levels across the intelligence services in question, SSR is used as the framework in this book. While the former is predominately concerned with the control and oversight relationship between civil authorities and the military (as the name suggests), SSR may encompass a wide variety of state actors. Neither, therefore, specifically has intelligence organizations in mind as its principal subject, but it is still possible to use both frameworks to analyze levels of intelligence democratization. Tom Bruneau, Cristiana Matei, and Steven Boraz, for example, argue that because many intelligence organizations derive their cultures and power from the military, CMR is best placed to progress democratic civilian control and effectiveness, with "efficiency," meanwhile, being too difficult to measure. The objective is to reconcile a "trinity of democratic civilian control, effectiveness (fulfilling the assigned roles and missions—from war, to peacekeeping, to intelligence, to counterterrorism), and efficiency (fulfilling the assigned roles and missions at a minimum cost) of the security forces."[65] Bringing these three variables together enhances human security and therefore pushes intelligence democratization forward. The same goes for intelligence services as part of a state's institutions within the SSR framework because entities that are part of the security sector tend to undergo sets of reform during and after their transition period to democracy.

SSR, on the other hand, offers a much broader interpretation of "human security," depending of course on the definition used, while being overtly linked to the notion of democratization through economic and political development.

Simply put, a peaceful and stable society can be created if the right resources are provided and the relevant actors are built up and developed. From Peter Gill and Lee Wilson's perspective, SSR may possibly be the ideal conceptual framework for measuring levels of democratic reform "precisely because it facilitates the study of the many different types of security actors operating at the neighbourhood, regional, and national levels."[66] When applied to nations in the midst of democratic reforms, the concept flexibly integrates with what Linz and Stepan suggest are the five interconnected and mutually reinforcing arenas of "modern consolidated democracy": the rule of law, economic society, political society, civil society, and the state apparatus. SSR does not specifically aim to achieve progress in each of these domains but is supposed to deliver more generally on three fronts: the provision of security, governance and rule of law, and effectiveness and efficiency. Summarized in brief, therefore, "the core objective of SSR is to enhance the effectiveness, efficiency and affordability of the security sector within a broader framework of democratic governance that ensures civilian oversight and democratic control."[67] This is similar to the stated approach of CMR, which entails civilian control, effectiveness, and efficiency, as highlighted above.[68] So valued is it in achieving these aims that the EU has even included SSR fulfillment in its preaccession criteria for membership of the organization since early 2006.[69]

The starting point for the development of SSR stemmed from attempts to formalize the different reform methodologies that external actors applied to countries in transition, such as Rwanda, Kosovo, and Sierra Leone, from the early 1990s to the early 2000s. During this period, as humanitarian crises erupted all over the world, a brief consensus was reached by the international community that "considerations of national sovereignty should not shelter a country's internal political arrangements from outside observation or criticism."[70] This agreement facilitated, in some cases, military action under the auspices of the United Nations (UN) in addition to the implementation of reforms led by external bodies and organizations. It was for this reason that the UN identified SSR as "a core element of multidimensional peacekeeping and peacebuilding, essential for addressing the roots of conflict and building the foundations of long-term peace and development."[71] This initial positioning of SSR as a "peacekeeping tool" had the inadvertent effect, however, of encouraging both practitioners and policymakers to focus on specific components over others. Within the definition used by the Development Assistance Committee (DAC) of the Organisation for Economic Co-operation and Development (OECD), there are three primary goals that SSR seeks to achieve:

1. Improve the democratic oversight of the security and justice system and its components

2. Improve the effective management of the security and justice system
3. Strengthen the security and justice system's effectiveness in delivering services.[72]

Although international organizations such as the UN identified SSR as a core peacekeeping and peacebuilding element, individual states have been more precise in their perception of SSR's role, with the UK's Department for International Development stating that it involves a focus on efficient resource management "to allow the provision of security that does not threaten democracy or human rights, or undermine other development goals."[73] In 2004 the OECD established guidelines on SSR that defined a state's security system as including core security actors from armed forces, police, gendarmerie, border guards, and intelligence and security services as well as security management and oversight bodies, such as ministries of defense and internal affairs. Justice and law enforcement institutions as well as nonstatutory security forces, such as private security companies, were also included.[74] As the Department for International Development (now merged with the Foreign and Commonwealth Office) has underlined further, the aim of SSR is to transform "the security system which includes all the actors, their roles, responsibilities and actions, so that it is managed and operated in a manner that is more consistent with democratic norms and sound principles of good governance."[75]

Albert Schnabel and Hans-Georg Erhart's *Security Sector Reform and Post-Conflict Peacebuilding*, for example, includes several chapters written by those with field experience implementing SSR in a variety of countries. In almost every case study, implementation of SSR involved developing civil-military relations, an important but by no means exclusive element of the framework.[76] This is a problem that Nina Wilén also identifies, stating that it is a common challenge to try to get countries and donors to pay attention to the holistic nature of SSR and not become confused or distracted by "the seemingly urgent demand for strong and operationally efficient security forces that are capable of both peacekeeping and, increasingly, counterterrorism operations."[77] As numerous governmental policy documents state, there is more to SSR than these objectives alone. Indeed, it requires a focus on efficient resource management "to allow the provision of security that does not threaten democracy or human rights, or undermine other development goals."[78] The aim is to transform "the security system which includes all the actors, their roles, responsibilities and actions, so that it is managed and operated in a manner that is more consistent with democratic norms and sound principles of good governance."[79] This includes security management and oversight bodies, such as ministries of defense and internal affairs, financial management bodies, and public complaints commissions; justice and law enforcement institutions, such as the judiciary, prisons, prosecution services, and traditional justice systems; and nonstatutory security forces, such as private security companies, guerrilla armies, and private militias.[80]

Accordingly, there is a great deal more to SSR than the simple "fixing" of any one organization or institution. The African experience in particular, showcasing that "SSR concerns not only militaries" but also "civil society, media, the private sector and traditional authorities, who should be drawn into the process."[81] Separately, Heiner Hänggi and Vincenza Scherrer also promote the importance of "national ownership" as having the best chance of establishing a democratic, accountable, and transparent security environment—characterized by good governance and the rule of law—stemming from external support of local actors.[82] National ownership of SSR is crucial for the sustainability of any change in the long term.[83] This includes national ownership of reform in the intelligence sector, which the Geneva Centre for the Democratic Control of Armed Forces (now called the Geneva Centre for Security Sector Governance) argues is likely to benefit intelligence services in a number of ways: because robust oversight "protects intelligence services from misuse of power, and improves their credibility and legitimacy," because "intelligence professionals benefit from fair treatment and working conditions when they work in institutions that are held accountable," and because "inclusive services" with "balanced workforces" can offer better intelligence analysis and assessments.[84] Ideally, the SSR transformation process is meant to occur in all areas simultaneously, yet, "while sound in theory, such a comprehensive approach presents problems in practice."[85]

Although SSR is a solid policy framework that can be applied to other aspects of government, when it comes to intelligence it faces a series of challenges. Transparency is usually the most challenging sticking point. While it is possible for uniformed police or military forces to operate in plain sight and still retain effectiveness, the same cannot be said for intelligence services. This is because the nature of their work means it needs to be out of sight for it to be effective. Precisely how much intelligence activity the public is meant to be aware of and how it is overseen is a contentious subject even in the most advanced democracies. The British government for example, did not even acknowledge the existence of the Secret Intelligence Service (MI6) until 1986, even though its existence was an open secret among the public.[86] Other disclosures, meanwhile, can be more damaging, particularly where they affect the trust between citizens and state actors. One such recent case would be the revelations of former US National Security Agency (NSA) contractor Edward Snowden, who in 2013 shocked the world with revelations about the extent of the NSA's data-collection programs.[87] Therefore, there exists a continuous process by which all democratic nations must continually review and amend practices and oversight mechanisms to achieve a delicate balance between operational requirements and democratic ideals.

As Matei and Bruneau acknowledge, the paradox faced by all democracies, "both new and long established," is that while a democracy, "which is based on accountability of the governors to the governed, requires transparency, intelligence at least at some level, requires secrecy to be effective, which negates to some degree both accountability and transparency."[88] Such confidentiality naturally puts limitations on the kind of openness that organizations can realistically agree to so as not to overtly compromise effectiveness. As a result, while declassification and "demystification" processes are very important for helping educate and shape citizens' understanding of their intelligence services' roles and activities, there often remains a wide gulf between public perceptions of current activities and what is going on in reality.[89] Therefore, attempting a process of democratization of an intelligence service is not the same as democratizing a military or police force.

There is no universally accepted definition of "intelligence." Throughout this book, it refers to a wide range of activities, from collection of information to its analysis and dissemination. These activities are conducted in secret and provide relevant policymakers with warning and time to make decisions that, when implemented, can also include covert action. The ultimate objective of each element is effectively to ensure the security of the state. Based on the above definition, any reference to "intelligence services" will mean the state intelligence organizations that use intelligence to help policymakers make national security decisions. This excludes military forces and the police, although reference to military intelligence divisions and political police bodies during authoritarian rules of government are included where they are considered relevant to the analysis.

When trying to understand what a democratized intelligence service is, therefore, one should look at "intelligence systems that fulfil their mandates effectively and within the framework of sound domestic and international partnerships, whilst accountable to the elected officials, and ultimately to the citizens."[90] The main difference between a nondemocratic intelligence service and a democratic one is that the former operates in an environment of nearly total secrecy and its effectiveness lies in defending the regime rather than its people. When transitioning from an authoritarian regime to democratic rule, therefore, what are the key reforms that should be undertaken to ensure a democratic intelligence system? As Timothy Edmunds notes, there are three levels that can help establish a democratized intelligence service: (1) "standards and procedures" of democratic civilian control and oversight over the intelligence services, (2) consolidated mechanisms that set the basis for this control, and (3) expertise and capabilities to support intelligence activities, most important including those for the removal of authoritarian elements.[91] The first and second levels are linked mostly to accountability and transparency, with the third one to effectiveness. It is key to bear in mind that intelligence services operating under authoritarian regimes can be "effective" in the sense that they are fulfilling assigned roles and missions set by that regime. These missions and duties focus on protecting that regime and result in human rights violations. However, in a democratic setting, these missions target real, current, and relevant threats while the staff who occupy these roles have been recruited meritocratically, based on their skills that pertain to these threats. Enacting laws that enforce effectiveness and transparency is key to ensure that the intelligence services no longer act oppressively or carry out any illegal activities. Establishing and strengthening control and oversight mechanisms is also fundamental because, if properly done, this will result in the intelligence service being accountable to the citizens it is meant to protect.[92] In addition to these elements, as argued by Matei and Bruneau, it is key to foster a society interested and invested in intelligence by raising awareness and educating the public about matters of intelligence, cultivate a "political culture that supports intelligence in society and inside the agencies," and "institutionalise processes that support transparency and effectiveness" as well as "professionalise the intelligence services."[93]

INTELLIGENCE DEMOCRATIZATION INDICATORS

From the above, it is clear that a democratized intelligence service should be institutionally effective and transparent with a solid legal framework, fair recruitment processes, and robust personnel standards, be under a strong control and oversight structure, and be in a position to increase openness in order to foster a more informed and engaged civil society.[94] An intelligence service will be able to achieve this level of democratization only after effectively excluding any remaining authoritarian legacies.

SSR focuses on the following key areas: transparency, accountability, and effectiveness. To achieve democratic control, both formal and informal, which civil society can assist to foster, and reach a level of accountability, a process of lustration is needed. This is fundamental because lustration helps establish transparency. This is then paired with proper recruitment processes. Lustration and recruitment are in a way interlinked, as we will see in following chapters. Fair recruitment also supports effectiveness with skilled personnel tackling real threats. Last, as control and oversight relate to transparency and accountability, targeting emerges as part of these two elements. This is because in a democratic status quo, intelligence services should focus on threats that target a state's citizens as opposed to the regime itself. This reinforces elements such as transparency and accountability further, while it ensures effectiveness within a democratic setup. As well as the available literature on (intelligence) democratization and the three case studies in question, key indicators to help measure the levels of intelligence democratization in Portugal, Greece, and Spain emerge:

- Lustration
- Control and oversight
- Recruitment
- Targeting
- Civil society

Lustration

There are several definitions of lustration, which is generally used in conjunction with a state's transition to democracy, not necessarily an intelligence service's transition. Some authors define it as "the exclusion of individuals from political life or their judicial punishment for past actions under a previous regime."[95] This can include criminal proceedings or screening procedures, including against collaborators and staff of state institutions.[96] Additionally, when "political decisions made in the immediate aftermath of the transition and directed towards individuals on the basis of what they did or what was done to them under the earlier regime" is defined as "transitional justice." This lustration process targets personnel only.[97] In this book, lustration is defined as the process by which a state that is transitioning to democracy removes officials and other insiders from the previous authoritarian regime. These individuals are often identified based on their past involvement in repression, including violations of human rights, and their affinity for the old regime or authoritarian ideology. As Gill notes, to achieve greater democratic control, a process of lustration is often required to establish transparency and root out unacceptable activities. To have maximum effect, this needs to be accompanied by fresh recruitment drives, including civilians with higher educational qualifications and skills that are relevant to actual current threats.[98] The depth of lustration can vary from case to case, ranging from merely cosmetic lustration by the party in office to an in-depth formal purging. Lustration should be the first step to true reform. If this first step has not been carried out, the other ones (including robust control and oversight, targeted collection that is limited to actual threats, and fair recruitment) will not be successful. The key questions the book will aim to answer with regard to this indicator are: Did each case study go through a robust lustration process, and if so, when? What was the (positive) effect of lustration for each country?

Control and Oversight

Under control and oversight, the analysis will focus on the legal groundwork needed before any mechanisms are put in place as well as the different types and levels of control and oversight for each country. "Control," in general and for the purposes of this book, is defined as the control, management, and direction that the director of the agency possesses. The director, of course, follows the ministerial direction, which is based on a legal framework.[99] "Oversight" on the other hand, is a "process of 'superintendence' that does not focus on the day-to-day management but with ensuring that the overall activities of the agency are consistent with its legal mandate."[100]

There are different levels of control and oversight, such as more immediate control and oversight structures, some of them from within the agency and external. For the purposes of this book, when referring to "immediate" control and oversight, the author refers to the first layer of control, exercised by the agency and the executive. This is done by the intelligence service's director via the direction of the executive branch or ministry. It is based on passed legislature. Additional levels or layering that comes after that is what we call "external oversight." This includes parliamentary, extraparliamentary, and judicial as well as informal, where we find the media, citizens, and NGOs. Therefore, is there a legal basis for oversight? Is there sufficient control? Is there proper parliamentary oversight? Are there any other established forms and levels of (external) oversight, such as judiciary? Can we make any observations where possible as to if those are practically applied?

Immediate Control and Oversight

In addition to the above, it should be noted that internal legal accountability mechanisms within intelligence organizations are important. These include, among others, general counsels and inspectors general, whose function is to review and assess intelligence activity.

External Oversight

External oversight involves processes and mechanisms that aim to oversee the intelligence services but come from the outside. *Parliamentary oversight* through parliamentary questions, usually directed to the director of an intelligence service, is one of the oversight mechanisms that is most common across Westernized democracies. In this book, the analysis will try to answer questions such as: Is there parliamentary oversight in each case study? What kind of questions does the parliament put to the service, and what type of answers does it get? Are there any parliamentary committees, and how independent are they?[101]

Additionally, other independent committees tend to be part of external oversight mechanisms and usually they are referred to as *extraparliamentary oversight*. Judicial bodies may also play a role in ensuring "agencies use their special powers according to the law and protect citizens' rights from the agencies' intrusive collection and searches."[102] This is what is known as *judicial oversight* and, as an example, involves judges who decide on whether any interception of communications is necessary and "proprietary" on the part of the intelligence service. Another aspect of external oversight involves *informal oversight*. This refers to external mechanisms, at both domestic and international levels, which involve the checking of the intelligence organizations by "outsiders," including a free press, independent think tanks, NGOs, and international organizations. In this book, the author will focus on informal oversight as part of the civil society chapter.

Recruitment

Recruitment is a key indicator because it is part of the professionalization process. The recruitment of qualified professional staff also relates to lustration. During an authoritarian regime, staff are being selected more for their loyalty to that regime than they are for their qualifications. When candidates are evaluated based on their academic and technical qualifications, it enhances democratic rule. Based on the above, key questions that this book will aim to answer in terms of recruitment include: Do the intelligence services hire based on merit and qualifications or loyalty to the regime/government? If yes to the former, when did they start doing so? What exactly were the staff recruited to do? And how were they approached—through open and transparent means? Are there police and/or military personnel present within the civilian intelligence services?

Targeting

Collection of information is the foundation of intelligence. In the intelligence process, the first stage is "planning and direction," referred to here as "targeting." Intelligence services in democratic regimes place limits on their targeting, especially when it comes to domestic spying. In a democracy, there should be an organizational process whereby real threats to national security are identified and targeted, as opposed to perceived enemies of the state as chosen by an authoritarian regime. Authoritarian regimes often see the domestic population as their number-one potential threat. The methods of collecting intelligence are another key element in the intelligence cycle. The intelligence service should not use national security as a justification for abuses of domestic law and human rights. Based on the above, the following key questions emerge: Do the intelligence services target actual threats to national security, and, if yes, when did they start doing so? Do the intelligence services violate domestic law to collect information? Is there a legal basis for oversight when it comes to targeting?[103] When looking at *targeting* in this book, therefore, we will look at targeting of threats as well as methods for collecting information.

Civil Society

An engaged civil society that enjoys freedom of inquiry and expression is fundamental for measuring intelligence democratization but also for driving it. As the main purpose of the intelligence services during democratic rule is to protect the citizens of a state (not the ruling regime), it is really important to examine the involvement as well as awareness of each civil society in Portugal, Greece, and Spain before and after their transition. Therefore, in each case are there civil society groups and a robust media presence that drive informal oversight? Are there established partnerships between universities and the intelligence services? Is there an open culture of intelligence?

TABLE 1.1. Indicators: Intelligence services under authoritarian versus democratic rule

	Intelligence service under authoritarian rule	Intelligence service under democratic rule
Lustration	N/A	A purging process is applied to remove authoritarian elements from the intelligence service.
Control and oversight	Rules based on executive decrees, military orders, or party directives. Head of the regime sets the rules. No external oversight mechanisms.	Proper legislation on the intelligence services' objectives, protection, and use of personal data. Responsible ministers appoint agency heads and set budgets—all this in agreement with the law. Solid external oversight.
Recruitment	Loyalty to the regime acts as the only criterion for recruitment.	Recruitment is based on merit and takes place from all sectors of society.
Targeting	Targeting of "perceived" enemies of the state, with illegal practices, such as torture and wiretapping.	Real, relevant threats to national security are targeted. Law sets out authorization processes for collection of information via covert operations. Notion of "proportionality" is key.
Civil society	Complete state secrecy. Repressed civil society actors, no free press, and fear and suspicion toward the regime.	Active civil society and informed media drive conversation around intelligence. Existing intelligence discipline. Ability to access information by the public.

Source: Inspired by and adapted from Peter Gill's snapshot of indicators before and after democratic transition in *Intelligence Governance and Democratisation: A Comparative Analysis of the Limits of Reform* (Abingdon, UK: Routledge, 2016).

NOTES

1. Matei and Bruneau, "Intelligence Reform in New Democracies," 602–30.
2. Matei and Bruneau, 615.
3. Francis Fukuyama, *The End of History and the Last Man* (New York: Free Press, 1992), xi.
4. Fukuyama, xi.
5. Carles Boix, Michael Miller, and Sebastian Rosato, "A Complete Data Set of Political Regimes, 1800–2007," *Comparative Political Studies* 46, no. 12 (2012): 1523–54. See also Rachel Kleinfeld, "Competing Definitions of the Rule-of-Law," in *Promoting the Rule-of-Law Abroad: In Search of Knowledge*, ed. Thomas Carothers (Washington, DC: Carnegie Endowment for International Peace, 2006); Tom Ginsburg, *Rule by Law: The Politics of Courts in Authoritarian Regimes* (Cambridge: Cambridge University Press, 2010); Christoph Bleiker and Marc Krupanski, *The Rule of Law and Security Sector Reform: Conceptualising a Complex Relationship* (Geneva: DCAF, 2012); David Beetham, "Civil Society: Market Economy and Democratic Polity," in *Civil Society in Democratisation*, ed. Peter Calvert and Peter Burnell (London: Frank Cass, 2004); Guillermo O'Donnell, "The Quality of Democracy: Why the Rule of Law Matters," *Journal of Democracy* 15, no. 4 (2004); John Peeler, *Building Democracy in Latin America*, 2nd ed. (Boulder, CO: Lynne Rienner, 2004); Juan Linz and Alfred Stepan, *Problems of Democratic Transition and Consolidation: Southern Europe, South America, and Post-Communist Europe* (Baltimore: Johns Hopkins University Press, 1998); Jean Grugel and Daniel Hammett, *The Palgrave Handbook of International Development* (London: Palgrave Macmillan, 2016); and Ronald Inglehart and Wayne E. Baker, "Modernization, Cultural Change, and the Persistence of Traditional Values," *American Sociological Review* 65, no. 1 (2000). See also Karl Marx, *Grundrisse: Foundations of the Critique of Political Economy* (New York: Random House, 1973), and Jean Grugel and Matthew Louis Bishop, *Democratization: A Critical Introduction*, 2nd ed. (New York: Palgrave Macmillan, 2014).
6. Larry Diamond, *Developing Democracy: Toward Consolidation* (Baltimore: Johns Hopkins University Press, 1999), 65–66.
7. Linz and Stepan, *Problems of Democratic Transition and Consolidation*, 5.
8. Diamond, *Developing Democracy*, 221.
9. Adam Jezard, "Who and What Is 'Civil Society'?," World Economic Forum, www.weforum.org/agenda/2018/04/what-is-civil-society/.
10. Grugel and Bishop, *Democratization*, 36. See also Todd Landman, "Violence, Democracy and Human Rights in Latin America," in *Violent Democracies in Latin America*, ed. Enrique Desmond Arias and Daniel Goldstein (Durham, NC: Duke University Press, 2010), 235–36.
11. Paul Q. Hirst, *From Statism to Pluralism: Democracy, Civil Society, and Global Politics* (Loudon: Routledge, 2013), 13.
12. Mary Kaldor and Ivan Vojevoda, *Democratization in Central and Eastern Europe* (London: Pinter, 1999), 3–4.
13. Gill and Andregg, *Comparing the Democratisation of Intelligence*, 489 (my italics).
14. Marina Caparini, "Controlling and Overseeing Intelligence Services in Democratic States," in *Democratic Control of Intelligence Services: Containing Rogue Elephants*, ed. Hans Born and Marina Caparini (Abingdon, UK: Routledge, 2007), 3.

15. Marcus G. Raskin, "Democracy versus the National Security State," *Law and Contemporary Problems* 40, no. 3 (1976): 189–220.

16. Raskin, 202–3.

17. Bruneau and Boraz, *Reforming Intelligence*, 15.

18. Bruneau and Boraz, 14.

19. Examples abound of such intelligence organizations. For the shah of Iran's SAVAK, see Carl Wege, "Iranian Intelligence Organizations," in Davies and Gustafson, *Intelligence Elsewhere*, 141–56.

20. Miroslav Hadžić, *Intelligence Governance in the Western Balkans: A Comparative Perspective* (Geneva: DCAF, 2012), 13.

21. Larry L. Watts, "Intelligence Reform in Europe's Emerging Democracies," CIA, June 27, 2008, www.cia.gov/library/center-for-the-study-of-intelligence/csi-publications/csi -studies/studies/vol48no1/article02.html.

22. Legislative Services Branch, "Consolidated Federal Laws of Canada, Canadian Security Intelligence Service Act," Canadian Security Intelligence Service Act, August 19, 2020, laws-lois.justice.gc.ca/eng/acts/c-23/FullText.html, as referred to in Hans Born and Ian Leigh, *Making Intelligence Accountable: Legal Standards and Best Practice for Oversight of Intelligence Agencies*, DCAF Handbook Series (Oslo: Publishing House of the Parliament of Norway, 2005), 55–56.

23. Intelligence and Security Services Act 2002, Netherlands, Article 2.

24. Andrei Soldatov and Irina Borogan, *The New Nobility: The Restoration of Russia's Security State and the Enduring Legacy of the KGB* (New York: PublicAffairs, 2010), 5–6.

25. Law on the Intelligence and Security Agency 2004, Bosnia and Herzegovina, Article 10.

26. Abram N. Shulsky and Gary J. Schmitt, *Silent Warfare: Understanding the World of Intelligence*, 3rd ed. (Washington, DC: Potomac Books, 2009), 101.

27. Shulsky and Schmitt, 101.

28. Jason Breslow, "Colin Powell: U.N. Speech 'Was a Great Intelligence Failure,'" Public Broadcasting Service, May 17, 2016, www.pbs.org/wgbh/frontline/article/colin -powell-u-n-speech-was-a-great-intelligence-failure/.

29. K. G. Robertson, "Recent Reform of Intelligence in the UK: Democratization or Risk Management?," *Intelligence and National Security* 13, no. 2 (1998): 145.

30. Bruneau and Boraz, *Reforming Intelligence*, 15.

31. Born and Leigh, *Making Intelligence Accountable*, 77.

32. Bruce Berkowitz, "Intelligence, Secrecy, and Democracy," Hoover Institution on War, Revolution, and Peace, Stanford University, accessed February 23, 2021, https://www.senado.gov.br/comissoes/CCAI/txtBerkowitz.htm.

33. Born and Leigh, *Making Intelligence Accountable*, 77.

34. Berkowitz, "Intelligence, Secrecy, and Democracy," 4.

35. Shulsky and Schmitt, *Silent Warfare*, 102.

36. Fred Schreier, "The Need for Efficient and Legitimate Intelligence," in Born and Caparini, *Democratic Control of Intelligence Services*, 25.

37. Matei and Bruneau, "Intelligence Reform in New Democracies," 606.

38. Peter Chalk and William Rosenau, *Confronting the "Enemy Within": Security Intelligence, the Police, and Counterterrorism in Four Democracies* (Santa Monica, CA: RAND Corp., 2004), 15. See also Ian Leigh, "The UK's Intelligence and

Security Committee," in Born and Caparini, *Democratic Control of Intelligence Services*.

39. H. Born, L. K. Johnson, and I. Leigh, *Who's Watching the Spies? Establishing Intelligence Service Accountability* (Washington, DC: Potomac Books, 2005).

40. James S. Van Wagenen, "A Review of Congressional Oversight," CIA, accessed February 23, 2019, https://www.cia.gov/static/Review-of-Congressional-Oversight.pdf.

41. K. G. Robertson, "Recent Reform of Intelligence in the UK: Democratization or Risk Management?," *Intelligence and National Security* 13, no. 2 (1998): 155.

42. B. Rittberger and K. H. Goetz, "Secrecy in Europe," *West European Politics* 41, no. 4 (2018): 839.

43. Michael Glennon, "National Security and Double Government," *Harvard National Security Journal* 5, no. 1 (2014): 109–10.

44. Gill and Andregg, *Comparing the Democratization of Intelligence*, 489.

45. Peter Gill, "Reasserting Control: Recent Changes in the Oversight of the UK Intelligence Community," *Intelligence and National Security* 11, no. 2 (1996): 315.

46. For an account of this episode and the underlying tensions between intelligence entities and those that oversee them in the US, see Spencer Ackerman, "Inside the Fight to Reveal the CIA's Torture Secrets," *Guardian*, September 9, 2016, www .theguardian.com/us-news/2016/sep/09/cia-insider-daniel-jones-senate-torture -investigation.

47. Bruneau, and Boraz, *Reforming Intelligence*, 15.

48. Matei and Bruneau, "Intelligence Reform in New Democracies," 606.

49. CSIS, "Accountability and Review," Backgrounder Series, January 1996, 2–3.

50. IPCO, accessed February 23, 2021, https://www.ipco.org.uk/investigatory-powers /useful-definitions/. See also IPCO's official website, https://www.ipco.org.uk/.

51. Ian Leigh, "National Courts and International Intelligence Cooperation," *International Intelligence Cooperation and Accountability*, ed. Hans Born, Ian Leigh, and Aidan Wills (London: Routledge, 2011) 231–51.

52. Thomas Boraz and Steven Bruneau, "Reforming Intelligence: Democracy and Effectiveness," *Journal of Democracy* 17, no. 3 (2006): 32.

53. Gill, *Intelligence Governance and Democratisation*, 136; Eduardo Estévez "Comparing Intelligence Democratization in Latin America: Argentina, Peru and Ecuador Cases," *Intelligence and National Security* 29, no. 4 (2014): 552–80.

54. Gill, *Intelligence Governance and Democratisation*, 136.

55. Matei and Bruneau, "Intelligence Reform in New Democracies," 620.

56. Florina Cristiana Matei, "Romania's Intelligence Community: From an Instrument of Dictatorship to Serving Democracy," *International Journal of Intelligence and CounterIntelligence* 20, no. 4 (2007): 629–60.

57. Rubén Arcos, "Spain," in *Routledge Companion to Intelligence Studies*, ed. Robert Dover, Michael Goodman, and Claudia Hillebrand (London: Routledge, 2014) 242.

58. Omar Rodríquez, "Intelligence and Professionalism in Mexico's Democratic Transition," in *Intelligence Professionalism in the Americas*, ed. Russell Swenson and Susana Lemozy (Washington, DC: Center for Strategic Intelligence Research and Joint Military Intelligence College, 2003) 247–48.

59. Seva Gunitsky, "Democratic Waves in Historical Perspective," *Perspectives on Politics* 16, no. 3 (2018): 634.

60. The Carnation Revolution started as a military coup by the Movimento das Forcas Armadas (MFA; Armed Forces Movement) and soon was supported by strong civil

resistance. This led to the fall of the Estado Novo (see chapter 2) and started a revolutionary process that in turn resulted in a democratic Portugal. See Samuel Phillips Huntington, *The Third Wave: Democratization in the Late Twentieth Century* (Norman: University of Oklahoma Press, 1993). See also Raquel da Silva, *Narratives of Political Violence: Life Stories of Former Militants*, Critical Terrorism Studies (Abingdon, UK: Routledge, 2018).

61. John Sislin, "Revolution Betrayed? Romania and the National Salvation Front," *Studies in Comparative Communism* 24, no. 4 (1991): 395–411.

62. Gen. Victor Stănculescu presented the personnel figures for the Fifth and Sixth Directorates (VIP protection and military counterintelligence) shortly after his appointment as defense minister in February 1990. SRI director Virgil Magureanu gave a fuller accounting in his first report to the parliament in November 1990, although he apparently undercounted personnel by about one thousand. See, e.g., Dennis Deletant, "The Successors to the Securitate: Old Habits Die Hard," in *Security Intelligence Services in New Democracies*, ed. K. Williams and Dennis Deletant (Basingstoke, UK: Palgrave, 2001), 215–17. The SRI has since reconstructed a more accurate roster and made it public.

63. Sinisa Jakov Marusic, "New Macedonia Lustration Commission Resumes Collaborator Probe," Balkan Insight, August 1, 2014, https://balkaninsight.com/2014/08/01/old-head-to-lead-macedonia-s-lustration-commission/.

64. Nicolás Misculin, "Argentina to Purge Disloyal Spies from Intelligence Agency: Sources," Thomson Reuters, February 27, 2015, www.reuters.com/article/us-argentina-prosecutor-spies/argentina-to-purge-disloyal-spies-from-intelligence-agency-sources-idUSKBN0LV29720150227.

65. Matei and Bruneau, "Intelligence Reform in New Democracies," 602. See also Florina Cristiana Matei and Andrés de Castro García, "Transitional Justice and Intelligence Democratization," *International Journal of Intelligence and CounterIntelligence* 32, no. 4 (2019): 717–36, and Zoltan Barany, *The Soldier and the Changing State: Building Democratic Armies in Africa, Asia, Europe, and the Americas* (Princeton, NJ: Princeton University Press, 2012).

66. Peter Gill and Lee Wilson, "Intelligence and Security-Sector Reform in Indonesia," in Davies and Gustafson, *Intelligence Elsewhere*, 157–81.

67. Bleiker and Krupanski, *Rule of Law and Security Sector Reform*, 45.

68. Matei and Bruneau, "Intelligence Reform in New Democracies," 602.

69. Matei and Bruneau, 602. See also Anja H. Ebnöther Philipp H. Fluri, and Predrag Jurekovic, eds., *Security Sector Governance in the Western Balkans: Self-Assessment Studies on Defence, Intelligence, Police and Border Management Reform* (Geneva: DCAF, 2007) 4.

70. Lise Rakner, Alina Rochal Menocal, and Verena Fritz, *Democratisation's Third Wave and the Challenges of Democratic Deepening: Assessing International Democracy Assistance and Lessons Learned* (London: Overseas Development Institute, 2007) 1.

71. "Security Sector Reform: United Nations Peacekeeping," United Nations, November 2017, www.un.org/en/peacekeeping/issues/security.shtml.

72. Geneva Centre for Security Sector Governance, accessed February 23, 2021, https://issat.dcaf.ch/Learn/SSR-Overview.

73. Department for International Development, *Understanding and Supporting Security Sector Reform* (London: DFID, 2002), 1–41, https://www.securitycouncilreport

.org/atf/cf/%7B65BFCF9B-6D27-4E9C-8CD3-CF6E4FF96FF9%7D/supporting security[1].pdf.

74. OECD, *OECD DAC Handbook on Security Sector Reform: Supporting Security and Justice*, (2008) https://doi.org/10.1787/9789264027862-en. See also Wilhelm N. Germann and Timothy Edmunds, *Towards Security Sector Reform in Post–Cold War Europe: A Framework for Assessment* (Baden-Baden: Nomos Verlagsgesellschaft, 2003), 11–25, and Alan Bryden and Hänggi Heiner, *Reform and Reconstruction of the Security Sector* (Münster: LIT Verlag, 2004), 1–9.

75. Department for International Development (DFID) et. al., *The Global Conflict Prevention Pool: A Joint UK Government Approach to Reducing Conflict* (London: FCO, 2003), 30.

76. Albrecht Schnabel and Hans-Georg Ehrhart, *Security Sector Reform and Post-Conflict Peacebuilding* (Tokyo: United Nations University Press, 2005).

77. Nina Wilén, "Examining the Links between Security Sector Reform and Peacekeeping Troop Contribution in Post-Conflict States," *Journal of Intervention and Statebuilding* 12, no. 1 (2018): 65.

78. Department for International Development, "Understanding and Supporting Security Sector Reform," 1–41.

79. DFID et al., "Global Conflict Prevention Pool," 30.

80. OECD, *OECD DAC Handbook*. See also Germann and Edmunds, *Towards Security Sector Reform*, 11–25, and Bryden and Heiner, *Reform and Reconstruction of the Security Sector*, 1–9.

81. Ján Kubiš, minister of foreign affairs of the Slovak Republic, introductory statement, *Developing a Security Sector Reform (SSR) Concept for the United Nations*, proceedings of the expert workshop held in Bratislava, Slovakia, on July 7, 2006, https://www.securitycouncilreport.org/atf/cf/%7B65BFCF9B-6D27-4E9C-8CD3 -CF6E4FF96FF9%7D/SSR%204%20Developing.pdf.

82. See H. Hänggi and V. Scherrer, "Towards an Integrated Security Sector Reform Approach in UN Peace Operations," *International Peacekeeping* 15, no. 4 (2008): 486–500.

83. Hänggi and Scherrer, 488–89.

84. DCAF, *Intelligence Oversight*, SSR Backgrounder Series (Geneva: DCAF, 2017), 7.

85. Bryden and Heiner, *Reform and Reconstruction of the Security Sector*, 124.

86. Luke Jones, "The Time When Spy Agencies Officially Didn't Exist," BBC News, November 8, 2014, www.bbc.co.uk/news/magazine-29938135.

87. Glenn Greenwald, "NSA Collecting Phone Records of Millions of Verizon Customers Daily," *Guardian*, June 6, 2013.

88. Matei and Bruneau, "Intelligence Reform in New Democracies," 603.

89. Three years after becoming chief of MI6, Sir Alex Younger elaborated on his efforts to demystify MI6 in an interview with the *Guardian* newspaper. Ewen MacAskill, "MI6 Boss: George Smiley a Better Role Model for Agents than James Bond," *Guardian*, September 28, 2017.

90. Matei and Bruneau, "Intelligence Reform in New Democracies," 604.

91. Germann and Edmunds, *Towards Security Sector Reform*. See also Peter Wilson, "Analysis: The Contribution of Intelligence Services to Security Sector Reform," *Conflict, Security and Development* 5, no. 1 (2005).

92. Wilson, "Analysis." See also Matei and Bruneau, "Intelligence Reform in New Democracies, 602–30.

93. Matei and Bruneau, "Intelligence Reform in New Democracies," 606, 616.

94. Matei and Bruneau, 602–30.

95. P. Goble, "Analysis from Washington: Toward Collective Innocence?," Radio Free Europe / Radio Liberty (RFE/RL) report, May 1996.

96. Susan Karstedt, "Coming to Terms with the Past in Germany after 1945 and 1989: Public Judgments on Procedures and Justice," *Law and Policy* 20, no. 1 (1998): 16.

97. Jon Elster, "Coming to Terms with the Past: A Framework for the Study of Justice in the Transition to Democracy," *European Journal of Sociology* 39, no. 1 (1998): 14; Letki, "Lustration and Democratisation in East-Central Europe," 529–52.

98. Gill and Andregg, *Democratization of Intelligence*, 23–24. Chapter 7 will discuss recruitment.

99. Peter Gill and Mark Phythian, *Intelligence in an Insecure World* (Cambridge, UK: Polity, 2006); Aidan Willis, *Understanding Intelligence Oversight* (Geneva: DCAF, 2007); Peter Gill, "Reasserting Control: Recent Changes in the Oversight of the UK Intelligence Community," *Intelligence and National Security* 11, no. 2 (1996); Peter Gill, "Of Intelligence Oversight and the Challenge of Surveillance Corporatism," *Intelligence and National Security* 35, no. 7 (2020).

100. Gill and Phythian, *Intelligence in an Insecure World*, chap. 8.

101. Gill and Phythian, chap. 8.

102. Gill and Phythian, chap. 8.

103. Gill, *Intelligence Governance and Democratisation*, 45. See also Gill and Phythian, *Intelligence in an Insecure World*, chap. 4.

2

The Legacy of History

This chapter will provide a brief twentieth-century political background on Portugal, Greece, and Spain and the origins of each country's intelligence organizations during authoritarian rule. What role did the intelligence services play, what laws were put in place, how were they governed, and what pathologies did they develop? All of these will be linked to the indicators described in the previous chapter.

Looking back to the twentieth century, it is possible to see many commonalities in the historic pathways across the case studies. Portugal, Greece, and Spain each entered the twentieth century in a state of powerful social, political, and economic transformation. New industries were being developed, old social norms were being reduced or discarded, and a broader group of citizens started pursuing power and enfranchisement. Common trends eventually emerged in the Portuguese, Greek, and Spanish societies in reaction to these developments, including the increased centralization of state power, the increased militarization of society, and an overt fear of communism as a political ideology. Often each of these trends supported one another, with the fear of communism or "dangerous political radicals" used by the military as justification for seizing power and ruling via the executive branch. Intelligence organizations, therefore, often served dictators rather than democrats, with their primary objective being to eliminate political opposition and identify subversives. In this way, they served leaders who were more interested in using them to boost their own rule rather than protect citizens.

To this end, oversight mechanisms were superficial or practically nonexistent, with intelligence organizations answering to a minister at times but usually to the prime minister or the president directly. Laws served the organization rather than set the limits within which they could operate. Constitutional rights and protections were amended or suspended altogether. The judiciary was used to rubber-stamp state decisions rather than judge cases on their own merits. Civil society was weakened, curtailed, or ignored. The press was censored and rendered ineffectual as a source of independent thought. Organizational transparency and ethical behavior remained alien concepts. As a result, an intelligence culture developed in each country that promoted the idea that it was normal to operate with relative impunity, to not face any consequences for one's actions, and even to be promoted and rewarded for questionable acts against one's countrymen. This was the kind of culture that democrats in Portugal, Greece, and Spain inherited from 1974 to 1976 and that affected the ensuing intelligence democratization process.

PORTUGAL

Throughout the majority of the twentieth century, Portugal lacked both strong civil society involvement in political affairs and an empowered media. This proved advantageous to various authoritarian rulers, particularly António de Oliveira Salazar (in power 1932–68) but also Marcello Caetano (1968–74) and Maj. Sidónio Pais (1917–18), each of whom exploited the relative weakness of Portuguese civil society in order to push their own agendas. For a long time, the only place that really mattered was Lisbon, the city housing the ruling elite who controlled the country's political affairs, set its economic policies, and dictated what the cultural norms were.[1] It is for this reason that Juan Linz argues that the political revolution that occurred during the early decades of the century "was largely a Lisbon phenomenon that found only limited echo in most of the country."[2] In the early decades of the twentieth century and during the period of the First Republic (1910–26), the urban masses and rural population had little to no voice, and what solace they found in major institutions, such as the Catholic Church, was treated with suspicion by Portugal's secular governments. This had culminated in the 1911 Law of Separation, which made the Church subordinate to the state, in addition to the reintroduction of various anticlerical laws and the confiscation of property.[3]

As Kerstin Hamann and Paul Christopher Manuel argue, "business groups and labour organizations were also frustrated by the lack of political stability and consequent economic disruptions during the 16 years of the First Republic." They point out that the majority of the forty-five administrations established from 1910 to 1926 "did not last longer than four months."[4] Furthermore, while political parties existed, they struggled to ever truly represent a significant part of the populace, instead devolving into organizations that represented the narrow personal interests of the Lisbon elite.[5] When the First World War broke out, therefore, Portugal was a deeply divided country, with the average person having little say or control over what happened.

The First Republic was ill-prepared to weather wartime reverses as it was not a unified state. Republicanism, for all the good it had done in introducing civic freedoms, representative government, and ideals of social justice, had also divided citizens radically along political, ideological, and class lines.[6] These divisions were not reconciled with Portugal's new democratic system because a major segment of society—namely Portuguese monarchists—were not able to legitimately express their political opinions, organize parties, or enter elections.[7] The result was a military coup led by Maj. Sidónio Pais, who mobilized fifteen hundred troops and supporters and took the capital in just three days after government forces found themselves cut off and the president realized he was without popular support.[8]

While Pais himself was popular with Portuguese society, especially Catholics, his brief rule did not facilitate an easing of the tensions that had developed within Portuguese society. When Pais was assassinated in December 1918, Portuguese political affairs devolved into further chaos. Monarchists attempted a brief but violent restoration, while in the North, young officers inspired by Pais's example looked to form a military government that would put the interests of the armed forces first.[9] Both efforts failed. At the heart of the matter was the inability of any one political party to form a viable majority that could oversee and govern the country. Accordingly, while the legal term of congressmen was three years, few actually lasted this long. The congress elected in June 1919, for example, was dissolved by decree on June 1, 1921. Its successor, meanwhile, was dissolved after an even shorter period, this time due to a military insurrection. Of the various governments to hold office in the early 1920s were "one that lasted one day and one that lasted six days during January 1920. Civic disorder was rampant and, as a result, public confidence in the very existence of the republic plummeted."[10]

GREECE

At the same time, Greece experienced significant social, political, and economic upheaval, specifically in 1922 when King Constantine I was forced to abdicate following military disaster in Turkey.[11] There followed a period during which the strength of the Second Republic—and citizens' endorsement of it—was severely tested. Four military coups were attempted in 1925, 1926, 1933, and 1935, with the prime minister himself almost being assassinated in 1933. This facilitated the rise of a new class of politicians in Greece, populists who promoted a message of law and order and decried the anarchy to which Greece was at risk of falling. Foremost among them was Gen. Ioannis Metaxas who, like Maj. Sidónio Pais in Portugal, exploited the fractures in Greece's political and social fabric to take power in a bloodless coup in 1936. A firm militarist, Metaxas had served in the Hellenic Army for thirty years and had occupied several positions in various Greek governments, most notably as minister of defense. The respect that this provided, as well as his friendship with the restored King George II, meant that many Greeks welcomed his suspension of democracy as a necessary antidote to the social and economic disturbances that were reducing business activities and aiding the development of "Bolshevik tendencies" within certain sections of society.[12] The general and academic Alexandros Mazarakis-Ainian noted in his diary, for example, that "the fear of communism by the middle classes and the events in Spain made many prefer to lose their liberties than their money."[13] Fear of communist punishments was especially strong among the many followers of the Greek Orthodox Church, who viewed communism as a direct threat to their ability to worship. It was for this reason that the church itself endorsed Metaxas's seizure of power and described it as "a blessing for Greece" in the long run.[14]

SPAIN

While Portugal and Greece were going through these tumultuous times, during Spain's Second Republic (1931–39) politicians were keen to empower and mobilize their supporters among different classes. This included "the urban petty bourgeoisie, small entrepreneurs, merchants and shopkeepers who saw in republicanism the vehicle with which the professional classes could assert their political independence after decades of nominal liberalism and actual autocracy."[15] These groups were eager to help change Spain after years of marginalization and economic decline. The problem this mass mobilization caused, however, was to intensify political disagreements.[16]

The culmination of this division was, of course, the Spanish Civil War (1936–39), whose history is more extensive that can allow discussion here. However, what is notable is the unprecedented mobilization of Spanish society that the war led to. On both sides of the conflict, individuals, organizations, businesses, and other entities provided the manpower, time, and resources needed to wage war. Yet whereas the Second Spanish Republic sought to harness the power of civil society in order to protect itself, the Nationalists sought to annihilate mass movements by means of repression and reeducation. It is estimated that this ultimately led to the detainment and processing of more than half a million Spaniards by Gen. Francisco Franco's Nationalist side between July 1936 and April 1939.[17] A total of 106,822 Republican prisoners passed before Francoist committees in 1937 alone, with a large number forced to join the Francoist army in order to make up for the time they had spent serving under the republic's flag.[18] This repression only intensified after Franco's victory in 1939.[19]

It is fundamental to understand the origins and pathologies of the intelligence services of the three case studies and align the historical discussion with the SSR benchmarking analysis. It is also key to understand the powerful significance of the intelligence services in all three democratization processes when those sparked as well as the wider significance of the intelligence services to the governments of the time. Indeed, all three services impacted the beginning of the transition. In Portugal, officials of the Polícia Internacional e de Defesa do Estado (PIDE; International and State Defense Police) were disillusioned by the nation's African adventures and were completely excluded from any developments within the military where the negative sentiment toward the Overseas War initially emerged.[20] Without any intelligence on this kind of sentiment, the government did not have sufficient or timely information on the upcoming resistance. Civil society played a key role here in helping drive the Carnation Revolution. In Greece, the agency Kentrikí Ypiresía Pliroforión (KYP; Central Information Service) experienced a powerful moment when it chose to provide truthful intelligence to Gen. Dimitrios Ioannidis (although very late) instead of continuing to act as a "creature of the regime." This intelligence "failure" was instrumental to the fall of the military junta, but it also highlights an interesting point—that of the relationship and limitations between the consumer and producer of intelligence. In Spain the security apparatus did its best to insulate itself from change and to act as a drag on reform. The Spanish system failed to engage while active resistance was noted. This resistance resulted in Spanish civil society adopting an "apathetic" approach to its "political reality."

In the remainder of this chapter these organizations will be examined in closer detail during their authoritarian periods in terms of four of the five SSR indicators: control and oversight, recruitment, targeting, and civil society. Lustration will not be covered here because it is a process that only takes place during a transition to democracy.

CONTROL AND OVERSIGHT

It is important to understand how control and oversight structures over the intelligence services, if any, operated during authoritarian rule in Portugal, Greece, and Spain. This will help the reader understand if these intelligence services changed their practices and moved closer to democratization after their dictatorships fell in the 1970s. Traditionally, under authoritarian rule, the rules are based on executive decrees. Usually no external oversight mechanisms exist, and if there are any, they tend to be cosmetic.

Portugal

Prior to its transition to democracy, Portugal had a history of weak oversight when it came to both intelligence activities and government affairs in general. This was a result of the involvement of the Portuguese military in the nation's political affairs, with military officers wielding their powers against domestic opponents. Salazar's dictatorship, during its extensive lifespan, accentuated the issue, with the legislature only serving the government, and laws written only to provide justification for the regime's actions, while the only oversight came from the executive branch itself. Despite attempts at liberalization during the later regime of Marcello Caetano, the core authoritarian setup remained more or less unchanged by the time of the Carnation Revolution in 1974. The state behaved as it willed, and nothing could ultimately compel it to do otherwise.

The decline of oversight in Portuguese political affairs began when Maj. Sidónio Pais marched on Lisbon with several hundred disaffected soldiers at the end of 1917.[21] Having deposed an unpopular democratic government, Pais used his relative prominence to embark on a self-proclaimed mission to "purify" the Portuguese Republic, which had "lost its way after seven years of mismanagement." Fulfillment of this "mission" soon saw the legislature relegated to playing a secondary role in matters of state, with the executive branch of government taking primacy in order to "get things done."[22] This was achieved through the passing of two laws that supplanted the 1911 constitution and granted Pais considerable executive powers. So powerful did Major Pais subsequently become that he began to be referred to as *presidente-rei* (president-king). This designation was used admirably among conservatives, Catholics, and the rural populace, all of whom welcomed his protection of "traditional values" and the promotion of the *pátria* (homeland) ideal.[23] Pais set up his own dedicated intelligence organization that was accountable only to him. This Polícia Preventiva (Preventative Police), established in January 1898 and reorganized in March 1918, was "given autonomy and powers to arrest or detain suspects implicated in political or social crimes."[24]

It was in response to such developments that one young Republican decided to assassinate Major Pais in December 1918. Within this void, the Polícia Preventiva began to operate increasingly autonomously, creating and maintaining a register of all political and social associations and their members.[25] That they could do so without formal authorization was a result of the framework formalized by Decree No. 5171 of February 22, 1919. This had made them accountable to local civil governors rather than any central authority, a patchwork arrangement that benefited them rather than those they were meant to serve.[26]

In the last thirteen months of the First Republic, four coup attempts were made, the last of which succeeded on May 28, 1926. The new military government—the Ditadura Nacional (National Dictatorship) as it became known—soon found, however, that the work was harder than it had originally imagined. Because of this, it looked to fill various key governmental positions not with more uniformed officers but with civilian technocrats. Among those chosen for such a role was António de Oliveira Salazar, a pious and reserved economics professor who in 1928 agreed to become Portugal's finance minister on the condition that he would have a free hand in managing the government's expenditure.[27] Equipped with special powers, Salazar balanced the books in just one year and began to provide the government with budget surpluses—a significant achievement in a country long afflicted by debts and budget deficits.[28]

Such successes made him a key asset to the Ditadura Nacional and soon the most viable choice for prime minister in a country still torn between conservative and liberal interests.[29] Salazar refused to settle there, however, and instead invoked the power of the state to remake the country in his image, declaring that change would be achieved by whatever means were necessary, including force.[30] Therefore, whereas Major Pais had attempted to merely "purify" the Republic, Salazar looked to destroy it and replace it with what he termed the Estado Novo (New State)—a corporatist authoritarian regime that took inspiration from Catholic interpretations of economics and antiparliamentarian viewpoints.[31] The latter in particular helped ensure that Salazar, as leader, was the sole arbiter of the state and the people's fate, with all ultimately being accountable to him alone. Salazar intended his Estado Novo to be a revived version of Portugal's medieval past. This placed an emphasis on respect of traditional authority and positioned the executive as the country's "guarantor"—its decisions to be respected and not questioned. Law and order were therefore essential components of the new regime, with the Polícia de Segurança Pública (PSP; Public Security Police) and the Guarda Nacional Republicana (GNR; Republican National Guard) pushed to the forefront of public life.[32]

The most important security functions, however, were placed in the hands of a new intelligence organization that aimed to build on the work done by the Polícia Preventiva: the Polícia de Vigilância e de Defesa do Estado (PVDE; Surveillance and State Defense Police). The PVDE "combined the functions of criminal investigative police, international police, internal security and counterintelligence, foreign intelligence, immigration and emigration services, border surveillance, and prison administration."[33] On paper, its organization closely resembled the British Security Service (MI5). At the top was a director who oversaw the operation of sections focused on each of the above—seven in all, an amount similar to MI5's six "A–F" sections in 1940.[34] One key difference, however, was that while MI5 was limited to collecting and passing on information, the PVDE received the power to arrest, from Decree 22,992 of August 1933.[35] This increased its powers and capabilities significantly and enabled it to act outside of traditional parameters set by the state. This was particularly the case given the way in which the PVDE was held accountable. Indeed, while on paper it reported to the minister of the interior, its director—Capt. Agostinho Lourenço—had such a close personal relationship with Salazar that he was trusted to operate independently, and the PVDE received almost unlimited funds.[36] This latter point was quite notable in the cost-cutting climate of the time and was indicative both of the emphasis that Salazar put on security and the power that he wielded in his role as president of the Council of Ministers.[37]

Toward the end of the Second World War, when economic difficulties led to visible discontent with the Estado Novo and Salazar's policies, Salazar came to value such close control more than ever. This was also when he became more convinced that only adherence to his vision could revive Portugal's fortunes. It was in this context that at a meeting of the Council of Ministers on February 9, 1945, Salazar spoke for over an hour about Portugal's internal crisis. His conclusion was that where the regime had made mistakes, it should fix them, but where it had "been right," it should continue to convince the people of its cause and fight its "enemies."[38] Granted increased amounts of autonomy and operational powers, the PVDE developed a reputation at home and abroad as a repressive part of the state apparatus that bore "Gestapo-like" features and tendencies (Gestapo: Geheime Staatspolizei; Secret State Police). It developed paramilitary functions after 1945, when it was transformed into PIDE. On paper the new intelligence organization was accountable to the Ministry of the Interior, but it contained "within a single structure all organisms and responsibilities for the prevention of and repression of political crimes against internal and external state security."[39] This made it so that its competencies did in fact cut across a number of areas, many of which were the responsibility of other departments and entities.

António Fortunato de Figueiredo records that after this Portugal "passed from an arbitrary but casual stage of repression to the development of a scientific system which, in its operative methods was tantamount to a neo-Inquisition."[40] This it did in a distinctly cynical manner as Salazar aimed to placate the Western allies with reforms that appeared to make PIDE less like Nazi Germany's infamous Gestapo but were in fact more symbolic than anything else. From 1945 this even allowed for a period of "limited opposition" before so-called elections were held. These stage-managed exercises, which acted as a release valve for any democratic aspirations, subsequently took place infrequently every four to seven years, with PIDE ensuring that opposition candidates never won a single seat, despite intensive campaigning.[41] The objective of this exercise in faux democracy was never to enable legitimate opposition to develop but to divide middle-class professionals from the dreaded Portuguese Communist Party (PCP) and undermine its "popular front" strategy.[42] Another false reform involved adjustments to PIDE's legal capabilities. Whereas the PVDE, PIDE's predecessor that resulted from the merger of the Portuguese International Police and the Political and Social Defense Police, had been allowed to conduct "unlimited detention," PIDE was limited by legal statute to detaining individuals without charge for up to three months.[43] After this, detention could be extended for two forty-five-day periods but only if the interior minister agreed.[44] In principle, this introduced an important check on PIDE's power. In reality, however, it was irrelevant because the interior ministers never opposed a single extension request that PIDE submitted, regardless of the merits the case put before them.[45] It did not help that the post was typically occupied by relatively weak individuals who struggled to assert their nominal power but who were more than happy to block any efforts by the Ministry of Justice to rein in PIDE. This helped facilitate the creation of a special plenary court, in addition to further general security measures in 1947 meant to cover the field of so-called political delinquency.[46] The government was henceforth able to dismiss armed forces officers who "shirked their loyalty to state institutions" and dismiss any public servants who "had taken part in acts of sedition."[47]

This power became increasingly utilized as Salazar began to fear that with the path to change through democratic means blocked, the only option open to reformers was to alter the state from within or overthrow it by military coup. To safeguard against the latter, further measures were adopted from 1949 that aimed to enhance the regime's security apparatus. Under Decree-Law No. 37,447, PIDE was given the power to intern individuals for up to three years in a "suitable establishment," although this period could be extended if PIDE so wished.[48] A Conselho de Segurança Pública (Public Security Council) was also created, chaired by the Portuguese interior minister and comprising the commanders or directors of the GNR, the PSP, the Judicial Police (Polícia Judiciária, which, among others, investigated criminal offenses), and PIDE.[49] Through this council and its dominant role in shaping Portugal's security posture, PIDE was able to expand its control over the other security organizations. It also began receiving significant cooperation from other government bodies, such as the Office of Political Affairs, the Ministry of Foreign Affairs, and the General Secretariat for National Defense.[50]

Some oversight of PIDE's activities was obtained through the creation of a Higher Police Council in 1949, which was set up specifically to provide special oversight of those who had already been found guilty of crimes against the state. These individuals were only allowed to be detained for up to three years, and PIDE was responsible for making the case for further detention as appropriate.[51] This became irrelevant from 1954 to 1960, however, when, in mockery of the judicial system, PIDE officers were free to become judges and the Ministry of Justice was blocked from monitoring any cases brought to court by the organization. Even in cases where individuals had been found not guilty, PIDE was legally able to hold prisoners for periods of six months up to three years, extendable throughout three successive periods of three years.[52] Such power put PIDE beyond the control of all but Salazar himself and enabled it "to keep indefinitely under arrest all those who were believed to be dangerous to society."[53] It was not until Salazar relinquished power in September 1968 in favor of Marcello Caetano that any attempt was made to rein in the organization, which had achieved almost omnipotence in security affairs. For many Portuguese, Caetano was a welcome change to Salazar. While the latter had become a reclusive and embittered individual, obsessed with maintaining Portugal's moral and patriotic well-being, Caetano seemed to be an engaging progressive. These qualities and goals were reflected in his leadership style, which was outgoing and friendly. He made numerous tours to "meet the people" of Portugal and the African colonies and held televised "fireside chats" about his programs. The slogans of his prime ministership were "evolution without revolution" and "renewal in continuity."[54]

However, "renewal in continuity" entailed few enhancements to structures controlling PIDE. Instead, it meant that the organization received a change in name, to the Direcção-Geral de Segurança (DGS; Directorate-General of Security), and little else. The period of "preventative detention" was shortened to three months, but this still gave the DGS enough time to mistreat detainees, particularly since Caetano refused to pass reforms that would have allowed them access to legal counsel during their internment.[55] Furthermore, many of the same personnel who had severed in PIDE continued their employment in the new organization. This was disappointing to many Portuguese. This disenchantment was one of the underlying motivating factors for the eventual Carnation Revolution.

Greece

In the early 1920s the Greek government decided to create a dedicated intelligence center on Corfu, the Ypiresía Amýnis Kérkyras (YAK; Corfu Defense Service), the purpose of which was to counter Italian espionage activity and propaganda and frustrate as much as possible Italian expansion in the Mediterranean.[56] In September 1925 YAK was transformed into the Ypiresía Genikís Asfaleías tou Kratous (YGAK; General Security Service). YGAK's primary purpose was to monitor "suspicious organizations," counter foreign espionage, and supervise aliens.[57] In this it was held accountable by the interior minister and through him the so-called constitutional dictator of the time, Gen. Theodoros Pangalos. Even this limited oversight structure was curtailed, however, in January 1926, when Pangalos, mistrustful of those around him, decided to remove the interior minister from the chain of command and to control YGAK himself.[58] This example was to be followed by several of the general's successors, all of whom valued the power that a personal intelligence service provided.

First and foremost among them was Gen. Ioannis Metaxas, who, like Maj. Sidónio Pais in Portugal, exploited fractures in Greece's political and social fabric in order to take power in a bloodless coup in 1936. Metaxas declared a state of emergency, adjourning the Greek parliament indefinitely and assuming the title of "o Archigos" (the Chief). In his first speech as leader, Metaxas announced that until further notice he would "hold all the power needed for saving Greece from the catastrophes which threaten her."[59] To help him combat this threat, Metaxas created his own personalized intelligence service—the Ministry for Public Security—in November 1936 under Compulsory Law 320. Granted almost complete autonomy, its minister—Konstantinos Maniadakis—was free to pass whatever laws he felt necessary to complete these objectives, whether that meant detention without charge, torture, or the mass destruction of literature.[60]

The Kentrikí Ypiresía Pliroforión kai Erevnón (KYPE; Central Intelligence and Research Service), which replaced the temporary Military Protection Department and General Directorate of Information in 1949, was made accountable only to the prime minister.[61] This not only increased the risk of it being exploited for personal political gain but also of it being unduly influenced by its foreign backers, specifically intelligence personnel from the United States. This was the result of huge amounts of American aid directed to Greece and other countries after the Second World War through the Marshall Plan. The American Agreement of Economic Help to Greece, for example, which was signed by Greece and the United States on June 29, 1947, established the American Mission for Aid to Greece.[62] The end product of such American input was the KYP, which was formally established by Law 2421/1953 in 1953.[63]

As with its predecessors, the KYP was accountable only to the prime minister and continued anticommunist activities at the behest of the executive branch. Little to no attempt was made to make the KYP more accountable for its actions.[64] In the early 1960s, Col. Georgios Papadopoulos served as a liaison officer between the KYP and the CIA before taking on the role of director for counterintelligence.[65] Indeed, such was the power of Papadopoulos and other middle-ranking officers in the 1960s that one Greek general later remarked, "It was common knowledge at the time that this group had become all-powerful, that [Dimitrios] Patilis [a member of the National Union of Young Officers, along with other members who were also officers from the KYP] could do whatever he wanted, just like Papadopoulos, who even won for himself the sobriquet, 'Greece's Nasser.'"[66]

Toward the end of 1973, Papadopoulos chose to experiment with liberalization. Most of the changes he administered, however, were purely symbolic, and the junta itself continued to function as an entity unto itself. For example, in August 1973, sentences of up to eighteen years' imprisonment were passed on six prominent Greeks accused of bombing activity and belonging to the resistance group Ellinikí Anti-Diktatorikí Neolaía (EAN; Greek Anti-Dictatorial Youth).[67] Among those observing the trial was the British Labour MP Stanley Clinton Davies, who concluded that instead of treating the case on its merits and providing an element of judicial oversight, the "court had made the decision to convict and that it would have been much quicker if it had simply called the accused to court and sentenced them without going through a pantomime designed to show the outside world that some due process of law was being applied."[68] The fact that the court allowed the prosecution to carry on despite the lack of due process was indicative of the way in which the state's version of events continued to be the only one that mattered, particularly when it came to matters of intelligence or security. This situation continued until Papadopoulos himself was deposed and replaced by the hardliner Ioannidis, at which point the functions of the state and the KYP became even further removed from democratic control. The resulting concentration of power ultimately led to the downfall of Ioannidis and the junta following his disastrous attempt to bring about *enosis* (union) between Greece and Cyprus.

Spain

Prior to its civil war, Spain endured a long period of social, economic, and political unrest, and in order to hold things together, the state resorted to increasing levels of repression. This popular apathy and resentment provided an opening for those who thought they could do better, particularly in the Spanish military. Among them was Capt. Gen. Miguel Primo de Rivera, who overthrew the Spanish government with the consent of King Alfonso XIII in September 1923.[69] There followed a period of rule when the Spanish military sought to influence every aspect of day-to-day life in order to create a generation of "new men" or "permanent soldiers." Supporting them was the Somatén Nacional, a militia that had been periodically used throughout Spanish history to provide functions to the Spanish Armed Forces. These included repression of common crimes in rural areas of Spain and of perceived crimes such as strikes. This role expanded, however, when a royal decree on February 4, 1929, bestowed the militia with "additional functions of vigilance and information" and called upon it for a further intervention in political repression.[70] These measures "marked a qualitative drive towards semi-totalitarian positions by the dictatorship. Party, militia, security forces and army were interlinked in the service of *primorriverista* repression in what constituted the *de facto* creation of a police state."[71] Primo de Rivera himself sat at the top of the command structure, and each element was ultimately accountable to him and him alone.

Only the king commanded more authority, and it was only after losing his and the armed forces' support that Primo de Rivera found his dictatorship replaced by democratic rule in 1930. Spanish Republicans erased the General's legacy and established safeguards against further military coups. This included the dissolution of the Somatén and the dissolution of the monarchy itself in 1931. A new constitution of the Second Republic, meanwhile, radically transformed Spanish society, establishing freedom of speech and freedom of association and extending suffrage to women for the first time. The government of Manuel Azaña (1931–33) introduced the Law for the Defense of the Republic.

Its text was very stringent and specified eleven categories of crime subject to its jurisdiction, among them incitement to resist or disobey the law, incitement to military indiscipline or conflict between the armed forces and the government, diffusion of news or rumors designed to disturb the peace or the economy, acts of violence against persons or property and incitement thereto, and any deed or statement calculated to cast discredit on the government and its institutions.[72]

The harshness of the punishments for committing any of the above—indefinite detention, exile, or a large fine—as well as the lack of any provisions for a citizen to appeal was indicative of just how much even Spain's democratic leaders appreciated unsupervised power when it was theirs to wield. In an echo of Primo de Rivera's earlier sentiments, Prime Minister Manuel Azaña claimed in 1933 that he had held "a power such as few have enjoyed in this country in modern times" and that he had "employed it in putting my foot down on the enemies of the Republic."[73] This established a very dangerous precedent for what came to be seen as acceptable uses of state power, particularly when it came to its use against Spanish citizens.

This was particularly the case after the Spanish Civil War (1936–39) when wartime intelligence organizations that had been governed under military regulations were put to use against Spanish civilians. Indeed, despite the cessation of hostilities, the nationalist Servicio de Information y Policia Militar (SIPM; Military Police and Information Service) never came off its "war footing." Instead, it continued to focus on hunting down former key Republican figures and persecuted anyone that was believed to be hostile to Gen. Francisco Franco's new regime. With SIPM reporting directly to Franco's Consejo de Defensa Nacional (National Defense Council), this would have been something that he would have known about and sanctioned.[74] Certainly, the legal basis for SIPM's continued activities during peacetime was not long in coming, with the Ley de Responsabilidades Políticas, or Law of Political Responsibilities, on February 13, 1939.[75] This law "declared the political guilt of persons who from October 1934 had contributed to creating or worsening subversion in Spain" or who, during the war, "had taken up the defence of the Republic or shown an uncooperative attitude towards the insurgents."[76] Altogether this placed millions of Spaniards at risk of sudden prosecution for "retroactive treason" or indictments for historical crimes against a state that never existed prior to 1939.

In 1941 the role of establishing who was worthy of suspicion fell to the Brigada Político-Social (BPS; Political-Social Brigade), which was set up under the Law of Vigilance and Security of March 8, 1941.[77] In addition to creating the BPS, the law incorporated all of Spain's police forces under the command and control of the DGS and, through it, the interior minister.[78] This applied an oversight structure to the BPS but only in order to ensure that it was fulfilling its key tasks and meeting the wants and needs of Franco himself. Indeed, with no monarchy to hold him back and the armed forces granting him their full support, Franco was head of state, the military, the Falange party, and head of the government. Franco held absolute authority and was not to be held accountable for his actions. A common quote by the dictator and his followers that captures this aura was "Franco only answers to God and history."[79]

This lack of accountability applied to the BPS through subsequent decades, all the way until 1968, when another highly militarized intelligence organization was created: the Organización Contrasubversiva Nacional (OCN: National Countersubversive Organization). Under the command of Col. José Ignacio San Martín, the OCN ostensibly reported to the Ministry of Education and Science, but in reality it answered to the Spanish Army. So successful was the OCN in its efforts that Vice President Luis Carrero Blanco, who was by 1967 the de facto ruler of Spain owing to Franco's ill-health, ordered the construction of an even larger intelligence organization based on the OCN's template. This was designated in 1972 as the Servicio Central de Documentación (SECED; Central Documentation Service) and under Decree 511/1972 was detailed to report directly to the Spanish prime minister alone.[80]

This was the legacy that was bequeathed to Spain when the Basque separatist group Euskadi ta Askatasuna (ETA; Basque Homeland and Liberty) assassinated Blanco with a car bomb in December 1973 in the aptly named Operation Ogre.[81] Instead of protecting their citizens, Spain's various militarized intelligence organizations continued to engage in activities that were designed purely to protect the Francoist regime and its institutions. In pursuit of this task, they were accountable not to the Spanish people but to the executive branch of government, the only element that had oversight of their activities. In this way, a clear line of continuity can be drawn from the original Francoist intelligence organizations established during the Spanish Civil War and those that remained when Franco died in November 1975.

RECRUITMENT

The key indicator of recruitment is fundamental to understanding the criteria under which intelligence staff were recruited during the authoritarian period of each case study. Areas such as loyalty to the regime, the level of education of the services' personnel, and the composition of the service with police and military personnel, as opposed to civilians, are key parameters to examine.

Portugal

Prior to 1984, when the Sistema de Informações da República Portuguesa (SIRP; Informations System of the Portuguese Republic) was created, Portugal had several intelligence organizations, almost all of them "civilian" entities. The first of these, the Preventative Police, came under Portugal's national police structure, reporting up the police chain of command through the Ministry of the Interior to President Pais. Under Decree No. 3673 of December 22, 1917, specific personnel were assigned to this organization, with a focus on those experienced in investigations and detective work.[82] Not long afterward, in 1918, a General Directorate for Public Security was created following an overall review of Portugal's police setup. Under Decree No. 4166 of April 27, 1918, the directorate absorbed the Preventative Police and began hiring a director, a staff of twenty agents, one secretary, and four assistants.[83] The decree also stipulated that the new organization could hire "auxiliary agents of all sexes and of all social classes." These would appear on a secret list and be responsible for surveillance and information-collection roles.[84] Despite the flurry of changes that occurred to this directorate and other police organizations during the 1920s, the police always maintained ownership of the state's intelligence functions. The Criminal Procedure Code of 1929 placed more emphasis on the investigative side of police work than ever before.[85]

This in turn culminated in the merger of the Portuguese International Police and the Political and Social Defense Police to form the PVDE in 1933. To begin with, the PVDE was weakened by an unwieldy command structure and a small staff. This quickly changed, however, with the outbreak of the Spanish Civil War next door in 1936 and the subsequent assassination attempt against Salazar in 1937. After this, the PVDE expanded rapidly, and its officers began to adhere to a progressively stricter series of rules and requirements. Prospective officers, for example, had to take an oath before being able to serve in government.[86] This required candidates to state, "I declare on my honour that I am devoted to the social order established by the Portuguese constitution of 1933 and that I actively repudiate communism and all subversive ideas."[87] Indeed, in order to work for the PVDE, it did not necessarily matter where a candidate came from, what their economic background was, or other distinctions that perhaps prevented applicants from succeeding in other government departments. What mattered was that the candidates display loyalty to both the state and Salazar as its head.[88]

Such requirements only became more pronounced when the PVDE's successor, PIDE, was formed in 1945. By the 1950s, PIDE had grown rapidly in size, hiring officers all over Portugal and also developing intelligence networks throughout Portuguese Africa.[89] A key consideration of whether or not they were hired was whether they were willing and able to adhere to Salazar's four ideals of "order," "discipline," "unity," and "hard work."[90] This became particularly important when the Overseas War began and PIDE was thrust into the heart of the fighting in Africa. At this point, PIDE went on a huge recruitment spree, with close to two thousand new staff members joining the organization from 1964 onward.[91] This large increase came at the expense of quality, however, with many staff members failing to live up to previously established standards. Indeed, with the hiring of recruits with lower educational standards, the rate of expulsion for "dereliction of duty" began to rise, as did all kinds of intelligence failures—most notably, the escape from prison of several high-profile prisoners.[92]

Although Caetano, upon becoming ruler of Portugal in 1968, looked to rein in PIDE after it was seen to have become a "state within a state," its dissolution and replacement with the DGS did not automatically end its long dominance of intelligence affairs. Instead, many officers were simply transferred to the new organization. Furthermore, its network of informers continued to grow. According to the Commission for the Extinction of PIDE, for example, the DGS operated a network of approximately twenty thousand informers by the time of the Carnation Revolution in 1974.[93] Indeed, those wishing to either apply for roles in the DGS or to become an informer continued to be received by the organization right up until the end of the Caetano regime. Such was the relative appeal of the organization and what it could offer, particular to those in the lower classes who valued the perks that a position in the intelligence service could offer, even if it only meant working as a driver or office cleaner.[94]

Greece

During the early twentieth century, Greece experimented with several different intelligence organizations, each with their own operational remit and purpose. First, there was YAK, which was staffed by a small number of military officers from 1924, followed by the creation of YGAK, in 1925. This latter organization was a joint product of the Hellenic Gendarmerie and British police officers who aimed to provide the Greek state with an internal investigatory capacity. To this end, they focused recruitment efforts on those police officers experienced in detective or investigatory work in order to help fulfill the objective of handling "suspicious individuals" and foreign spies. In January 1936 the Greek military briefly reclaimed intelligence functions for themselves under its own Defense Intelligence Branch, before Metaxas effectively merged both domestic and foreign intelligence functions in November 1936 under his own Ministry of Public Security (MPS).[95] As a result, intelligence roles became filled by a mix of military officers and police personnel.

This arrangement continued after the Second World War, by which point Greece again experimented with various intelligence organizations—including the Military Protection Department, the General Directorate of Information, and the Central Intelligence and Research Office—before settling on the KYP in 1953.[96] Although ostensibly a civilian intelligence organization, the KYP continued the practice of filling roles with either police officers or military personnel. Accordingly, the vast majority of staff wore one uniform or another and were typically appointed or volunteered for service within the organization at the behest of their commanders rather than recruited through open competition. This was the case when it came to the appointment of the KYP's directors, a power that was granted to the Greek prime minister. Starting with Col. Alexandros Natsinas in 1953, the KYP was controlled by a series of high-ranking military officers, each of whom had trained in Greece's elite artillery school. Natsinas was joined by Colonel Papadopoulos, who took control of the KYP's internal security section in 1959, and Col. Nikolaos Makarezos, who was responsible for foreign espionage from 1966.[97]

Following the junta's takeover of power in April 1967, the KYP's organizational makeup did not change as the military already had close relations with the majority of its staff, with several even being key coup plotters themselves. Staff continued to be "assigned" to the KYP, including its new head, Brig. Gen. Alexandros Hadjipetros.[98] The only notable difference were the expectations that began to be placed upon new and existing members of staff as the junta began to consolidate its power. This included making them, other civil servants, magistrates, and educational employees sign before their respective minister a loyalty declaration that included answers to sensitive questions about family and social relations.[99] Anyone who refused or was suspected of disloyalty was removed from their position. This included a number of outspoken democrats and those who were perceived to be "political moderates" unsuited to performing in the new political environment the junta was trying to build. As the CIA understood it at the time, this process was part of an attempt to ensure that the government bureaucracy was only staffed with "nonpartisan functionaries who combine occupational skill with integrity."[100] It was also indicative of the value that the junta assigned to the KYP, viewing it as an essential component of the state security infrastructure that would help it maintain its power. Notably, however, the KYP's number of staff did not increase dramatically during the junta period, as might be expected, thanks in part to competition from General Ioannidis's Ellinikí Stratiotikí Astynomía (ESA; Hellenic Military Police). The ESA became infamous during the junta period for the heavy-handed way in which it conducted arrests and investigations and well known as a user of torture to solicit confessions out of prisoners and other suspects.

Spain

Unlike Portugal, which historically created police-based intelligence organizations, and Greece, which decided to mix military and police officers together, Spain predominantly adopted a military-like structure for its intelligence organizations. This began with the assignment of intelligence functions to the

Somatén Nacional militia in 1929, before intelligence functions were assigned to the paramilitary Guardia de Asalto (Assault Guards) and the Guardia Civil (Civil Guard) in the 1930s. The outbreak of the Spanish Civil War saw the militarization of intelligence taken to new levels, with both sides developing military-based intelligence organizations that recruited from the existing ranks in order to suppress resistance and counter the enemy. This included the Departamento Especial de Información del Estado (DEDIDE; Special Information Department of the State), the information services of the army, navy, and air force, the Nationalists' Servicio de Información y Policía Militar (SIPM; Military Police and Information Service), and the Republicans' Servicio de Investigación Militar (SIM; Military Information Service).[101] In addition, there were organizations such as the Servicio de Información de la Frontera Noroeste de España (SIFNE; Information Service of the Northeast of Spain) and the International Brigades' own information section.

Each of these organizations recruited soldiers, either for the Nationalist cause or the Republican cause, and although the former won in the end, those who had served in security or intelligence roles never fully came off their "war footing." It is for this reason that the BPS, when it was established in 1941, was built using a cadre of former SIPM officers, each of whom had served in a military capacity during the war.[102] These soldiers were subsequently augmented by an influx of police detectives and investigators, and the BPS was placed under the General Police Corps. During its collaboration with the Gestapo, José Finat y Escrivá de Romaní (the general director of Security) established a secret Special Brigade. One of its objectives was to "control Jews residing in Spain."[103] It was especially important that its members were not only skilled professionally but also committed to Francoism and to anticommunism in general.

These criteria remained in place when the OCN was created in 1968 from the ranks of the Spanish Armed Forces. Indeed, this latter organization became the pet project of the Sección de Información del Alto Estado Mayor (SIAEM; Information Section of the General Staff)—the military information section—after the minister of education requested military support in undermining the student protest movement.[104] Undersecretary of Education Alberto Monreal later specified that the objective of the new organization would be to offer "technical support to prevent subversion in the universities from placing the regime in a situation similar to that which the French in May placed de Gaulle."[105] Soon the organization's head, Col. José Ignacio San Martín, recruited two individuals, one to form and direct its "action groups," another to coordinate "psychological actions."[106] After two years of development, San Martín estimated that the OCN had recruited "about forty chiefs and officers of the three branches [of the armed forces], most of them full-time, although others dedicated to reading and documentation work would be assigned on a part-time basis."[107] At the same time, the OCN had succeeded in recruiting just under four hundred "collaborators" of both sexes from all over Spain.[108] To some in the Spanish high command, the explicit use of the military in such fashion was detestable and beneath its standing. Gen. Manuel Díez-Alegría, for example, commented that "having a bunch of captains and commanders on the loose at universities was an aberration," something better suited to policemen and not military officers.[109] The fact that the OCN had the backing of Franco's heir apparent, Adm. Carrero Blanco, rendered General Díez-Alegría's opinion moot, however, and in turn prevented the military from not participating in the development of the SECED. This organization, which was built from the OCN's successes, was again an entirely military-run affair. The SECED decided by default how it recruited, with officers being appointed by commanders who deemed them worthy and able to fulfill such roles essential in the fight against "the domestic enemy."

TARGETING

Examining the "threats" that the intelligence services of a nondemocratic era targeted, as well as the methods they used, is fundamental to understanding whether the targets changed after the dictatorships fell. The authoritarian governments of Portugal, Greece, and Spain all focused on repression and targeted their own citizens who were perceived to be enemies of the regime. Anticommunism was at the top of their agendas and remained a principal concern until long after their transition to democracy. Illegal methods such as torture were applied constantly to induce fear and extract information.

Portugal

The main purpose of Portugal's intelligence services in the run-up to the Carnation Revolution, which took place on April 25, 1974, was to ensure law and order—regardless of the political or economic impact on society. The primacy of such an objective had its roots in the chaos of the First Republic (1910–26) and the perceived period of calm under Maj. Sidónio Pais's executive rule in the last year of the First World War. For António de Oliveira Salazar, who became president of the Council of Ministers in 1932, the former was something to be avoided at all costs and the latter emulated as much as possible. It was to this end that he created the PVDE in 1933, which was developed into PIDE in 1945. PIDE featured prominently in Salazar's efforts to protect and maintain Portugal's overseas empire throughout the 1950s and 1960s, to a point where its security role became almost as broad as the Portuguese Armed Forces. Although Salazar's successor, Marcello Caetano, attempted to reverse this trend and make PIDE more palatable to Portuguese citizens and soldiers alike, its reputation as a service that "held the regime up whilst keeping the people down" was one that would have important consequences both for it and Portuguese intelligence when democratization began.[110]

Having received responsibility for the combined functions of almost all of the state's investigatory and administration organizations, including the police, domestic intelligence, foreign intelligence, border surveillance, and others, the PVDE developed immense powers of collection. As well as setting up a huge domestic information-gathering network, the PVDE also developed networks in the Madeira Islands and in Africa.[111] Although he was technically supposed to report to the interior minister, the organization's director, Capt. Agostinho Lourenço, developed a close working relationship with Salazar himself. This soon gave him a reputation for being one of the most powerful men in the state, and he used this power to try to make the PVDE a professional intelligence organization. Lourenço lamented, for example, the lack of foreign language proficiency among the PVDE's staff and its inability to compete with its other European counterparts when it came to gathering information abroad.[112] This was all the more problematic due to the amount of pressure that he came under to ensure the state's security. In Salazar's mind, communism was the biggest threat to Portugal's interests and the most important intelligence-collection target was therefore Portuguese communists and their supporters. He stated in 1933, "There is no such thing as Portuguese, French, or British communism, only international communism, which strives to impair and destroy national independence."[113] Consequently, when the Spanish Civil War broke out in July 1936, Salazar looked to deploy the PVDE's considerable resources on both sides of the border. If the Spanish Nationalists lost, Salazar feared that a communist takeover of the Iberian Peninsula would eventually occur, with anarchy and violence the natural result.[114]

The PVDE was soon turning over Spanish Republicans and communists to Franco's forces, refusing entry to Spanish refugees, and collecting intelligence on the Republican administration's ambassador in Lisbon.[115] Franco's own intelligence services were even granted permission to operate on Portuguese territory unimpeded, with the PVDE's full support.[116] In the eyes of anti-Franco forces, such cooperation made Salazar complicit in the general's campaign against the Spanish Republic and therefore a target for reprisal. Retaliation ultimately came on July 4, 1937, when Emídio Santana, founder of the Sindicato Nacional dos Metalúrgicos (National Union of Metallurgists) tried to blow up Salazar as he was heading for mass.[117] This incident was illustrative of both how exposed Portugal was to the Spanish Civil War and the PVDE's relative inability to fully contain it. As a result, Lourenço sought aid from two countries that shared Salazar's antipathy for communism and a desire for order at any costs: fascist Italy and Nazi Germany.

With both Italy and Germany flooding Spain with troops, munitions, and matériel in order to aid Franco, it was not difficult for them to increase their activities into Portugal. Indeed, the fascist Italian police already maintained a mission in Portugal, and the Nazi Sicherheitsdienst (SD, the intelligence service of the Schutzstaffel [SS; Protection Squad] and the Nazi Party) and Gestapo were also keen to expand their presence in such places as Lisbon.[118] To this end, they readily agreed to export instructors "to provide training in the latest police state techniques of the 1930s. The end product was a force that infiltrated most areas of national life and had a summary way of dealing with malcontents."[119] Spanish Republicans and communists were the test subjects of the PVDE's updated techniques, and concerted action led to the arrest and deportation of approximately a thousand suspected "malcontents" from 1936 to 1939.[120] It was not just Spanish citizens who had reason to be fearful, however, as during this time the PVDE began collecting information on those Portuguese it deemed to be "domestic subversives." In this, they were supported by the newly created Portuguese Legion, a far-right militia sanctioned by the Portuguese government on the understanding that it would act "always in obedience to the government and regularly under the orders of the civilian or military authority."[121] Those citizens who were unfortunate enough to be targeted by the PVDE were arrested and processed through institutions such as the Tribunal Militar Especial (TME; Special Military Court). This was a court created specifically to adjudicate on "crimes against the security of the state" and the "organs of sovereignty."[122] As the 1930s went on, such crimes could include anything from being a Freemason to voicing opposition to Salazar's political positions or policies.[123] No one was safe from persecution.

As in Metaxas's Greece, the solution to the resultant prison overcrowding was exile to Portugal's various isolated islands and colonies, including a dedicated penal colony on the Cape Verde peninsula.[124] The PVDE was able to effectively carry out such policies through detailed record keeping and by exploiting its links with the Polícia de Investigação Criminal (PIC; Criminal Investigation Police) and the PSP. The PVDE's dedicated presence in outposts outside of Lisbon—in Porto, Funchal (on Madeira Island), Coimbra, Angola, Portuguese Guinea (later Guinea-Bissau), and Mozambique—also granted it a limited external capability. Both this and its new training proved essential by the time the Second World War broke out in 1939, when the PVDE found itself needing to collect information on a new set of targets.

While sympathetic to the Axis powers' anticommunist stance and happy to purchase their arms, Salazar had little interest in helping achieve a victory that would likely make Portugal subservient to Nazi Germany. He also, however, could not see how they could lose, particularly after France fell and Britain stood alone.[125] Consequently, Salazar looked to keep his options open. To do so required intense diplomatic acrobatics and the entertaining of entreaties from both sides. Given its importance in the structure of Salazar's regime, the PVDE was right in the middle of such interactions. Its officers soon became the target of British and German "inducements" in the form of medals and decorations, official invitations to visit, and, of course, large sums of money.[126] Such offers were essential for acquiring Portuguese entry and exit visas, knowledge of each side's comings and goings, and even the acquiescence or aiding of espionage on Portuguese soil. Thus did the PVDE perpetuate cat-and-mouse games between rival intelligence officers in grand hotels in Lisbon and coastal towns throughout Portugal at the same time as it was meant to be securing the country's neutrality. At the Palacio Hotel in Lisbon, for example, *Life* magazine journalist William D. Bayles recorded the presence of "rich Jews," Englishmen, and Americans mixing with Gestapo officers identifiable by their "freshly Alpine-tanned faces." Later, upon his return to his room, he found PVDE officers calmly going through his belongings.[127] Such corruption and paranoia were indicative of a wider malaise present in the Estado Novo and one that was to become only more pronounced before the war ended.

PIDE inherited the majority of the PVDE's powers and competencies when it was formed in 1945 and made responsible "for the prevention of and repression of political crimes against internal and external state security," requiring it "to spy on individuals . . . even where they have been handed over to the supervision of the Ministry of Justice."[128] To this end, it continued to cultivate and exploit a vast network of spies and informers across Portugal. "The eyes and ears of the service, they operated in all public places—cafés, railway stations, post offices, hospitals, offices, universities, and factories. . . . Known as *bufos*, these eavesdroppers were heartily despised by their fellow citizens who for nearly half a century never dared to discuss politics in the open."[129] Although never acknowledged by the state, the frequent disappearance or torture of those targeted by PIDE was well known by the Portuguese public.[130] As the country's economic situation worsened, Salazar relied more and more on the fear that PIDE created in order to stabilize his rule and undermine his enemies. This was particularly the case when the Estado Novo transitioned from the 1950s into the 1960s and further threats to it began to evolve both in Portugal and its colonies overseas.

During the Overseas War, for example, PIDE began channeling greater resources into collecting information in Africa and using this to help shore up the Portuguese military. As time went on and the war effort continued to deteriorate, PIDE also began actively participating in the fighting, namely through the development and coordination of its own militia networks dubbed the *flechas* (arrows). These were locally raised troops who were used to track and harass rebel forces as well as support Portugal's own forces.[131] Drawing on its domestic experience, PIDE also developed "thousands of informants that sometimes stretched all the way to rebel command headquarters in Dar es Salaam, Kinshasa, Conakry, and Dakar."[132] They allowed PIDE to report on not just tactical situations but also the state of rebel supply networks and political support far from the battlefront. Other information was "derived from good old-fashioned sleuthing on the ground, coupled to information brought in from patrols, cross-border travellers, captives, documents taken during or after contacts, as well as air and naval reconnaissance."[133]

To help sort through this intelligence, and coordinate military actions, PIDE drew upon the local Serviços de Centralização e Coordenação de Informações (Information Centralization and Coordination Services). Following on from the unrest in Angola, these administrative services had been set up there and in Guinea and Mozambique in 1961, before a formal PIDE Overseas Office had been created in 1962. In each country, the service's objective was to collect, analyze, and disseminate intelligence regarding colonial politics, administration, and defense to safeguard the stability of the Portuguese colonial rule.[134] In Mozambique, for example, "it was the responsibility of the Mozambican Information Centralisation and Coordination Services to orient, coordinate and activate the investigations deemed essential to keep the populations from the 'state of subversion' in which they were located."[135] After the Frente de Libertação de Moçambique (FRELIMO; Mozambique Liberation Front) began to fight against Portuguese rule in September 1964, the local information service helped inform Portuguese strategy not just in Mozambique but also across the whole Portuguese Empire.

While the war saw PIDE reach the apex of its power, it also acted as a prologue to its eventual dismantling. On paper PIDE benefited immensely as it received more men and more resources with which to perform its tasks. In addition, as Salazar himself grew more infirm, he relied increasingly on those like Fernando Silva Pais, PIDE's director, who was said to meet the dictator nearly every day and succeeded in making the organization "a state within a state."[136] When the DGS was formed, it was not markedly different from PIDE in either its composition or competencies. Opposition groups were key targets of the DGS. Shielded from DGS surveillance by the directives of their own senior commanders, these opposition groups were able to plot in secret until the day came in April 1974 when they completely surprised the government with a military coup. The DGS's only comfort came from knowing that it had predicted that a plot was in motion but had been deliberately misled about the date by its informer.[137]

Greece

Although Greece began the twentieth century concerned about Italian intentions in the Mediterranean, its main intelligence organization—YAK—ended up spending most of its time focusing on Greek citizens believed to have links to the newly formed Soviet Union.[138] As part of this, YAK "set up networks of informers all over Greece (mostly recruited from the underworld but, increasingly, also within the ranks of the labour movement) and built working relations with the gendarmerie and the military."[139] The underlying legal basis for these actions were "decrees introduced in 1924 [which] promoted the notion of *ante delictum* 'crimes of opinion,' and established special Committees for Public Safety."[140] Possessing any kind of sympathy for communist or left-wing ideals was effectively deemed a "thought crime," and the "constitutional dictator" of the time, Gen. Theodoros Pangalos, was quick to identify communists in general as the main threat to his regime. To this end, "his best known measures . . . were the outlawing of the Communist Party—and smashing of a number of militant front organisations belonging to the peasantry."[141] When YAK was transformed into YGAK, its main purpose remained combating communism. Only Pangalos's overthrow in August 1926 brought an end to YGAK's operations and its official dissolution within the same month. Greece would not have another official intelligence service for approximately eight years, but the legacy of what YGAK had done would survive its dissolution and transfer directly to its successor, the MPS.

This latter organization was created by the 4th of August Regime, otherwise known as the regime of General Metaxas, who as mentioned earlier took power by military coup in 1936. Under the leadership of Konstantinos Maniadakis, the MPS revived YGAK's practice of targeting Greek communists rather than investigating external threats to Greek security. Indeed, so enthusiastically did Maniadakis pursue this task that he quickly began to be referred by his detractors as "the Himmler of Greece."[142] His main successes were to turn the Kommounistikó Kómma Elládas (KKE; Greek Communist Party) against itself, first by pressuring members to sign statements denouncing their ideology and party, and second by establishing a parallel KKE under the control of the MPS itself.[143] So effective were these methods that until 1942 most communists believed that the "Old Central Committee" had become traitors and fifth columnists.[144] They also attracted the attention of external parties, most notably Heinrich Himmler himself, who, in addition to pursuing closer ties with the Portuguese and Spanish intelligence services, looked to develop ties with Greece. This led to a formal understanding in November 1936 for the MPS to begin sharing information with the Gestapo in order to defend both Greece and Germany against "Bolshevik agitation."[145] This was then followed by a further invitation from Himmler to Maniadakis directly, inviting him to a congress where methods to fight communism were to be discussed.[146] So close was the alleged relationship between Himmler and Maniadakis that when German forces entered Athens in 1941 as conquerors, the latter apparently "handed over to the Gestapo his very complete dossiers of all persons suspected of Republican sympathies and a number of officers detained for opposition to the regime."[147]

From March 1946, tensions between the Greek government, royalists, socialists, communists, and anticommunists boiled over into open warfare. Operating primarily in the country's northern mountainous region, the Yugoslavian- and Albanian-backed Dimokratikós Stratós Elládas (DSE; Democratic Army of Greece) began a guerrilla war against police and military forces in the interior. To begin with, the insurgents "avoided direct engagements with the GNA [Greek National Army], thus succeeding in keeping the widely dispersed Greek forces fully occupied in northern and central Greece."[148] This allowed them to avoid the fate of the guerrillas of the Ellinikós Laïkos Apeleftherotikos Stratos (ELAS; Greek People's Liberation Army) who had taken on Greek forces and the British Army directly in December 1944 and been destroyed.[149] It did not make them capable of beating the Greek government, however, which from 1947 began receiving large amounts of aid from the United States. Eventual defeat of the communists in 1949 saw the Military Protection Department first reorganized into the General Directorate of Information and later KYPE.[150]

While the word "military" may have been removed from its title, the new organization was still very much a militarized organization owing to the fact that soldiers made up much of its staff. To them, the war against communism was not something that had ended in 1949, and so the same struggle waged by their predecessors was carried on. In the political climate of the time, whether this interfered with the liberties of the Greek people was not something that overtly concerned the country's largest backer: the United States. Undersecretary of State Dean Acheson had articulated this school of thought when he addressed Congress in 1947. In comparing Greece to rotten apples, Acheson stated that "as the apples in the barrel get infected by one single apple, [communist] corruption in Greece would infect Iran and further east. It would also carry the infection to Africa through Asia Minor and Egypt, and Europe via Italy and France which are already threatened by strong domestic parties in Western Europe."[151] To counter such threats, KYPE (and its 1953 successor, the KYP) collaborated with other Western intelligence services to monitor the movement of Warsaw Pact troops in the Balkans and any Soviet fleet movements in the Black Sea. American organizations such as the CIA were also granted greater autonomy to operate on Greek soil at the expense of the country's sovereignty.[152]

The KYP was then redirected to focus its energies again against communist subversion and report any relevant intelligence to the regime's appointed prime minister, Konstantinos Kollias. Subsequently, the organization was expected to work closely with the Greek military and police that carried out day-to-day security operations and maintained law and order.[153] Soon this allowed a degree of normalcy to return to most Greeks' lives. As the CIA described it in May

1967, "although they did not begin their take-over armed with a ready-made five-year plan for Greece, the coup leaders have achieved impressive results in some of the things they have set out to do."[154] Restoration of public order was top of the list of the junta's perceived successes, yet to maintain its power base it soon became necessary to stir fears of resurgent communist forces subverting Greek society.

Not long after taking power, for example, one of the junta members, Colonel Makarezos, announced, "We [the coup leaders] are certain that the communist threat is over." When later pressed on why the regime was still suppressing opposition members, he reversed course and underlined the junta's intention to "never permit Greece to become a second Vietnam."[155] Although no stranger to pursuing communist threats, both real and imagined, such inconsistent posturing quickly reduced the KYP's mission to blindly trying to satisfy the changing whims and fancies of its new leaders. Such incentives to deliver information emboldened those at the bottom and reduced the quality of the information that consumers received. This included prison authorities who received few incentives to offer anything other than basic care for their wards but strong encouragement to gather information if they could. This provision allowed guards to torture and interrogate prisoners at their own whim, even if it served no useful purpose.

In an expansion of the KYP's operational remit, the junta tasked the service with disrupting any organization or group believed to be against the new government, regardless of its politics.[156] They were empowered to do this by the junta's suspension of all guarantees relating to personal security and also citizens' political rights. Following its coup, the junta informed its compatriots of this new status by radio communiqué. By emergency decree, rights of association, freedom of the press, and the inviolability of personal correspondence and one's domicile were all suspended indefinitely. Political meetings and gatherings were also banned, and arrests and searches could be made any time the security forces saw fit.[157] Those arrested were kept at assembly points before being dispatched to various places throughout the country. For anyone deemed to be of high value, the punishment was often to be sent to one of Greece's many remote islands. There they were often treated badly and, in some cases, tortured.[158] All this was made possible by the junta's suspension of basic rights and protections that Greeks had hitherto enjoyed. Decree No. 280 in particular suspended all rights and freedoms of Greek citizens as formerly guaranteed by the Greek constitution. These rights included the protections of Article 18, which condemned torture and forbade capital punishment for political offenses.[159] The junta's decree also invoked selected parts of Article 91 of the constitution, which allowed for the declaration of a state of emergency in case of war, general mobilization, or social disorder.[160] Thus did the junta attempt to add a semblance of legitimacy to its actions by promoting the idea that all of them were necessary and legal per the country's own democratic constitution.

This was quickly dispelled by Constitutional Act No. 1 of May 1967. It attributed constituent competence to the government, to be exercised by the Council of Ministers, without the king's cooperation. Instead, he was to exercise legislative power under the responsibility of the government.[161] The same act stated that a new constitution modifying the "non-fundamental" dispositions of the preceding one would be put to the vote in a referendum, something that meant the abolition of the constitution as a whole, including Article 91, which had originally been used to justify the alleged state of emergency.[162] Other laws soon followed that reinforced the junta's existing powers and gave it greater control over different aspects of Greek society. This included a growing collection of "laws of necessity," which gave junta ministers and officials carte blanche to carry out actions and initiatives as they saw fit, without legal interference. The purpose of these stringent laws was to help fulfill the junta's vision of a revolution that would "save the nation" and safeguard its traditional ideals of "homeland, religion, and family."[163] In the junta's mind, each of these were threatened by domestic enemies and international communism. Only a strong military leadership could hope to protect the country from such threats, and if that entailed the suspension of democracy and then rule through decree, so be it. As far as Papadopoulos and the other junta members were concerned, if Metaxas had not needed democratic institutions to rule Greece effectively and maintain an intelligence organization, then neither did they.[164]

Despite its wide-ranging powers, the KYP was not overtly successful in its new enterprises. Indeed, the perceived failure of the organization after 1967 to "achieve results" led to much of its operational responsibilities being exported to the gendarmerie and the ESA. Under the latter's commander, Gen. Dimitrios Ioannidis, the ESA thrived during the dictatorship and frequently boosted its own profile and jurisdiction at the expense of the KYP.[165] This was facilitated by Ioannidis's creation of a dedicated intelligence and interrogation unit "at whose headquarters opponents of the regime, both civilian and military, were systematically tortured." In a macabre expression of symbolism, their building even hosted the motto "He who enters here exits friend or cripple."[166] Although some detainees were treated well, many more were tortured for information or as extrajudicial punishment. A document addressed to the European Human Rights Commission, dated March 1969, told of Poly Savvinidou, a student of architecture who was beaten on the soles of her feet in the Agia Sophia police station in Piraeus. Another student, Maria Kallorgi, was similarly tortured and interrogated for forty days at a military camp in Dionysos.[167]

Ioannidis's subsequent ascension to power at the expense of Papadopoulos signaled the end of the junta's previous experimentation with liberalization, as he began ordering the KYP and his own military police to carry out repressive measures not seen since 1967.[168] As before, the majority of those arrested posed little threat to the regime and had a negligible intelligence value. Ioannidis was smart enough to realize that repression was not enough to maintain his regime, however, and soon began plotting a course of action that he believed would make him a genuinely popular leader. The target of his attentions was Cyprus, which since 1960 had existed as an independent, sovereign nation. *Enosis*—the union of Greek peoples—had always been an ideological objective of Greek nationalists, and in July 1974 Ioannidis tried to achieve union with Cyprus by military coup.[169] Ioannides, however, in the words of one of his junta colleagues, did not work with others for the benefit of Greece but instead "regarded the ministers and career civil servants who composed the official government as a 'logistical base' for his own power."[170] From late 1973 this approach put him at odds with the KYP and its director, Gen. Lambros Stathopoulos, who had a habit of warning about Turkey's potential responses to a Greek-sponsored coup in Cyprus. Having grown increasingly frustrated with what he viewed as the overt pessimism of Stathopoulos's reporting, Ioannidis attempted to have him removed from his position.[171] Although unsuccessful in this regard, the episode ensured that any such risk assessments became increasingly marginalized in the KYP's subsequent analyses, despite the growing amount of intelligence that indicated Turkey's readiness to intervene in Cyprus.[172] This included warnings made by Turkey that any direct Greek effort to topple the president of Cyprus, Archbishop Makarios III, would result in a parallel Turkish intervention.[173] Instead, what Ioannidis received from the KYP was information that reinforced his existing views. One such piece of intelligence focused on the individual belief of Cypriot minister Tasos Papadopoulos that diplomatic efforts were pointless since Turkey would never actually go to war for the sake of the Turkish Cypriot minority.[174]

The turning point for the KYP came on July 18 when Turkish units and supplies were spotted embarking upon landing craft from Mersin port.[175] It is only at this point, when a Turkish invasion appeared so near, that General Stathopoulos decided to abandon his stance of providing only reassuring intelligence to Ioannides and his coplotters. Stathopoulos's mistake was to not have delivered such an assessment earlier and to have continued to frame Turkey's troop movements as "regular exercises" until it was too late.[176] However, even if he had, it is questionable as to whether he would have found a receptive audience. For even after Turkish forces began landing in Cyprus on the morning of July 20, the junta appeared divided on how to respond, with Ioannides ordering a partial mobilization of the Hellenic Army while the chief of the armed forces, Grigorios Bonanos, ordered a general one.[177] Having lost any chance of securing *enosis* and with it what remained of their legitimacy, both General Stathopoulos and his remaining entourage voluntarily decided to abdicate, in an attempt to secure some goodwill ahead of what they knew would be a lengthy trial.[178]

Spain

Whereas both Portugal and Greece established formal intelligence organizations quite early on in the twentieth century, Spain differed by making intelligence collection the additional responsibility of an existing organization: the paramilitary Somatén. This organization, which was used by the dictator General Primo de Rivera from 1923, began collecting intelligence on "domestic threats" in 1929. It did this through Citizens' Investigation and Information Centers, which placed a Somatén representative in every district, village, or neighborhood in order to collect information and establish databases on political opponents.[179] Once enough such information had been gathered, violence was authorized against those found to be "compromising public order."[180] As a result, the Somatén quickly earned a reputation as a heavy-handed group, whose members roamed towns and neighborhoods encouraging citizens to denounce one another for crimes against the state. So alienating was its behavior that following Primo de Rivera's overthrow a group of mayors wrote to the new Republican interior minister in 1931 to demand its abolition, given the way that Primo de Rivera had perverted the institution's original dignified local Catalan spirit and turned the militia into a vulgar tragicomedy performed "by a bunch of gunmen servile to dictator and king."[181]

Unfortunately for such concerned citizens, intelligence collection did not become any more palatable during the period of the Second Republic (1931–39). In urban areas, political opposition and civil society groups faced intimidation by the newly formed Guardia de Asalto, a uniformed police force specifically designed to combat public unrest, while in the countryside, the Guardia Civil kept restless workers, farmers, and landowners in check.[182] This meant that intelligence collection became fragmented. As the general in charge of the DGS, which was responsible for coordinating police forces, made clear, "each governor, as well as some generals, industrialists and businessmen relied on their [own] information structures, which at times were more effective than official channels."[183] Accordingly, by 1934, when a central intelligence organization was badly needed, numerous complaints began to be raised by officers tasked with responding to threats, saying they lacked the information they needed to achieve results.[184] Because of this, social and political tensions only rose as the Guardia de Asalto and Guardia Civil responded to unrest in a heavy-handed manner, suffering several casualties and causing several deaths in incidents in the industrial north and agrarian south. Prime Minister Azaña took no action to rectify this situation, however. As far as he was concerned, violence was natural: "Knowing as I do how deeply rooted violence is in the Spanish character, this cannot be proscribed by decree, yet, we still hope that the time will come when Spaniards will stop shooting each other."[185] To José María Gil-Robles, leader of the Catholic-conservative Confederación Española de Derechas Autónomas (CEDA; Spanish Confederation of Autonomous Rights), such irresponsibility was likely only to lead to disaster.[186] Indeed, lacking reliable information about the threats facing the country, Azaña was more or less unaware of how far along several military officers were in their plot against the government. It was because of this that little was done to prevent the rebellion of Spanish forces in Africa on July 17, 1936, an event that marked the start of the Spanish Civil War.

With the outbreak of military conflict and the division of the country into Republicans and Nationalists, intelligence collection became a military responsibility on both sides. One of these included the SIM, built in August 1937.[187] The SIM's main purpose was to neutralize the effectiveness of the Nationalists' SIPM and combat fifth columnists within Republican-held territory.[188] The SIM was known to rely on torture to get the information it needed and carry out extrajudicial executions of subjects at will.[189] By the end of the Spanish Civil War in 1939, for example, it is estimated the SIM had executed approximately one thousand individuals and arbitrarily detained many more.[190] Such actions illustrated the viciousness by which the war was fought as well as the negative impact that Soviet influence had over organizations. Instead of collecting and analyzing information, the SIM became focused on repressing dissent against communist and Soviet directives. It was steered in this regard by one Alexander Orlov, who developed "a network of terror" that focused on uncovering and eliminating suspected Trotskyites rather than Nationalists. This development much hindered the Republic's ability to prosecute the war effectively, for while the SIM had been "conceived to respond to the undeniable counter-espionage needs of the fascist Fifth Column, [it] ended up mobilising all the military might of the nation to serve the interest of the socialist-communist factions in absorbing the functions of government."[191]

After winning the Civil War in 1939, Franco embarked on a period of intelligence expansion, creating numerous organizations, among them the Servicio de Información de la Dirección General de Seguridad (Information Service of the General Directorate of Security). Other political information was gathered by the Servicio de Información del Movimiento (Movement Information Service), while foreign intelligence collection and counterintelligence became the responsibility of the armed forces' SIAEM.[192] Intelligence functions were also granted to the second section of the General Staff—Central-Servicio de Información Bis del Ejército (CESIBE; Central Information Service of the Army)—under the army, navy, and air force's own information services.[193] It was this military organization that was tasked with collecting information on anti-Franco activities and combating domestic subversion. To train new officers to do this, specialist schools were established to teach about the threats posed by communism, anarchism, and socialism. The key message they received was that opposition to the Franco regime was illegitimate and therefore a threat that needed to be contained. Such was the subsequent paranoia of the security forces that when Franco traveled Spain or went on vacation, citizens of the places he would stay in would be temporarily imprisoned as a precautionary measure.[194]

The creation of a new German-sponsored intelligence organization, the BPS, in March 1941 through the passage of the Law on Operation of the Superior Police Headquarters and the Law on Surveillance and Security worsened the situation.[195] Its first head was Gen. José Ungría Jiménez, who had gained a wealth of experience as the head of SIPM. To help him in his endeavors, Jiménez recruited many of his former colleagues to the new organization and liaised closely with Gestapo advisers in the art of suppression.[196] This facilitated what become referred to later as the White Terror or Francoist Repression, a series of large-scale arrests, assassinations, and purges that ultimately characterized the first nine years of Franco's rule.[197] To this end, the BPS was seen to define the desire of the Francoist regime to completely eliminate any chance of a potential coup or a return to republicanism.[198] It tried to do this by working in conjunction with the regular police and other intelligence services such as the DGS to uncover alleged networks of spies, saboteurs, and terrorists.[199] These actions affected the entirety of Spain's society and included the employment of Gestapo torture methods, which had previously only been used during the civil war on dissidents and Republicans.[200] The main targets "were of course communists, Jews and freemasons, but enemies comprised all supporters of the republican regime including the defenders of Separate Basque and Catalan identities."[201] In total, 130,199 such victims had been positively identified by 2010.[202] In addition, it has been estimated that up to half a million more had passed through concentration and forced-labor camps that operated from 1937 to 1947.[203]

As time went on, one of the most important tasks of the BPS and the DGS was to prepare reports for Franco and his ministers on what was going on in the country. This involved collecting enough information for bimonthly reports focused on internal and external opposition groups, crime, the country's economic situation, public reaction to international events, and activities of foreigners and diplomats in Spain. It also listed as threats a wide range of groups and organizations, including "Traditionalists (Carlists), dissident monarchists, radical Falangists, Basques, Communists . . . freemasons . . . and family members of Communists and fugitives."[204] This kind of information was particularly valued toward the end of the Second World War when "health and work conditions deteriorated to the point that, by 1945, hunger and related diseases had killed as many if not more Spaniards than had direct political repression."[205] Accordingly, the task of those in the BPS and other organizations, such as the

Falangist Servicio de Información e Investigación (Information Research Service), became ever more important. Hidden from public view, their methods also became even more severe. As one British report recorded of Franco's Spain in 1949, "its archives are based on the Nazi model, ensuring systematic surveillance of all suspected enemies of the State." The interrogation of a prisoner may include the use of "cruel artefacts, tending to force statements later called 'confessions.'" As they receive a bonus for them, the poorly paid police tend to use increasingly violent methods and prolong as much as possible the isolation of the prisoners to obtain a confession.[206]

The Francoist regime became even more reliant on this tried and tested methodology when it came to dealing with the ETA from the 1950s onward.[207] This group—which would become internationally infamous as time went on—had a rather inauspicious start. Originally it was no more than a "small group of university students who began meeting in 1952 to discuss Basque politics, increase their awareness of the Basque nationalist movement, and promote the use of Euskera [the native Basque language]."[208] This group, calling itself Ekin—"To Act"—originally aligned itself with the Partido Nacionalista Vasco (PNV; Basque Nationalist Party) but soon broke away after it became clear that the party would not seek anything more than "autonomous status" when Spain eventually became democratic again. For members of Ekin, passively waiting for such an event and deciding not to seek full independence was unacceptable betrayal of Basque interests. Thus, after rallying many disaffected PNV militants to its cause, Ekin became the ETA on July 31, 1959.[209]

The ETA's initial actions were limited to daubing nationalist-themed graffiti in Basque towns and cities, but it soon attempted a "spectacular" that brought them instant notoriety among Franco's intelligence organizations. On July 18, 1961, the group attempted to derail a train carrying Franco supporters and civil war veterans to a commemorative event. Although the attack ultimately failed, the response of the security forces was swift and uncompromising: "More than a hundred activists were arrested, and many of them were tortured and jailed" overnight. However, the "ETA had become a respected name, not just in nationalist circles, but in the anti-Francoist underground generally."[210] The experience, and the subsequent crackdown, gave the ETA its modus operandi for the future. It would conduct an attack and await the state's indiscriminate response, which it would then use to generate support for further action.[211]

The security forces played their role as required by treating all Basques as potential enemies subject to progressively tighter and harsher controls. This included strong responses from the BPS, which quickly made the Basque region its main area of operation.[212] In order to obtain information or secure confessions from suspects, the BPS began employing torture on a larger scale. So common was its use that it eventually became used not just to elicit information but also to instill fear into Basque nationalists. Indeed, "even when detainees had no knowledge to reveal, torture was . . . in order to intimidate the general Basque population, and to seek revenge."[213] This backfired, however, as the more that citizens were directly affected by the state, the more they began to support the ETA—the only organization that appeared to be willing to challenge the state's behavior.[214] There followed a campaign of bombing against signs of Spanish authority—Francoist statues in particular—and a spate of bank robberies.[215] The catalyst, however, only came in a year of turmoil around the world—1968— when a leading ETA member shot and killed a young Guarda Civil officer before being shot dead himself twenty-four hours later.[216] Thousands attended the ETA member's funeral and hailed the young Basques who were prepared to fight Franco's security apparatus head on.[217] The ETA's next move was to assassinate the head of the BPS's presence in Gipuzkoa. This led to the first of many "states of emergency" and the application of laws enabled by the 1960 Decree on Military Rebellion, Banditry and Terrorism.[218] The few rights that Basque citizens had were suspended, political opponents were classified as traitors, and the leaders of opposition groups received either long prison or death sentences. As a result, even more so than before, many citizens who had no involvement with the ETA became targets of the regime's intelligence-collection process, liable to be arrested arbitrarily and mistreated.

In addition to the war against the ETA, the Spanish authorities also had to contend with internal dissent as the 1960s went on. The years 1967 to 1972 in particular marked an era of student radicalism around the world, most prominently in the United States and France. It did not take long before the political ideals and ideas of such students began to reach their counterparts in Spain and cause concern among Francoist intelligence officers. The result was the creation of the OCN, which collected information on real or imaginary enemies of the Francoist regime, particularly university students who were becoming confident in displaying opposition to the government.[219] Indeed, the OCN tasked its officers with monitoring an ever-growing list of targets and launching operations to "infiltrate the academic world, labour organisations, and religious circles to neutralise dissent without exercising repressive police measures."[220] During its brief life, the OCN "achieved immense power."[221] Indeed, so successful was it that it was ultimately upgraded into an entirely new intelligence organization, the SECED. Whereas the BPS focused on collecting intelligence on dissidents, and the OCN had focused primarily on collecting intelligence on students and professors, the SECED's purpose was to "gather systematic information about political attitudes and activities, including possible subversion, in key sectors of Spanish society and intuitions, including the military."[222]

As a result, in the large crackdowns that marked the transfer of power from Franco to Blanco from 1967 onward, the SECED and its counterparts helped enable the detainment, punishment, and death of up to four hundred thousand Spanish citizens.[223] Even foreign intelligence when it was collected had a repressive focus, with the SECED ultimately spending "more time monitoring Republicans, Catalans, Basques, and anarchists living in exile in France, Belgium, Argentina, and Mexico than it did checking in on developments in the [Spanish] Sahara or gauging the opinion of the Franco regime in other European polities."[224]

At the end of Franco's lifetime, then, Spain had developed an extensive and capable set of intelligence organizations, each able to collect information on a wide range of "threats" and challenges. The role of both the BPS and the SECED was to protect Franco's Spain, and in this they succeeded, at least until Franco and his chosen successor died. Following this, they became authoritarian intelligence organizations without an authoritarian leader to serve.

CIVIL SOCIETY

A robust civil society was missing from all three countries in the case studies before their transition to democracy. Available literature on civil society before the 1970s focuses primarily on public sentiment toward the government rather than intelligence affairs per se. This is because the government was equated with the intelligence organizations as well as the fact that each government applied rules that took from citizens every right to be involved in political life. Additionally, a strong media oversight mechanism was absent because the media was heavily controlled by the state. Using the intelligence services of that time to enforce the governments' rules and punish those who broke them had become standard practice, with any potential for civil society involvement being completely abolished. When more liberal approaches by governments started to take place, civil society groups started to be created for the first time.

Portugal

The notion of the Republic itself came into question as it fundamentally lacked the support and engagement needed to function. After several attempts, the military took power, first on May 28, 1926. This move was in fact welcomed by labor and business organizations, with the chronic instability witnessed during the First Republic having won democracy few advocates among those civic groups that existed. They were even willing to overlook the suspension of the 1911 constitution and the censorship of the media if it allowed people "to get back to work" and get on with their lives.[225] Moreover, many even joined the new dictatorship when it became clear to the soldiers in charge that governing a country was not as easy as it once appeared. It was in this way that the reticent economics professor António de Oliveira Salazar became first finance minister and in 1933 prime minister. Under Salazar's rule, sweeping changes were made to the way that the state interacted with civil society. One key action that Salazar took, for example, was to depoliticize civil society, ending its ability to influence political affairs. As far as Salazar was concerned, the only things that the Portuguese should concern themselves with were family and the church—the two constituent elements of his traditional view of society.[226] To make sure that this happened and that he alone retained control of the direction the country was heading, Salazar did five things. The first was to effectively ban any kind of political activism, which the PVDE enforced, thus preventing the public from receiving competing information. The second was to invoke a tight control of the media, including even literature, films, and theaters, in order to present that which the government agreed with.[227] The third was to make public employment conditional upon loyalty to the regime. The fourth was to alter the education system to instill corporatist and traditionalist values, including by making participation in the Mocidade Portuguesa (Portuguese Youth) organization compulsory from the ages of seven to fourteen.[228] Furthermore, while the constitution continued to offer citizens various rights and freedoms, all of them could be invalidated and suspended at the state's pleasure "for the common good."[229] In this way, Salazar aimed to not only dominate Portuguese society unchallenged in the present but also ensure that future generations would be receptive to his rule.

This arrangement only altered after the Second World War, when Salazar attempted to restore his image with the victorious Allies by making attempts to liberalize his rule. This included allowing the development of the Movimento de Unidade Democrática (MUD; United Democratic Movement), which replaced the Movimento de Unidade Nacional Antifascista (MUNAF; Movement of National Antifascist Unity) as the main source of opposition to the regime. Unfortunately for democratic activists, MUD was no more than a mechanism designed to waste the energies of those involved, an organization that was allowed to function in order to grant the impression that Portugal was a democracy rather than actually help make it one. Those who did not understand this and challenged Salazar's consistent landslide electoral victories were targeted by PIDE.[230] This included the independent candidate Gen. Humberto Delgado, who, after nearly winning the 1958 presidential election—something that would have granted him the power to dismiss Salazar—was dismissed from the military, exiled abroad, and eventually assassinated by PIDE in 1965.[231] Business and labor groups also remained tightly controlled, with the state administering its own system of employer associations and trade unions. These were designed to promote class harmony rather than class conflict—or agitation against the corporatist state—with the good of the individual being ranked below that of the common good.[232] This nullified the organic development of groups that could genuinely represent popular interests because the state effectively decided what was and was not in the interests of its people.

To escape such constrictions and the country's dire economy, many Portuguese emigrated. In the 1960s Portugal still maintained a large overseas empire. The jewel in the colonial crown was Angola, which had first experienced Portuguese colonialization in the sixteenth century before finally becoming an official overseas province of Portugal in 1951. Just ten years later, however, Portugal's hold on the country became threatened by the nationalist Uniao das Populações de Angola (UPA; Union of Angolan Peoples), led by Holden Roberto. When the Belgian Congo became independent on June 30, 1960, "its government began to give Roberto practical assistance, including permission to establish a radio station and a training camp within its borders."[233] The UPA used this base of operations to gather enough forces for what they believed would be a brief struggle but that would mark the start of the prolonged Guerra do Ultramar, or Overseas War. On March 15, 1961, his force of approximately five thousand armed men entered northern Angola, "destroyed whatever lay in its path and killed men, women, black, white, young, and old." Around seven hundred European farms, trading points, and government posts were ruined.[234] Roberto himself admitted to his group's exploits, stating that "this time the slaves [the UPA] did not cower. They massacred everything."[235] The deadly assault shocked the Portuguese government but did not result in its rapid retreat as Roberto had planned. Instead, the level of violence perpetrated by the UPA against Portuguese and Angolan civilians caused outrage in Portuguese society and led to sympathy around the world for the settlers.[236] This helped facilitate a brutal counteroffensive by PIDE and four companies of Caçadores Especiais (Special Hunter) troops, which succeeded in driving the UPA to the edges of Angola by September 20, 1961.[237]

Portugal was not as effective in Guinea, where fighting against the Marxist Partido Africano para da Independência da Guiné e Cabo Verde (PAIGC; African Party for the Independence of Guinea and Cape Verde) began in January 1963. Although a military approach had proven effective in helping to pacify Angola, this was not the case in Guinea, where the country's jungles and porous borders stymied the effectiveness of Portuguese counterattacks. Accordingly, "PAIGC gained control over huge swathes [of territory], despite Portugal's vast commitment of troops, weaponry, and merciless counterinsurgency tactics borrowed from prior and ongoing American and European campaigns against guerrilla opponents in Africa and Asia."[238] This was a testament to the skill and determination of PAIGC as much as it was to the weakness and low morale of Portugal's largely conscript army. Indeed, aside from "elite units—the army's commandos and rangers, the air force's paratroopers, and the navy's marines—the Portuguese armed forces had great difficulties in utilising conscripts and conventionally trained officers in counter-insurgency operations."[239] This quickly earned the Portuguese the contempt of their Rhodesian and South African allies during the war in Angola, who criticized the colonial forces in Guinea for defending urban centers and isolated outposts instead of taking the initiative.[240]

This decline in respect for military and political authority was soon matched on the home front where the drawn out "low-intensity" conflict started placing a huge burden on Portuguese society. This in turn led to a notable amount of criticism among the country's seven largest economic groups, which argued that the war was leading to a domestic labor shortage as well as being an increasing waste of money.[241] In a society were dissent was rarely tolerated, this criticism was indicative of the growing confidence of citizens, particularly those at the top of the corporatist hierarchy, to challenge regime policies. This only increased as the Portuguese government resorted to opening up the country's economy in order to try to generate new revenue streams. With foreign investment increasing and the power of the state weakening, civil society groups began for the first time to promote independent paths. They were led by industrialists who were "impatient with the inadequate banking and financial institutions of the country and the lack of reliable information for economic decision-making."[242] Salazar remained unaffected by any popular sentiments, however, up until 1968, when a severe stroke stopped him from continuing in office. Certainly, so strong were his perceived colonial interests that after Salazar died in 1970, PAIGC founder and leader Amílcar Cabral reflected that he had been "unable to survive the affirmation of Africa's existence: the victorious armed resistance of the African peoples to the Portuguese colonial war." Thus, mused Cabral, while it may have been a stroke that struck him down, ultimately Africa itself was "the sickness which killed Salazar."[243] While a believer in Portugal's imperial rights, Salazar's replacement as national leader, Marcello Caetano, believed that he could bring an end to the Overseas War while saving face through a new colonial policy of "progressive autonomy and participation."[244]

Caetano's ultimate goal was the creation of a federation between Portugal and its colonies whereby power was to be "handed over to settlers and to the upper strata of the middle class *mestizo* and *assimilados*."[245] A key part of Caetano's strategy of so-called renovation in continuity involved presenting a "friendlier face" to the citizens of Angola, Guinea, and Mozambique as well as Portugal itself.[246] Indeed, in one of his first speeches, Caetano proclaimed that "faithfulness to the doctrine brilliantly taught by Dr Salazar should not be confused with stubborn adherence to formulae or solutions that he, at some time, may have adopted."[247] To this end, efforts were also made to further liberalize the Portuguese economy and to open up political life to outsiders, newcomers, and those previously deemed subversive. Various restrictions and laws limiting political liberty that had developed under Salazar were gradually relaxed.

Censorship conditions were reduced, political exiles were allowed home, and the electoral franchise was expanded. Even the dreaded PIDE was replaced with the DGS in 1969, the former being perceived as an organization that had tortured and manipulated its way into almost every aspect of Portuguese society.[248] Rather than be feared by his people, Caetano sought their respect and admiration, and it is for this reason that liberalization formed a key part of his political agenda. However, this emboldened political opponents of the regime, including the PCP, which was able to call out one hundred thousand members on strikes by 1974.[249] It also emboldened military opposition groups that cynically derided Caetano's pledges to end the Overseas War while it continued to escalate and more Portuguese soldiers continued to perish in Africa.

As promising as Caetano's initiatives were, they could not undo the political, economic, and social damage caused by the continuation of the Overseas War. Most prominent was the fact that the cost of running the conflict was absorbing most of the state's budget by the early 1970s as well as drawing in 282,000 members of the workforce on an annual basis as part of the official draft.[250] With the various African independence movements having rejected Caetano's "hand of friendship" and no end in sight to the conflict, the morale of rank-and-file soldiers plummeted. A major exogenous shock came in 1973 when, with world oil prices spiraling out of control, inflation rose 8 percent higher than the average Portuguese citizen's wages.[251] Junior army officers, "who often exhibited even less enthusiasm for the war than the troops under their command," viewed this as a critical juncture and soon began looking to men such as Gen. António de Spínola for leadership outside of the political chain of command.[252]

While rebel forces continued to receive domestic and foreign support, Salazar's Portugal grew both increasingly isolated and financially weakened as the war dragged on. Its people, meanwhile, also became more aware of both their immediate plight and the system that constrained them. Indeed, drawn together from all parts of Portugal, the conflict "allowed young Portuguese servicemen with very distinct upbringings to socialise with each other, broadening their socio-cultural horizons via sharing ideas, worldviews, cultural products, and reflections on their position."[253] This accelerated levels of apathy within the lower ranks and began a process of radicalization in some that would ultimately result in the development of antiregime groups. José Teixeira, for example, who was stationed in Angola from 1970 to 1972, recalled that he acquired "a new political awareness" from the southerners who believed that they were fighting an unsustainable and unfair war.[254] Rather than fighting patriotically for Portugal and Salazar, most soldiers were only interested in getting home safely. As one Portuguese conscript described it, "I was there defending my skin—not my motherland. . . . That was a fight for survival."[255] While obvious to a growing number of Portuguese, the risks of such increasing antipathy was not automatically registered by PIDE. This is because while it had almost a complete monopoly on the collection of information that involved domestic organizations, private citizens, and foreigners, it had not been granted entry into the military's affairs, except on rare occasions.[256] If a member of the armed forces acted out of line, it was handled internally, and the firmness with which the armed forces kept PIDE out of its affairs insulated it from the level of intrusion that other Portuguese otherwise regularly experienced.

In 1974 General Spínola published the innocuous-sounding *Portugal and the Future*.[257] In the book, however, he openly argued that "Portugal could not win a military victory against the liberation movements in its African colonies."[258] The subsequent displays of outrage by ultranationalists and the general's dismissal only galvanized opponents of the regime, and soon instances of open defiance were being displayed by students, soldiers, and civilians alike. The DGS, not having access to the same powers that PIDE had come to rely on in Salazar's last days, was incapable of stopping the dissent from developing into an existential threat.[259] Consequently, with Caetano displaying erratic leadership, "power slowly gravitated into the hands of diehard *situacionistas* who favoured internationally unacceptable solutions such as the total integration of Portugal and Africa or a hand-over of responsibility to white colonists."[260] It was within this period of political, economic, and social turmoil that the MFA was able to develop and, on April 25, 1974, bring down Caetano's Estado Social.

Greece

Having arrested leading collaborationists and dissolved the major institutions of Axis power in Greece, the Allies set about reestablishing democratic order. In an attempt to turn things around, the Military Protection Department was created to give the British-trained Hellenic Army an intelligence capability. The army's frontline role in providing security in Greece, however, ensured that the first use of the country's new intelligence organization was against its own citizens, many of whom just happened to be communists. The rejection of the thoughts and ideals of this portion of society was a major blow against civil society in general because, though ostracized, Greek communists remained one of the few groups that actively challenged the government of the day. In fact, it was perhaps because of their ostracism that they were able to challenge the government, having not been enmeshed as deeply in the traditional clientelist relationships that had undermined the independence of other civil society entities.

By the 1960s this structure had grown to include the Greek media, which became rabidly partisan and frequently acted as the mouthpiece for individual politicians rather than a representative of the public interest. A key reason for this was the press's lack of financial independence—most newspapers were privately owned and maintained and often struggled to achieve profitability. To survive in such an environment, newspapers "relied on indirect government subsides: duty-free newsprint, government backed bank loans for plant expansion, large advertising accounts from government institutions and bloc purchase orders by state agencies."[261] None of these benefits came for free. Indeed, there was even a period when several newspapers regularly sent potential articles to the National Radical Union party in order for them to be edited before they were printed. Seeing what was happening, individual journalists began to sell their talents to political patrons, either leaking or suppressing news per their clients' orders. Sometimes this even included warning about the publication of damning news, which the government often stopped with a simple word-of-mouth warning "vaguely analogous to the British D-Notice system."[262]

Consequently, when the junta took power in 1967, it looked to return the press "to its rightful mission," Papadopoulos announcing on the day of the coup that "freedom of the press does not mean irresponsibility, shamelessness, 'yellow press writing,' and the betrayal of national values."[263] Indeed, the junta's idea of a free press was one that reported its ideas and ideals without question. Those who resisted or opposed the junta from the outset were crushed. This included the staff of the two leading communist papers, staff and editors of the leading liberal papers, and even some of the leading conservative dailies—for example, *Kathimerini* (Daily) and *Messimvrini* (Noon). These two belonged to Helen Vlachou, who, being one of the most solvent Greek newspaper owners, was able to resist falling into line with other conservative publishers.[264] The majority of the papers to survive intact were those on the extreme right and royalist papers like *Apoyevmatini* (Afternoon). In order to ensure their loyalty, the government suspended Article 14 of the constitution, which had guaranteed press freedom. In its place, the junta gave itself the right to "ban the announcement or publication of information in any way; to seize newspapers, either before or after publication, and suspend newspapers for a certain period."[265] Furthermore, publication guidance was subsequently developed and issued to all print media outlets, outlining in detail the kinds of things that the media could not print. This included:

- Any article, commentary or news item . . . which criticises the Premier and members of the Government or their actions. . . .
- Historical accounts which by reference to the past can reawaken passions and sow discord.
- Communiqués from any organisation of the Left, including the EDA party and its affiliates.

In addition to things that it could print:

- The speeches, declarations or communiqués of the Premier and members of the government.
- At least one commentary per day referring to the government and its work.[266]

The KYP, which had never greatly concerned itself with policing such matters beforehand, was suddenly thrust into the position acting as an enforcer of such rules. As the junta became more entrenched in its views and less tolerant of dissent, this role expanded beyond press articles to include other literature and media products that Greek citizens consumed.

Public paranoia about the KYP (and other government organizations) increased after the 1967 coup as it appeared to have been complicit, if not an essential component, in the plotters' takeover plan. By exploiting the KYP's surveillance networks, Papadopoulos and the other coup plotters were able to quickly round up their opponents.[267] They included members of the Greek parliament, lawyers, journalists, unionists, and anyone else deemed to be of questionable loyalty. The speed and effectiveness of the coup shocked and surprised many observers, to the point where it became widely believed that it could not have occurred without American help.[268] The CIA for its part did not expect the new regime to last, given that it was opposed by the full spectrum of Greek political parties and the king.[269] Yet the detention and exiling of key political opponents and the imprisonment of thousands of others went a long way to helping the junta consolidate its power. Additionally, the US being more involved in Greece's political spectrum led to distorted views about the agency's reach and capabilities within Greece and concerns about what information it was collecting with the KYP's permission.

Furthermore, as it became known to work with torturers, "the average Greek put KYP, along with the military and the Gendarmerie, on the same level of responsibility and mistrust for all his suffering."[270] The KYP was forced into this position through the junta's drive for total commitment from those who served it. As observed by R. Roufos, although citizens did not need to worry about politics before the coup, "today, when the government represents 'the totality of the nation' it is unacceptable to remain aloof. Government employees, great and small, are forced to compromise more with the regime."[271] Accordingly, the reputation of the organization rapidly shifted from that of a benign entity, unknown to most citizens, to another component of the junta state.

What the regime was particularly afraid of was a loss of popular support, and to this end it went out of its way to try to maintain "a legitimate image," even if this was artificially supported by the kind of media manipulation listed above.

Outside of the families of military and police personnel and the Church, their base of support came from the middle and upper classes, which had actively identified with the anticommunists that had fought to maintain the country's independence since 1949. Their enthusiasm for the junta regime had always been tepid, however, and it is argued that they tolerated the junta rather than actively endorsed it.[272] It is because of this that they became more reliant on repressive measures in order to ensure effective control over society, a course of action that ironically only became less effective as time went on and more citizens became aware of the regime's crimes. This became especially clear during the trials of "traitors" because defendants were often not only prosecuted on flimsy evidence but were also rarely granted access to legal counsel or allowed to gather evidence that would have helped their cases. It was because of this growing trend that Papadopoulos tried to adopt a new governing strategy in early 1973. Its core was an attempt to "legitimize" his regime in the eyes of his opponents and reduce outside pressure to remove himself from Greek political affairs. The first step was the public release of many prisoners and detainees, including several Greek professors, lawyers, and students who had been arrested without charge.[273] However, although ostensibly free, the former prisoners were restricted in their activities and movements. Consequently, the 190 former members of parliament as well as retired officers, lawyers, and journalists who were released in July 1973 were prevented from leaving the country or returning to their former occupations.[274] Furthermore, once international observers and media outlets moved on to cover other interests, many of these individuals were simply rearrested. In other situations, quieter methods were used. Rather than being removed from their jobs, opposition civil servants, military officers, and others were instead replaced on grounds of "retirement" or "ill health." Those who were not government employees, meanwhile, such as students, were often forced into the army where their ability to organize and subvert the regime was nullified.[275]

While many privately disdained such developments but otherwise accepted the junta's authority, Greek students who actively challenged decided after six years of authoritarian rule that this situation was untenable. It was because of this that students of Athens Polytechnic University decided to occupy their campus on November 14, 1973, and turn it into a bastion of antiregime sentiment. Although relatively few in number and not formally organized, they openly challenged the junta's legitimacy and created an amateur radio transmitter to call for open rebellion against the regime and encourage a return to liberal democracy.[276] As thousands of others from across the capital began massing around the campus, Papadopoulos was forced to impose martial law on November 17, with the university itself cleared by armored vehicles and Ioannidis's dreaded ESA. As well as leading to the deaths of two dozen civilians, Papadopoulos's decision spelled the end of his position as the junta's leader. After having been blamed by his colleagues for allowing opposition to develop and not putting the uprising down sooner, he was forced out by the ruthless hardliner Ioannidis.[277] Though this and the crushing of the uprising bought the regime time, it came at the expense of its image as a protector of Greeks and Greek values. If the junta was prepared to use tanks against its own people, it could not be said to be the "free and fair" government that it claimed to be.

Spain

Civil society in Francoist Spain was not only incredibly divided but also incredibly weakened, particularly as an independent force. With the unions, communists, and other left-wing and opposition organizations rendered ineffectual, the only entities left were those that closely identified with the regime. This included the Spanish Catholic Church, which had supported the Nationalist cause as part of an anticommunist "crusade"; the Acción Española, Spain's own version of political nationalism comparable with the Action Française; and, of course, the fascist Falange. The latter perhaps was the only organization that threatened Franco's own grip on the country's political direction following his victory in the Civil War. In order to retain control and to direct the people's energies into activities that ultimately supported the state, Franco created the Falange Española Tradicionalista y de las Juntas de Ofensiva Nacional Sindicalista (Traditionalist Spanish Phalanx of the Councils of the National Syndicalist Offensive). This sanctioned fascism as the de facto political ideology of Francoist Spain "as the regime adopted fascist legislation and organisations of social control, including party and the militia, as well as youth, women's and trade unions, and gave the fascists seemingly total control of the press, official propaganda and the streets."[278] Yet, the compromise was that this would take place in an environment in which Franco remained the unchallenged leader of the state, the church retained its primacy in educational and spiritual affairs, the military maintained control over security and public order, and well-connected businessmen retained control over the economy.[279] Thus, the state involved outsiders heavily in its affairs, providing that they were active supporters of the Francoist state and unlikely to challenge either its ideals or policy choices.

As occurred later under the Greek military junta, this included subsuming the media and press under its control. This process began with the Press Law in 1938 when the Civil War was still ongoing. Technically the law was "provisional," but this did not stop it from remaining in effect for the next three decades because it remained such a useful tool for the authoritarian type of government that Franco presided over. To this end, it allowed the state to prevent publication of information unless specifically authorized and also enabled the state to suspend publication rights without any kind of appeal.[280] Newspaper editors could be appointed or dismissed on a whim, even if their papers were privately owned, and journalists themselves had to register officially with the government, belong to government-run associations, and offer their sources and material for inspection. Thus, even though the press ostensibly remained independent, its credentials as a source of criticism were rendered ineffectual by the government's impositions. This included obligations to interpret and report on news items in a certain fashion, as well as to avoid certain issues—such as state security and intelligence matters—altogether. Eventually, these obligations became so detail-orientated that they even specified what kind of headlines and photographs should be used as part of stories.[281] As if this was not bad enough, the "independent" press also had to compete with a growing number of pro-Francoist media outlets and newspapers. These included the Prensa del Movimiento (Press of the Movement), which ended up presiding over multiple newspapers and magazines.[282] The only consolidation for the "free press" was that despite their enormous disadvantages in terms of resources and authorized protocols, they could still boast about selling approximately two-thirds more copies than their state-backed rivals.[283]

Fortunately for the regime, buying "independent" newspapers was often the extent that public resistance or opposition took during Franco's time in power. Indeed, the strength of both the state and its entities, such as the BPS and later the SECED, remained more or less unchallenged, even during periods of crisis. This included the 1950s, by which time "the economy was so plagued by rising inflation and continually increasing balance of payment deficits stemming from the overvalued peseta and un-competitiveness, that it was on the verge of breakdown."[284] One remaining guerrilla commander reported to exiled Socialist Party leaders, "Those who trust in the possibilities of an armed revolt know nothing of the internal situation in Spain. Whereas most people wanted both economic and political 'normality,' they also understood that any attempt to show defiance would be 'drowned in blood.'"[285] Such comments were indicative of the strength and effectiveness of the methods used by Franco's intelligence services to suppress dissent among "disloyal" civil society groups as well as the effectiveness of their policies when it came to the media. Instead of actively resisting the regime, therefore, most Spaniards, including those who had previously been politically active, chose instead to focus on coming to terms with their new political reality.[286] Only one group chose to challenge the Francoist regime when it was at its strongest and thus to escalate matters further. This was the ETA, an organization that sought to challenge the unchallenged power of the state through the only means that appeared left to citizens: violence. It is key to note that most of the worst measures were applied to the Basque region alone. This further added to the perception that rather than acting to protect their interests, the Spanish state was a direct enemy of its citizens.[287]

CONCLUSION

This analysis of the Portuguese, Greek, and Spanish intelligence services' history based on the chosen indicators showcases their origins, their institutional and legal setups, and the pathologies that became standard practice during their nondemocratic rule. These created inherent limitations, a few of which persisted even after their dictatorships fell. Indeed, when it came to control and oversight, recruitment, targeting, and civil society, all three cases showed similarities.

***Control and oversight* came only from the executive branch that used each intelligence service for its own benefit.** Started from even before the dictatorship period, the Preventative Police, the Special Security Service, and the National Militia collected information against their own citizens, and they did so unaccountable to anyone but the executive branch, with control and oversight mechanisms often comprising nothing more than meetings and contact between director and minister or minister and prime minister (or, in one case, minister and "president-king"). This became even more pronounced when António de Oliveira Salazar, Gen. Ioannis Metaxas, and Gen. Francisco Franco each began their periods of dictatorship. Through the passing of executive decrees, intelligence services were established with the specific purpose of political repression. In Portugal PIDE had immense powers, including the power to arrest and detain for a long period by law while the service was effectively controlled by Salazar. Additionally, any laws to apply oversight structures to the service were cosmetic because PIDE could circumvent them and act as Salazar directed it. Greece followed the same example, with Gen. Theodoros Pangalos and Gen. Dimitrios Ioannidis controlling the Greek intelligence services, while a judiciary function was nonexistent with courts sentencing "enemies of the state" without proof. In Spain, Franco was head of state, the military, the Falange, and the government. Any oversight mechanisms to "control" the BPS were only in place to ensure that it was acting based on Franco's wants.

***Recruitment* was based on loyalty to the regime, while educational qualifications were not a requirement. The civilian percentage within each service was minimal in all three cases.** PVDE officers had to take an oath before being able to serve the government, while candidates with lower educational standards were recruited. By the time of the Carnation Revolution, PIDE's network had reached approximately twenty thousand staff. In Greece, the KYP was controlled by military officers, while the majority of its personnel came from the police and military. Like in Portugal, all staff had to make a loyalty declaration. In Spain, a predominantly military-focused structure was applied in the intelligence organizations. The BPS, though, focused on recruiting police specialists to help it become more like the Gestapo, with all staff being committed to Francoism as well as anticommunism. As an example of the composition of one service, the SECED's personnel consisted of only 10 percent civilians. Across the three cases, the above resulted in high volumes of unqualified uniformed personnel.

In all three countries, collection practices violated human rights, while *targeting* **focused on perceived threats against the regime.** More than anything else, intelligence services before the 1970s looked to protect the interests of the ruling head of state and their institutions of power. Protection of the people was only pursued in the most oblique sense and part of an overarching need to defend against such dangers as "international communism." The people therefore were repressed in order to save them. This facilitated some of the worst behaviors that intelligence organizations are often indicted of—unexplained arrests, imprisonment without charge, extrajudicial killing, and torture. The last of these occurred in each of the countries analyzed and on explicit behalf of the regimes that the relevant intelligence organizations served. In Portugal, for Salazar, communism was the biggest threat, with communists and Spanish Republicans being subject to PVDE's/PIDE's updated techniques as well as arrest and deportation. A Special Military Court was also founded to process those Portuguese citizens who were targeted and arrested by the PVDE. Communism was at the top of the agenda for the Greek dictators too, with Ioannidis also creating a dedicated intelligence and interrogation unit that used torture. In Spain, collection focused on perceived anti-Franco activities and combating domestic subversion with the BPS's White Terror and Gestapo torture methods. The OCN infiltrated, among others, the academic world, and the SECED monitored Republicans, Catalans, Basques, and anarchists living in exile in France, Belgium, Argentina, and Mexico.

Civil society **was repressed by the respective governments through the intelligence services.** Any kind of opposition was crushed until social upheaval emerged in one case. In Portugal, Salazar banned any kind of political activism, while there was strict control of the media and press. Public employment was conditional upon loyalty to the regime. In Greece, Greek communists were one of the few groups that challenged the government, while the Greek media was highly partisan. With the KYP being used to apply those rules, the reputation of the organization changed to it being equated to another element of the junta. In Spain, a similar trend is observed. Any unions, communists, and other left-wing and opposition organizations became ineffectual while the media was under the government's control. On top of the general strategy to suppress the media as it happened in Portugal and Greece, Spain established a big volume of pro-Francoist press. The result of the above was that most of the Spanish civil society chose to come to terms with the new regime, the only exception being the ETA, which used violence against it.

The relationship between intelligence producers and intelligence consumers is another important theme that emerges organically. Greece's KYP and its analysis during the crisis over Cyprus is probably one of the most prominent examples. Indeed, the KYP provided valuable information, although too late in the process, deciding that it would act as a separate entity to the junta regime. Ioannidis's obsession with marginalizing and politicizing intelligence is a common limitation that comes up in the relationship between intelligence services and policymakers. This is a theme that persisted even after the end of the dictatorship. As important as it is for intelligence services to produce valuable intelligence and disseminate it in a timely manner, it is equally important for decision-makers to be properly educated on intelligence and intelligence matters in order to be in a position to use it for the benefit of their citizens.

The routines and norms that were created by an early period of militarization and the development of particular methods in wartime, followed by a period of entrenchment and intense repression, survived the eventual collapse of the Estado Novo, the Greek junta regime, and the Francoist state. This kind of culture survived in decrees, laws, and operational guidelines of the states they had served and in the memories of the intelligence officers that followed them as well as in civil society sentiment. Indeed, challenges such as poor control and oversight structures, targeting of perceived rather than real threats, unfair recruitment practices, and a closed civil society persisted in Greece and Spain after their dictatorships fell. Portugal was the only one among the three cases that demonstrated positive change early on, as we will see in subsequent chapters.

NOTES

1. Stanley Payne, *A History of Fascism, 1914–1945* (Madison: University of Wisconsin Press, 1995), 139–41.
2. Juan Linz, "Spain and Portugal: Critical Choices," in *Western Europe: The Trials of Partnership*, ed. David S. Landes (Lexington, MA: Lexington Books, 1977), 241.
3. Douglas L. Wheeler, *Republican Portugal: A Political History, 1910–1926* (Madison: University of Wisconsin Press, 1998), 62–92.
4. Kerstin Hamann and Paul Christopher Manuel, "Regime Changes and Civil Society in Twentieth-Century Portugal," *South European Society and Politics* 4, no. 1 (2007): 74.
5. Walter Opello, *Portugal's Political Development: A Comparative Approach* (Abingdon, UK: Routledge, 1985), 40.
6. Raphael Costa, *From Dictatorship to Democracy in Twentieth-Century Portugal* (London: Palgrave Macmillan, 2016), 2.
7. Wheeler, *Republican Portugal*, 91–92.

8. Wheeler, 137.

9. Wheeler, 195.

10. Wheeler, 200.

11. T. D. Sfikas, "The Tale of Parallel Lives: The Second Greek Republic and the Second Spanish Republic, 1924–36," *European History Quarterly* 29, no. 2 (1999): 226. Constantine I abdicated in 1922 after Greece lost the Greco-Turkish War (1919–22).

12. Harry Cliadakis, "The Political and Diplomatic Background to the Metaxas Dictatorship, 1935–36," *Journal of Contemporary History* 14, no. 1 (1979): 124.

13. A. Mazarakis-Ainian, *Apomnimonevmata* [Memoirs] (Athens: Elliniki Protoporia, 1948), 475.

14. Alexandros Sakellariou, "Authoritarianism and the Greek Orthodox Church," Rosa-Luxemburg-Stiftung, September 2, 2019, www.rosalux.de/en/publication/id/40942/#_ftn6.

15. Sfikas, "Tale of Parallel Lives," 236.

16. Sfikas, 239.

17. Xosé-Manoel Núñez, "New Interpretations of the Spanish Civil War," *Contemporary European History* 13, no. 4 (2004): 520.

18. Núñez, 520.

19. Antonio Cazorla Sanchez, "Surviving Franco's Peace: Spanish Popular Opinion during the Second World War," *European History Quarterly* 32, no. 3 (2002): 391.

20. The Overseas War, also known as the Portuguese Colonial War (Guerra Colonial Portuguesa), lasted thirteen years (1961–74) and was between Portugal's military and the nationalist movements in its African colonies.

21. Commander H. B., *Espionaje y servicio secreto (ensayo de una metodologia)* [Espionage and secret service (essay of methodology)] (Madrid: Rivadeneyra, 1936), 137.

22. Commander H. B., 138.

23. Darlene J. Sadlier, *An Introduction to Fernando Pessoa: Modernism and the Paradoxes of Authorship* (Gainesville: University Press of Florida, 2009), 45.

24. "História das Informações" [Information history], SIRP, July 20, 2020, www.sirp.pt/quem-somos/historia.

25. "História das Informações."

26. "História das Informações."

27. Filipe Ribeiro de Meneses, *Salazar: A Political Biography* (New York: Enigma, 2010), 45.

28. Howard J. Wiarda, *Corporatism and Development: The Portuguese Experience* (Amherst: University of Massachusetts Press, 1977), 94.

29. Wiarda, 80.

30. Meneses, *Salazar*, 82.

31. Hugh Kay, *Salazar and Modern Portugal* (New York: Hawthorn Books, 1970), 63.

32. Kay, 150.

33. Douglas L. Wheeler, "In the Service of Order: The Portuguese Political Police and the British, German and Spanish Intelligence, 1932–1945," *Journal of Contemporary History* 18, no. 1 (1983): 3.

34. Wheeler, 4.

35. Wheeler, 5.

36. Wheeler, 5.

37. De Meneses, *Salazar*, 150.

38. Salazar e Caetano, doc. C 46, Conselho de Ministros de 9 de Fevereiro de 1945, 148.

39. Helena Gonçalves da Silva, Adriana Alves de Paula Martins, Filomena Viana Guarda, and José Miguel Sardica, *Conflict, Memory Transfers and the Reshaping of Europe* (Newcastle upon Tyne: Cambridge Scholars Publishing, 2010), 156.

40. António de Figueiredo, *Portugal: Fifty Years of Dictatorship* (New York: Holmes & Meier, 1976), 115–16

41. Tom Gallagher, "Controlled Repression in Salazar's Portugal," *Journal of Contemporary History* 14, no. 3 (1979): 390.

42. Gallagher, 390. The largest opposition during the dictatorship in Portugal, the PCP advocated for an alliance against fascism and across social class.

43. It is alleged that this initial period is when most detainees were subject to torture in order to facilitate further investigation of the political crimes they had committed. Sleep deprivation, "statue torture," beatings, insults, and blackmail were the most common forms of abuse used by PIDE, and their applications were developed over time. Initially, beatings were very common, but from the 1950s onward, methods that left no visible marks became more widely used, in particular sleep torture (even though beatings still continued). The intensity of the torture also tended to vary according to social class (and was more severe for workers and peasants, particularly if they were members of the Portuguese Communist Party). See Irene Flunser Pimentel, *A história da PIDE* [A history of PIDE] (Lisbon: Círculo de Leitores, 2007). See also chapter 6 of the present volume for more detail.

44. Gonçalves da Silva, *Conflict, Memory Transfers and Reshaping of Europe*, 157.

45. Gonçalves da Silva, 159.

46. Tom Gallagher, *Portugal: A Twentieth-Century Interpretation* (Manchester: Manchester University Press, 1983), 118–19.

47. De Figueiredo, *Portugal*, 122.

48. Neville Vincent, "The Shame of Portugal," *Spectator*, April 13, 1962, http://archive .spectator.co.uk/article/13th-april-1962/11/the-shame-of-portugal.

49. Manuel Lucena, *Os lugar-tenentes de Salazar* [The lieutenants of Salazar] (Lisbon: Alêtheia Editores, 2015), 320.

50. "História das Informações."

51. Gonçalves da Silva, *Conflict, Memory Transfers and Reshaping of Europe*, 160.

52. Gonçalves da Silva, 160.

53. Gallagher, *Portugal*, 119.

54. Walter C. Opello, *Portugal: From Monarchy to Pluralist Democracy* (Boulder, CO: Westview, 1991), 96.

55. Gonçalves da Silva, *Conflict, Memory Transfers and Reshaping of Europe*, 167.

56. "A Brief Chronicle of the Greek Intelligence Services before EYP (1924–1953)," National Intelligence Service, http://www.nis.gr/portal/page/portal/NIS/History /BeforeEYP.

57. "Brief Chronicle of Greek Intelligence Services."

58. "Brief Chronicle of Greek Intelligence Services."

59. Jeremy Mitchell, *Conditions of Democracy in Europe, 1919–39: Systematic Case-Studies* (New York: St. Martin's / International Political Science Association, 2000), 234.

60. Marina Petrakis, *The Metaxas Myth: Dictatorship and Propaganda in Greece* (London: I. B. Tauris, 2011), 34–38.

61. "Brief Chronicle of Greek Intelligence Services."
62. S. Beckmann, "American Aid to Greece: The Marshall Plan as a Model for Development Aid," *Clocks and Clouds* 1, no. 1 (2012).
63. John Nomikos and Andrew Liaropoulos. "Truly Reforming or Just Responding to Failures? Lessons Learned from the Modernisation of the Greek National Intelligence Service," *Journal of Policing, Intelligence and Counter Terrorism* 5, no. 1 (2010): 31.
64. D. Tsarouhas, "Explaining an Activist Military: Greece until 1975," *Southeast European Politics* 6, no. 1 (2005): 1–13.
65. James Miller, *The United States and the Making of Modern Greece: History and Power, 1950–1974* (Chapel Hill: University of North Carolina Press, 2009), 150.
66. "Report of P. Panourgias," *Akropolis*, August 17–21, 1974. Part of this report was also published in Constantine Svolopoulos, *Constantine Karamanlis* 7, 18–19, cited in Leonidas Kallivretakis, "The Known Unknown 'April' Conspirators," *Kathimerini*, June 15, 1975, 35.
67. "18-year Greek Sentences," *Guardian*, August 13, 1973. See also Donald C. Munn, "Military Dictatorship in Greece (1967–1974): The Genesis of Greek Anti-Americanism" (master's thesis, Naval Postgraduate School, 1980).
68. "18-year Greek Sentences," *Guardian*, August 13, 1973.
69. Alejeandro Quiroga, *Making Spaniards: Primo de Rivera and the Nationalization of the Masses 1923–30* (Basingstoke, UK: Palgrave Macmillan, 2014), 32.
70. RD 4.2.1929, El Somatén, February, 1929, in Quiroga, *Making Spaniards*.
71. Quiroga, *Making Spaniards*, 162.
72. Payne, *History of Fascism*, 73.
73. Payne, 74.
74. Antonio Díaz, "Spanish Intelligence during the Second Republic and the Civil War: 1931–1939," *Journal of Intelligence History* 6, no. 1 (2006): 41–65.
75. *Boletín Oficial del Estado* [Official Bulletin of the State; hereafter BOE] no. 44, de 13 de febrero de 1939, *Gazeta histórica, Referencia*: 1939/1451.
76. Alison Ribeiro de Menezes, Antonio Cazorla-Sánchez, and Adrian Shubert, *Public Humanities and the Spanish Civil War: Connected and Contested Histories* (Cham: Palgrave Macmillan, 2018), 51.
77. Ana Domínguez Rama, *Enrique Ruano: Memoria viva de la impunidad del Franquismo* [Enrique Ruano: Living memory of the impunity of Francoism] (Madrid: Complutense, 2011), 198–99.
78. Article 1, Ley de Vigilancia y Seguridad [Surveillance and Security Law], March 8, 1941, BOE no. 65, 1627.
79. José Javier Olivas Osuna, *Iberian Military Politics: Controlling the Armed Forces during Dictatorship and Democratisation* (Basingstoke: Palgrave Macmillan, 2014), 117.
80. Decree 511/1972 of March 3, which gives new wording to paragraph 2 of Article 2 of Decree 245/1968, of February 15, on reorganization of the presidency of the government, BOE no. 60, March 10, 1972.
81. Luis R. Aizpeolea, "The Day ETA Struck a Lethal Blow to the Franco Regime," *El País*, December 18, 2013, https://english.elpais.com/elpais/2013/12/18/inenglish /1387374599_382537.html.
82. Decree 3673, December 21, 1917, Diário do Govêrno no. 222/1917, series I of 1917-12-21.

83. Decree No. 4166, Diário do Govêrno No. 91/1918, 1st supplement, series I of 1918-04-29.

84. Decree No. 4166.

85. "História das Informações."

86. Wheeler, "In the Service of Order," 2.

87. R. G. Cardwell, *Affairs of Portugal* (Washington, DC: Department of State, 1936).

88. Wheeler, "In the Service of Order," 20.

89. Wheeler.

90. Wheeler.

91. Gallagher, "Controlled Repression in Salazar's Portugal," 398.

92. Gallagher, *Portugal*, 120.

93. Pimentel, *História da PIDE*, 315.

94. Duncan Simpson, "Approaching the PIDE 'from Below': Petitions, Spontaneous Applications and Denunciation Letters to Salazar's Secret Police in 1964," *Contemporary European History* 30, no. 3 (2020): 14–15.

95. John Nomikos, "The Internal Modernization of the Greek Intelligence Service (NIS-EYP)," *International Journal of Intelligence and CounterIntelligence* 17, no. 3 (2004): 436–37.

96. Nomikos, 437.

97. "Past Directors," National Intelligence Service, http://www.nis.gr/.

98. "Past Directors."

99. "Past Directors."

100. CIA, "The Greek Junta," memorandum, May 24, 1967, no. 1113/67, 7.

101. CIA, 304.

102. Enric Hernàndez, "La Brigada Político Social" [The Social Political Brigade], *El Periódico*, November 4, 2014, www.elperiodico.com/es/opinion/20141101/la -brigada-politico-social-3653067.

103. "La Huella de la Gestapo en la Brigada Político Social" [The Trace of the Gestapo in the Social Political Brigade], elDiario.es, January 12, 2019, www.eldiario.es /comunitat-valenciana/eldiario-de-la-cultura/huella-gestapo-brigada-politico -social_132_1752338.html.

104. Carlos Barrachina Lison, "El regreso a los cuarteles: Militares y cambio politico en Espana (1976–1981)" [The return to the barracks: Military and political change in Spain (1976–1981)], March 1, 2002, http://www.resdal.org/Archivo/d0000195.htm.

105. José Ignacio San Martín, *Servicio especial: A las órdenes de Carrero Blanco; De Castellana a El Aaiun* [Special service: Under the orders of Carrero Blanco; From Castellana to El Aaiun] (Barcelona: Planeta, 1984), 21.

106. San Martín 22.

107. San Martín, 23.

108. San Martín, 28.

109. Carlos Barrachina Lison, "El regreso a los cuarteles: Militares y cambio politico en Espana (1976–1981)" [The return to the barracks: Military and political change in Spain (1976–1981)], Departamento de Ciencias Políticas y de la Administración, Facultad de Ciencias Políticas y Sociología, Universidad Nacional de Educación a Distancia, 2002.

110. Wheeler, "In the Service of Order." See also Pimentel, *Historia da PIDE* [History of PIDE]. See also María da Conceição Ribeiro, *A Polícia Política no Estado Novo (1926–1945)* [A Political Police in the New State (1926–1945)] (Lisbon: Editorial

Estampa, 1995). Pimentel covers key aspects of PIDE throughout Salazar's and Caetano's rule, including the institution itself, its powers and recruitment practices, its monitoring of the public and persecution of "opponents" of the regime (such as the Portuguese Communist Party), the attempted military coup, PIDE's methods, political arrests (including but not limited to investigation), torture to extract information, PIDE's prisons, and its sentencing powers.

111. Conceição Ribeiro, 3.

112. Conceição Ribeiro, 6.

113. Antonio Ferro, *Salazar: Portugal and Her Leader* (London: Faber & Faber, 1939); "Constitui um grande exito: O primeiro espetáculo gratuito promovido pelo Secretariado de Propaganda Nacional" [It's a big hit: The first free show promoted by the National Advertising Secretariat], *Diário da Manhã* [Daily Morning], November 6, 1933.

114. Portugal Ministério dos Negócios Estrangeiros, *Dez anos de política externa (1936–1947): A nação portuguesa e a Segunda Guerra Mundial* [Ten years of foreign policy (1936–1947): The Portuguese nation and the Second World War] (Lisbon: Imprensa Nacional, 1961), 49–51.

115. Wheeler, "In the Service of Order," 15.

116. Wheeler, 15.

117. De Meneses, *Salazar*, 216. Emídio Santana was one of the key Portuguese activists of anarcho-syndicalism in Portugal.

118. "História das Informações."

119. Gallagher, "Controlled Repression in Salazar's Portugal," 387.

120. Gallagher, 387.

121. Decree-Law 27058, September 30, 1936, Oliveira Salazar's Archive, CO/PC/21. See also Luís Nuno Rodrigues, "The Creation of the Portuguese Legion in 1936," *Luso-Brazilian Review* 34, no. 2 (1997).

122. Decree-Law 23, 203, in *Legislação repressiva e antidemocrática do regime fascista* [Repressive and undemocratic legislation of the fascist regime] (Lisbon: Comissão do Livro Negro Sobre o Regime Fascista, 1985), 144–54.

123. Freemasons and other "secret societies" were particular targets of the Salazar regime, which abhorred their perceived "subversive tendencies." See de Meneses, *Salazar*, 150.

124. "História das Informações.

125. De Meneses, *Salazar*, 241.

126. Neill Lochery, *Lisbon: War in the Shadows of the City of Light, 1939–45* (Melbourne: Scribe Publications, 2011), 60–61.

127. Ronald Weber, *The Lisbon Route: Entry and Escape in Nazi Europe* (Lanham, MD: Ivan R. Dee, 2011), 21.

128. Gonçalves da Silva. *Conflict, Memory Transfers and Reshaping of Europe*, 156.

129. Gallagher, "Controlled Repression in Salazar's Portugal," 387.

130. One law passed in 1956 allowed PIDE to indefinitely detain anyone it suspected of being "dangerous to society." Gallagher, 119.

131. John P. Cann, *The Flechas: Insurgent Hunting in Eastern Angola, 1965–1974* (Solihull, UK: Hellion, 2013).

132. Al J. Venter, *Portugal's Guerrilla Wars in Africa: Lisbon's Three Wars in Angola, Mozambique and Portuguese Guinea, 1961–74* (Solihull, UK: Helion, 2015), 213.

133. Venter, 213.

134. Conor O'Reilly, ed., *Colonial Policing and the Transnational Legacy: The Global Dynamics of Policing across the Lusophone Community* (London: Routledge, 2018).

135. "Information Centralization and Coordination Services of Mozambique," AATT—PIDE/DGS, Associação dos Amigos da Torre do Tombo, www.aatt.org/site/index .php?op=Nucleo&id=1533.

136. Kenneth Maxwell, "Portugal under Pressure," *New York Review of Books*, May 29, 1975, 10.

137. Neil Bruce, *Portugal: The Last Empire* (Newtown Abbot, UK: David & Charles, 1975), 108.

138. Joseph Fitsanakis, *Ethniki asfalia ke sighrones ipiresies kataskopias stin Ellada* [National security and modern intelligence services in Greece] (Athens: Potamos, 2015), 78–79; A. Dagkas, Ο χαφιές: Το κράτος κατά του κομμουνισμού [The informer: The state against communism] (Athens: Ellinika Grammata, 1995); Παρακράτος στη Θεσσαλονίκη [Parastate in Thessaloniki], *Eleftherotipia*, May 15, 1998, 91.

139. British Legation, dispatch of January 25, 1927, FO 286/1009 in Seraphim Seferiades, "The Coercive Impulse: Policing Labour in Interwar Greece," *Journal of Contemporary History* 40, no. 1 (2005).

140. Seferiades, "Coercive Impulse," 59.

141. Seferiades, 59.

142. Cháris Vlavianós, *Greece, 1941–49: From Resistance to Civil War; The Strategy of the Greek Communist Party* (New York: Macmillan, 1992), 16.

143. Vlavianós, 16.

144. Vlavianós, 16.

145. Gert Sørensen and Robert Mallett, *International Fascism: 1919–45* (London: Frank Cass, 2002), 158.

146. PRO, FO 286/1142/71/71/49/37 in Sorensen and Mallett, 170. See also Mogens Pelt, *Tobacco Arms and Politics Greece and Germany from World Crisis to World War 1929-41* (Copenhagen: Museum Tusculanum Press / University of Copenhagen Press, 1998).

147. Department of State, Office of Intelligence Coordination and Liaison, "*The Role of the Army in Greek Politics*," I.R. No. OCL-3745, August 15, 1946, 7 NADB, OSS File.

148. Amikam Nachmani, "Civil War and Foreign Intervention in Greece: 1946–49," *Journal of Contemporary History* 25, no. 4 (1990): 494.

149. CIA, "Greece," March 1948, no. SR-10, I-I, Truman Library, President's Secretary's File, box 259.

150. "Brief Chronicle of Greek Intelligence Services."

151. Robert L. Beisner, *Dean Acheson: A Life in the Cold War* (Oxford: Oxford University Press, 2009), 57.

152. Tim Weiner, *Legacy of Ashes: The History of the CIA* (New York: Doubleday, 2007), 39: "We were in charge. . . . We ran things. We were seen as kings."

153. Fitsanakis, *Ethniki asfalia ke sighrones ipiresies kataskopias stin Ellada*, 119; Philip Agee and Louis Wolf, *Dirty Work: The CIA in Western Europe* (Secaucus, NJ: Lyle Stuart, 1978), 154; "I Kataskeui tou Hafie" [The creation of the informer], *Eleutherotupia*, June 23, 1996, http://www.iospress.gr/ios1996/ios19960623a.htm.

154. CIA, "Greek Junta," 7.

155. CIA, 6.

156. Nomikos and Liaropoulos, "Truly Reforming or Just Responding to Failures?," 32.

157. Tasos Egollopoulos, general secretary of the Greek Association of Lawyers, "Greece under the Junta," UK National Archives, 1968, 135.

158. Egollopoulos, 135.

159. Decree No. 280 ΦΕΚ Α'58/ 21/04/1967. See also *Εφημερίς της Κυβερνήσεως του Βασιλείου της Ελλάδας* [The Government Gazette of the Kingdom of Greece], April 21, 1967.

160. Decree No. 280 ΦΕΚ Α'58/ 21/04/1967.

161. Constitutional Act No. 1, Greek parliament, Athens, 1967.

162. Egollopoulos, "Greece under the Junta," 136.

163. G. Van Steen, "Parading War and Victory under the Greek Military Dictatorship: The Histrionics of 1967–74," in *War as Spectacle: Ancient and Modern Perspectives on the Display of Armed Conflict*, ed. Anastasia Bakogianni and Valerie M. Hope (London: Bloomsbury Academic, 2016).

164. Kostis Kornetis, *Children of the Dictatorship: Student Resistance, Cultural Politics, and the Long 1960s in Greece* (New York: Berghahn, 2016), 21.

165. Fitsanakis, *Ethniki asfalia ke sighrones ipiresies kataskopias stin Ellada*, 120.

166. "Dimitrios Ioannidis," *Telegraph*, August 17, 2010, www.telegraph.co.uk/news /obituaries/military-obituaries/7950781/Dimitrios-Ioannidis.html.

167. "Report on Female Prisoners," League for Democracy in Greece, April 8, 1968.

168. Dimitri A. Sotiropoulos, "The Authoritarian Past and Contemporary Greek Democracy," *South European Society and Politics* 15, no. 3 (2010): 451.

169. Sotiropoulos, 451.

170. Laurence Stern, "Bitter Lessons: How We Failed in Cyprus," *Foreign Policy*, no. 19 (1975): 41.

171. Pavlos Apostolidis, *Mystiki Drasi: Ipiresies Pliroforion stin Ellada* [Secret action: Intelligence services in Greece] (Athens: Papazisis, 2014), 214.

172. Apostolidis, 214.

173. Athens-Ankara contacts on Makarios, dispatched from Henry Kissinger to Henry Tasca, March 13, 1974 in Apostolidis, 210–14.

174. Apostolidis, 210.

175. Christos Kassimeris, "Greek Response to the Cyprus Invasion," *Small Wars and Insurgencies* 19, no. 2 (2008): 258.

176. Apostolidis, *Mystiki Drasi*, 216.

177. William Mallinson, *Cyprus: A Modern History* (London: I. B. Tauris, 2005), 81.

178. Sotiropoulos, "Authoritarian Past and Contemporary Greek Democracy," 451.

179. RD 4.2.1929 and ROC 8.2.1929, *El Somatén*, February 1929; ROC, 16.4.1929, CLE, no. 147, 86–87, in Quiroga, *Making Spaniards*. See also Rodrigues, "Creation of the Portuguese Legion."

180. ROC 8.2.1929 in Quiroga, Additional Disposition; ROC, 16.4.1929. See also Rodrigues, "Creation of the Portuguese Legion."

181. Collective letter of the mayors of the district of Falset (Tarragona) to the Spanish interior minister, 3.9.1931, AHN, Gobernación, series A, bundle 59, box 2. Also in Quiroga, *Making Spaniards*.

182. Stanley G. Payne, *Spain's First Democracy: The Second Republic, 1931–1936* (Madison: University of Wisconsin Press, 1993), 73–75.

183. Emilio Mola Vidal, *Obras completas* [Complete works] (Valladolid: Libreria Santaren, 1940), 320–21.

184. Julio Garrido Ramos, *La información en la guerra: Misión de la 2a sección de un E. M. en campaña y actuación de todas las armas* [Information in the war: Mission of the 2nd section of an E. M. in campaign and performance of all weapons] (Madrid: Agencia Española de Librerías, 1931), 175–76.

185. Stanley G. Payne, *The Collapse of the Spanish Republic, 1933–1936: Origins of the Civil War* (New Haven, CT: Yale University Press, 2006), 234.

186. Payne, 235.

187. Payne, 304.

188. Payne, 305.

189. Payne, 757.

190. Gabriel Jackson, *The Spanish Republic and the Civil War 1931–1939* (Princeton, NJ: Princeton University Press, 1971), 533.

191. Díaz, "Spanish Intelligence," 41–65.

192. *"CNI-Centro Nacional de Inteligencia,"—¿Qué Es?* ["CNI-National Intelligence Center,"—What is it?].

193. Juan J. Alcade, *Los servicios secretos en España: La represión contra el movimiento libertario español (1936–1995)* [The secret services in Spain: Repression against the Spanish libertarian movement] (Madrid: Juan J. Alcalde, 2008), 2.

194. Alcade, 3.

195. Domínguez Rama, *Enrique Ruano*, 198–99.

196. Andrew Szanajda and David A. Messenger, "The German Secret State Police in Spain: Extending the Reach of National Socialism," *International History Review* 40, no. 2 (2018): 403.

197. Antony Beevor, *The Battle for Spain: The Spanish Civil War, 1936–1939* (London: Phoenix 2007), 89–94.

198. Javier García, "High Police Commanders Come from the Former Political-Social Brigade," *El País*, February 7, 1983.

199. Antonio Díaz Fernández, "The Intelligence Services and the Mass Media in Spain," *Journal of Intelligence History* 9, no. 1–2 (2009): 92.

200. Jill Edwards, *Anglo-American Relations and the Franco Question, 1945–1955* (Oxford: Clarendon Press, 1999), 57.

201. Carsten Humlebæk, *Spain: Inventing the Nation* (London: Bloomsbury, 2015), 68–69.

202. Espinosa Maestre, *Violencia roja y azul: España, 1936–1950* [Red and blue violence: Spain, 1936–1950] (Barcelona: Crítica, 2010), 77–78.

203. Humlebæk, *Spain*, 69.

204. Wayne H. Bowen, *Spain during World War II* (Columbia: University of Missouri Press, 2006), 229–30.

205. Antonio Cazorla-Sánchez, "Beyond They Shall Not Pass: How the Experience of Violence Reshaped Political Values in Franco's Spain," *Journal of Contemporary History* 40, no. 3, (2005): 509.

206. Bravo Gutmaro Gómez, *Puig Antich: La transición inacabada* [Puig Antich: The unfinished transition] (Madrid: Taurus, 2014), 38.

207. Luís A. Gil-Alana and Carlos P. Barros, "A Note on the Effectiveness of National Anti-Terrorist Policies: Evidence from ETA," *Conflict Management and Peace Science* 27, no. 1 (2010): 29.

208. Wayne Anderson, *The ETA: Spain's Basque Terrorists* (New York: Rosen Publishing Group, 2004), 16.

209. Gil-Alana and Barros, "Note on the Effectiveness, 17–18.

210. Paddy Woodworth, *Dirty War, Clean Hands: ETA, the GAL and Spanish Democracy* (New Haven, CT: Yale University Press, 2002), 36.

211. Woodworth, 36.

212. Stanley G. Payne, *The Franco Regime, 1936–1975* (Madison: University of Wisconsin Press, 2011), 558.

213. Robert P. Clark, *The Basques: The Franco Years and Beyond* (Reno: University of Nevada Press, 1979), 174.

214. Paddy Woodworth, "In 1973, I Applauded an Eta Killing. Not Now," *Irish Times*, April 8, 2017, www.irishtimes.com/news/world/europe/in-1973-i-applauded-an-eta-killing-not-now-1.3039065.

215. Woodworth, *Dirty War, Clean Hands*, 37.

216. Luís A. Gil-Alana and Carlos P. Barros, "A Note on the Effectiveness of National Anti-Terrorist Policies: Evidence from ETA," *Conflict Management and Peace Science* 27, no. 1 (2010): 30.

217. Woodworth, *Dirty War, Clean Hands*, 38.

218. Payne, *Franco Regime*, 456.

219. Florina Cristiana Matei, Andrés de Castro García, and Carolyn C. Halladay, "On Balance: Intelligence Democratization in Post-Franco Spain," *International Journal of Intelligence and Counterintelligence* 31, no. 4 (2018): 772.

220. Matei, de Castro García, and Halladay, 771.

221. Antonio Díaz Fernández, "The Need and Role of Intelligence Services in a Democracy: Balancing Effectiveness and Transparency," as cited in Matei, de Castro García, and Halladay, 771.

222. Payne, *Franco Regime*, 571.

223. Matei, de Castro García, and Halladay, "On Balance," 772.

224. Matei, de Castro García, and Halladay, 772.

225. Hamann and Manuel, "Regime Changes and Civil Society," 74.

226. Payne, *History of Fascism*, 158.

227. D. L. Raby, *Fascism and Resistance in Portugal* (Manchester: Manchester University Press, 1988), 6.

228. Richard Robinson, *Contemporary Portugal: A History* (London: Allen & Unwin, 1979), 58–59.

229. Gallagher, *Portugal*, 65.

230. Hugo Gil Ferreira and Michael W. Marshall, *Portugal's Revolution Ten Years On* (Cambridge: Cambridge University Press, 1986), 25.

231. James Badcock, "Did Portugal's Dictator Salazar Order Killing of Rival?," BBC News, February 13, 2015, www.bbc.co.uk/news/world-europe-31427521.

232. Howard J. Wiarda, *Corporatism and Development: The Portuguese Experience* (Amherst: University of Massachusetts Press, 1977), 107–8.

233. John P. Cann, "The Artful Use of National Power: Portuguese Angola (1961–1974)," *Small Wars and Insurgencies* 22, no. 1 (2011): 201.

234. René Pélissier, *Le naufrage des caravelles: Études sur la fin de l'empire portugais (1961–1975)* [The shipwreck of the caravels: Studies on the end of the Portuguese Empire (1961–1975)] (Orgeval: *Éditions* Pelissier, 1979), 147.

235. Cann, "Artful Use of National Power," 201.

236. Edward George, *The Cuban Intervention in Angola, 1965–1991* (New York: Frank Cass, 2005), 9–10.

237. George, 9–10.
238. Elizabeth Buettner, *Europe after Empire: Decolonization, Society, and Culture* (Cambridge: Cambridge University Press, 2016), 204.
239. Filipe Ribeiro de Meneses and Robert McNamara, "Parallel Diplomacy, Parallel War: The PIDE/DGS's Dealings with Rhodesia and South Africa, 1961–74," *Journal of Contemporary History* 49, no. 2 (2014): 370.
240. De Meneses and McNamara, 371.
241. Hamann and Manuel, "Regime Changes and Civil Society," 78.
242. Kenneth Maxwell, "The Transition in Portugal," working paper, Columbia University and Tinker Foundation, 1982, 11–14.
243. Amílcar Lopes da Costa Cabral was a major anticolonial leader in Portuguese Guinea. From 1963 until his assassination in 1973, he led the PAIGC against Portuguese forces. See Amílcar Cabral, *Return to the Source,* Africa Information Service, 1973, 26.
244. Fernando Tavares Pimenta, "Decolonisation Postponed: The Failure of the Colonial Politics of Marcelo Caetano (1968–1974)," *Social Dynamics* 42, no. 1 (2016): 17.
245. Pimenta, 18.
246. Ronald H. Chilcote, Stylianos Hadjiyannis, Fred A. III Lopez, Daniel Nataf, and Elizabeth Sammis, *Transitions from Dictatorship to Democracy: Comparative Studies of Spain, Portugal, and Greece* (London: Routledge, 2016), 84.
247. Gallagher, *Portugal,* 166.
248. "História das Informações.
249. Chilcote et al., *Transitions from Dictatorship to Democracy.*
250. Jian Chen, *The Routledge Handbook of the Global Sixties: Between Protest and Nation-Building* (Abingdon, UK: Routledge, 2018), 87.
251. Gallagher, *Portugal,* 173.
252. Ângela Campos, *An Oral History of the Portuguese Colonial War Conscripted Generation* (Cham: Springer International Publishing, 2018), 77.
253. Campos, 77.
254. Campos, 77.
255. Campos, 148.
256. This included the Beja Uprising of January 1962, the only forceful attempt to overthrow the government prior to 1974. See Gallagher, "Controlled Repression in Salazar's Portugal," 394.
257. Buettner, *Europe after Empire,* 205.
258. "Antonio de Spinola, "A Bridge to Democracy for the Portuguese," *New York Times,* August 14, 1996, www.nytimes.com/1996/08/14/world/antonio-de-spinola-86-a-bridge-to-democracy-for-the-portuguese.html.
259. "História das Informações.
260. Gallagher, *Portugal,* 184.
261. Richard McDonald, "The Greek Press under the Colonels," *Index on Censorship* 3, no. 4 (1974): 27.
262. McDonald, 27. A D-Notice (Defence and Security Media Advisory Notice) is an official request to news editors not to publish in any form items on subjects for reasons of national security.
263. McDonald, 27.
264. McDonald, 28.

265. McDonald, 28–29.

266. Taken from the full list compiled in "How a Free Press Vanished," *IPI Report* 16, no. 8 (1967): 5.

267. Robert V. Keeley, *The Colonel's Coup and the American Embassy: A Diplomat's View of the Breakdown of Democracy in Cold War Greece* (University Park: Pennsylvania State Press, 2011), 89.

268. At least one member of the US administration present in Greece at the time argued that the opposite was the case, that "both the US embassy in Athens and the CIA were caught by surprise, not so much by the coup, but by the composition of its perpetrators. The reports by the CIA's Athens station in the first hours of the coup were characterized by confusion and uncertainties and it took several days before the agency could confirm the identity of those who masterminded it. One of the key reasons for this had been the fact that, while the CIA had been expecting a coup at the time, they believed it would come from a group of disaffected Greek generals rather than mid-ranking officers." Keeley, 88.

269. See telegram from the embassy in Greece to the Department of State, Athens, April 21, 1967, *Foreign Relations of the United States: Cyprus, Greece, Turkey*, vol. 16 (Washington, DC: Government Printing Office, 2000), document no. 275: "King Constantine, blazingly angry, has just told me that neither he nor General officers control the Greek army tonight. 'Incredibly stupid ultra-right-wing bastards, having gained control of tanks, have brought disaster to Greece.'"

270. Former NIS director Ioannis Corantis, press conference, December 17, 2015.

271. "Athenian," *Inside the Colonels' Greece* (New York: Norton, 1972).

272. Sotiropoulos, "Authoritarian Past and Contemporary Greek Democracy," 451.

273. Sotiropoulos, 451.

274. Sotiropoulos, 451.

275. Sotiropoulos, 451.

276. "Greece Marks '73 Student Uprising," *Athens News*, November 17, 1999.

277. CIA, "The Situation in Greece," memorandum, November 25, 1973, 1.

278. Ismael Saz Campos, "Fascism, Fascistization and Developmentalism in Franco's Dictatorship," *Social History* 29, no. 3 (2004): 347.

279. Saz Campos, 347.

280. Javier Terrón, *La prensa en España durante el régimen de Franco: Un intento de análisis político* [The press in Spain during the Franco regime: An attempt at political analysis] (Centro de Investigaciones Sociológicas, 1981), 55–56.

281. Alejandro Pizarroso, "Política informativa: Información y propaganda (1939–1966)" [Information policy: Information and propaganda (1939–1966)], in *Historia de los medios de comunicación en España: Periodismo, imagen y publicidad (1900–1990)* [History of the media in Spain: Journalism, image and advertising (1900–1990)], ed. Jesús T. Alvarez (Barcelona: Editorial Ariel, 1989), 241–42.

282. Juan Montabes, *La prensa del estado durante la transición política española* [The state press during the Spanish political transition], (Centro de Investigaciones Sociológicas, 1989), 24.

283. Justino Sinova, "La difícil evolución de la prensa no estatal" [The difficult evolution of the non-state press], in Alvarez, *Historia de los medios de comunicación en España*, 270–71.

284. Humlebæk, *Spain*, 70.

285. *Informe absolutamente reservado a la CE de la Unión General de Trabajadores en el exilio* [Report absolutely reserved to the EC of the General Union of Workers in exile], Toulouse, November 1948, Archivo de la Fundación Largo Caballero; *Secretariado de Cataluña de la UGT de España a la comisión ejecutiva de la UGT en el exili* [Secretariat of Catalonia of the UGT of Spain to the executive commission of the UGT in exile), June 2, 1948, 358–401.
286. Cazorla-Sánchez, "Beyond They Shall Not Pass," 512.
287. Woodworth, *Dirty War, Clean Hands*, 38.

PART II

SECURITY SECTOR REFORM INDICATORS AND INTELLIGENCE

3

Lustration

Although the available work on democratization is robust, systematic pieces of work on lustration are scarce, especially when it comes to its application in the intelligence field and intelligence democratization specifically. In the limited available literature, there are opinions that are "emotional and critical" toward lustration as a process. However, despite this general popular opinion, lustration can "contribute to the consolidation of democracy."[1] Indeed, there is a positive correlation between lustration and democratization. It is key to note that the relationship between them is *not* causal. Applying lustration processes will not certainly lead to the consolidation of democratic institutions, but at the same time it could aid this process.[2] As A. Przeworski argues, "a country which successfully puts a lustration law into force marks its break with the past, as well as radically limiting the influence of the elite with experience of (and presumably preferences for) non-democratic practices."[3] When applied to intelligence services, it can contribute to their democratization as part of a state's institutions. This chapter will examine lustration as one of the SSR indicators chosen for this book that helps measure levels of intelligence democratization. In addition, it will argue that lustration had a positive effect on the intelligence democratization in Portugal. Greece and Spain, which did not follow a robust purging process, were met with resistance to democratization later because nondemocratic elements remained within the services.

Lustration is the process that a state applies during its transition from a nondemocratic form of government to a democratic one. It mainly, but not only, focuses on the removal of regime officials and insiders through a purging process.[4] Indeed, the absence of lustration and the opening of intelligence files results in the "stickiness" of the old regime.[5] Individuals who are targeted for lustration are often leaders who directed and benefited from nondemocratic rule, especially those who were involved in human rights abuses. The intensity and length of lustration proceedings can vary dramatically and either take place in a broad or even arbitrary manner in order to achieve "revolutionary justice" or on a more limited and surgical basis, sometimes in the form of a public inquiry or tribunal of a more formal nature. More often than not, though, events occur behind the scenes, with those who are known or perceived to be of questionable loyalty to the new regime put into early retirement, transferred to less sensitive posts, or in some cases dismissed altogether. Ideally, what follows is the establishment of more rigorous vetting and hiring processes designed to bring in officers who will support the new democracy. Although liable to reduce the effectiveness of any intelligence organization in the short term, purification in this manner serves to enhance control in the long term, in addition to making any organization more open to oversight measures. As Peter Gill notes, to achieve greater democratic control, a process of lustration is often required to establish transparency and root out unacceptable activities. To have maximum effect, it needs to be accompanied by fresh recruitment drives, ideally among civilians with higher educational qualifications.[6]

A key aspect that we need to consider when looking at lustration is who made the political decision to carry out the formal process. Natalia Letki argues that there are three possible "sources of such a decision: popular will, the will of the elite, and external factors." She continues: "Of course, these three dimensions are present in each political decision, but the balance between them differs in different contexts, e.g., the importance of the external situation should be the greatest in the case of a transition imposed by another regime or international community," while when democratization is the result of a revolution, "the element of public opinion should be of primary importance: the society should be interested in 'judging itself.'"[7]

Lustration of the Portuguese intelligence service was indeed a process that was driven by Portuguese society, which wanted to deal with the authoritarian past, which was heavily linked to PIDE. Another key point that needs to be highlighted is that to be able to understand the impact lustration had on an intelligence service, one should examine if that process was successful or not. Although there are no quantifiable elements that can provide a measurable approach, a more qualitative one is possible. The three main criteria to establish if lustration was successful are "its actual implementation, the practicality of the scope, and the impartiality of the act."[8] The scope relates to elements such as how many people were purged. With regard to impartiality, one should look at who is the target of the process—for instance, the nondemocratic elements that are legacies of the authoritarian regime or the political opposition.

Lustration is the first step toward true (intelligence) reform during a democratic transition. The Portuguese intelligence service was the only one that underwent an intensive purging process that led to the uprooting of authoritarian elements. This resulted in a more robust control and oversight structure as well as fairer recruitment drives. In terms of its implementation, impact, and success, the Portuguese lustration of the authoritarian intelligence service was indeed holistic, and although at times too broad, it did target authoritarian elements rather than any democratic political opposition. Contrary to Portugal, Greece and Spain did not experience a period of proper lustration. Authoritarian elements, including nondemocratic personnel and behavior, persisted for a long time, impeding the reform process.

This chapter is an analysis of lustration as an indicator within the SSR framework that helps measure the levels of intelligence democratization in the Portuguese, Greek, and Spanish intelligence services after their dictatorships fell in the 1970s. Although all indicators in subsequent chapters examine developments up until recently, the current chapter is the only one that focuses specifically on the very first years of the transition period across the three case studies because this is when the lustration process took place (or not).[9] The main questions that we are going to examine in this chapter are: Did each country's intelligence services go through a robust lustration process and, if so, when? What was the positive effect of lustration for each country?

PORTUGAL

On April 25, 1974, a military coup took place in Portugal, which marked the beginning of the so-called third wave of democratization that ended with Spain adopting a democratic system of governance in November 1975.[10] The driving force behind the coup was the MFA. This organization was made up of a broad collection of lieutenants, captains, and majors in the Portuguese Armed Forces with disparate grievances. Some, for example, particularly resented a planned law that would grant militia officers the same level of standing as university graduates.[11] Others, meanwhile, were bitterly disappointed with the government's handling of the Overseas War and the disastrous effect that it was having on Portugal's economy. This latter grievance was the key unifying factor for many members of the MFA who had been left "embittered by their colonial war experience in Africa" and positively "influenced by the ideology of the very African liberation movements they were fighting."[12] This had led them to first question the policies and then the legitimacy of the very government they served and not only to overthrow it but also to dismantle its enforced empire through grants of independence. This, they believed, would allow them to refocus what resources Portugal had left to address the country's own pressing internal problems.[13]

The very way that the MFA was constructed and operated meant that no one individual ever became its designated leader. Although without a clear figurehead, the movement was not without clear democratic ideals that ran counter to the ingrained militarism and conservatism defining the Estado Novo. Accordingly, as António Costa Pinto makes clear, the position of the MFA as the driving force behind the Carnation Revolution "opened a space for social and political mobilisation that exacerbated the crisis of the state." This made it so that "moderate elites were incapable of directing [the institutionalization of democracy] 'from above.'"[14] Instead, power was distributed across a loose network of collective alliances, with the MFA making all major decisions through a revolutionary coordination committee. It is for this reason that the movement's actions have subsequently been termed as a "military coup, but with certain peculiarities."[15] Most notably, this included the decision by the MFA's Revolutionary Council to implement a progressive political agenda while it was dismantling the Estado Novo rather than simply taking over existing state institutions and its security apparatus.

The effect, in contrast to Greece and Spain, was to usher in a period of intense turmoil. As the MFA haphazardly attempted to build a new Portugal, conflict flared between three factions: MFA loyalists, right-wing reactionaries (later led General Sebastião Ribeiro de Spínola himself), and far-left activists who thought the MFA was not radical enough. In one notable incident in the spring of 1975, the loyalist First Light Artillery Regiment based outside of Lisbon was attacked by counterrevolutionary paratroopers and rogue air force personnel using ground-attack aircraft.[16] Although swiftly contained by the MFA's revolutionary forces, this abortive coup attempt only marked the beginning of what was developed into the "hot summer of 1975."[17] In this period, Portugal's competing factions waged a war for the heart of Portuguese society while the MFA did what it could to maintain control without the benefit of a formal intelligence organization that could know what was going on across Portugal. Indeed, in its rush to draw a line on the repressive era of Caetano and Salazar, one of the first major actions the MFA had taken after its successful coup was to completely disband Portugal's main intelligence organization, the despised DGS.[18] Just over a year later, they did the same to the *Polícia de Informação Militar* (PIM; Military Information Police), which had collected intelligence from Portugal's wartorn colonies.[19] The MFA and the population at large resented the DGS—often then referred to by the name of its infamous predecessor, PIDE—and the Revolutionary Council believed its maintenance to be incompatible with its agenda of democratization, decolonization, and development.[20] Because of this, the MFA did not attempt to merely purge the DGS of "bad elements" but instead purge Portuguese society of the DGS. Its chosen method was the aptly named Comissão de Extinção da PIDE-DGS, MP e LP (CEMPL; Commission for the Abolition of the Political Police, Portuguese Legion and Portuguese Youth), which was given legitimacy under Law 171/74.[21]

CEMPL had the extraordinary role of preparing "criminal proceedings of the trial of former police agents and cooperating with other purge institutions, given its monopolistic access to about three million files kept on individual citizens."[22] With its power emanating from its "revolutionary legitimacy," CEMPL was able to bypass the traditional Portuguese judiciary.[23] Its resultant unrestrained actions thus "prevented the re-composition of the State apparatus . . . and was the main factor explaining why, in the Portuguese case, the movement for the dissolution of institutions and purges exceeded those of [other] classical purges."[24] Indeed, although Spain would go on to build a "new" organization out of the remains of its discredited old ones, the MFA willingly opted for a "root and branch" reform. To have been an employee of the DGS or PIDE was retroactively listed as criminal offense, and soon both Spain and Brazil experienced a rapid influx of former intelligence officers eager to avoid prosecution by revolutionary tribunals.[25] This marked the start of intensive purges (*saneamentos*) and a prolonged period of "transitional justice." Initially this process was relatively orderly in nature and limited to affecting only specific parts of the old regime. Former leading figures, including Caetano, were exiled to such places as Madeira and Brazil (if they had not already left the country). In addition, other more visible members of the political elite and some conservative military officers were removed from office or granted early retirement.[26] Soon, however, popular resentment and anger boiled over, and MFA revolutionaries began targeting all manner of individuals. This unregulated expansion quickly spread to those who had no ties to the former regime but were perceived to have benefited under it either economically or socially.[27] As Costa Pinto describes it, "the concept of 'collaborator' changed during this period of 'exception.'"

In 1974 the first purge was based on a strict concept of collaboration, but in 1975, "with the burgeoning anti-capitalist wave, a number of traditional attitudes held by industrialists were also considered as symbols of the old regime."[28] This lasted all through 1975.[29] Appropriately enough, this period was termed the Processo Revolucionario em Curso (PREC; Ongoing Revolutionary Process). It was not until the elections of 1976, where the Partido Socialista (PS; Socialist Party of Portugal) won a majority that a degree of stability was returned, and a new constitution was adopted in April 1976.[30] By then, those PIDE and DGS officers who had chosen to stay in Portugal were detained in the same prisons in which the enemies of Salazar and Caetano had once been kept. A Captain Sousa e Castro, after being named superintendent of CEMPL, found that the government was holding about one thousand PIDE members in prison across the country, many of whom had been in jail for over a year without charges and without a trial. He also mentioned that in some cases, the conditions were "substandard."[31]

The incarcerations had been made legal by Article 292 of the new constitution regarding indictment and trial of PIDE/DGS agents and officials. This enshrined in the constitution three laws that were rapidly brought into effect in 1975 in order to offer "revolutionary legitimacy for the trial in special military courts of members of PIDE [DGS] and government officials who were considered directly responsible for repression."[32] Among them was Constitutional

Law 8/75, "which provided for the trial in a military tribunal of members of the political police and government officials directly responsible for repression."[33] The law also enabled those ruling to pass sentences of from two to twelve years and did not set a statute of limitations for criminal proceedings.[34] Aside from a minority of extreme conservatives and right-wing forces, such as the Portuguese Legion, these actions were not opposed by major portions of Portuguese society. In fact, they were extremely popular. In 1974, for example, the punishment of former intelligence officers was the third most popular demand in 149 recorded disputes and was the top demand in 1975.[35] Following the Carnation Revolution, new officers would be required as well as an entirely new intelligence-collection process. Portugal's lustration process was indeed strict, but it ensured the complete uprooting of all authoritarian elements from the security institutions, allowing it to build a democratized intelligence service from scratch and early on.

GREECE

In Greece the initial punishment of individuals and groups with perceived links to the junta regime was also very popular, especially among students. This latter group had had a key role in the mainstream opposition to the junta government and had suffered greatly after events such as the 1973 Athens Polytechnic uprising.[36] Yet a key difference was that while in Portugal the armed forces formed the vanguard of democratic change, in Greece the armed forces acted as a major barrier. This was the case for several reasons. First, the Greek officer corps was inherently conservative and prejudiced against anything that resembled left-wing or communist ideologies. Second, the Greek military in general was still divided by its preferences for authoritarian rule, republican rule, or the institution of the monarchy. This latter fratricidal issue had divided the country for close to sixty years and was only settled by referendum on December 8, 1974.[37] In the event, 69 percent of the country voted against the return of the king and in favor of a presidential democracy, yet strong sympathies remained among members of the armed forces, which had previously equated loyalty to the monarch with anticommunism and patriotism in general.[38]

Thus, for the wide range of academics, civil servants, bankers, police, and military officers who were perceived to be against democratization, the process of *apohountopoiisi* the "de-juntification" of the "deep state"—was highly risky. The main difficulty facing Konstantinos Karamanlis, who had returned as prime minister on July 24, 1974, lay in the fact that while he had to be seen to be taking action against adherents and collaborators of the junta, he also had to keep members of the Greek military and security sector onside.[39] Accordingly, Karamanlis decided to adopt a strategy of cautious, contained, and limited change, in contrast to Portugal's rapid, widespread, and radical change.[40] From September 1974 "sanctions were imposed on professors, whilst judges who had been purged by the junta because of their democratic beliefs were readmitted to the judiciary." Meanwhile, "those who had collaborated with the junta were punished, either by being demoted or by being forced into retirement."[41] It was only in October 1974—three months after the junta's collapse—that senior military officers began to be arrested and Karamanlis felt secure enough to issue a decree stating that "there would be no amnesty for criminal offences, such as high treason committed by those involved in the 1967 coup."[42] In response, twenty-three far-right military officers began plotting another coup d'état but were stopped in February 1975 after a tip-off to the KYP.[43]

The climax of the country's period of transitional justice came with the widely observed trials of the leaders of the Greek junta. Starting on July 28, 1975, these trials culminated with "the most severe punishments of any Southern European process of criminal transitional justice."[44] The three leaders of the 1967 coup were sentenced to death, eight of their followers were sentenced to life imprisonment, and seven more received sentences of five to twenty years.[45] As Dimitri Sotiropoulos states, however, while "the sanctions imposed on the protagonists of the breakdown of democracy were severe, . . . accomplices, such as members of the authoritarian cabinets between 1967 and 1974 and the Junta's rank and file—including torturers—received mild treatment."[46] The main problem hindering the efforts of prosecutors was a lack of evidence upon which to charge offenders. Many incriminating files belonging to the military police "were never recovered and were not used in any of the trials. In fact, documents which were initially exhibited in court by senior EAT-ESA officers later disappeared without ever being found."[47] The country's period of "transitional justice" was also much shorter than that of Portugal, lasting only from the autumn of 1974 to late 1975.[48] It was for this reason that an element of "business as usual" continued in some areas of the military and security forces several years after democracy had been restored and changes had been made to increase transparency and the rule of law. This was particularly the case in the KYP, which aside from the trial of former director Maj. Gen. Michael Roufogalis, remained more or less untouched by postjunta lustration. Many officers who had been present since the start remained in place, including those who had performed duties under the junta in service of the state.[49]

SPAIN

The conservatism of Greece's approach to lustration was nothing, however, compared to that adopted by the leaders of post-Franco Spain. Less than two months before the general's death in November 1975, the Spanish authorities had spent much of their time coordinating huge crackdowns against anti-regime forces and passing laws such as Decree No. 10/1975. This decree had lengthened the list of terrorist offenses that citizens could be tried for. It also allowed for the death penalty to be imposed if a terrorist attack resulted in the death of a member of the armed forces or security services.[50] Even after Franco died, these kinds of policies were not dropped overnight, and Francoism itself remained broadly entrenched until the king felt sufficiently secure to force the resignation of his Francoist prime minister in July 1976.[51] It is only at this point, when Adolfo Suárez became prime minister, that any lustration activities were entertained. Rather than confront the past head-on, however, as in Portugal, or tacitly acknowledge it, as in Greece, Suárez decided to bury it almost entirely. This was done through what was officially termed the 1977 Amnesty Law but popularly known as *el pacto del olvido,* or "the pact of forgetting."[52] The passage of such a law made it so that the collective decision of Spain's democrats was to "deal with a difficult and painful past by choosing not to deal with it at all."[53] Unlike in Portugal, there was no rush to dismantle major state institutions or purge those who were believed to have orchestrated or collaborated in state repression.

By needing to appease both traditionalists looking to maintain Franco's legacy and radicals who wished to forge a new democratic path for Spain's institutions, the 1977 Amnesty Law made large-scale purges impossible. It also provided the basis for the release of most political prisoners, even those who had committed capital crimes, and prevented the prosecution of government torturers who had worked for Spain's intelligence and security forces. Indeed, it "amnestied crimes and misdemeanours that the authorities or security officers and agents may have committed . . . [and] crimes committed by security officials and agents that violate the rights of persons."[54] There was little public debate about the impact that this ruling might have because both "Congress and the Senate focused almost exclusively on forgetting and pardoning," and there was little to no debate about the inclusion of such articles prior to voting.[55] This meant that many in Spain were not even aware of what had been agreed to until afterward, when the debate was over and the chance to influence events had passed. Even if more citizens had been aware, however, it is not clear that they would have demanded more stringent punishments or greater democratic controls over the security services.

Rather than demanding the establishment of an investigative commission along the lines of the Argentine report *Nunca* Más (Never again), the majority of Spanish citizens appeared content to turn the page of history and leave the crimes of the past where they were.[56] Major newspapers such as *El País* argued at the time that "democratic Spain must from now on look to the future, forget the events and responsibilities of the Civil War and distance itself from forty years of dictatorship. . . . A people cannot and must not lack historical memory: but the latter must serve to encourage projects for peaceful future coexistence rather than promote rancor about the past."[57] Only Francisco Letamendia, a radical Basque nationalist, called for meaningful actions that would have affected the removal of inappropriate actors, such as "a measure to complement the amnesty by replacing the security forces inherited from the dictatorship by others dependent on the autonomous provinces."[58] Most other deputies, meanwhile, were happy to side with those like Deputy Prime Minister Alfonso Osorio, who was anxious to bring matters to a close and take "the first step toward national reconciliation and concord among all Spaniards."[59]

CONCLUSION

In analyzing the lustration process affecting the intelligence agencies of Portugal, Greece, and Spain in their postdictatorship periods, it is not difficult to see how much the legacies of the past affected the scope and pace of change later. Both the length and depth of the lustration process, which began in each country soon after the fall of each dictatorship, varied widely.

The background and policy of each policymaker affected how the lustration process would be run. This meant that in Portugal, where young, radical military officers found themselves making all the decisions, change was total, as there was no place for the old, tainted components of the state, such as the DGS, in the new world they wanted to build. The MFA's objectives of democracy and development meant that authoritarian elements had to be completely removed. Certainly, the revolution that took place in Portugal and operated as a critical juncture facilitated this sentiment and process. Comparatively, the elevation of the conservative Konstantinos Karamanlis back into power after several years of exile in turn meant that a conservative approach to change was initially adopted in Greece. Far from building the country anew, therefore, Karamanlis for the most part simply aimed to revive what had existed before the junta, regardless of whether it was ultimately flawed and in desperate need of reform. Indeed, Karamanlis applied a decapitating rather than uprooting approach to lustration, opposite to the MFA's in Portugal. Only the top-level junta elements received severe punishments, including death sentences (which were then commuted to life imprisonment shortly after the trial) and life imprisonment, whereas multiple accomplices or collaborators of that regime remained untouched, some even taking on high-ranking office positions in security institutions. Such replication of the status quo was nothing, however, compared to Spain. The pact of forgetting essentially illustrated how democracy had not been gained as in Portugal or revived as in Greece but *granted* by the consent of the monarchy. Time and time again, therefore, actions were taken to appease former regime insiders in order to achieve democratization without rupture despite the structural and cultural problems this caused.

Civil society was a key element that supported or impeded change across the three cases. Portuguese citizens were tremendously vocal in needing the punishment and purging of the security sector, to the point where for a short time methods to carry out those punishments were quite extreme. Spanish citizens, on the other hand, were very keen to forget the past and move forward, something that was reinforced by the 1977 Amnesty Law as well as the Spanish media. Civil society, therefore, acted more as a barrier for reform in Spain. Similarly to Spain but not to that extent, the different factions within Greece had created further obstacles for the government. Unable to start over with a clean slate, Karamanlis needed on one hand to get rid of any junta remnants while on the other keep the military and security sector onside. This is linked to our earlier point on critical junctures and key events and the power they can have on change. Indeed, Portugal experienced a drive to reform from within with the armed forces and civil society that operated as a catalyst for change leading to the Carnation Revolution, a critical juncture. This was a major component that drove reform in Portugal—a component that was absent from both Greece and Spain.

Lustration as a process can have a positive effect on democratization. The main advantage of lustration is that it takes place for the "public interest."[60] This is the case across all institutions and, of course, intelligence services too because their main objective is to protect a state's citizens. These services therefore should be democratic to protect them, and going through a lustration process can help exclude any nondemocratic elements, ultimately for the citizens' benefit. A lustration process's main objective is to bring about positive change, but it is important to consider the risks it might also carry. The main arguments include the "moral aspect of creating a new democracy on the basis of exclusion."[61] R. A. Dahl states that "a reasonable argument may be presented in behalf of a particular judgment as to the proper boundaries of inclusion and exclusion. But the exact location of any boundary is necessarily a highly debatable issue."[62] Lustration is not the equivalent of exclusion. At times, though, it can limit certain civil as well as political rights. However, it is key to emphasize that if a "reasonable argument" for this kind of "limitation" is made, it would first be the lustrated elements' adherence to authoritarian practices and, second, the general discussion about the "legality" of authoritarian groups in a democratic state.[63] Although the above are highlighted in the available literature as "risks" or conceived as disadvantages, they "depend on the context and thus are open to debate."[64]

Bureaucratic institutions, some of which are intelligence services, can be influenced by lustration. The result of a lustration process can be "depoliticised officials." This, in turn, results in effective administration of the bureaucratic institutions.[65] Lustration's objective is twofold. On one hand, lustration focuses on the removal of the personnel who have been loyal to the nondemocratic regime. On the other, lustration acts as a screening mechanism whereby the moral standards as well as technical skills of the staff that hold high-ranking positions are checked. As a result, the popular distrust of the state institutions is decreased as "the usability of the state bureaucracy by the democrats" increases.[66] So, lustration can have a positive effect on a few areas, including the recruitment process of a state's institutions as well as civil society, by establishing an open culture between intelligence services and the state's citizens. Indeed, although there might be a few problematic elements to it, lustration is valuable in removing nondemocratic legacies. This is demonstrated by institution lustration examples elsewhere, including the former East Germany, the Czech Republic, Hungary, and Poland.[67]

Lustration was one of the most visible aspects of change in each of the three countries, but when it came to the intelligence field, its scope ranged from the extreme—organizational dissolution and criminalization of previous employment—to the cosmetic—organizational rebranding with the same personnel. There were benefits and drawbacks to both approaches. Even though some of the methods of the lustration process in Portugal were at times extreme, Portugal's overall regulated lustration body managed to completely uproot authoritarian components from its security institutions and start anew, which can only be considered a successful reform process. This places Portugal ahead of Greece and Spain, which continued to maintain authoritarian elements within such institutions in the long run. These authoritarian elements would act as major barriers to reform later.

Last, lustration in general and its relationship with intelligence democratization in particular have been understudied areas. In this chapter, we have demonstrated that lustration can act as a positive catalyst for intelligence democratization and can substantially aid reform. One hopes that this chapter will drive more conversation about lustration and how it can act as a facilitator for reform while also serving as a measure for intelligence democratization within the SSR framework.

NOTES

1. Letki, "Lustration and Democratisation in East-Central Europe," 529.
2. Letki, 529–52.
3. A. Przeworski, M. Alvarez, J. A. Cheibub, and F. Limongi, "What Makes Democracies Endure?," *Journal of Democracy* 7, no. 1 (1996): 50.
4. Gill, *Intelligence Governance and Democratisation*, chap. 7.
5. Gill, chap. 7.
6. Gill and Andregg, *Democratization of Intelligence*, 23–24. See also Lavinia Stan, *Transitional Justice in Eastern Europe and the Former Soviet Union: Reckoning*

with the Communist Past (London: Routledge, 2009). See also Matei and de Castro García, "Transitional Justice and Intelligence Democratization," 717–36.

7. Letki, "Lustration and Democratisation in East-Central Europe," 535. See also Timothy Garton Ash, *We the People: The Revolution of '89 Witnessed in Warsaw, Budapest, Berlin and Prague* (Cambridge, UK: Granta, 1990), and J. Elster, "Coming to Terms with the Past: A Framework for the Study of Justice in the Transition to Democracy," *Archives Européennes de Sociologie* 39 (1998): 7–48.

8. Letki, "Lustration and Democratisation in East-Central Europe," 543.

9. Periods of transition: Portugal, April 1976, when the new constitution was proclaimed; Greece, autumn of 1974 to late 1975; Spain, November 1975 to June 1977, when first general elections took place. See Gill and Michael Andregg, *Democratization of Intelligence.*

10. Linz and Stepan, *Problems of Democratic Transition and Consolidation.*

11. Rui Cunha Martins, *Portugal 1974: Transição política em perspectiva histórica* [Political transition in the historical perspective] (Coimbra: Imprensa da Universidade de Coimbra, 2011), 184.

12. J. P. Davies, "Revolution of the Red Carnations," *New York Times,* July 13, 1975.

13. Antonio Costa Pinto, "Political Purges and State Crisis in Portugal's Transition to Democracy, 1975–76," *Journal of Contemporary History* 43, no. 2 (2008): 307.

14. António Costa Pinto, "Authoritarian Legacies, Transitional Justice and State Crisis in Portugal's Democratization," *Democratization* 13, no. 2 (2006): 177.

15. Hugo Gil Ferreira and Michael W. Marshall, *Portugal's Revolution: Ten Years On* (Cambridge: Cambridge University Press, 2010), 76.

16. "Lisbon Says It Foiled Coup after Attack on Loyal Unit," *New York Times,* March 12, 1975, www.nytimes.com/1975/03/12/archives/lisbon-says-it-foiled-coup -after-attack-on-loyal-unit-lisbon-says.html.

17. CIA, "Memorandum: Coup Attempt in Portugal," March 11, 1975, 1.

18. José Javier Olivas Osuna, *Iberian Military Politics: Controlling the Armed Forces during Dictatorship and Democratisation* (New York: Palgrave Macmillan, 2014), 71.

19. Costa Pinto, "Political Purges and State Crisis," 313.

20. Ferreira and Marshall, *Portugal's Revolution,* 76.

21. Olivas Osuna, *Iberian Military Politics,* 71.

22. Costa Pinto, "Political Purges and State Crisis," 180.

23. António Costa Pinto and Leonardo Morlino, eds., *Dealing with the Legacy of Authoritarianism: The 'Politics of the Past' in Southern European Democracies* (Abingdon, UK: Routledge, 2013), 56.

24. Costa Pinto, "Political Purges and State Crisis," 308.

25. Kathryn Sikkink, *Justice Cascade: How Human Rights Prosecutions Are Changing World Politics* (New York: W. W. Norton, 2012), 53–54.

26. Costa Pinto, "Political Purges and State Crisis," 177.

27. Costa Pinto, 179.

28. Neil J. Kritz, *Transitional Justice: How Emerging Democracies Reckon with Former Regimes* (Washington, DC: United States Institute of Peace Press, 1995), 293.

29. Costa Pinto, "Political Purges and State Crisis," 179.

30. Marina Costa Lobo and Pedro C. Magalhães, "Portuguese Democratisation 40 Years On: Its Meaning and Enduring Legacies," *South European Society and Politics* 21, no. 2 (2016): 163.

31. Sikkink, *Justice Cascade,* 54.

32. Costa Pinto and Morlino, *Dealing with the Legacy of Authoritarianism*, 59. See also Law No. 8/75, dated July 25, 1975, as revised by Law No. 16/75, dated December 23, 1975, and by Law No. 18/75, dated December 26, 1975.

33. Costa Pinto, "Authoritarian Legacies, Transitional Justice and State Crisis," 180.

34. Artur Costa, "O julgamento da PIDE-DGS e o direito (transitorio) à *memoria*'" [The PIDE-DGS trial and the (transitional) right to "memory"], in *De Pinochet a Timor Lorosae: Impunidade e direito à memória* [From Pinochet to Timor Lorosae: Impunity and the right to memory], ed. Iva Delgado, Manuel Loff, Antonio Cluny, Carlos Pacheco, and Ricardo Monteiro (Lisbon: Cosmos, 2000), 39–53.

35. Fátima Patriarca, "A revolução e a questão social: Que justiça social?" [The revolution and the social question: What social justice?], in *Portugal e a transição para a democracia (1974–1976): 1º Curso Livre de História Contemporânea, Lisboa, 23 a 28 de Novembro 1998* [Portugal and the transition to democracy (1974–1976): 1st Free Course on Contemporary History, Lisbon, 23 to 28 November 1998], ed. Fernando Rosas (Edições Colibri, 1999), 141.

36. The 1973 Athens Polytechnic uprising saw Greek students and workers occupy the university in a demonstration of opposition to the junta regime. The resulting security crackdown led to the deaths of dozens of people. For more information, see George Psacharopoulos and Andreas M. Kazamias, "Student Activism in Greece: A Historical and Empirical Analysis," *Higher Education* 9, no. 2 (1980): 127–38.

37. George Kassimeris, *Europe's Last Red Terrorists: The Revolutionary Organization 17 November* (London: C. Hurst, 2001), 24.

38. Christos Kassimeris, *Greece and the American Embrace: Greek Foreign Policy towards Turkey, the US and the Western Alliance* (London: I. B. Tauris, December 18, 2009), 50.

39. Richard Clogg, *A Concise History of Greece* (Cambridge: Cambridge University Press, 2002), 173.

40. Harry J. Psomiades, "Greece: From the Colonels' Rule to Democracy," in *From Dictatorship to Democracy*, ed. John H. Herz (London: Greenwood Press, 1982), 256.

41. Costa Pinto and Morlino, *Dealing with the Legacy of Authoritarianism*, 14.

42. Costa Pinto and Morlino, 14.

43. Fotios Moustakis, *The Greek-Turkish Relationship and NATO* (London: Routledge, 2003), 140.

44. Costa Pinto and Morlino, *Dealing with the Legacy of Authoritarianism*, 15.

45. Costa Pinto and Morlino, 15.

46. Sotiropoulos, "Authoritarian Past and Contemporary Greek Democracy," 1.

47. Nico Wouters, *Transitional Justice and Memory in Europe (1945–2013)* (Cambridge, UK: Intersentia, 2014), 273.

48. Wouters, 273.

49. Neil J. Kritz, *Transitional Justice: How Emerging Democracies Reckon with Former Regimes*, (Washington, DC: United States Institute of Peace, 1995), 266.

50. See "Decreto ley 10/1975, de 26 de agosto, sobre prevención del terrorismo" [Decree law 10/1975 of 26 August on the prevention of terrorism], www.boe.es/buscar/doc.php?id=BOE-A-1975-18072.

51. Henry Ginger, "Spanish Premier Resigns, Apparently at King's Wish," *New York Times*, July 2, 1976, www.nytimes.com/1976/07/02/archives/spanish-premier-resigns-apparently-at-kings-wish-spains-prime.html.

52. Madeline Davis, "Is Spain Recovering Its Memory? Breaking the *Pacto del Olvido*," *Human Rights Quarterly* 27, no. 3 (2005): 863.

53. Omar G. Encarnación, "Reconciliation after Democratization: Coping with the Past in Spain," *Political Science Quarterly* 123, no. 3 (2008): 436.

54. See Paloma Aguilar, "Justice, Politics, and Memory in the Spanish Transition", in eds. Alexandra Barahona de Brito, Carmen Gonzalez Enriquez, and Paloma Aguilar, *The Politics of Memory and Democratization* (Oxford: Oxford University Press, 2001), 102, https://academic.oup.com/book/27029/chapter-abstract/19629 9879?redirectedFrom=fulltext.

55. Aguilar, 102.

56. Encarnación, "Reconciliation after Democratization," 437.

57. *El País*, October 15, 1977.

58. Francisco (Ortzi) Letamendia, *Breve historia de Euskadi: De la prehistoria a nuestros días* [Brief history of the Basque Country: From prehistory to present day] (Barcelona: Ruedo Iberico, 1980), 49.

59. Alfonso Osorio, *Trayectoria política de un ministro de la Corona* [Political trajectory of a minister of the Crown] (Barcelona: Planeta, 1980), 161.

60. Letki, "Lustration and Democratisation in East-Central Europe," 540.

61. Letki, 541.

62. R. A. Dahl, *Democracy and Its Critics* (New Haven, CT: Yale University Press, 1989), 128.

63. Letki, "Lustration and Democratisation in East-Central Europe," 542.

64. Letki, 542.

65. Letki, 546.

66. Linz and Stepan, *Problems of Democratic Transition and Consolidation*, 11.

67. Letki, "Lustration and Democratisation in East-Central Europe," 537.

4

Control and Oversight

"Democratic intelligence" is an oxymoronic notion in some respects because intelligence services are, to varying degrees, secretive and opaque rather than open and transparent. Yet most democracies see intelligence services as a necessity for security and informed decision-making, so they have sought to put in place democratic oversight and clearer limits on intelligence activities.[1] After the fall of nondemocratic regimes in South America and Southern and Eastern Europe in the 1970s and 1980s, the concept of intelligence oversight gained momentum.[2] This was due to the elevation of human rights issues and the documentation of abuses conducted by the intelligence services of these countries during their authoritarian periods. In some cases, subsequent intelligence scandals also made the case for additional regulation and oversight. In line with the SSR framework, therefore, this chapter will focus on the intelligence control and oversight systems of Portugal, Greece, and Spain after their dictatorships and up to the present day. The main questions we will seek to answer are: Is there a legal basis for oversight? Is there sufficient control? Is there proper parliamentary oversight? Are there any other established forms and levels of external oversight, such as judiciary? Can we make observations about their applicability? Although one of the main aspects of this chapter is the existence (or not) of a robust control and oversight structure across the three cases, subsequent chapters will also look to make observations about their possible applicability.

The previous chapter established that a process of lustration can have a positive effect on the democratization process of any government institution, including intelligence services. A robust lustration process can indeed set the parameters not only for removing authoritarian sympathizers and promoting a fairer recruitment process but also help enhance the control and oversight system in the long term. Because of the removal of any authoritarian elements, the organization can also be more receptive to oversight structures. Peter Gill and Michael Andregg argue that lustration leads to greater democratic control through a process that helps establish a degree of transparency and the removal of authoritarian elements.[3] This chapter will argue that this is exactly what happened in Portugal, which underwent a purging process as well as a critical juncture through the Carnation Revolution. This further facilitated change. Indeed, Portugal established a holistic and robust control and oversight system that was not impeded by authoritarian legacies. As Roberto Manuel Henriqueto Goucha argues, control over the Portuguese intelligence service has been "highly institutionalised," especially after 2004. He continues: "This is thanks to a clear break with the legacy of authoritarianism, and in particular the Political Police, presenting a consistent pattern of demilitarization, with the separation of civil and military intelligence functions."[4] This is contrary to Greece and Spain, which continued to suffer from nondemocratic elements, including the centralized power of the executive, cosmetic parliamentary oversight, the legacy personnel, and the stickiness of bureaucracy due to the militarized nature of the services. This meant that the control and oversight systems of these two countries were never properly established. Furthermore, this negatively impacted recruitment, targeting, and the awareness of civil society.[5]

An important by-product of strong oversight mechanisms which adhere to the rule of law is an increase in the amount of trust citizens place in their national intelligence organization(s). Without proper mechanisms that ensure government employees are held accountable, this would not be possible, and the citizens' trust would be reduced or completely nonexistent. We briefly analyzed this in chapter 2, while an in-depth analysis will be provided in the following chapters.

Before we dive into the comparison of the control and oversight systems in Portugal, Greece, and Spain, it is important to point out that in addition to legacies of the past, there were other factors that arrested change. The main one was the unwillingness of policymakers to associate themselves with controversial intelligence activities, especially in Spain. This highlights an important issue—that of the relationship between consumers and producers of intelligence. This is a constant issue that exists and creates limitations in finding the balance between transparency and effectiveness. Educating policymakers on the importance and role of intelligence organizations is key. It is lacking in Greece, though, and until more recently in Spain too.

CONTROL AND OVERSIGHT: A BRIEF OVERVIEW OF DEFINITIONS

The terms "control" and "oversight" tend to be conflated. To distinguish between the two: When talking about control within an intelligence organization, one refers to the head of an agency, who must have enough power to manage and direct its operations. The term "oversight" "describes a system of accountability in which those vested with the executive authority in an organisation have their actions reviewed" by an independent group or body that has the power to do so.[6]

Oversight is a "process of 'superintendence' that does not focus on the day-to-day management but with ensuring that the overall policies of the agency are consistent with its legal mandate."[7] The basic principles on which oversight can take place are "clear lines of authority and responsibility, auditing and inspection."[8]

As Peter Gill and Mark Phythian argue, although different approaches to establishing oversight mechanisms vary between countries based on political histories and cultures, a "common set of challenges" has arisen.[9] These include, among others:

a. Organizational problems: After the fall of nondemocratic regimes in particular, political executives tend to create intelligence services without going through a parliamentary approval process. This means that the established agencies are mostly a result of the executive's vision and wants.[10] To avoid such an issue, there need to be four layers of control and oversight. The first two include the agency itself and the executive. This means that the "immediate" control of an agency falls under its director within the framework of ministerial directions, which "are, in turn, required by the relevant statute passed by the legislature." The statute should mirror the "preferences" of the party in office and certain groups, including NGOs. At the same time, oversight should start in the agency but be coupled with "reinforcement by the executive branch," parliamentary committees, and judicial oversight. The media, citizens, and groups—such as NGOs, think tanks or universities—should offer an additional layer of oversight.[11]

b. Questions surrounding collection: These include the targeting of real threats rather than perceived enemies and the types of methods used to collect information. Are those methods legal and ethical, meaning in line with the respect for human rights? Should the oversight structure be reactive, whereby overseers respond to issues when they arise, or should the overseers be proactive too?

c. Questions about the oversight of analysis: Among others, these include: Are the agencies interpreting information accurately? Are they sharing intelligence with others in the national security community? Are the actions taken toward the perceived threat "proportionate"? What mechanisms exist to check if that is the case? Are there any checks to mitigate the politicization of intelligence?[12]

When looking at all of the above questions and issues, one understands that a holistic approach is needed for democratic oversight, a system that addresses not just the "legality" but also the "propriety" with regard to ethics and human rights in the intelligence sphere.[13]

LEGAL FRAMEWORK FOR OVERSIGHT

A key part of regulating and monitoring the appropriateness of intelligence organizations' activities involves evaluating their compliance with domestic laws and regulations—in particular, enabling legislation designed to protect institutions, citizens, and businesses. In many cases, the legislation is codified at the constitutional level, but it can also exist in additional laws designed to progress matters and boost overall governmental transparency levels, such as freedom of information legislation. In short, laws relating to intelligence set the parameters within which intelligence organizations are supposed to operate. If they subsequently break these laws or utilize them in a way that legislators did not intend, then numerous parties have a right to hold them accountable through appropriate mechanisms. This can include judicial proceedings in addition to the amendment or replacement of specific legislation.[14] In modern democracies, there exists a general expectation that representatives of the people and public sector workers should operate in accordance with the moral standards of the day. This in turn has facilitated the production of statues, codes of practice, and operational guidelines with ethical and moral standards as a core concern.[15] Another key point worth highlighting is that in areas that experience a transition from a nondemocratic to democratic rule of government, policymakers tend to "divide the responsibility for the production of intelligence amongst various services and monitor their functioning through mechanisms of external control."[16] This is something that Portugal was successful in applying.

International organizations and meetings, including the EU, the UN, the Summit of Americas, and the OECD, have specified that "legislation of clear legal standards for the establishment of agencies and their possession of special powers" is key in helping to control intelligence services robustly.[17] In connection to this, the legal framework for intelligence should clearly specify the threats to national security the intelligence services should focus on as well as the powers given to them to do so. This includes elements such as the collection and analysis of information as well as powers given to the services such as the power to arrest.[18] Legal rules are key as they will result in effectiveness of security and "propriety."[19]

With such demands placed upon them, intelligence organizations have resultingly been forced to introspectively consider how to best perform their roles. For them, the task is more difficult than almost all other public entities for the way in which the nature of their work prevents complete transparency or the complete avoidance of the unethical.[20] Gill and Phythian argue that on a pragmatic level "states cannot achieve long-term democratic legitimacy unless they respect human rights and freedoms."[21] Any subsequent violation of such rights therefore must always be considered "proportionate" to the "alleged threat," with targeting only specific individuals and in a way that does not entail threat or intimidation.[22]

Portugal

In the years following the Carnation Revolution, there was little to no legislative oversight of intelligence in Portugal due to the intensive process of lustration that followed as well as the absence of political and societal calls for a new intelligence service. It was only around a decade after Marcello Caetano had been deposed that any such demand arose, and this came directly as a result of threats to Portugal's reputation as a safe and stable country rather than due to popular request. Toward the end of the 1970s, Portugal experienced a flurry of violent incidents. The first of these occurred on November 13, 1979, when the Israeli ambassador to Portugal and three others were wounded in a gun attack on the Israeli embassy.[23] This was followed on July 27, 1983, by the storming of the Turkish embassy by an armed Armenian group.[24] In the same year, a moderate leader of the Palestinian Liberation Organization (PLO) was also assassinated in public by the Abu Nidal Organization.[25] The 1982 Penal Code acknowledged that terrorism was an issue that "needed to be combated severely by criminal law" but that reliance on the law alone had "very little preventative effect."[26] As the police and military were unable to stop terrorist entities from operating on Portuguese soil and prevent violent acts, the creation of new civilian intelligence entities was deemed necessary in 1984. This took place with Law No. 30 of September 5, 1984—the Framework Law of the Information System of the Portuguese Republic. This enabling legislation established the general basis for the creation of SIRP.[27] The law underlined the limits within which the organization and its planned subsidiaries were to operate and the behavior they were expected to display.

As the law stated, the purpose of SIRP was to "ensure, in compliance with the Constitution and the law, the production of information necessary to safeguard national independence and guarantee internal security."[28] To achieve this, the law provided for the creation of three suborganizations: the Serviço de Informações Estratégicas de Defesa (SIED; Strategic Information Service of Defense), the Serviço de Informações de Segurança (SIS; Security Information Service), and the SIM.[29] Operational limits and restrictions were built in under Article 3: "Limit of the information services activities." This legally forbade activities that went against rights, freedoms, and guarantees enshrined in the constitution.[30] They also could not "take advantage of their quality, their position or their function for any action of a different nature from that established within the scope of the respective service."[31] If they did, they would be punished accordingly, either by the organization itself, its supervisory board, or the National Data Protection Commission. These limitations extended into the laws specifically laid for the SIS when it became operational in 1984 and 1985. Article 3 of Law 225/85, for example, reiterated that SIS officers could perform research functions only. They could not, as had been the case in the past, perform any acts that resembled "police functions" or detain any person or prosecute criminal proceedings.[32] The breach of these regulations would constitute a "serious violation of functional duties" and make the officer responsible liable to "disciplinary sanction" up to and including dismissal.[33] These limits and sanctions remained in place through the 1991 amendment to the law as well as the 1995 amendment. Given the hurtful memory of PIDE during the dictatorship period in Portugal, legislators decided to separate intelligence services from the police. This meant that only the SIS and SIED were responsible for the production of security intelligence, whereas the police forces were entitled to produce police intelligence for "the purposes of criminal prevention, investigation, and police action."[34] This is particularly key, as there was a willingness from Portugal's policymakers to drive reform in addition to the complete uprooting of any authoritarian elements that had taken place during the lustration process and was driven by Portuguese civil society. Indeed, the policymakers' willingness had a robust democratic footing, and they could actually apply the above policies, as opposed to being impeded due to authoritarian remnants.

During this same period, several other major pieces of legislation were passed that played an important role in determining the scope and depth of activities performed by Portuguese intelligence organizations. The starting point was, of course, legislation relating to the armed forces, which had ownership of intelligence functions prior to the creation of SIRP. The central component was the 1982 National Defense and Armed Forces Law, which codified the nation's defense policy and its underlying principles, objectives, and guidelines.[35] This included setting out the purpose and function of the SIM, which was to "deal exclusively with military information, with the scope of the missions assigned to them by the Constitution and by this law."[36] Notably, the law also anticipated new additions to the intelligence space by stating that "coordination between the military intelligence services and other intelligence services existing *or to be created* [my italics], namely in the other areas of national defense, will be regulated by decree/law."[37] The 1984 SIRP framework law began this process, but it was also followed by several other important additions, particularly the 1987 Internal Security Law. This set out to formalize the activities by which the state would "ensure public order, security and tranquility, protect pensions and property, prevent crime and help ensure the normal functioning of democratic institutions, the regular exercise of citizens' fundamental rights and freedoms, and respect for democratic legality."[38] The objective was to protect "the life and integrity of persons, public peace and the democratic order against violent or highly organized crime, including sabotage, espionage, or terrorism."[39] Importantly, however, all such activities were to be done in line with several fundamental principles, among them that "the prevention of crimes, including that of crimes against the security of the state, can only be done with observance of the general rules on police and with respect for the rights, freedoms and guarantees of citizens."[40] The above legislation and regulations, along with the 1976 constitution, ensured that intelligence services were protected by potential instances of abuse from the get-go.

The 1987 Internal Security Law also mandated the Portuguese government having responsibility for establishing, "in accordance with the law, the rules for classification and control of circulation of official documents, as well as the accreditation of persons who should have access to classified documents."[41] This was later built upon by the Law of the Secret State, which entered into force on April 7, 1994, and sought to define Portugal's approach to classifying state secrets, appropriate access to secret information, and its use.[42] A "state secret" was specifically defined as "documents and information, which if known by unauthorized persons, are liable to jeopardize or cause damage to national independence, to the unity and integrity of the State and to its internal and external security."[43] From the outset, secrecy was postulated to be the exception rather than the rule when applied to government-held information, with classifications being made "on a case-by-case basis in view of their specific circumstances, not automatically resulting from the nature of the matters to be treated."[44] This ruling therefore forced Portuguese intelligence entities to make sure that they had a clear reason for the classification of information. They could not simply apply classification by default to all the information they held.[45]

This included the 1995 revision of the 1984 SIRP framework law. This change abandoned the original idea of creating and maintaining three intelligence services separately focused on internal, external, and military matters. Instead, Portuguese politicians decided to consolidate intelligence under two. The SIS would continue to focus on internal security, while a new service, the Serviço de Informações Estratégicas de Defesa e Militares (SIEDM; Strategic Defense and Military Information Service), would focus on both external *and* military intelligence. Indeed, as the relevant article stated, SIEDM was to be "the body responsible for producing information that contributes to safeguarding national independence, national interests, the external security of the Portuguese State, the accomplishment of the missions of the Armed Forces and the military's security."[46] This merged the responsibilities it was envisaged would be carried out by SIED and the SIM when the original 1984 law was drafted. Practically, implementing such a change was not overly difficult given that the creation of the two organizations had never actually been realized.[47] It also simplified oversight arrangements because the inclusion of military commitments meant that the organization was accountable to the prime minister via the defense minister and required to meet all existing requirements on data security and state secrets.[48] As with the SIS when it was created, stringent limitations to SIEDM's activities were built into its enabling legislation. Almost identical wording was taken from the earlier SIS law and included in the sections that defined the parameters within which SIEDM's officers could operate and the punishments that would result if such parameters were breached.[49]

Following 9/11, much intelligence and security legislation focused on enabling Portugal's intelligence organizations to respond to terrorism more effectively. This was an issue that received supranational legislative attention, specifically by the EU. This resulted in the establishment of the European Council's 475/2002 framework decision on combating terrorism being transposed into Portuguese national law under Law 53/2003.[50] This took those elements of the 1982 Penal Code focused on terrorism and expanded them into their own separate law. Notably it defined terrorist groups, terrorism, and the penalties associated with conducting with terrorist activity.[51] This assisted the SIS in particular by setting the criteria by which it could pursue investigations of terrorist groups under the 1987 Internal Security Law, in addition to the criminal charges that would result from any subsequent prosecution. This formalization aligned with the standards set out at the same time by the 2003 Strategic Defense Concept that the "democratic rule of law must, in pursuit of its strategic objectives, have an information system that proceeds, under the terms of the law and subject to democratic inspection, to the collection, treatment, sharing and appropriate use of information."[52] Per the law, the relevant bodies could utilize legislation, such as Law 53/2003, to evaluate whether the SIS was operating in line with the standards set by the Assembly of the Republic. Additionally, they could also change existing laws in order to adapt to the times and ensure that SIRP, the SIS, and SIED were operating in line with such "democratic rule."

In 2004, for example, the supervisory powers of the Conselho de Fiscalização do SIRP (CFSIRP; Supervisory Board of the Information System of the Portuguese Republic) were strengthened with the establishment of a secretary-general of SIRP. The secretary-general was responsible for the "direction, inspection, supervision and coordination of the intelligence services and common bodies."[53] This included revisions made to the 1987 Internal Security Law in 2008, the passing of further state secret legislation in 2014 and 2015, the passing of a dedicated cybersecurity strategy in 2015, and further counterterrorism legislation in 2017. It is in light of the adherence to such laws that SIRP proudly posits on its website that its activities are guided by the following five principles: constitutionality, legality, specialty, need, and proportionality.[54] SIRP advocates have highlighted that SIRP "maximized operational synergies, created doctrinal unity, optimized human resources, provided for a better coordination of forces and improvement of the relationship with national security forces and services and foreign intelligence services, and improved operational flexibility within the framework of an early warning system and of a culture of integrated information."[55]

Greece

Greece's approach to legal oversight differed due to the fact that it decided to maintain its existing intelligence organization after the fall of the junta in 1974. Efforts were thus made to reset the parameters within which the organization operated. Of greatest importance was National Decree 75/1974, "on the replacement and supplementation of Law 380/1969." This reorientated the Greek intelligence service, the KYP, away from the antidemocratic activities to which it had been assigned under the junta, most specifically its focus on members of the Greek Communist Party and left-wing activists and generally on political opponents, rather than those who actively sought to do harm to Greek interests or citizens.[56] This was followed by the creation of a new Greek Constitution, which from the outset set the standards by which all government organizations, including the KYP, would be held accountable. The final draft, produced in 1975, reinstated eleven key articles that the junta had done away with and had a pronounced effect on the subsequent oversight of the KYP. The articles contained provisions that prevented the authorities from arresting citizens without a warrant and stopping lawful assemblies, and they prohibited "torture, any bodily maltreatment, impairment of health or use of psychological violence, as well as any other offence against human dignity."[57] In contrast to junta-era protocols, post-1974 citizens were also entitled to not be "arrested or imprisoned without a reasoned judicial warrant which must be served at the moment of arrest or detention pending trial, except when caught in the act of committing a crime."[58] While not specifically related to intelligence in the traditional sense, these moves were important due to the legacy left by members of the junta security forces, specifically the military police, and the need to dispel the idea that such behavior would ever again be acceptable.

More relevant legislation did not follow until 1986, when Andreas Papandreou decided to remodel the KYP during his second term as prime minister. Through Presidential Decree ND 1645/1986, the KYP was renamed Ethnikí Ypiresía Pliroforión (EYP; National Intelligence Service). Its remit was also expanded from "the collection and processing of information concerning the national security of the country" to include counterintelligence, the coordination and distribution of intelligence, and "any other mission assigned to it by the National Security Council or the Prime Minister."[59] This latter point was notable, however, given that no explicit mention was made in the law about carrying out such missions in compliance with the constitution or other laws designed to protect personal freedoms and rights.[60] Indeed, through the entire text, no mention is made of the constitution; instead, it simply focuses on the purpose, organization, and composition of the new service. This would not be such a substantial issue were it not for the fact that so few other laws have been passed that might regulate the EYP's activities or provide a better understanding of its operational parameters around this time. Presidential Decree 360/1992, for example, was also very good at setting out how the EYP should conduct recruitment—how many people should be recruited, from which areas, and what education they needed, as it will be explained in more detail in chapter 5—but less explanatory when it came to setting out how the organization would operate.[61] Remarkably, even the overall purpose of the organization was not made clear in the law, such objectives instead being buried within the job description of each individual component in Article 2.[62]

This only changed in 2008 with the passing of Law 3649/2008, National Intelligence Service, and other provisions. This set out from the outset that the EYP was to perform its mission within the framework of the constitution. Within this framework, the EYP would have to search, collect, process, and disclose information to the competent authorities of the information concerning:

a. The protection and promotion of the political, economic, military and in general national strategic interests of the Country.
b. The prevention and confrontation of activities that pose a threat to the democratic state, the fundamental human rights, the territorial integrity and the national security of the Greek State, as well as the national wealth of the Country.
c. Preventing and dealing with the activities of terrorist organizations, as well as other organized crime groups.[63]

This was the first time that adherence to the articles posited in the post-junta constitution was acknowledged and respect for human rights and democratic rule was codified. Beyond this, however, there have been almost no other enabling legislation or rules that the EYP's activities could be measured against.

Spain

The post-Franco Spanish Constitution provided the foundation for much of the subsequent laws and regulations relating to intelligence and intelligence oversight. Approved on December 6, 1978, the constitution limited from the outset the ability of citizens to request information held by the government if it concerned the security or defense of the state, the investigation of crimes, or the privacy of individuals.[64] From the outset, therefore, there existed a hurdle on transparency. This was to have a substantial impact upon subsequent transparency laws governing access to administrative documents held by public entities. The 1978 constitution also contained numerous articles that were intended to govern the country's new intelligence service—the Centro Superior de Información de la Defensa (CESID; Superior Center for Defense Information), created on July 14, 1977—and ostensibly prevent it from repeating the kind of activities that had occurred under Franco. Sections 53 and 54 of chapter 4 of the constitution focused specifically on "the guarantee of fundamental rights and freedoms," while section 55 laid out the precise parameters within which the state could suspend those same rights and freedoms.[65] Thus, according to the new constitution, only an organic act could "determine the manner and circumstances in which, on an individual basis and with the necessary participation of the courts and proper parliamentary control . . . [a citizen's rights] may be suspended for specific persons *in connection with investigations of the activities of armed bands or terrorist groups* [my italics]."[66] This was important for two reasons. First, it made the suspension or reduction of a citizen's rights dependent on laws agreed upon by the legislature. It also established the kind of criteria upon which the legitimacy of such suspensions rested. No longer could the state's intelligence organizations legally gather information on whomever they wanted, including political opponents. Instead, any investigation was dependent on there being a clear and present danger. Accordingly, while the Amnesty Law may have prevented those intelligence officers who had conducted crimes in the past from being held accountable, the final point of section 55 attempted to make it clear that illegal behavior would not be tolerated from 1979 onward: "Unwarranted or abusive use of the powers recognized in the foregoing organic act shall give rise to criminal liability as a violation of the rights and freedoms recognized by the laws."[67] That this was included in the Spanish Constitution, as opposed to any other law, carried substantial weight when it came to promoting a new culture of accountability and adherence to the rule of law.

This somewhat negated the absence of any specific mention of the above in either the initial law that restructured the Spanish Ministry of Defense and created CESID in 1977—Royal Decree 1558/77—or the follow-up law that set out the organization's purpose and objective.[68] The same was also the case for Organic Law 6/1980, which set out the rules governing Spain's national defense (and to which CESID was ultimately held responsible, given its placement in the Ministry of Defense).[69] That was in addition to Order 135/1982, which again set out the role and organization of CESID but gave little to no information as to the enabling legislation or regulations upon which it carried out its duties.[70] It was only with the passing of the Spanish Anti-Terrorism Law in 1984 that it was possible to see—beyond the criteria already included in the constitution—the legal basis upon which intelligence collection was being carried out. Perceived terrorists were notified if their rights and protections have been suspended, except on occasions where it would compromise investigations.[71]

The importance of compliance with such rulings was as such alluded to in 1995 when Royal Decree 1324 was issued. This stated in its "General Duties" section that all CESID staff were required to "maintain compliance with the Constitution and the rest of the legal system." One potential pitfall followed in the next line, however, which made it clear that staff also were to "comply strictly, loyally, impartially and diligently with the obligations of the service, faithfully obeying the orders issued by their hierarchical superiors."[72] This raised the question, therefore, as to which would be placed first in the event of conflict: compliance with the rule of law or compliance with the organization's hierarchy. It did not take long for the latter to be shown as the victor, when several scandals with CESID at their center led to calls for the laws to be revisited and the organization to be overseen more stringently.[73] Popular anger motivated those such as Eduardo Serra—the Partido Popular government's defense minister in 1997—to promote the idea that to stop CESID from acting in a dangerously independent manner, the best course of action would be to formally set out its objectives once and for all.[74] This idea was "noted" by the wider Spanish cabinet but never acted upon. The result was that intelligence consumers could then deny any knowledge of events should they ever face legal action. Unlike in Greece, therefore, policymakers' willingness to apply proper reform was limited. This aligns with what Florina Cristiana Matei and Thomas Bruneau call "transition fatigue," "a post-transition stagnation in political and social changes—which curbs any interest and keenness for reform." This is further reinforced by the fact that policymakers tend to want to be able to deny any knowledge of illegal activities to avoid being accused of being involved in illegal actions.[75]

It was not until the exogenous shock of September 11, 2001, which acted as a critical juncture, that the political impetus was generated to finally address such major issues. The result were two major laws. The first, Law 11/2002 of May 6, 2002, ushered in a new era in Spanish intelligence affairs through the creation of "efficient, specialized and modern intelligence services, capable of facing the new challenges of the current national and international scenario, governed by the principles of control and full submission to the legal system."[76] The specified action was the abolition of the widely maligned and flawed CESID and its replacement with the CNI. This was necessary given the ad hoc and irregular way in which CESID had been created and governed. Or, as the problem was described at an official level in 2002, "the current regulation of the Higher Information Center of Defense is contained in a plurality of provisions, none of them of a legal nature."[77]

Furthermore, any such laws that had been passed up to this point lacked "a unitary and systematic regulation and with the appropriate legal rank in light of the Constitution."[78] Prior to 2002, therefore, intelligence activities in Spain were more or less unregulated, at least compared to the levels seen in other countries. With political willpower determining that such an issue could no longer stand, the CNI was created with legal oversight in mind from the outset.[79] In light of this, it was defined as "the public body responsible for providing the President of the Government and the Government of the Nation with the information, analysis, studies or proposals to prevent and avoid any danger, threat or aggression against the independence or territorial integrity of Spain, national interests and the stability of the rule of law and its institutions."[80] Consequently, if it were to later emerge that more death squads had been created or sponsored by the CNI or that the king's telecommunications had been tapped, then the onus would be on the government to show that it did not sign off on any such "proposal."

This resulted in behavior the exact opposite from before 2002, with policymakers showing more willingness to reform. Since then, nineteen laws have been passed relating to the CNI, its structure, its organization, and the regulations affecting it. The willingness to introduce additional laws was reinforced by the Madrid attacks of 2004. Several of these laws have introduced new regulatory requirements or obliged the CNI to act in a certain way. They have included Royal Decree 421/2004, which set out the regulations by which a newly created National Cryptological Center (CCN) would operate and function within the CNI. They have also included the Law of National Defense in 2005, the 2010 Royal Decree on Preventing Terrorist Financing, the 2011 Law on Public Sector Contracts, the 2011 Law for the Protection of Critical Infrastructure, the 2015 Law of National Security, and finally the 2015 Judicial Regulation of the Public Sector. All of them were summarized in the detailed compendium produced by the CNI in 2016 titled *Regulatory Regulations*.[81] As a result, any citizen can now understand what role the CNI plays in national defense, how it carries out this role, and under which rules it is able to do so. The above progress came only as a result of critical junctures that acted as factors that support progress. These were 9/11 and the Madrid attacks in 2004.

IMMEDIATE CONTROL AND OVERSIGHT

Without effective control, government organizations risk not only failing to perform according to the objectives set out by law, but democratic society also risks suffering abuses of power. When looking at intelligence organizations, the risk runs higher due to the less open or secret environment in which they operate. For a government organization to be able to perform in accordance to the law, a layer of accountability is necessary. In a parliamentary system, accountability—both by the intelligence organization and the government controlling it—comes through the form of ministerial responsibility. Without this link, the organization cannot be held to account by either the legislature or the public via the relevant minister. These are the elements that control over intelligence agencies comprises.

Portugal

Until legislation was passed for the creation of SIRP in 1984, control of and accountability for Portugal's remaining intelligence functions sat with the country's defense minister—at the time Carlos Alberto da Mota Pinto.[82] This was a result of the dismantling of Portugal's civilian intelligence organization following the Carnation Revolution and the decision to rely purely on the armed forces' own military intelligence section from 1975 to 1984. The 1984 SIRP framework law quickly changed all this by creating an entirely new intelligence setup, with different levels of oversight and control. Under the new law, the ultimate authority for intelligence matters was the prime minister of Portugal. It was the prime minister who was responsible for informing the president of the republic of any misconduct by the intelligence services, coordinating the action of responsible ministers, chairing the Superior Information Council, and exercising any other functions "assigned by law."[83] It is at the Superior Information Council specifically where the prime minister wielded the most control. The council is "the interministerial body for consultation and coordination in matters of information" and is composed of a wide range of ministers, the chief of the General Staff of the armed forces, and all the directors of the planned intelligence organizations. The council's responsibilities are outlined in the SIRP framework law (Article 18, number 4) and include to "advise and assist the Prime Minister in coordinating information services; pronounce on all matters submitted to it with regard to information by the Prime Minister or, with his authorization, by any of its members; propose the orientation of the research activity by the various information services."[84] In short, the council advises on matters relating to intelligence and tasks the relevant organizations into taking follow-up actions.

Fulfillment of these actions was to be the responsibility of several standalone intelligence organizations, including SIED, the SIM, and the SIS.[85] Each would be controlled and run internally by a director, but under the law the ultimate responsibility for the running of SIED would be the prime minister's, with the defense minister—via the chief of staff of the armed forces—being responsible for the SIM and the minister for internal administration being responsible for the SIS.[86] At no point could one responsible minister influence or oversee the actions of another, with each being responsible for their assigned organization alone.[87] If there were disagreements in practice, these were to be resolved at the Superior Information Council, with the prime minister adjudicating.

Within the SIS—the only organization immediately created following the SIRP framework law—an almost identical control setup was enacted, with the minister of internal administration leading an "advisory council" that "functions as a body for technical consultation and coordination in matters of internal security information."[88] Beneath this council was the Executive Board, composed of the director and deputy director. Together they were responsible for a wide range of duties, among them directing "the service in order to ensure the effective pursuit of their institutional purposes, issuing the service orders and instructions that it deems convenient," enacting the policies of "the Minister for Internal Administration and the deliberations of the supervisory bodies," and appointing and dismissing personnel.[89] Per Article 3 of the relevant law, all of these activities were to be performed within strictly defined limits.[90] When SIEDM was eventually created in 1995, the exact same template was used. The defense minister also chaired an "advisory council," which advised "in matters of strategic defense and military information when making decisions regarding the exercise of their own or delegated powers" and proposed "the adoption of appropriate measures for the centralization, exploitation and use of all information that is of interest to the pursuit of the objectives legally committed to SIEDM."[91] These objectives in turn were to be enacted by a director-general and two deputies who were to "supervise the activities of the services and exercise their inspection, oversight and coordination, in order to ensure the effective pursuit of their institutional purposes," issue "the service orders and instructions that it deems convenient, within the scope of the duties legally committed to SIEDM," appoint and dismiss staff, and more.[92] From the outset, therefore, it was clear to all involved, in addition to the public, how their nation's intelligence organizations were controlled and their activities directed. A clear chain of responsibility was established by the laws passed, which led from the most junior employee up to the director's level and through to cabinet ministers and beyond. With this being the case, the opportunities for one or more of the national intelligence organizations to begin performing undemocratically were much reduced.

All of this changed quite substantially in 2004 when major amendments to the 1984 SIRP framework law were made. SIEDM, which had existed only since 1995, was broken up. Its military intelligence functions were returned to the armed forces and the control that the defense minister and minister of internal administration had previously had over both it and the SIS was removed. Indeed, under Law 4/2004, the SIS and the reformed "SIED" became the responsibility of SIRP alone, with the new position of secretary-general being under the direct authority of the Portuguese prime minister.[93] This secretary-general had total control over the SIS and SIED, managing their activities through their directors and executing the instructions of the prime minister. They also absorbed many of the responsibilities previously held by directors up to that point, including presiding over each service's advisory and administrative councils, directing the activity of data centers, preparing budgets, and managing recruitment.[94] This change simplified the control mechanisms that had existed up to that point and placed a greater emphasis on the relationship between the prime minister and the secretary-general they appointed. The directors of both SIED and the SIS continued to "direct responsibility for the normal activity and for the regular functioning of each service" but under the supervision of the secretary-general rather than government ministers.[95] This setup remained unchanged when the SIRP framework was most recently amended in 2014, and the secretary-general, under the prime minister, continued to wield control over Portugal's two intelligence organizations.

Greece

Since it was established in 1953, the KYP had a tight control structure whereby the organization's director answered directly to the Greek prime minister. Despite the problems that this caused prior to 1967, Konstantinos Karamanlis decided to maintain control when he became prime minister in 1974. It is possible that this was done in order to offer the executive its own sources of information, separate from the Ministry of Defense and the armed forces, which had conspired to overthrow the government in 1967. In any case, the result was that control of the postjunta KYP resembled very much the type of control that had been exerted before the junta had taken power. This made the appointment of the right kind of director more important than ever and is one of the underlying reasons that both Karamanlis and later Andreas Papandreou hired and fired different elements of the organization's management early on in their premierships.

Karamanlis's and Papandreou's tug-of-war for control of the Greek state extended to control of the KYP when Karamanlis came into office in 1980 and Papandreou in 1981. Given that Papandreou had decided to take on the defense portfolio from 1981 onward, this gave him total control over the organization's activities and affairs from that point.[96] Law 1415/1984 formalized this arrangement by making it clear that the KYP "is an independent political service under the direct control of the Prime Minister."[97] This brief law also enabled the prime minister and them alone to enact further laws relating to the KYP's development and regulation, transferring such responsibilities only at a time of their choosing.[98] The result was Law 1645/1986. This created a new intelligence organization from the foundation of the old one (the EYP) but again outlined that it was "an independent political public service with the mission of the country's security and reports directly to the Prime Minister."[99] Indeed, in addition to collecting and processing information and tackling "the spying activities of foreign intelligence agencies," the EYP was to carry out "any other mission related to the above responsibilities assigned to it by the National Security Council or the Prime Minister."[100] The prime minister was also, again, made responsible for appointing the organization's commander and deputies. Furthermore, they were to receive "special duties" determined "in secret" by the prime minister.[101] Consequently, the executive branch of the Greek government continued to wield enormous control over the Greek intelligence organization, the exact nature of which, however, remained hidden from view.

What is notable is that this was the setup that was legislated by the Greek parliament. Whereas the Portuguese legislature had assured itself of some input through its accompanying civilian supervisory board, no such mechanism was established in Greece between 1986 and 2008. It is possible that this would have occurred had there been more political debate prior to the implementation of the law, yet at the time Papandreou appeared to only be concerned with rapid change. Major political and public debate about what kind of intelligence service Greece needed and how and whether it could be independently regulated never really took place.[102] Indeed, further details only emerged by decree. Under Presidential Decree 360/1992, for example, the roles and responsibilities of all of the EYP's staff and operational components were more clearly defined to the public. The organization's commander was still appointed and had their strategic duties defined by the prime minister, but the decree otherwise clarified that they

a. Have the highest management of the services of the EYP, control and coordinate its work. Within the scope of its competence, the Commander issues Standing Circulars and Orders.
b. They are the disciplinary head of all the personnel of the EYP Civil and Military and exercise disciplinary power in accordance with the existing provisions and the provisions of the present.

This came on top of financial powers and recruitment activities. Certainly, the only things they were not in control of in 1992 were "appointments, permanent appointments of employees, transfers and secondments outside the EYP."[103] In other words, this was the coming and going of uniformed staff, which was admittedly no small thing when a large percentage of personnel continued to hail from the Greek military and police, as it will be shown in chapter 5.

Law 3649/2008 further altered the equation by making the interior minister responsible for controlling the EYP.[104] This was notable due to the fact that it marked the first time that the organization had come under the control of this minister, having long been the responsibility of either the defense minister or the prime minister directly. The law was also notable due to the way in which it created an Information Council staffed by the EYP's commander, the general secretaries of the Ministry of the Interior and the Ministry of Foreign Affairs, and others. This council had the remit of coordinating all state intelligence and security services in the field of information collection and distribution as well as identifying and formulating new information requirements—in other words, tasking the country's intelligence entities in collecting information pertinent for the EYP.[105] The commander, meanwhile, continued to exercise the administration of the service—"direct, coordinate, supervise and control its work"—while being ultimately accountable to the "Minister of Interior for the exercise of his duties." (This focus of "he/him/his" in the wording had also been present in the previous 1992 law and was indicative of the cultural norms present within the service when it came to expectations as to who would be in charge at one time or another.[106]) This kind of "stability" was in contrast to the additional cabinet portfolio changes that occurred from 2008 onward. For example, the EYP was under the minister of civil protection from October 13, 2009, under Law 3817/2010 before it was once again returned to the prime minister in 2020 under Law 4704/2020.[107] The result is that control has been passed full circle, with the same setup that was present before democratization being more or less present afterward.

Spain

The 1977 law that established CESID following the dissolution of the Franco-era intelligence organizations was unique in that it placed the organizations within the domain of military as opposed to under civilian control. This was made possible through an understanding that the Ministry of Defense would be "integrated into the old Military Ministries and receive functions and responsibilities that go beyond the strictly military field."[108] To this end, although the Spanish defense minister technically had control over CESID, ultimate authority for its actions rested with the General Staff of the armed forces, which served the king. This arrangement somewhat isolated the elected component of CESID's command structure, enhancing the powers of the unelected officials and uniformed officers who served in its ranks. The director of CESID in particular was approved on the recommendation of the defense minister. The director was to "ensure the execution of the missions entrusted to the center," "arrange its internal organization and territorial deployment," and, most important, "maintain close contact and collaboration with the information bodies of the Joint Chiefs of Staff and General Staff of the three Armies."[109] Accordingly, this facilitated behavior and activities not exactly in sync with the democratic ideals of the time, as Antonio M. Díaz Fernández makes clear: "Adapting to new democratic practices proved to be difficult for many members of the military, who formed part of the intelligence services and were all too used to undertaking acts of espionage on an independent footing."[110]

The decision, meanwhile, to merge many of Franco's old intelligence and security services into one organization—CESID—without any meaningful lustration meant that problems of control were not isolated to any one event in particular. Instead, a culture of rogue operational practices was allowed to develop. Among the most prominent breakers of trust were CESID's elite Agrupación Operativa de Misiones Especiales (AOME; Special Operations Group), led by Maj. José Luís Cortina. By the late 1970s and early 1980s, Major Cortina "enjoyed almost complete autonomy; his only hierarchical link to CESID was Calderón [Javier Calderón, CESID's then director], who didn't supervise the unit in practice but simply requested from it, on behalf of the various divisions of the centre; information, the major would later obtain without answering to anybody about his manner of obtaining it."[111] Such an arrangement easily facilitated bad behavior that could be kept secret from others, whether outside legislators or even the defense minister. Consequently, with such a wide gap between the amount of control that was in place on paper and what was applicable in reality, Spain's government was left vulnerable to threats emanating from some of the same individuals that had sworn to protect it. With the protection that *el pacto del olvido* had given them, Franco-era officials were free to take up positions in CESID and elsewhere and propagate the ideology and methodology of the Franco-era intelligence services.

Part of the reasoning for not undertaking thorough lustration was a desire to maintain the kind of expertise that was needed for Spain to fulfill its growing list of international obligations. Spain's accession to the North Atlantic Treaty Organization in June 1982, for example, "required the establishment of a National Security Authority responsible for protecting and controlling the Classified Information originated by the parties of the Treaty."[112] This authority would also have to "co-ordinate and supervise the protection measures for the NATO Classified Information handed over to Spain by the Alliance."[113] By order of the Ministry of Defense on September 30, 1982, CESID was entrusted with this task, and the result was a general tightening up of Spain's handling of classified and sensitive information. A key step was the creation of the Oficina Nacional de Seguridad (ONS; National Security Office) in 1983. Its primary task was ensuring that civil servants followed the relevant rules when handling classified information that originated nationally or came from foreign partners. Beyond this, however, the ONS was also intended to be available to help CESID's director "in the discharge of his duties related to the protection of Classified Information."[114] What this meant was that the organization was put in a position where it could help oversee which information was classified and which was not. The amount of power invested in CESID without comparable control being exerted was all the more incredible given what had happened prior to and during Lt. Col. Antonio Tejero's abortive coup attempt in 1981, for not only did CESID fail to prevent the attempt, but it also was implicated in supporting it either directly or via AOME.[115] It is evident, therefore, that authoritarian practices continued to take place, with the Spanish intelligence service acting as a catalyst in favor of the government as opposed to its people. Resistance to change came from within the service as legacies of the authoritarian regime persisted.

This situation changed only in 1984 and 1985 with the invocation of Royal Decree 135/1984, which split control of CESID between the president and the minister of defense, and Royal Decree 2632/1985, which outlined the purposes of the organization and the role that its "general director" would play in providing "adequate levels of security to the people."[116] Royal Decree 1324/1995, thereafter, set out in detail the recruitment practices that CESID would adopt and the regulations that officers would be expected to abide by. Yet it also maintained the duality of power that existed not only between the president and defense minister but also between the cabinet and the Spanish military, which maintained a huge influence of power given the number of officers it continued to place in CESID directly.

A few years later and despite the other major changes wrought by the passing of Law 11/2002, which regulated the CNI, this arrangement was one that did not substantially change. The CNI, as when it was created, continued to operate under the control of the Ministry of Defense and with military officers in its ranks. The difference, however, was the introduction of new parties responsible for controlling the organization's activities. These will be analyzed in detail in the external oversight section of this chapter, but it is important to briefly touch on a couple in this section as part of their connection to the director(s) of the service(s). For the first time, the law specifically contemplated the principle of parliamentary control of the activities of the CNI.[117] While the Spanish parliament could not necessarily control the development of every single source or the launching of operations, it could control what funds were allocated to which activities, a substantial power that had the potential to rein in any major abuses of power. The long-term isolation of Spain's only intelligence organization was also ended through the creation of a Government Delegate Commission for Intelligence Affairs. This was to be chaired by the vice president of the government designated by its president and made up of the ministers of foreign affairs and cooperation, defense, interior, economy, and competitiveness; the director of the cabinet of the presidency of the government; the secretary of state for security; the secretary of state; and the director of the CNI, who will act as its secretary.[118] The purpose of this group was to meet and

a. Propose to the President of the Government the annual objectives of the National Intelligence Center that must be part of the Intelligence Directive.
b. To monitor and evaluate the development of the objectives of the National Intelligence Center.
c. Oversee the coordination of the National Intelligence Center, the information services of the State Security Forces and Corps, and the organs of the civil and military Administration.[119]

The responsibility for fulfilling any such objectives proposed by the commission then fell to the director and secretary-general of the CNI, acting in concert with the regulations set out by both the commission and parliament.[120] This setup has remained in place with minor amendments up to 2020, when Arturo Relanzón Sánchez-Gabriel, a civilian, was appointed secretary-general of the CNI at the behest of the Spanish defense minister.

EXTERNAL OVERSIGHT

Although a legal framework is necessary, it alone is not enough. In the first section of this chapter, emphasis was put on the immediate control and oversight structures and mechanisms that were established in Portugal, Greece, and Spain after their dictatorships fell in the 1970s as well as the legal framework that encompasses them. In addition to those structures and mechanisms, there are also external oversight structures that can be used to oversee an intelligence service.

External oversight involves different types of mechanisms, including parliamentary and extraparliamentary, judiciary, and informal. The latter will be analyzed in chapter 7. Before we dive into the three case studies, we should revisit the definitions of the different types of external oversight. *Parliamentary oversight* involves parliamentary questions usually for the director of an intelligence service. In this book, given that all three cases have parliamentary systems, the analysis will aim to answer questions such as: Is there parliamentary oversight in each case study, what kind of questions does the parliament put to the service, are there any parliamentary committees adjacent to that process, and how independent are they? What type of answers do the intelligence services provide the parliament with, and is there a legal framework that gives enough oversight powers to each parliament and their committees? Other, independent committees tend to be part of external oversight mechanisms, known as *extraparliamentary oversight*. Additionally, *judicial oversight* involves judges who decide on whether any interception of communications is necessary and proper as a method to collect information or run searches. We will aim to answer questions such as: Are there any additional external oversight structures in addition to parliamentary? Can we make observations about their effectiveness and independent action?

Portugal

Portugal is unique among the three case studies in that it introduced dedicated external oversight measures at the point of creating its new intelligence organizations in 1984. As stated in SIRP'S website, "SIRP's activity and its possible impact on citizens' rights and freedom means that it must have suitable oversight mechanisms." Accordingly, SIRP is monitored by CFSIRP, an oversight council whose members are elected by the Portuguese parliament.[121] This SIRP supervisory board is also elected by the Portuguese parliament, for the specific purpose of monitoring SIRP's (and by extension SIS's and SIED's) activities. Although SIRP's secretary-general answers to the prime minister, CFSIRP is separate and above the secretary-general. It has no relationship with the PM and only focuses on SIRP's activities for the benefit of the Assembly of the Republic. It is composed of three citizens "of recognized standing and in full enjoyment of their civil and political rights, elected by the Assembly of the Republic by secret ballot and a majority of two thirds of the Members present."[122] These three citizens would supervise the control of Portugal's information services for a period of up to four years, unless decided otherwise by the Assembly of the Republic.[123] CFSIRP is responsible for overseeing the secretary-general as well as the activities and the relationship among the services.[124] The services that the law envisaged would be created—the SIS, SIED, and the SIM—were expected thereafter to submit annual reports on their activities, with the board having "the right to request and obtain from the information services, through the respective supervising ministers, any additional clarifications to the reports that it deems necessary for the full exercise of its supervisory powers."[125] Following review of these reports, CFSIRP would then itself submit an "opinion" to the legislature on how it thought the information services were being managed.[126] It was expected to do so "with the independence, exemption and sense of mission inherent in the function [it] exercise[s]."[127] To help it do this, the board was to be advised by a "technical commission" composed of "the Director of the Strategic Defence Information Service, the Director of the Security Intelligence Service, the Chief of the Information Division of the General Staff of the Armed Forces and the Secretary-General."[128]

The Assembly of the Republic approves the appointment of SIRP's leadership, elects the members of CFSIRP, and can request the presence of CFSIRP whenever it wants. CFSIRP "is made up of three citizens of recognized repute and in full enjoyment of their civil and political rights, whose profile provides guarantees of respecting, during the exercise of functions and after their termination, the duties arising from the position, namely those of independence, impartiality and discretion."[129] At the same time, the SIRP data inspection committee, which consists of three magistrates from the public ministry designated and sworn in by the attorney general, would supervise the access of public data in order to ensure "the cancelation or rectification of collected data that involves violation of the rights, freedoms and guarantees enshrined in the Constitution and the law and, if necessary, exercise the corresponding criminal action."[130] Consequently, from its inception, the Portuguese intelligence system not only had legislative oversight that was built in but also external. Another entity for oversight was created in 1987. This was the Conselho Superior de Segurança Interna (Higher Council for Internal Security), which included the Portuguese prime minister, ministers of state, and the director-general of the SIS.[131] Whereas CFSIRP facilitated transparency, the Higher Council assisted "the Prime Minister in the exercise of his powers in matters of internal security, in particular the adoption of the necessary measures in situations of serious internal security threats."[132] Although suitably vague, this kind of language was still in strong contrast to that previously used in the decrees of Salazar and Caetano, which were liable to refer to certain groups and individuals as "public enemies." It was also open to revision, with further legislation and organizational changes relating to intelligence occurring on an almost annual basis in Portugal from 1987 onward. This included the Council of Ministers' approval of the the SIS's first data center in November 1988.[133] It also included the transfer of the PIDE and DGS archives to the Portuguese National Archive in 1990, something that facilitated open study of Portugal's repressive past and particularly the role that the national intelligence service had played.[134] These files were open to the public. Transparency, therefore, was one of the key elements that Portugal established.

As the years went by, SIRP's board's responsibilities continued to expand and get strengthened. In 1995 CFSIRP was no longer just to "report" to the Assembly of the Republic on its opinion of how Portugal's intelligence organizations were performing but also actively ensure "compliance with the Constitution and the law, particularly with regard to the fundamental rights, freedoms and guarantees of citizens."[135] To do this, the board was expected to:

a. Request additional clarifications, reports and other elements deemed necessary for the full exercise of their supervisory powers.
b. Know the governmental guidance criteria for the information search effort.
c. Annually issue opinions on the functioning of the information services to the Assembly of the Republic. SIRP reports to the Assembly of the

Republic twice a year. The first report covers the first six months of the year. The second report covers the whole year.

d. Suggest investigations and corrections procedures when the facts justified it.[136]

In this task, it was to receive the full weight of support from the Assembly of the Republic, which would provide it with secretarial staff, sufficient logistical support, and budgetary allocations in order to "assure it of the indispensable means to fulfill its attributions and competences."[137] In 1996 these powers were further strengthened, with CFSIRP empowered to receive on a bimonthly basis "a complete list of processes in progress" from the directors of the SIS and the newly created SIEDM.[138] It could also carry out independent inspections of either organization at any time and request that the government do the same. That year, the commission of public prosecutors responsible for supervising the use of public data was also granted the ability to conduct independent inspections.[139] In this way, both supervisory entities were given real power when it came to making sure that bad behavior was prevented and/or dealt with in a timely manner. It is key to point out that the supervisory board provides the assembly with its opinion but that it is up to the assembly to take actions in response.

With the remodeling of SIEDM in 2004 and the removal of both the defense minister and minister of the interior from the chain of command, external oversight shifted focus to the newly created secretary-general of SIRP. To begin with, the Assembly of the Republic had the right to sign off on any nominee that the prime minister put up for the post, with a hearing before a parliamentary committee being mandatory prior to their actual appointment.[140] After this, CFSIRP was then tasked with monitoring and supervising "the activity of the Secretary-General and the intelligence services, ensuring compliance with the Constitution and the law, particularly the system of fundamental rights, freedoms and guarantees for citizens."[141]

To further assure that the independence of the board was beyond reproach, the SIRP framework was amended again in 2014 to boost its already substantial impartial credentials. To this end, the board was to be "elected by the Assembly of the Republic by secret ballot and a two-thirds majority of the Deputies present, not inferior to the absolute majority of the Deputies in office," with the election of the members "preceded by a hearing by the parliamentary committee responsible for constitutional matters, rights, freedoms and guarantees." Dismissal would be the result of any "manifest violation of the duties of independence, impartiality and discretion."[142] The inspection visits were also made a mandatory requirement, to occur at least quarterly with or without warning. In addition, they were to "verify the regularity of the internal rules and regulations related to operational safety procedures, as well as to assess any deviations from the standard in relation to international standards and good practices." This was in addition to a host of enhanced duties involving assuring the integrity of recruitment practices, and previously listed requirements.[143] Additionally, it is key to emphasize that all opinions and communiqués issued by the board are today available to the public on its website and that the themes covered are relevant and current to Portuguese society. As an illustrative example, in its most recent opinion of the first semester of 2020, the board spoke about the "focus on the work and priorities of CFSIRP in the face of the reality of information services in the face of the immediate deficits erected by the pandemic of Covid-19, which essentially manifest themselves as challenges inherent to national security and the respective response capacities including efficient and effective articulation between these."[144] Additionally, the first-ever board report emphasized, "As indicators of respect for the Constitution and the laws, it seems to us from the analyzed elements that recruitment is being carried out according to the legal requirements and training is oriented toward defense of democratic institutions" and "due to the elements collected so far, we believe we can affirm that the rights, freedoms and guarantees of the citizens enshrined in the Constitution and the law have been guaranteed."[145] This report demonstrated early on that the board has access to information it requires and has confirmed that the service abides by the law and respects the citizens' human rights.

Last, there is the Data Supervision Commission, which is manned by three prosecutors appointed by the attorney general's office and is responsible for overseeing the intelligence services' data centers.[146] Accordingly, between CFSIRP and the Data Supervision Commission, there was little going on in SIRP, the SIS, or SIED that was not being monitored, investigated, or reported on by external entities. This remarkable level of oversight was made possible through the early introduction and adoption of such practices in 1984 and their subsequent maintenance and expansion through the various amendments to the SIRP framework thereafter. Furthermore, the institutionalization of the intelligence services and the oversight mechanisms as well as their legitimacy within Portuguese society have also increased.[147] This robust oversight structure and openness have increased trust across Portuguese society, which now has access to and can analyze documentation on intelligence matters. This has helped establish an engaged citizenry.

Greece

Historically, there has been little external oversight of the Greek intelligence organization since its inception in 1953. With the executive having nearly total control over its activities, the only form of oversight came via parliamentary questions. Even then there was no guarantee that ministers would get a meaningful response. This was the case from 1974 to 1986, when the law founding the EYP was passed. Even at this latter point, however, little oversight was built into the new organization. The only additional mechanism established for the EYP to receive outside input was via an "information council" consisting of the EYP's director, the head of the Ministry of Public Order's security branch, the director of the General Secretariat for National Defense, and a representative from the Foreign Ministry.[148] Even then, the council was designed to support the EYP in performing its primary functions under Article 2 of the law rather than ensure that it was complying with other regulatory statutes. Certainly, the areas of "supervision" or "regulation" did not even feature in the law as either separate sections or standalone articles.

This remained the case through to National Decree 360/1992, and it was only in 1994 that a degree of outside oversight was introduced, via Law 2225/1994 for the protection of freedom and response and communication and other provisions. This marked an attempt to regulate the EYP's intrusive activities by setting out the circumstances under which it could intercept communications. For the most part, this meant invoking articles of the Greek Penal Code and submitting requests to a "competent judicial council" to show that the investigation of a case or the verification of a place of residence was impossible without intercepting communications.[149] Only after the Supreme Judicial Council and/or public prosecutor had signed off could interception proceed. This introduced a legal check to any request by the EYP to intercept public communications.[150] Despite this strengthening of judicial oversight, additional changes made in 1997 insulated the EYP from it. This was most evidently displayed through the decision to exempt EYP personnel from the authority of the Greek Ombudsman. This agency had been established under Law 2477/97 in order to facilitate the prosecution of crimes committed by public officials, specifically public services that violate the rights or encroach on the legitimate interests of citizens—for example, by infringing on a right protected by the constitution or the law.[151] The above exemption was a curious choice despite further regulation of the EYP's investigatory powers in the same year through Law 2472/1997 for the protection of individual personal data. This expanded the protections afforded to individuals but granted the EYP the ability to circumvent them, providing of course, that a "representative of the prosecutor's office" agreed that there was a serious danger to public order and security.[152] The question remained, for example, as to how it was possible to confirm that the EYP was verifying all its practices via the public prosecutor and not keeping anything "off the books." Revisions made in 1999 to the 1986 law governing public access to administrative documents certainly did not make it more likely that such breaches might be unearthed by concerned citizens. Although not granting as broad a power to reject requests for information as the original text, the 1999 law still allowed "the competent administrative authority" the ability to deny requests if satisfaction would "complicate the investigation of judicial, administrative, police or military authorities in relation to the commission of a crime or administrative breach."[153] Up until the end of the twentieth century, therefore, Greek laws were still quite loose with regard to the organization's objectives as well as what was kept secret from the parliament and/or the public. This approach is completely different from the one in Portugal. Indeed, in Greece citizens were effectively cut off, with no access to any documentation on intelligence matters. There existed a closed intelligence culture.

So far in the twenty-first century, the pace of change has been slow. Indeed, changes made in 2002 simply passed the responsibility for the EYP from the prime minister to the minister of public order. Parliamentary questions have been the main way to receive information about the EYP through formal methods. The permanent Committee of Institutions and Transparency was also established to manage the parliamentary control of "independent" administrative institutions, including the EYP. Based on the *Rules of Procedure of the Parliament*, the committee can request from the government documents that focus on the activities of the EYP. The government, however, can deny to provide these documents for "reasons of national security." The committee can invite the director of the intelligence service while the responsible minister is present and ask relevant questions. These discussions are classified. However, the committee can publish its findings if it so wishes. None of those "opinions" are available on the parliament's website when it comes to the EYP specifically.[154] This is completely opposite from the Portuguese CFSIRP, which has a dedicated website where all documentation on its findings is publicly available.[155]

Although the committee's sessions are classified, one can find questions posed to the responsible minister by other MPs, along with their answers, on the Greek parliament's website. Indicatively, an example of a question from an MP of one of the opposition parties (who also acted as the EYP's director from 2004 to 2009) was, What was the assigned amount in the EYP's budget for "secret" missions in 2010? The responsible minister responded that the amount was €8,456,000 and provided additional information for the subsequent year, for which the sum was €4,200,000. Another question from the same MP to the minister responsible for the EYP was based on news that had emerged about portable wiretapping equipment sold to certain "businessmen": Is the minister going to take any steps to investigate the issue via the intelligence service that falls under his remit? The answer was that both the EYP and the police were aware of the issue and were working in harmony "on issues of common interest" to counter criminal activities.[156] Contrary to the Portuguese website of CFSIRP, the website of the Greek parliament is not user-friendly, and it is extremely difficult for the public to locate any information related to the EYP and any oversight mechanisms that pertain to it.

Additional oversight was introduced through the creation of the Authority for Ensuring the Confidentiality of Communications (ADAE) under Law 3115/2003. The purpose of this independent authority was recorded as being to ensure the confidentiality of mail and all other forms of free correspondence or communication.[157] Remarkably, it was empowered to do so by issuing regulations and performing audits on communications network service providers and public entities, including the EYP. It could hold hearings that such providers and entities would be obliged to attend and respond to complaints raised by the public and evidence gathered by special investigative powers.[158] Any findings would be forwarded to the minister of justice, the Speaker of the parliament, and the leaders of the parties represented there.[159] While the law established this oversight, however, it limited ADAE to simply monitoring compliance with the procedural terms and conditions set out by other national legislation. Only the judiciary was allowed to decide whether any interception of communications was necessary and lawful per laws passed since 1994. Law 3115 was important nonetheless due to the way in which it changed the power dynamic between the EYP and others. Whereas before 2003 the judiciary had only become aware of investigatory activities when the EYP had approached them, after 2003 it and members of the legislature could theoretically audit the EYP whenever they so wished.

This involvement of the legal profession in the EYP's affairs gathered pace under Law 3649/2008, which reaffirmed that the EYP's operations and duties were viable only through compliance with the provisions of Law 2472/1997, Law 3115/2003, and Law 3471/2006. To make sure that the EYP was adhering to such provisions, the new law mandated the appointment of a public prosecutor whose job was to check "the legality of its [the EYP's] special operational actions which concern human rights, and other responsibilities assigned to it."[160] Remarkably, however, any breaches of such rights could actually be kept secret for up to fifty years, only being declassified if so approved by a newly created three-member "declassification committee" and only based on requesting information for personal purposes.[161] This again put a limit on just how much external oversight others were capable of conducting over the EYP, particularly given the maintenance of legislative barriers. Throughout the decades and as of 2020, the main means to apply external scrutiny over the EYP's activities has been parliamentary oversight, including the parliament's Committee of Institutions and Transparency, with the responsible ministers being at the forefront of the process. This was the minister of civil protection since October 18, 2009, under Law 3817/2010, before control was once again returned to the prime minister in 2020 under Law 4704/2020.[162] As analyzed above, this mechanism embodies several limitations, including a closed intelligence culture with inadequate transparency.

Spain

At the creation of CESID in 1977, the law mandated only a very limited degree of outside oversight of the intelligence service. As CESID was highly military in nature, the only external input came not from any civilian entity but the military itself, through the Supreme Council of Military Justice. This was a body that, "in matters of Military Justice, exercises the Superior Jurisdiction with the organization, missions and powers attributed to it by current legislation."[163] Other than this, the only mechanism for others to raise questions about CESID was to pose them directly to the defense minister in the Spanish parliament. Spain differed from Greece, however, by not simply settling with this arrangement. As part of their legislative efforts, Spanish lawmakers aimed to empower themselves to be able to learn about and put an end to any abuses by reforming the 1968 Ley de Secretos Oficiales (Official Secrets Law). In the revised text of October 11, 1978, the Spanish parliament was for the first time exempted from traditional restrictions on classified information. These had effectively blocked anyone outside of a small circle of ministers, civil servants, and military personnel from knowing anything about the state's intelligence activities.[164] As a result, when it came the time to formulate the new restrictions, lawmakers did not hold back from promoting their own interests. Indeed, in the revised text it was clearly stated that "the declaration of 'classified matters' will not affect the Congress of Deputies or the Senate, which will always have access to all the information they claim, in the manner determined by the respective regulations and, as the case may be, in secret sessions."[165] On paper, this was a groundbreaking development that marked the first time in modern history that a degree of democratic governance was applied over Spanish intelligence. As was to be seen, however, it marked only the start of a long battle to gain some kind of oversight over CESID rather than the end.

In March 1987, for example, Catalan deputy Miguel Roca and sixty-six other parliamentary deputies appealed to the Constitutional Court against the Presidential Resolution of July 18, 1986. This resolution had come in response to earlier claims that deputies were unable to review classified information and carry out their duties in line with the provisions of the constitution because of technical rulings. The presidential resolution, however, still "excluded individual deputies from gaining access and conferred it only to commissions and a group(s) that included at least a quarter of the members of Congress."[166] However, according to the resolution the appeal was turned down on grounds that the Court considered that the resolution of the presidency of Congress was a "decision or act of no legal standing and, as a consequence, could not be appealed against on legal grounds."[167] In this way, parliamentary oversight was reduced on the grounds of technical matters, rather than substantive arguments against external regulation. In this case, the respective regulations underlined that specific documentation was required to gain access to the required "secret sessions" where CESID's activities could be reviewed. However, "since no reference was made in the rulebook on parliamentary procedure to gaining access to this sort of documentation . . . the Chamber of Deputies systematically blocked deputies from consulting classified information."[168]

An interesting example relating to the issue of oversight is referenced by Díaz Fernández, who writes that on January 4, 1979, during the burial of Constantino Ortín Gil, the military ruler of Madrid who was assassinated by the ETA, Vice President Manuel Gutiérrez Mellado was confronted by numerous soldiers. When Gutiérrez Mellado demanded a list with the names of the troublemakers from José María Bourgon López-Dóriga, the head of CESID refused to provide it, saying "he was not there to spy on his colleagues."[169] Thus, although on paper Spanish parliamentarians could oversee the running of CESID and help set its annual objectives, in reality they were firmly blocked from achieving any meaningful supervision. After escalating protests, the presidency sought to resolve the issue by approving "the resolution of 18 July 1986, which established a procedure for deputies to access classified files. However, the resolution excluded access by individual deputies and granted it solely to committees or to one or more parliamentary groups that made up at least a quarter of all deputies in Congress."[170] This further frustrated parliamentary efforts to review the information that CESID was classifying on a regular basis and went a long way to hindering the regulatory procedures that the 1978 constitution was meant to prescribe.

After continued political pressure and the reiteration of complaints in 1989, the presidency of Congress put forward on June 2, 1992, another resolution for the disclosure of classified information to deputies. However, this resolution did little to placate those who had the most interest in reviewing what Spain's intelligence service was doing—namely the Grupo Mixto, a loose collective of Basque, Catalan, communist, and other deputies who did not hold enough seats to belong to a defined political group but who were automatically incorporated by law into a single definable entity.[171] The result were a series of parliamentary sessions that appeared to show the willingness of CESID to submit to independent oversight but that frequently ended without any meaningful discussion. In one such case, where deputies began to ask the director of CESID about what the organization did, the chair decided to end the session so as not to break the relevant rules.[172]

Issues with this legal setup was most prominently felt during the infamous GAL affair, which involved the cooperation between the ministry of interior and

CESID to establish a government-sponsored terrorist group, the Grupos Anti-terroristas de Liberación (GAL; Antiterrorist Liberation Groups).[173] Incredibly, despite such monumental political turmoil, the affair resulted in only minor improvements to the laws regulating CESID. The most meaningful of them was Act 11/1995 of May 11, 1995, which sought to regulate the government's use of *fondos reservados*, or confidential funds.[174] This act meant that Spanish deputies had the power for the first time to influence how much money the Spanish intelligence service received and help establish what the money was used for. This key point was established in Article 7.1, stating that "the appropriations destined for reserved expenses will be subject to the control of the Congress of Deputies, through a Parliamentary Committee composed of the President of the Chamber, who will preside over it, and those Deputies who, in accordance with parliamentary regulations, have access to official secrets."[175] It was henceforth the responsibility of those like the director of CESID to report twice a year to the presiding committee, where in secret sessions they would detail "to the Commission on the application and use of the corresponding budgetary funds."[176] This information was then to be used to help construct an annual report "for submission to the Presidents of the Government and the Court of Auditors."[177] Although an important step, given that all such proceedings and their resulting reporting remained secret and that not all deputies could participate due to established restrictions, the initiative of discussions still remained with CESID. This was certainly still the case for judicial proceedings in which CESID could still refuse to participate as it willed. Not only that, but as Díaz Fernández surmises, "65% of parliamentary oversight was initiated by press reporting." He continues: "When it came to allegations of illegalities by the services, this went up to 89%."[178] This impasse remained unresolved at the end of the twentieth century despite popular and political pressure to establish clear external oversight.

Further improvements were made possible through the eventual dissolution of CESID and its replacement by the CNI in 2002, after 9/11. Under the enabling Law 11/2002, the actions of the CNI were to "be subject to parliamentary and judicial control in the terms that this Law and the Organic Law regulating prior judicial control of the National Intelligence Center determine."[179] As a result, Law 11/2002 included entire sections on parliamentary involvement. The CNI had to "submit to the knowledge of the Congress of Deputies, in the manner provided for by its Regulations . . . the appropriate information on its operation and activities."[180] The Congress of Deputies had to keep any such information it received secret but still had the ability to "be aware of the intelligence objectives established annually by the Government and of the report that, also on an annual basis, shall be prepared by the Director of the National Intelligence Center for the evaluation of activities."[181]

At the same time that Law 11/2002 was passed, a regulatory law was passed setting out in detail how the CNI would be supervised and held accountable from then on. This piece of legislation—Organic Law 2/2002—was formulated "for the purpose of establishing a judicial control of the activities of the afore-mentioned Center that affect the fundamental rights recognized in Article 18.2 and 3 of the Spanish Constitution,"[182] namely activities that may affect the inviolability of the home and the secrecy of communications. When such activities needed to be carried out legally, the director of the CNI was to request the relevant authorization by formally detailing the specification of the requested measures, the facts supporting the request, the identification of those affected, the place they would be carried out, and for how long. These "measures" are allowed to last only twenty-four hours in cases of entering private grounds or three months if the issue at hand was interception of communications.[183] If an extension is needed, which cannot be longer than the periods of equal duration of the above, the magistrate has to "within a period of 72 hours that cannot be extended, concede or refuse the requested authorization," with the context of these secrets classified as "secret."[184]

All of this would be closely monitored by a "Delegate Commission of the Government for Intelligence Matters." This was to be chaired "by the Vice President of the Government designated by its President and composed of the Ministers of Foreign Affairs, Defence, Interior and Economy, as well as by the Secretary General of the Presidency, the Secretary of State for Security and the Secretary of the Director State of the National Intelligence Center."[185] The purpose was to "oversee the coordination of the National Intelligence Center, the information services of the State Security Forces and the civil and military administration bodies."[186] Since 2002 the majority of laws that have been passed have been made to facilitate structural and organizational changes to the CNI and the wider governmental security network. For example, Royal Decree 1886/2011 established various governmental commissions, including a National Security Council, of which the director of the CNI was a member. This council now approves the National Security Report that is presented annually to the Cortes Generales on the activities of the CNI.[187] Perhaps owing to the victories it has already achieved, the legislature has made little additional effort to lobby for further regulatory powers or oversight mechanisms.

CONCLUSION

When comparing the control and oversight mechanisms of the three countries, there are several key points showcasing that Portugal is ahead of the other two, which it managed decades before Greece and Spain made any relevant progress. It is key to note that this chapter mainly focuses on the existence or not of these structures, while observations have been made on their applicability. In subsequent chapters, their levels of effectiveness will become more evident.

Portugal established a holistic oversight structure early on. By the end of 1984, Portugal had democratically established the authority for an intelligence supervisory board and several intelligence services with defined operational remits. Elements such as internal terrorism did indeed push for the creation of an intelligence service. The intensive process of lustration that preceded the establishment of the new services, as well as their control and oversight frameworks, was another key catalyst that aided this. Unlike the Greek and Spanish services, Portugal not only created a new service to respond to actual threats but also established the legal parameters by which they would conduct their activities and linked them to the Portuguese constitution. This was contrary to Greece, whose legal framework was not linked to the constitution for a very long time. To keep them on this "straight path," there existed control and oversight in the form of individual directors and ministers but also an "independent" supervisory body composed of "high-standing" citizens. As a result, although only SIRP and the SIS were ultimately made operational between 1984 and 1986, Portugal's politicians established from the outset a process of accountability, oversight, and, most important, transparency. The Portuguese supervisory board CFSIRP has access to information upon which it can make assessments and recommendations. Indeed, its publicly available "opinions" have indicated the services' effectiveness and their adherence to protecting Portuguese citizens' human rights. This was not the case for Greece or for Spain, whose legal framework for oversight was poor, with key elements of the government and the judiciary being completely excluded. This was evident by also the several scandals and failures that emerged, as will be analyzed in following chapters. This robust control and oversight in Portugal set the parameters for targeting real threats, recruiting based on merit, and establishing an open civil society, as we will see later.

The inspections approach varied between country intelligence services, with Portugal at the forefront. Since the 1980s Portugal has added to that structure by further strengthening the oversight powers of several bodies. It is interesting to note, for example, that the Assembly of the Republic has to sign off on whom to appoint as the secretary-general of the service. This is a key difference seen when comparing Portugal to Greece, for example, where the minister responsible for the EYP decides whom to appoint. Additionally, whereas in Portugal the assembly's supervisory board runs mandatory inspections on a quarterly basis, in Greece the judiciary theoretically can audit the EYP whenever it wishes, but no mandatory regular inspections or audits are required. This is a key element in the comparison as it not only highlights the level of oversight within these case studies but also demonstrates its nature. It is clear from the above that Portugal aimed to establish a more proactive method when it came to overseeing its intelligence services, by allowing a scheduled as well as an ad hoc inspections approach, whereas Greece was mostly reactive, in the events where it actually did act against any violations.

In Greece, executive control and parliamentary questions are the main ways to exercise oversight over the EYP. Parliamentary questions remain the main component to exert oversight on the EYP. However, as with Spain, the service's director can deny answering any of the questions posed by the parliament on grounds of national security. It is interesting that there are no published documents by the relevant parliamentary committees in Greece.[188] This contrary to the complete openness Portugal has established with the publication of the "opinions" of the oversight supervisory board. Any additional effort to establish further external oversight has been cosmetic in Greece. In 1994, ten years after Portugal had established the SIRP framework law, Greece wrote its first decree for external oversight, with a focus on how the EYP could intercept communications. This was a flawed step because the service's personnel could bypass the authority of the Greek Ombudsman, an agency aiming to facilitate the prosecution of crimes committed by public officials. This was completely opposite from regulation in Portugal, where the SIRP data inspection committee is responsible for supervising the access of public data with the aim of canceling or rectifying the collection of any data that involves violations of human rights, as established by the constitution. Indeed, although in Portugal laws are clear in what are the key responsibilities for each intelligence agency within the law, Greece is suffering from a blurry outline of responsibilities, which started in the 1980s and in key areas persists today. As highlighted in the introduction of this chapter, during a transition period, when executives establish a service without conversations with the parliament, a danger exists whereby executives' visions and wants become part of that service. This was the case with Greece. Papandreou wanted a quick change and therefore, without parliamentary debate and via presidential decrees, rendered himself alone as the key component for control over the Greek intelligence agency. This kind of approach has persisted to date. Indeed, executive control is one of the most prominent types of oversight in Greece. This is a very interesting point because the legacy of its authoritarian past to ensure the power lies with the executive is something that has not really changed.

Spain's oversight structure was poor. Even though Spain established a legal framework before Portugal did, it became apparent quickly that this was mostly symbolic and at times conflicting. Indeed, the parliament was exempt from traditional restrictions of classified information as early as 1978. Although good on paper, technical rulings impeded a variety of deputies from having access to classified information, including Basque and Catalan deputies. Additionally, like in Greece, CESID's representatives in the secret sessions had the authority to end sessions as they saw fit and used it. Moreover, Portugal was the only case study that established a link with the constitution in its laws. In Spanish intelligence-related laws on the other hand, the constitution was mentioned with caveats, creating a conflict of interest among personnel who were not sure which to obey—the constitution or the CECID-relevant laws.

A series of scandals pushed for some reform. In 1995 deputies had the authority to influence how much money would be assigned to CESID as well as what it was used for. Despite this extra layer of oversight, however, issues kept arising, as when it came to judicial oversight, CECID could decide which information could be shared or not. Additionally, the issue of classification also arose when comparing Portugal to Spain. Portugal managed to establish a robust legal framework where classification was the exception rather than the rule, contrary to Spain whose ONS could help oversee what information was classified. Given the above, it is evident that even in more recent decades, elements of the Franco era have remained in Spain. Starting with CESID's "elite" control in 1977 when the agency was put under military control by the Spanish Ministry of Defense, the General Staff, and the king, who all used the service as they saw fit, the service operated under high levels of secrecy until the early 2000s and ensured that any political opposition from, for instance, the Basque region was excluded from the oversight processes. Even the emergence of probably the biggest scandal in Spain's recent history, the GAL affair, did not support proper reform. This aligns with our earlier argument on a critical juncture having to take place to foster change such as a revolution, as happened in Portugal, or a terrorist attack.[189]

The year 2002 was a key one for reform for all three countries as a result of the 9/11 critical juncture. It was a landmark year for the development of laws and regulations affecting Spanish intelligence as well as Greek. Not only was parliamentary oversight legislated for the first time but also preliminary judicial oversight of a kind not seen previously in Spain. Emphasis was put on the laws and rules designed to regulate the CNI's activities from the outset and enable effective oversight from other areas, such as the judiciary. One of the most important developments was the establishment of the National Security Report, which was presented annually to the Cortes Generales on activities of the CNI, and, of course, the assembly's supervisory board. Indeed, Spain has made progress in the past twenty years, especially since 2014, by adding more and more rulings to its armory and creating a robust legal process. On the other hand, Greece has fallen behind in regulating, let alone applying, this level of oversight. Spain, however, experienced its own critical juncture in 2004 when the Madrid attacks took place, unlike Greece, which tried to respond to the changing international landscape.

The presence of a legal framework is key and, indeed, the first step to establishing the road map of the objectives and rules for any intelligence service. A legal framework on its own is not enough, however, to ensure democratic rule in the intelligence sphere. This is why robust control and oversight mechanisms are key to overseeing the intelligence services and ensuring that they are not involved in authoritarian-like activities. Portugal is a great example of doing just that. After going through a vigorous lustration process that helped it uproot authoritarian remnants, it had the ability to create a strong basis for control and oversight early on before it continued to build onto it on a regular basis. Contrary to Portugal, Greece and Spain continued to experience issues of nondemocratic nature within their control and oversight systems. Indeed, in Greece the executive and poor parliamentary oversight remains the main way to monitor the EYP. Equally, Spain suffered for many decades from a loophole framework, with key members of the political opposition being completely excluded from any oversight procedure, very similar to what was the case under Franco. This continued until critical junctures emerged and a proper effort to create solid control and oversight systems started in the early 2000s.

NOTES

1. Gill and Phythian, *Intelligence in an Insecure World*, chap. 8. See also Gill, *Intelligence Governance and Democratisation*, and Gill and Andregg, *Democratization of Intelligence*.
2. Gill and Phythian, *Intelligence in an Insecure World*. See also Gill and Andregg, *Democratization of Intelligence*.
3. Gill and Andregg, *Democratization of Intelligence*, 23–24.
4. Roberto Manuel Henriqueto Goucha, "O sistema de informações em Portugal" [The information system in Portugal] (master's diss., Instituto Universitário de Lisboa, 2011). See also Carlos S. Arturi and Júlio C. Rodriguez, "Democratization and Intelligence and Internal Security Agencies: A Comparative Analysis of the Cases of Brazil and Portugal (1974–2014)," *Brazilian Political Science Review* 13, no. 2 (2019).
5. More in-depth detail on civil society will be provided in chapter 7.
6. Frederic F. Manget, "Another System of Oversight: Intelligence and the Rise of Judicial Intervention," in *Intelligence and National Security: The Secret World of Spies; An Anthology*, ed. Loch K. Johnson and James J. Wirtz (New York: Oxford University Press, 2008), 385.
7. Gill and Phythian, *Intelligence in an Insecure World*, chap. 8.
8. Gill and Phythian, chap. 8.
9. Gill and Phythian, chap. 8.
10. In a simplified way, forms of control within the executive branch include ministerial directions, institutions of control include attorney generals, and institutions of oversight include inspector generals. For more information on control and oversight, see Gill and Phythian, chap. 8.
11. Gill and Phythian, chap. 8.
12. For all three points (a, b, and c), see Gill and Phythian, chap. 6. See also Caparini, "Controlling and Overseeing Intelligence"; Claudia Hillebrand, "The Role

of News Media in Intelligence Oversight," *Intelligence and National Security* 27, no. 5 (2012); and Gill, "Of Intelligence Oversight and the Challenge of Surveillance Corporatism."

13. Gill and Phythian, *Intelligence in an Insecure World*, 155.

14. Gill, *Intelligence Governance and Democratisation*, 3–5.

15. The increased relevance of ethics in the public sector space often underpins work carried out in order to increase overall trust in government because "citizens expect public servants to serve the public interest with fairness and to manage public resources properly on a daily basis. Fair and reliable public services inspire public trust and create a favourable environment for businesses, thus contributing to well-functioning markets and economic growth. Public ethics are a prerequisite to, and underpin, public trust and are a keystone of good governance." Organisation for Economic Co-operation and Development, *Trust in Government: Ethics Measures in OECD Countries* (Paris: OECD, 2000), 1–329.

16. Maria do Céu Pinto Arena, "Portugal's Intelligence Evolution in the Post-9/11 World," *International Journal of Intelligence and CounterIntelligence* 25, no. 1 (2012): 165.

17. Gill and Phythian, *Intelligence in an Insecure World*, chap. 8; Born and Leigh, *Making Intelligence Accountable*.

18. Gill and Phythian, *Intelligence in an Insecure World*, chap. 8.

19. Gill and Phythian, chap. 8; Laurence Lustgarten and Ian Leigh, *In from the Cold: National Security and Parliamentary Democracy* (Oxford: Oxford University Press, 1994).

20. Gill and Phythian, *Intelligence in an Insecure World*, chap. 8; Toni Erskine, "'As Rays of Light to the Human Soul'? Moral Agents and Intelligence Gathering," *Intelligence and National Security* 19, no. 2 (2010); Phillip Knightley, *The Second Oldest Profession: Spies and Spying in the Twentieth Century* (New York: W. W. Norton, 1987).

21. Gill and Phythian, *Intelligence in an Insecure World*, chap. 8.

22. Gill and Phythian, chap. 8.

23. "Israeli Envoy in Lisbon Is Wounded and Guard Slain in Embassy Raid; Arafat's Visit Cited," *New York Times*, November 14, 1979, https://www.nytimes.com/1979/11/14/archives/israeli-envoy-in-lisbon-is-wounded-and-guard-slain-in-embassy-raid.html.

24. John Darnton, "7 Dead in Lisbon in Armenian Raid," *New York Times*, July 28, 1983, https://www.nytimes.com/1983/07/28/world/7-dead-in-lisbon-in-armenian-raid.html.

25. Peter Wise, "Moderate PLO Leader Assassinated," *Washington Post*, April 11, 1983, https://www.washingtonpost.com/archive/politics/1983/04/11/moderate-plo-leader-assassinated/98ccd878-1cca-4f6d-99ad-ebe07b8218bf/.

26. Section 32, Part III (Special Part), Portuguese Criminal Code Decree-Law No. 400/82, *Diário da República*, no. 221/1982, 1st supplement, series I of 1982-09-23.

27. Law No. 30/84 of September 5, 1984, Article 1, http://www.pgdlisboa.pt/leis/lei_mostra_articulado.php?nid=764&tabela=leis.

28. Law No. 30/84 of September 5, 1984, Article 2, http://www.pgdlisboa.pt/leis/lei_mostra_articulado.php?nid=764&tabela=leis.

29. Law No. 30/84 of September 5, 1984, Articles 20–21, http://www.pgdlisboa.pt/leis/lei_mostra_articulado.php?nid=764&tabela=leis.

30. Article 3, Limit of Information Services Activities, Chapter I, General Principles of Law No. 30/84 of September 5, 1984, Information System of the Portuguese Republic.

31. Article 29, Misuse of Functions, Chapter V, Duties and Responsibilities of Law No. 30/84 of September 5, 1984, Information System of the Portuguese Republic.

32. Article 3, Activity Limits, Chapter I, Nature Duties and Powers of DL No. 225/85 of July 4, 1985, SIS.

33. Article 3, Activity Limits, Chapter I, Nature Duties and Powers of DL No. 225/85 of July 4, 1985 SIS.

34. Article 2, No. 1, and Article 6, Framework Law of SIRP, and Law No. 9/2007 of February 10, 2007, especially Article 3. See also Rui Pereira, "Terrorismo e insegurança: A resposta portuguesa" [Terrorism and insecurity: The Portuguese response], *Revista do Ministério Público*, no. 98 (2004): 100.

35. Law 29/82, National Defense and Armed Forces Law, *Diário da República*, no. 285/1982, series I of 1982-12-11.

36. Article 67, Military Information of Law 29/82, National Defense and Armed Forces Law, *Diário da República*, no. 285/1982, series I of 1982-12-11.

37. Paragraph 4, Article 67, Military Information of Law 29/82, National Defense and Armed Forces Law, *Diário da República*, no. 285/1982, series I of 1982-12-11.

38. Article I, "Definição e fins de Segurança Interna" [Definition and purposes of homeland security], Law No. 20/1987 of June 12, 1987, Lei de Segurança Interna (Homeland Security Law).

39. Section I, Article 1, "Definição e fins de Segurança Interna" [Definition and purposes of homeland security], Law No. 20/1987 of June 12, 1987, Lei de Segurança Interna (Homeland Security Law).

40. Paragraph 3, Article 1, Definition and Purposes of Internal Security Law 20/87, Internal Security Law, *Diário da República*, no. 134/1987, series I of 1987-06-12.

41. Section I, Article 8, "Definição e fins de Segurança Interna" [Definition and purposes of homeland security], Law No. 20/1987 of June 12, 1987, Lei de Segurança Interna (Homeland Security Law).

42. Article 1, points 1–3, Law No. 6/94 of April 7, 1994, Assembly of the Republic, *Diário da República*, no. 81/1994, series IA of 1994-04-07.

43. Article 2, points 1–3f, Law No. 6/94 of April 7, 1994, Assembly of the Republic, *Diário da República*, no. 81/1994, series IA of 1994-04-07. Contrasted against Article 2 of Spain's Law 48/1978 of October 7, 1978, Ref. BOE-A-1978-25567: "For the purposes of this Law, matters, acts, documents, information, data and objects whose knowledge by unauthorized persons may damage or endanger the security and defense of the State may be declared 'classified matters.'"

44. Paragraph 3 of Article 2, State of Secrecy of Law No. 6/94, State Secrets, *Diário da República*, no. 81/1994, series IA of 1994-04-07.

45. This matter was alluded to within the law itself in paragraph 2 of Article 1, "Objective," which included details on "restrictions on access to administrative and judicial archives, processes and records, for reasons related to criminal investigation or to the privacy of individuals, as well as those relating to the information services of the Portuguese Republic and other systems for classifying matters, if by own legislation."

46. Article 19.1 of Law 4/95 of February 21, 1995, Assembly of the Republic, *Diário da República*, no. 44/1995, series IA of 1995-02-21.

47. Bob de Graaff and James M. Nyce, eds., *Handbook of European Intelligence Cultures* (Lanham, MD: Rowman & Littlefield, 2018), 299.

48. Article 19.2, Article 23, Article 26, Article 28, and Article 32 of Law 4/95, of February 21, 1995, Assembly of the Republic, *Diário da República*, no. 44/1995, series IA of 1995-02-21.

49. Article 4, Activity Limits, and Article 4, Misuse of Duties in Chapter I, Nature, Duties, and Powers in DL No. 254/95 of September 30, 1995, Defense and Military Strategic Information Service.

50. Law 52/2003, Law on Combating Terrorism, *Diário da República*, no. 193/2003, series IA of 2003-08-22.

51. Articles 2–9 of Law 52/2003, Law on Combating Terrorism, *Diário da República*, no. 193/2003, series IA of 2003-08-22.

52. Article 9.2 of Resolution 6/2003 *Diário da República*, no. 16/2003, series IB of 2003-01-20.

53. Júlio Pereira, "El sistema de intelligencia de la Republica de Portugal (SIRP)" [The intelligence system of the Republic of Portugal (SIRP)], *Inteligencia y Securidad*, no. 12 (2012): 18–19.

54. "Principles and Means of Operation," SIRP, www.sirp.pt/quem-somos/missao -meios-de-atuacao-valores-e-visao.

55. Heitor B. Romana, "Informações: uma reflexão teórica" [Information: a theoretical reflection], *Segurança e Defesa*, no. 6, April–June (2008): 100.

56. Law 1415, *Government Gazette*, AD11, 7.2.1984.

57 Articles 5, 7, and 11 of the Greek constitution, http://www.hri.org/docs/syntagma /artcl25.html#A6.

58. Article 6 of the Greek constitution, http://www.hri.org/docs/syntagma/artcl25 .html#A6.

59. Article 2, paragraphs A–D of Law 1645, *Government Gazette*, AD132, 26.8.1986.

60. Law 1645, *Government Gazette*, AD132, 26.8.1986, The National Intelligence Service.

61. Presidential Decree No. 360, *Government Gazette*, A 183, 25.11.1992.

62. Article 2, Responsibilities of EYP Services, Presidential Decree No. 360, *Government Gazette*, A 183 / 25.11.1992.

63. Article 2, Mission of Law 3649/2008, National Intelligence Service and other provisions, *Government Gazette*, A 39 / 3.3.2008. See also chapter 6.

64. Paragraph B of Article 105 of the 1978 Constitution Ratified on December 7, 1978, and sanctioned on December 27, 1978.

65. Spanish Constitution, chapter 5, Section 55(2), 15.

66. Spanish Constitution, chapter 5, Section 55(2), 15.

67. Spanish Constitution, chapter 5, Section 55(2), 15.

68. Royal Decree 1558/1977 of July 4, 1977, which restructures certain Bodies of the Central State Administration, BOE no. 159, July 5, 1977, and Royal Decree 2723/1977 of November 2, 1977, which organically and functionally structures the Ministry of Defense, BOE no. 265, November 5, 1977. The latter in fact contains only a brief mention of CESID: "In order for the Defence to have the information it needs to carry out its functions, the Higher Defence Information Center has been created, which will take charge of those activities that are determined and that, although they had been carried out by other organizations, it is estimated, should be integrated into the area corresponding to Defence. Those that, due to

their special nature, correspond exclusively to the informational organs of the military chain of command are outside its jurisdiction."

69. Organic Law 6/1980 of July 1, 1980, which regulates the basic criteria of national defense and military organization, BOE no. 165, July 10, 1980.

70. Order 135/1982 of September 30, 1982, which regulates the structure and relationships to be maintained by the Higher Defense Information Center, BOE no. 254, October 23, 1982.

71. Paragraph 1 of Article 18, Guarantee and Control of Measures, in Organic Law 9/1984 of December 26, against the action of armed gangs and terrorist elements and the development of Article 55.2 of the Constitution, BOE no. 3, January 3, 1985.

72. Paragraphs 2a and 2b, Article 37, General Duties in Royal Decree 1324/1995 of July 28, 1995, which establishes the staff regulations of the CESID, BOE no. 198, August 19, 1995.

73. The GAL affair was one of the key scandals that emerged in the Spanish media. A detailed overview of it will be provided in chapter 7.

74. "The government, gentlemen, has not only given it a general order to act within the law, but has made it clear to the Center what information constitutes the objectives that it must pursue. It has fixed the objectives, has said which courses of action are open to it in order to accomplish all of the objectives set by the Ministry of Defense." Speech by the minister of defense, Eduardo Serra, in the Defense Committee no. 287 of the VI legislature, October 7, 1997, 8263.

75. Matei and Bruneau, "Intelligence Reform in New Democracies," 610.

76. Opening Explanatory Memorandum of Law 11/2002 of May 6, regulating the CNI, BOE no. 109, July 5, 2002.

77. Opening Explanatory Memorandum of Law 11/2002.

78. Opening Explanatory Memorandum of Law 11/2002.

79. Opening Explanatory Memorandum of Law 11/2002. This deemed the laws underpinning the creation of the CNI "necessary to address a new regulation of the intelligence services through a standard with the status of Law, in which the nature, objectives, principles, functions, substantial aspects of its organization and administrative legal regime are collected in a unitary and systematic manner; as well as parliamentary and judicial controls, constituting the essence of their efficient and transparent functioning."

80. Article 1 of Law 11/2002 of May 6, 2002, regulating the CNI, BOE no. 109, 05/07/2002.

81. National Intelligence Center, *Regulatory Regulations*, Legal Department of the CNI, Ministry of the President, July 2016.

82. "Galeria de Ministros" [Gallery of Ministers], Portal da Defesa na Internet, www .defesa.gov.pt/pt/defesa/historia/galeriaministros/Paginas/default.aspx.

83. Article 17, Powers of the Prime Minister, Law No. 30/84 of September 5, 1984, Information System of the Portuguese Republic.

84. Article 18, Superior Information Council, Law No. 30/84 of September 5, 1984, Information System of the Portuguese Republic.

85. Article 13, Structure, Nature and Dependency, Chapter III, System Structure, Law No. 30/84 of September 5, 1984, Information System of the Portuguese Republic.

86. Articles 19–21, Chapter III, System Structure, of Law No. 30/84 of September 5, 1984, Information System of the Portuguese Republic.

87. Article 15, Organic Dependency, Chapter III, System Structure, Law No. 30/84 of September 5, 1984, Information System of the Portuguese Republic.

88. Article 12, Composition, Chapter II, Advisory Council, Decree-Law (DL) No. 225/85 of July 4, 1985, SIS.

89. Articles 16 and 17, Chapter III, Organs, Services and Powers, DL No. 225/85 of July 4, 1985, SIS.

90. Article 3, Activity Limits, Chapter I, Nature, Duties, and Powers, DL No. 225/85 of July 4, 1985, SIS.

91. Article 13, Competence, Chapter II, Advisory Council in Law, DL No. 254/95 of September 30, 1995, Defense and Military Strategic Information Service.

92. Articles 14 and 16, Chapter III, Organs, Services, and Powers, Law DL No. 254/95 of September 30, 1995, Defense and Military Strategic Information Service.

93. Article 17, Powers of the Prime Minister, Organic Law No. 4/2004 of November 6, 2004, Information System of the Portuguese Republic.

94. Organic Law No. 4/2004 of November 6, 2004, Information System of the Portuguese Republic.

95. Paragraph 3, Article 22, Directors of the Information Services, Organic Law No. 4/2004 of November 6, 2004, Information System of the Portuguese Republic.

96. Loren Jenkins, "Papandreou Takes Over, Warns Military," *Washington Post*, October 22, 1981, www.washingtonpost.com/archive/politics/1981/10/22/papandreou-takes-over-warns-military/a1d5c07f-5931-4429-9bc6-0d149a1e4d62/.

97. Paragraph 1, Article 1, Law 1415/1984.

98. Paragraph 3, Article 1, Law 1415/1984.

99. Article 1, Title Submission, Law 1645, *Government Gazette*, AD132, August 26, 1986.

100. Article 2, Work, Law 1645, *Government Gazette*, AD132, August 26, 1986.

101. Paragraph 5, Article 5, Commander, Deputy Commander, Law 1645, *Government Gazette*, AD132, August 26, 1986.

102. Musa Tuzner, *Intelligence Cooperation Practices in the 21st Century: Towards a Culture of Sharing* (Amsterdam: IOS Press, 2010), 23.

103. Article 3, Commander, Presidential Decree No. 360, *Government Gazette*, A 183, November 25, 1992.

104. Article 1, National Intelligence Service and other provisions, Law No. 3649, *Government Gazette*, A 39, March 3, 2008.

105. Article 8, Information Council, Law No. 3649, *Government Gazette*, A 39, March 3, 2008.

106. Article 9, Commander–Deputy Commander, Law No. 3649, *Government Gazette*, A 39, March 3, 2008.

107. Law No. 3817, *Government Gazette*, A 16, February 16, 2010, Ratification of the Legislative Content Act of October 13, 2009, "Submission of the National Intelligence Service to the Minister of Citizen Protection." See also Article 5, Presidential Decree No. 81, Issue A 119, July 8, 2019.

108. Royal Decree 2723/1977 of November 2, which organically and functionally structures the Ministry of Defense, BOE no. 265, November 5, 1977.

109. Article 7.1, Order 135/1982 of September 30, which regulates the structure and relationships to be maintained by the CESID. BOE no. 254, October 23, 1982.

110. Antonio M. Díaz Fernández, "Halfway down the Road to Supervision of the Spanish Intelligence Services," *Intelligence and National Security* 21, no. 3 (2006): 441.

111. Javier Cercas, *The Anatomy of a Moment* (London: Bloomsbury, 2011), 199.
112. "What Is the CNI? Protection of Classified Information," National Intelligence Center, https://www.cni.es/en/whatisthecni/ans/.
113. "What Is the CNI?"
114. "What Is the CNI?"
115. On February 23, 1981, Lt. Col. Antonio Tejero and two hundred armed Civil Guard officers marched into the Congress of Deputies chamber in Madrid during the vote to elect Leopoldo Calvo-Sotelo as president of the government. This was the last serious attempt to bring back the Francoist government.
116. Royal Decree 2632/1985 of December 27, which regulates the internal structure and relations of the CESID, BOE no. 17, January 20, 1986.
117. Statement of Motives, Law 11/2002 of May 6, regulating the CNI, BOE no. 109, May 7, 2002.
118. Statement of Motives. There can be more than one vice president in Spain within a given government. For example, Suárez's government after the dictatorship had three vice presidents at the same time.
119. Article 6, Government Delegate Commission for Intelligence Affairs, Chapter II, Organization and Legal Regime, Law 11/2002 of May 6 2002, regulating the CNI, BOE no. 109, May 7, 2002.
120. Articles 9 and 10, Chapter II, Organization and Legal Regime, Law 11/2002 of May 6 2002, regulating the CNI, BOE no. 109, May 7, 2002.
121. SIRP official website, https://www.sirp.pt/en.
122. Law No. 30/84 of September 5, 1984, Article 7.
123. Law No. 30/84 of September 5, 1984, Article 7.
124. Pereira, "El sistema de intelligencia," 26.
125. Article 8, Competence, Chapter II, Inspection, Law No. 30/84 of September 5, 1984, Information System of the Portuguese Republic.
126. Paragraph 3, Article 8, Competence, Chapter II, Inspection, Law No. 30/84 of September 5, 1984, Information System of the Portuguese Republic.
127. Paragraph 1a, Article 11, Duties, Chapter II, Inspection, Law No. 30/84 of September 5, 1984, Information System of the Portuguese Republic.
128. Law No. 30/84 of September 5, 1984, Article 22, Technical Commission.
129. Official site of CFSIRP, https://cfsirp.pt/#!/membros.
130. Article 26, Supervision of Data, Chapter IV, Use of Technology, Law No. 30/84 of September 5, 1984, Information System of the Portuguese Republic.
131. Translated from Section II, Article 10, Conselho Superior de Segurança Interna (Higher Council for Homeland Security), Law No. 20/1987 of June 12, 1987, Lei de Segurança Interna (Homeland Security Law).
132. Translated from Section II, Article 10, Conselho Superior de Segurança Interna.
133. Presidência do Conselho de Ministros (Presidency of the Council of Minsters), Resolução do Conselho de Ministros 47/88, de 5 de Novembro (Resolution of the Council of Ministers 47/88 of 5 November), *Diário da República*, no. 256/1988, 1 Suplemento, Série I de November 5, 1988.
134. Colin Darch and Jon Woronoff, *Historical Dictionary of Mozambique* (Lanham, MD: Rowman & Littlefield, 2019). For more detail on the relocation of archives, see National Archives da Torre do Tombo, https://portal.ehri-project.eu/institutions/pt-005468.
135. Paragraph 1, Article 8, Competence, Chapter II, Inspection, Law No. 4/95 of February 21, 1995, Information System of the Portuguese Republic.

136. Article 8, Competence, Chapter II, Inspection, Law No. 4/95 of February 21, 1995, Information System of the Portuguese Republic.

137. Paragraphs 7–8, Article 8, Competence, Chapter II, Inspection, Law No. 4/95 of February 21, 1995, Information System of the Portuguese Republic.

138. Article 8.2b, Law 15/96 of April 3, Assembly of the Republic, *Diário da República*, no. 101/1996, series IA of April 3, 1996.

139. Article 26, Supervision of Data, Chapter IV, Use of Information Technology, Law No. 15/96 of April 3, 1996, Information System of the Portuguese Republic.

140. Article 15, Dependency and Appointment Process, Chapter III, System Structure in Law No. 4/2004 of November 6, 2004, Information System of the Portuguese Republic.

141. Paragraph 1, Article 9, Competence, Chapter II, Inspection, Organic Law No. 4/2004 of November 6, 2004, Information System of the Portuguese Republic.

142. Article 8, Supervisory Board of the Information System of the Portuguese Republic, Chapter II, Inspection, Organic Law No. 4/2014 of August 13, 2014, Information System of the Portuguese Republic.

143. Article 9, Competence, Chapter II, Inspection, Organic Law No. 4/2014 of August 13, 2014, Information System of the Portuguese Republic.

144. Official CFSIRP website, https://cfsirp.pt/. See also https://cfsirp.pt/wpcontent/uploads/2020/07/parecer_cfsirp_1semestre_2020.pdf and the Portuguese parliament website, https://www.parlamento.pt/sites/EN/Parliament/Paginas/Indepedent-administrative-bodies.aspx.

145. Official CFSIRP website, Information Services Supervisory Board report, 1988, https://www.cfsirp.pt/images/documentos/parecer%201986-87.pdf.

146. Pereira, El sistema de intelligencia, 26.

147. Carlos S. Arturi and Júlio C. Rodriguez, "Democratization and Intelligence and Internal Security Agencies: A Comparative Analysis of the Cases of Brazil and Portugal (1974–2014)," *Brazilian Political Science Review* 13, no. 2 (2019).

148. Article 6, Law 1645, *Government Gazette*, AD132 August 26, 1986, The National Intelligence Service.

149. Paragraph 2, Article 4, Law No. 2225, *Government Gazette*, 121, July 20, 1994.

150. Paragraphs 2–6, Article 4, Law No. 2225, *Government Gazette*, 121, July 20, 1994.

151. Paragraph 2, Article 3, Law No. 2477, *Government Gazette*, A 59, April 18, 1997, Ombudsman and Body of Inspectors–Auditors of Public Administration.

152. Paragraph 2, Article 3, Law No. 2477.

153. Paragraph 5, Article 3, Law No. 2690, *Government Gazette*, A 45, March 9, 1999, Ratification of the Code of Administrative Procedure and other provisions.

154. *Rules of Procedure of the Parliament*, accessed February 4, 2021, https://www.hellenicparliament.gr/userfiles/ebooks/KtV-2019-GR/54/index.html#zoom=z.

155. Official CFSIRP website, https://cfsirp.pt/.

156. Official website of the Greek Parliament, accessed February 4, 2020, https://www.hellenicparliament.gr/search/?searchText=%ce%ba%ce%bf%ce%b9%ce%bd%ce%bf%ce%b2%ce%bf%cf%85%ce%bb%ce%b5%cf%85%cf%84%ce%b9%ce%ba%cf%8c%cf%82+%ce%ad%ce%bb%ce%b5%ce%b3%ce%bf%cf%82+%ce%95%ce%a5%ce%a0&pageNo=4. See also answers no. 10018 of January 18, 2011, and no. 6177 of February 29, 2012.

157. Paragraph 1, Article 1, Law No. 3115, *Government Gazette*, A 47, February 27, 2003.

158. Paragraph 2, Article 1, Law No. 3115, *Government Gazette*, A February 27, 2003.

159. Article 9, Law No. 3115, *Government Gazette*, A 47, February 27, 2003.
160. Paragraph 3, Article 5, Supervision: How to Exercise Responsibilities, Law No. 3649 *Government Gazette*, A 39, March 3, 2008 National Intelligence Service and other provisions.
161. Article 4, Law No. 3649, *Government Gazette*, A 39, March 3, 2008.
162. Law No. 3817, *Government Gazette*, A 16, 16.2.2010, Ratification of the Legislative Content Act of October 13, 2009, Submission of the National Intelligence Service to the Minister of Citizen Protection, *Government Gazette*, 215 A. See also Article 5, Presidential Decree No. 81, Issue A 119, July 8, 2019.
163. Article 4, Chapter I, Minister and General Structure of the Ministry, Royal Decree 2723/1977 of November 2, 1977, which organically and functionally structures the Ministry of Defense.
164. The original text of Law 9/1968 on official secrets, Article 4, original text June 4, 1968, https://www.boe.es/buscar/act.php?id=BOE-A-1968-444&b=11&tn=1&p= 19680406#adiez.
165. Law 9/1968 of April 5 on official secrets, Article 10 (2), updated November 10, 1978, effective as of October, 31, 1978, https://www.boe.es/buscar/act.php?id= BOE-A-1968-444&b=11&tn=1&p=19781011#adiez.
166. Díaz Fernández, *Los servicios de inteligencia españoles*, 304.
167. Sentence of Tribunal Constitucional 118/1988 of June 20, 1988, and the particular opinion of Magistrate Francisco Rubio Llorente. For commentary on this appeal, see Juan Cano Bueso, *Información parlamentaria y secretos oficiales* [Parliamentary information and official secrets] (Barcelona: Institut de Ciencies Politiques i Socials, 1997).
168. Díaz Fernández, *Los servicios de inteligencia españoles*, 304.
169. Díaz Fernández, 195.
170. Díaz Fernández, 304.
171. Díaz Fernández, 305.
172. Budgetary Committee No. 55, IV Legislature, March 21, 1990. Intervention of the chair: "Ladies and gentlemen, Deputies, for all of these committee appearances, we have I believe been guided by a very broad interpretation with respect to the limits that were supposedly to lay out budgetary procedures more clearly. There may be other items in play here, which is not only procedural, and therefore, with great regret and referring you to what may be said in other committees, I do hereby draw this debate to a close. You will have to understand me, Señor Romero," 1301.
173. José M. Magone, *Contemporary Spanish Politics* (London: Routledge, 2018), 117.
174. Law 11/1995 of May 11, 1995, regulating the use and control of the credits destined to reserved expenses, BOE no. 113, May 12, 1995.
175. Article 7.1 of Law 11/1995 of May 11, 1995, regulating the use and control of the credits destined to reserved expenses, BOE no. 113, May 12, 1995.
176. Article 7.2 of Law 11/1995 of May 11, 1995, regulating the use and control of the credits destined to reserved expenses, BOE no. 113, May 12, 1995.
177. Article 7.4 of Law 11/1995 of May 11, 1995, regulating the use and control of the credits destined to reserved expenses, BOE no. 113, May 12, 1995.
178. Díaz Fernández, *Los servicios de inteligencia españoles*, 295.
179. Article 2, Principles, Chapter I, General Disposition, Law 11/2002 of May 6 2002, regulating the CNI, BOE no. 109, May 7, 2002.
180. Article 11, Parliamentary Control, Chapter III, Control, Law 11/2002 of May 6 2002, regulating the CNI, BOE no. 109, May 7, 2002.

181. Paragraph 4, Article 11, Parliamentary Control, Chapter III, Control, Law 11/2002 of May 6, 2002, regulating the CNI, BOE no. 109, May 7, 2002.

182. Opening Explanatory Memorandum of Organic Law 2/2002 of May 6, 2002, regulating the prior judicial control of the CNI, BOE no. 109, May 7, 2002.

183. Article 1 of Organic Law 2/2002 of May 6, 2002, regulating the prior judicial control of the CNI, BOE no. 109, May 7, 2002.

184. Antonio M. Díaz Fernández, "Spanish Intelligence in the Mediterranean Context," in *Intelligence beyond the Anglosphere*, ed. John Nomikos and Joseph Finatsakis (Athens: RIEAS, 2017), 154.

185. Article 6.2, Organic Law 2/2002 of May 6, 2002, regulating the prior judicial control of the CNI, BOE no. 109, May 7, 2002.

186. Article 6.4c, Organic Law 2/2002 of May 6, 2002, regulating the prior judicial control of the CNI, BOE no. 109, May 7, 2002.

187. Article 3, Royal Decree 1886/2011 of December 30, 2011, BOE no. 315, December, 31, 2011.

188. Article 3, Royal Decree 1886/2011 of December 30, 2011.

189. Eduardo E. Estévez, "Intelligence Community Reforms: The Case of Argentina," in *Intelligence Elsewhere: Spies and Espionage Outside the Anglosphere*, ed. Philip H. J. Davies and Kristian C. Gustafson (Washington, DC: Georgetown University Press, 2013), 219–38.

5

Recruitment

We have established that Portugal managed to uproot authoritarian elements by applying a process of lustration, an approach that the other two countries did not follow. By doing so, Portugal was able to create a robust control and oversight framework. Both Greece and Spain suffered from poor oversight structures. In line with transitioning to democratic standards and apart from the control and oversight mechanisms, all three countries were meant to focus on recruiting qualified personnel through fair recruitment methods.

The available literature on intelligence democratization identifies recruitment as a key indicator by which the level of intelligence democratization can be measured. This is reinforced by data within the case studies in question, which includes recruitment as an analytical marker for both development and cultural change. Under authoritarian rule, loyalty to the regime is the primary standard by which prospective candidates are evaluated, while training under authoritarian systems emphasizes technical skills that promote state security.[1] This contrasts with what takes precedence in democratic regime types, where recruitment is conducted on the basis of merit and training emphasizes technical skills that are appropriate within the context of the law and the rules protecting freedom of expression, association, and movement.[2] Often we find authoritarian elements remaining after a transition period, impeding the democratization process. Authoritarian practices and tendencies often remain concealed in situations where "the old-guard" continues to select new staff or recruitment practices remain disconnected from a liberal democratic doctrine.[3]

Indeed, in this chapter, we will observe that both Spain and Greece suffered from residual authoritarianism. Militarism in outlook and nepotism in hiring and promotion lasted in the services for a long time after the transition. This only changed substantially in Spain after two key events: 9/11 and the Madrid train bombings of May 2004 (11M). These shocks spurred the direction of more resources to the intelligence organizations and the recruitment of qualified personnel equipped to fight new, relevant threats.

Limited progress was made in Greece as it boosted the quantity of personnel. However, issues with quality persisted. Portugal again comes up as the only one among the three that did not suffer from authoritarian legacies and used recruitment to focus on actual threats. Although recruitment in Portugal presented a few limitations—due to the lustration process, the intelligence organizations had to start recruiting from scratch as the need for more personnel emerged after 9/11 and 11M—they were overcome quickly.

This chapter will assess Portugal, Greece, and Spain from the immediate postauthoritarian period through the SSR indicator of recruitment. Of prime interest are questions such as: Do the intelligence services hire based on merit and qualifications or loyalty to the regime/government? If yes to the former, when did they start doing so? Are there legacy members of the police and/or military who remain in the civilian intelligence service? Reference will also be made to the relevant legal rules that underpin recruitment processes: Are there any rules, and do they support democratic recruitment procedures? Recruitment therefore is both the process and the type of personnel that staffs the intelligence service of each country. Based on democratic practices, the process of recruitment has to be meritocratic, while any extensive presence of police or military personnel should be limited.

PORTUGAL

When looking at recruitment specifically, Portugal had to try a few different approaches before establishing a new civilian intelligence organization in 1984. Even so, Portugal was the only case study among the three that managed to launch a solid basis for staffing its intelligence services from the 1980s. As we will see later in the chapter, Greece is facing recruitment issues to this day, while Spain's recruitment practices became less nepotistic after 9/11 and 11M. With the Salazar- and Caetano-era intelligence organizations dissolved and their former members discredited, those aspiring to a career in Portuguese intelligence had a limited set of options from 1974 onward. To begin with, they would have had to join the Portuguese military. This was the only route to gaining a role in the Second Division of the Armed Forces General Staff, which until March 1975 was responsible for coordinating the activity of the SIM.[4] In May 1975, the Serviço Director e Coordenador da Informação (SDCI; Information Direction and Coordination Service) was created as the revolution's own trusted intelligence service. It was also military in nature, run by a navy captain-lieutenant, an army engineer, and a major aerodrome engineer with sufficient revolutionary credentials.[5] Indeed, this aspect weighed heavily when it came to recruiting SDCI's wider staff, with more than half coming from the wider MFA and the rest, though civilians, belonging to either the PCP or other Far Left political bodies.[6] Such a discerning recruitment process quickly distanced the revolution's new intelligence body from wider Portuguese society, which quickly resented the arbitrary manner within which it began to conduct itself.[7] It also put it at odds with moderates in the MFA who disapproved of its development along Soviet lines and emphasis on politics as much as intelligence.[8]

This was just one of the reasons that the Portuguese government decided to shut down the SDCI following the Far Left's coup attempt in November 1975. There followed six months within which Maj. Gen. Renato Marques Pinto was tasked with figuring out what to do with SDCI's staff and how to replace personnel who had been dismissed.[9] As there were not enough competent or reliable military officers left at this point to take on intelligence roles, the government found it necessary to recruit civil servants who had previously worked in the Information Centralization and Coordination Services of Angola and Mozambique.[10] In May 1976 these elements were reconstituted into a revived Second Division, and by November a plan was laid to merge the military's remaining information sections with it so as to have one overall intelligence function. When this plan ultimately was shelved due to the reluctance of certain generals to give up their intelligence capabilities, a new working group was formed in May 1977 to develop a model for a Republican Information Service. This would recruit civilians rather than military personnel, the latter instead being channeled into the Second Division, or Divisão de Informações (DINFO: Division of Intelligence [1977–93]) as it soon became known.[11] Despite the logic behind such an arrangement, however, the legacy that PIDE and the DGS had left was one of intense suspicion and hostility toward any intelligence organization. This was particularly the case for the new political class, many of whom had suffered under Salazar's and Caetano's rule and had little interest in spending time creating a new potential adversary.[12] Thus, recruitment for intelligence purposes proceeded along military lines, with the armed forces providing the bulk of personnel for DINFO and its subsidiary apparatuses.

This remained the case until 1982, when Portugal's democratic politicians decided to draw a line on the recent past with major revisions to the country's constitution. Among the most important changes was the abolition of the MFA's Revolutionary Council and DIFNO's restriction to military intelligence collection by a new defense law.[13] With these two actions, the way was clear in 1984 for the creation of a new civilian intelligence organization, which was also reinforced by the emergence of terrorist threats. Creating an intelligence organization from scratch after a lustration process meant that the potential pool of suitable recruits for intelligence roles was rather shallow. In the 1990s, during a public recruitment campaign, only eighty personnel were recruited at the SIS office in Lisbon.[14] Certainly, the low number of employees was not for want of trying or due to overt discrimination. Instead, the relatively unknown nature of the organization, combined with the public's lingering hostility to PIDE, made it an unattractive career path for most citizens. This changed somewhat with the eventual creation of SIEDM in 1997, which channeled military intelligence away from the control of DIFNO and opened up more positions for citizens to fill. It was 9/11, however, that was to have the most effect. It galvanized the Portuguese government and its officials into investing resources into intelligence matters at a level that had not occurred since before the Carnation Revolution.

From 2001 Portugal embarked upon a number of changes designed to boost its overall security posture. This included strengthening the laws overseeing defense and security matters, cracking down on different types of criminal activity, and modernizing its national intelligence organizations further.[15] The latter meant more resources and the ability to recruit more staff. However, it also entailed the challenge that plagued many other countries' intelligence organizations at that time: how to recruit and train the right kind of people capable of handling a new kind of threat. With greater public awareness and support for the work that SIRP, the SIS, and SIEDM were then doing, it was not difficult to fill positions, and the overall number of employees quickly rose. As António José Vilela describes it, however, recruitment was primarily aimed at people with existing experience in the public, security, or military sectors. As citizens who were of African, Asian, or Arab origin often did not have such experience, the number who were present in Portuguese intelligence roles by 2007 "could be counted using the fingers of two hands."[16] Elaborating on this issue in 2008, José Vegar summarized that recruiters "completely ignore people of African, Arab, Slav, and Chinese origins as well as Muslim and Orthodox believers who completed their studies in Portuguese schools." This was despite the fact that they had higher qualifications sometimes and could obtain information "much more easily and recruit informers in important circles," such as terrorism, illegal immigration, and organized crime.[17] The perpetuation of this issue was reflective of an inherent bias in the recruitment process. It also raised questions about whether resources were being invested correctly. In 2012, for example, *Diário de News* reported on how "three dozen recently reinforced personnel" were employed in SIS's countersubversion section analyzing the risks of demonstrations and political protests.[18] The main question posed was whether recruiting for such work was worthwhile, particularly when such analysis had proven to overestimate risks and dangers.

Further questions of the integrity of SIS's and SIED's recruitment practices were raised in 2015 after a security lapse resulted in the leaking of the names of 383 candidates seeking intelligence positions. The leak occurred after the candidates received a collective email from SIRP acknowledging their applications as opposed to a direct message. The result was the revelation of applications from staff in the GNR, the Autoridade Tributária (Tax Authority), the Foreigners and Borders Service, and the Autoridade de Segurança Alimentar e Económica (ASAE; Economic and Food Safety Authority).[19] Jorge Bacelar

Gouveia, the president of CFSIRP, SIRP's supervisory board, stated that because "confidentiality had been compromised," the solution was to cancel the recruitment campaign and start all over again.[20] This occurred in December 2015, when, in response to the rise of the Islamic State of Iraq and Syria (ISIS), SIS and SIED sought to recruit thirty people between them. Given that this would have taken the total number of Portuguese intelligence officers to just above seven hundred, the two organizations were criticized for not doing enough to recruit the numbers necessary to respond to the new terrorist threat.[21] The news came in the form of further revelations about the kinds of questions that candidates were subjected to as part of the so-called General Access Test: "What meat do Muslims not eat?" "Where is Damascus?" "What is a URL?"[22] This seventy-question test included fourteen in English or French, with the candidates faced with seven subjects such as history and politics as well as religion and sociology. This emphasis on Islamic culture, cyber threats, and wider issues showcased progression from just ten years before.[23]

Presently SIRP's, the SIS's, and SIED's recruitment practices indicate a balance between fulfilling operational requirements and presenting openings to wider Portuguese society. For entry into any of these organizations, citizens must not only be of a certain age, be of Portuguese nationality, and "enjoy good health"—they must also "possess academic qualifications suitable to the role they are applying for."[24] This and other conditions, such as the need to agree to a security assessment and commit to a duty of secrecy, are set out in law, meaning that the legislature has purposefully crafted and overseen how intelligence personnel are recruited into each service and the rules they must abide by thereafter.[25] If they meet such conditions, Portuguese citizens can choose to either submit "speculative applications" listing their details and background for general consideration of suitability or apply for specific roles listed on SIRP's website. The standards set also encourage fairer competition and reduce the chance of nepotism and cronyism that can otherwise plague public entities. Indeed, the high standards set are in fact indicative of the process working as idealized, with only those who *should* be employed recruited and trained. Accordingly, in 2020 Portugal operates in this area to a very high standard, with recruitment and training both aligning with upcoming operational needs in addition to legal and ethical standards.

GREECE

Following the fall of the junta, Greece bore witness to a slow but sustained withdrawal of the military from public affairs. Given Greece's history, however, the withdrawal was not total. This was most pronounced when it came to intelligence matters, due to the composition of the KYP. Ostensibly this was a civilian organization that recruited civilians. The reality, however, was that it was an organization dominated by military personnel and police officers recruited under entirely different processes than the wider civilian staff, who typically occupied minor administrative posts. In his term as prime minister after the junta, Konstantinos Karamanlis did not radically change this arrangement. The KYP's director, Lt. Gen. Labros Stahopoulos, for example, was initially replaced by Lt. Gen. Constantine Fetsis—who was brought out of retirement for the director's post—who was in turn replaced by Lt. Gen. Pantelis Kalamakis.[26] Independent scrutiny would have revealed that neither general had any major intelligence experience. Instead, each was appointed because he had been perceived as an enemy of the junta. This is an interesting point because targeting perceived threats had an impact on recruitment too, with the intelligence services being staffed with members who could be "trusted" by the government and not because they were qualified. Indeed, legacies of the authoritarian past persisted, with the recruitment process becoming increasingly politicized. Fetsis, among others, for example, had previously been implicated in trying to foster a general mutiny among the Hellenic Navy in the summer of 1973.[27] Kalamakis, meanwhile, had twice been arrested and tortured by the regime's officials, many of whom had previously been his subordinates.[28] Such "qualifications," however, formed the basis for recruiting a cadre of other military officers to Karamanlis's "new" KYP, most of whom were employed based solely on their presence within the junta's blacklist of alleged communists, socialists, and independents.[29] A long-term change was enacted in 1975, however, through a decision to open up entry-level positions to university graduates and managerial positions to internal civilian staff. This not only increased the possibility of more civilians being recruited over time but also their chances of becoming just as senior as the uniformed counterparts. Because of the glass ceiling then, many civilians would occupy the same positions for years, even though they often had more experience and were often more qualified than their military colleagues. In the short term, meanwhile, things remained very much the same, with the KYP continuing to recruit uniformed personnel at preferential levels over civilians right up to the beginning of the 1980s. This was both indicative of the military's continued dominance over security affairs in the postjunta environment and a perpetuation of the status quo that Karamanlis, despite his best efforts, was ill-placed to change.

This was not so much the case for Andreas Papandreou, who ran his 1981 election campaign literally on the slogan of "Change" in an effort to appeal to Greeks tired of almost a decade's rule by the political Right. Curiously, rather than build on Karamanlis's earlier efforts and expand civilian recruitment over time while curtailing the numbers of uniformed personnel brought into the KYP, Papandreou instead adopted his own unique approach. The purpose was to help reduce the institutional suspicion of Greek citizens who were in the center or on the left of the political spectrum.[30] In addition, he hoped to convince ordinary Greeks that the KYP was no longer just focused on securing the state but also interested in improving the quality of their everyday lives.[31] They included the large number of former Soviet citizens who had settled in Greece from 1968 to 1984 as well as returning members of the KKE and the Democratic Army of Greece (DSE).[32] Papandreou also had personal reasons for appointing what he saw as a reliable cadre of loyalists to the KYP's ranks. Having observed its activities as an adviser to his father's brief 1963 and 1964 governments, Papandreou had come to believe that the organization was prone to putting American security interests ahead of Greece's.[33] Consequently, he signed Law 1232/82, which led to the purging of the senior layers of the civil service for their alleged hostility toward the new regime. The new law abolished the ranks of general director and deputy general director, which were filled by tenured civil servants from all Greek ministries. The change was part of the attack by the Panellínio Sosialistikó Kínima (PASOK; Panhellenic Socialist Movement) on the inherited "establishment" of the Right and was accompanied by the arrival of a large number of party personnel alongside ministers. These were soon dubbed the "green guards" by critics, reflecting PASOK's campaign color.[34] Although theoretically Papandreou's intentions behind replacing personnel were good—to change public opinion toward the service—practically the result was that the KYP continued to become more and more politicized and staffed with unqualified politicized personnel who targeted perceived rather than real threats.

This was paired with the parallel recruitment of senior military officers to its command structure, including the appointment of Lt. Gen. George Politis as the KYP's new director in November 1981.[35] Indeed, Papandreou's decision to pack the KYP with PASOK members of questionable competence rather than enact more rigorous recruitment practices served only to make the organization *more* reliant on the acquisition of uniformed personnel to fulfill its objectives. This occurred in the face of changes made elsewhere, such as the passing of Law 1299/82.[36] It "designated a total of 113 posts, including fifty senior staff spread over six main offices or deployed on specific tasks assigned to them directly by the Prime Minister."[37] Among them were several individuals specifically assigned by Papandreou to intelligence-related activities. They reported to the Ministry of the Presidency of the Government until February 1984, at which time they began reporting directly to Papandreou himself in his capacity as minister of defense.[38] Legacies of the past therefore persisted well after the transition period, with a politicized and militarized intelligence service that was staffed with unqualified personnel.

Certainly, in the course of his administration, Papandreou acquired a great deal of executive power but made little use of it initially to reform the KYP, whether in how it recruited staff or generally conducted itself. This presented problems in Papandreou's second term when he decided to embark on an ambitious government-wide transformation plan.[39] By 1985 many of the civilian intelligence officers serving in the KYP were unhappy with the dominance that the Greek military continued to have over the organization.[40] One KYP officer at the time explained to an American journalist, "We work long hours, receive small salaries and have no chances of promotion because senior positions in the service are automatically occupied by military officers."[41] What this testimony illustrated even as late as 1985 was that the KYP remained in thrall to uniformed personnel. An engrained sense of tribal protectionism and years of tradition were certainly difficult to overcome, and as far as many military officers were concerned, this was the natural way of things. Kyriakos Papageorgopoulos, who had been the director of the KYP prior to the 1967 coup, argued at the time, for example, that military dominance of the KYP was necessary from the point of view of effectiveness since military officers' "training allows them to evaluate information at a strategic and tactical level, something a KYP civilian employee cannot do."[42]

It was only because of such pressure that Papandreou decided to change things through Presidential Decree 1645/1986. This decree also opened up further positions to "nonuniformed citizens," allowing for chiefs of divisions and deputy directors of the organizations A Directorate and B Directorate to be appointed civilians.[43] This included recruits from universities and technical colleges who were believed to be able to provide the kind of skills and knowledge needed to face "new international challenges."[44] As with Karamanlis' changes, however, little was actually different. The KYP, now known as Ethnikι Ypiresιa Pliroforion (EYP; National Intelligence Service), was not obliged to hire civilians over uniformed officers, regardless of how many roles were officially open to civilians. Papandreou also continued to undermine things through politically minded appointments. These were not conducive to long-term sustainable recruitment practices and set a dangerous precedent for what was to come. Although instances of cronyism had also been prevalent in Greece, Papandreou's administration took things to new levels through its decision to choose "easy fixes" as opposed to the hard work of legislating and enforcing changes to the EYP's engrained culture. Ahead of the 1989 general election, for instance, four hundred positions were given away in the EYP in order to help shore up support for Papandreou's ruling party, PASOK.[45] The implication was that only PASOK and Papandreou could be trusted to reward their supporters for their loyalty, regardless of whether said supporters would have actually qualified for the roles under normal conditions.

With PASOK briefly out of power from 1992 to 1993, this situation changed somewhat, with a key law enacted that formalized the EYP's recruitment process. Presidential Decree ND 360/1992 did not fundamentally change *whom* the EYP recruited, but it did change *how*. Under the decree, for instance, the Greek interior minister was made responsible for appointing a director, "a Greek or equivalent foreign university or other equivalent domestic or foreign faculty degree holder who has administrative experience in the public or private sector."[46] Notably the law designated the relevant director "disciplinarily superior to the NIS's [EYP's] civil and military personnel" but excluded them from having a say over "appointments, tenure of apprentice personnel, integrations, transfers and relocations outside of NIS [EYP]."[47] This inconsistency reflected the way in which the EYP continued to host military and police personnel, nominally under the director's command but in reality responsible to their own external command chains. Further disparity was apparent in the different criteria that civilian, military, and police personnel had to meet prior to receiving promotion to the highest positions within the EYP. Permanent civil servants, for example, needed to fulfill four sets of criteria: "previous experience," "initiative," "employee performance," and having completed "degree and graduate studies as well as training within NIS [EYP]."[48] Their military and police counterparts, meanwhile, merely needed to have "proven administrative experience" and training from their host departments to be eligible for senior ranks.[49] The barriers were equalized slightly more at the lower levels, however, with over a dozen pages of the 1992 decree listing in detail the exact criteria that civilian applicants had to fulfill thereafter in order to qualify for postings. To cite one example, applicants to one of forty-eight administrative staff positions had to have the following:

a. A degree in law, political sciences or finance from the University of Athens or the Panteion University of Political Sciences or the University of Piraeus or the University of Macedonia or any equivalent Degree from a foreign faculty.
b. Very good knowledge of one of the foreign languages that interest EYP.
c. Typing skills in the Greek language.[50]

Similar requirements, particularly when it came to higher education, were set for 726 other civilian positions, with the remainder requiring at least a high school education or technical training.[51] It was a similar case for uniformed personnel from either the military, coast guard, or police. The decree setting aside up to 865 positions for uniformed personnel who had to "remain in EYP for an obligatory 5 years unless removed for reasons pertaining to EYP's interests."[52] Candidates for these positions had to have graduated from their relevant academies or higher educational institutes. Moreover, they had to "have been deemed worthy of promotion per selection during the last evaluation before their placement by the relevant Board of the Army, Police, or Coast Guard sector."[53] The

1992 decree therefore leveled the playing field somewhat for civilians keen to enter the EYP but who had up until then not benefited from a patron in PASOK or a military commission.

From 1999 there were a flurry of changes that all altered how the EYP could recruit. The first came as part of Law 2683/1999, which set out the employment code for civil servants and employees of other public interests. The most important part of this law when it came to the EYP was Article 4, which formally stated that only Greek citizens could be appointed as employees of public bodies, nonnationals only being allowed in special cases and nationalized citizens only being eligible after a year as citizens.[54] This was followed in 2001 by a new presidential decree setting out recruitment criteria for the new PE7 Division of translators, interpreters, "listeners," and researchers of computer networks, which was to include eighty-three positions in total.[55] This brief decree put further emphasis on higher educational standard and technical training as a prerequisite for recruitment, with additional modifications being made in 2002 in order to recruit for sixty-five new positions in the DE2 Staff Intelligence Division and sixty-five vacancies in the TE5 Radio Telegraph Division.[56]

In the aftermath of 9/11 and the subsequent "modernization" of the EYP, efforts to recruit and train staff took on new importance, with the then minister of public order Mihalis Chryssokhoidis announcing that the "EYP is being called to play a new, significant role in consolidating national security. The Greek government is evidently aware of the increased demands and will secure the requisite funds in light of the debate on the new budget in the Greek Parliament."[57] Regrettably, the EYP's ability to meet such demands was undercut by the continuation of long-standing practices, most notably the kind of cronyism that had occurred extensively under Papandreou. According to Pavlos Apostolidis, who was the EYP's director from 1999 to 2004, uniformed officers often made use of patron networks in order to secure positions due to the benefits they offered: a posting in Athens, office work, and extra pay. Officers who were loyal to particular parties or ministers would typically benefit from such arrangements before leaving after three to five years. The EYP was thus not only the victim of short-termism when it came to strategy and leadership but also tactical challenges brought on by rarely receiving the kind of recruits it actually needed.[58] None of this was really addressed by the last major law passed in respect of the EYP, Law 3649/2008.[59] It again sanctioned the recruitment of both civilians and "active officers and noncommissioned officers of the Armed Forces and the Coast Guard, officers of the Fire Service and Hellenic Police."[60] Consequently, the status quo remained in place until 2010, when, in light of Greece's economic situation following the 2008–9 global financial crisis, the EYP ceased almost all recruitment from 2009 onward. Throughout that time, some authors underlined more recruitment issues within the service. One of the key problems was the fact that all intelligence officers, both high school and university graduates, had the same duties.[61]

Incredibly, this remained the case until almost ten years later, until 2019, when the EYP announced that it was recruiting for 302 staff in an effort to fill outstanding positions and reduce the organization's overall age, which was by then "very high."[62] To this end, applicants with university and technology education "must have been born between 1984 and 1998," while applicants with secondary education "must have been born between 1989 and 1998."[63] Criteria for the top spot, however—that of the EYP's director—was relaxed, with the Greek parliament passing a provision stipulating that a candidate could qualify with ten years of professional experience, not needing to be a university graduate as before.[64] These changes, along with the creation of the post of national security adviser to the prime minister and three new deputy commanders in the EYP, were indicative of a new period of modernization following many years of stagnation.[65] Whereas previously the EYP could not recruit despite the increase in multiple threats facing Greece, it now could, especially when the threat appears to be close in proximity. The age-old threat of Turkey, for instance, appeared to be enough to galvanize the hiring of eighty hackers following Turkish attacks on various Greek websites at the beginning of 2020.[66] Although this was hailed at the start of a "new era," it would only be a minor adjustment compared to the overhaul that was rumored to be planned in July 2020: "an overhaul of the country's National Intelligence Service (EYP) foreseeing, among other things, the controversial transfer of one of its key departments to the Defense Ministry."[67] If this were to include changes to the EYP's recruitment practices, it would represent a long overdue update and ideally align the organization's processes with other Western counterparts. Indeed, authoritarian legacies persisted in Greece for a long time and negatively impacted the recruitment process. Some progress was made immediately after 9/11 but with no substantial changes for another ten years after that. The Greek case will have to continue to be monitored to see if positive steps have been taken to move away from politicization practices when it comes to the staffing of its intelligence service.

SPAIN

If one wanted a career in intelligence in post-Franco Spain, the main difficulty, at least initially, was deciding which organization to apply to. In a reflection of both the Franco regime's paranoia and the pervasiveness of its bureaucracy, Spain had a multitude of organizations all engaged in some form of intelligence collection or another when the king appointed Adolfo Suárez prime minister in 1976. These included the Ministry of Foreign Affairs, the Ministry of Information and Tourism, the Ministry of Trade Union Relations, and the army, navy, and air force, whose Second Sections advised on military intelligence matters.[68] These entities were in addition to the country's two primary intelligence organizations—the BPS and the SECED—the former having been in operation since 1941. In short, there were many intelligence organizations recruiting new personnel, and none was exactly discerning about the previous roles that potential staff may have played in upholding the Francoist regime. Indeed, the primary effect of the 1977 Amnesty Law was to absolve former regime insiders of their sins and extend them employment opportunities in post-Franco organizations.[69] As with many other implications of the law, this was not widely acknowledged or reflected upon until quite later, by which time, many former Francoists had taken roles across the Spanish public sector.[70] Many roles were found, for example, in the new "democratic" intelligence organization of CESID, which from July 14, 1977, replaced many of the Francoist intelligence organizations, including the SECED.

CESID was the brainchild of Suárez's vice president, Manuel Gutiérrez Mellado. Having been given the power to create Spain's new intelligence organization, Gutiérrez Mellado made the curious decision to have the Spanish army and the SECED draw up a plan for what it should look like.[71] Gutiérrez Mellado invited "the High Staff of the Army and SECED to form a joint committee to develop a preliminary plan for a new intelligence service with new structures and new information priorities that would be better aligned to the democratic reality of Spain."[72] This, combined with Gutiérrez Mellado's past in the Spanish military, meant the outcome was a military-dominated intelligence organization that combined SIAEM and the SECED under the newly constituted Spanish Ministry of Defense.[73] Undermining any efforts to create a new, completely civilian organization, however, was the fact that Gutiérrez Mellado was a firm military man who had served Franco loyally since his uprising in 1936. This tipped the balance of the negotiations in favor of the Spanish military. After rejecting the name "Defense Intelligence Service," President Suárez himself decided to call the new organization CESID. This choice was peculiar for three reasons, as Antonio M. Díaz Fernández states: "Spain opted for a model of one service, one close to authoritarian regimes. The Spanish model was alien to the 'Western' model, based on one organism for domestic and another for foreign espionage. This model had thus embedded in it from the start a whole series of problems that would accompany it until the services' reform in May 2002."[74]

Díaz Fernández writes, however, that the resources available were inadequate to support the new structure of the organization and that this caused a "significant exodus of staff seconded from the Guardia Civil, police force, and military from the original but now extinct SECED." The first two saw interesting professional opportunities and promotion in the creation of new management bodies for their forces and the accompanying sweeping modernization.

However, many in the military did not feel able to adapt to the norms and habits of a democratic intelligence service, above all when a few months earlier they had been conducting very different work for another regime with whom they had developed strong bounds of loyalty and partnership.[75] Authoritarian elements had deep roots within the Spanish intelligence services, with legacy personnel still within their ranks. This resulted in authoritarian practices with a focus on perceived threats and collection methods that were far from democratic, as will be seen in chapter 6.

Consequently, despite whatever plans had been made to create a "civilian intelligence organization," CESID was thoroughly military in nature and primarily recruited military officers to its ranks. This, therefore, facilitated the creation of an intelligence service that was quite apart from wider Spanish society. It did not recruit based on individual merit, nor did it open itself up to fair and honest competition. Roles were essentially doled out to those with the right connections or appointed to "the right sort" of military personel. All of this was justified on the basis that this was the only way that CESID could inoculate itself against infiltration by foreign intelligence services.[76] The old guard agreed to the dismantling of tarnished organizations such as the BPS and the SECED on the basis that their personnel would still be granted their "proper place" in Spanish society, thus perpetuating the challenge of democratization.[77] The 1981 coup attempt brought to a head the dangers that this could pose, with CESID members subsequently implicated in the planning and coordination of the debacle. It is also what inspired the appointment of Lt. Gen. Emilio Alanso Manglano as head of the organization in an effort to modernize it and make it more professional.[78] Part of this involved efforts to recruit civilians from 1982 and into 1983. As *El País* predicted in May of the latter year, CESID would "shortly have women integrated in intelligence or counterintelligence missions, according to senior military officials." These women would not only come from groups already integrated into the armed forces but also be people who have no direct relationship with the military.[79] The result was that six years later, in 1988, CESID employed around two thousand staff in total, six hundred of whom were civilians.[80] While a welcome start in terms of diversification, it was also reported that many of the latter had been recruited on the basis of either being friends with, or related to, existing members of staff, rather than through open competition.[81]

It was not until as late as 1995 that recruitment practices began to be codified in law with Royal Decree 1324/1995 of July 28, which set out the specific staff regulations relevant to CESID.[82] This was the result of more criticism of CESID emerging from the media about the GAL affair, which had shocked the Spanish public. The need to reform the Spanish intelligence service became apparent. Remarkably, one of the foremost effects of the law was to reduce all personnel to temporary status, with those who were considered suitable being offered the possibility of being employed permanently, depending on how many years they had already served. At the front of the queue were those who had served more than nine years, who could access permanent recruitment options after just six months. Those who had served just over three years, however, needed to wait until 1998.[83] While the recruitment of uniformed personnel did not change, the process did substantially. No longer were recruits considered based on their personal connections. Instead, they needed to show that they

a. held Spanish nationality and were of legal age;
b. were in possession of the qualification required for the group that is assigned, in the list of jobs, the position in which they intend to join;
c. have not been released from public sector service, nor have been disqualified from the exercise of public functions for disciplinary reasons; and
d. do not suffer from illness or physical defect that incapacitates them for the exercise of their functions.[84]

They were then to undergo an assessment of suitability ranging from one to two years in duration, depending on which group of posts they were applying for. Only after a total of three years would CESID consider the possibility of offering a permanent position, the decision ultimately being made "based on the analysis of the circumstances of the affected personnel in the aspects of their personality, competence, performance and professional performance."[85] This ultimately meant that new recruits and existing staff needed to participate in a performance review several years long, without any guarantee of employment at the end of it. Although small steps were made, CESID continued to suffer from authoritarian legacies that included high volumes of present and former military personnel within its ranks as well as favoritism. This only changed after 9/11, which operated as a critical juncture.

By 2001 CESID's total number of staff had risen to approximately twenty-three hundred, a modest increase from what it had been in 1988. The events of 9/11 caused the legislature to allocate more resources to increase this figure further, with the organization's budget allocation increasing from €100 million in 2001 to €138 million in 2003.[86] This funding increase reflected not only the Spanish government's interest in protecting the country against international terrorism but also the development of the CNI, which replaced CESID in 2002. The first test of the new organization occurred in 2004, when al-Qaeda attacked the Madrid rail network. Immediately after the bombings, which acted as another critical juncture, new legislation was laid to combat the threat of international terrorism. Key points within this new legislation focused on coordination between law enforcement and intelligence agencies, international cooperation, and, of course, increasing intelligence capabilities.[87] Special attention was given to strengthening the capabilities of the National Police and the Guardia Civil as well as regional police forces in Catalonia and the Basque region. The main element of the above was to strengthen the counterterrorism services of the National Police and the Guardia Civil in order to equip them with the necessary skills and capabilities to face and respond to threats, such as international terrorism. Indeed, over the four years following the attacks, about one thousand National Police and Guardia Civil officers were hired. These new hires were being recruited "at a pace that responded not so much to political will as to the practical capacity of the various police external information units to take on new human resources specialized in international terrorism."[88] Overall, the public sector roles in counterterrorism increased by almost 35 percent, with three quarters of these involving external information work. Personnel in external information services grew by 72 percent in the National Police force and 22 percent in the Guardia Civil.[89] Within the CNI itself, 250 new officers were recruited for the specific purpose of combatting terrorism in Spain, followed by many more on a year-by-year basis.[90] Accordingly, by 2010 the total staff headcount had increased to 3,500, with civilians for the first time forming the majority at 59.88 percent of all staff, followed by active-duty military officers at 28.55 percent and 11.57 percent from the security forces.[91] This was a significant change compared to the composition at the end of the 1980s and in the early 1990s, with an emphasis put on real and relevant threats.

Part of this was a result of the streamlining of admission, training, and professionalization processes affecting staff since 1995, in addition to the CNI's movement away from military matters toward collection and analysis of modern threats. Notably, despite various changes to the role and remit of the organization from 2002, the staff regulations laid out by royal decree in 1995 for intelligence personnel continued to remain in force. What did develop further were the CNI's specific requirements for entry—for example, knowledge of foreign languages, specialized technical training, and a series of specific professional qualities. Accordingly, it was no longer enough to simply have a military or security background—one had to have the right sort of professional skills for the job. Analytical capabilities and abstract reasoning became prerequisites for intelligence officials and technicians, while good abilities of reasoning, speaking, and management of ideas became required of translators and interpreters.[92] Accordingly, while there were some roles that were more appropriate for military personnel, the greater proportion of jobs could be filled by civilians, whether directly recruited or drawn from the civil servants of the State Security Corps (CSE), the latter being typically approached due to their training and experience in information gathering, counterterrorism, or foreign operations.[93] From the early 2000s, Web-based communication became an important feature of the CNI's recruitment efforts, with the organization rebranding CESID's old website in order to offer potential recruits the opportunity to post speculative CVs from 2002 onward. Others were recruited directly from prominent universities, the CNI working with tutors and lecturers to identify the students with "the highest aptitudes" in order to fill roles.[94] This recruitment behind the scenes also extended to the continued invocation of personal contacts in order to facilitate job offers, with candidates pursued based on recommendations by existing members of the CNI. This controversial practice was one of the many reasons for the dismissal of the CNI's director in 2009 on allegations that he had secured positions for three of his nephews, while another senior intelligence official had done the same for his son and two granddaughters.[95] We can observe that after two critical junctures, 9/11 and 11M, substantial progress was made in terms of moving toward more democratic and professional recruitment processes that target relevant threats, such as international terrorism. Despite this progress, some elements of nepotism remained. This raises questions such as, Would a more robust oversight framework that would have resulted after a lustration process helped mitigate nepotism issues, as happened in Portugal? Indeed, there is no data that proves a direct causation relationship here, but a correlation link is visible. This is not to suggest that emphasis should not be put on other key factors that can push for reform, such as the media, which tends to reveal scandals, and/or critical junctures that help drive change.

In terms of the practicalities of the recruitment process, one should look at the CNI's Recruitment Sources Database, a system available to the CNI's human resources department and by which the CNI analyzed potential candidates from its various recruitment sources, grouped by professional areas.[96] Those fortunate enough not to be screened out were then contacted to see if they were willing to participate in the recruitment process for an anonymous job at the Ministry of Defense. If they accepted, they were then invited to begin selection either at the organization's headquarters or one of its subsidiary properties. It was via this system that eight hundred potential recruits were processed in 2010 alone, with each tested against the conditions and requirements of the relevant positions.[97] In this way, the 1995 regulation requiring that candidates pass tests to "determine whether they fulfill the necessary conditions to carry out the job they are applying for" was introduced.[98] The result was a weeding-out process involving six stages lasting anywhere from six to twelve months and consisting of cultural, aptitude, and general intelligence tests to assess a recruit's intellectual potential. There were also personality questionnaires to build a better understanding of each candidate's psychology.[99] Thereafter, candidates were subject to a competency-based selection system using the CNI's own skill profiles "in which the knowledge, skills, abilities and personality traits that lead to success in a given organization are expressed in concrete behaviors that are assessable in the selection process."[100] Only after these steps had been passed and security checks had been completed were candidates finally appointed.

Indeed, this process continued to be adhered to over the next ten years as Spain found itself once again the target of a renewed terrorist threat, this time from ISIS. In 2016, for example, a further €60 million was allocated to the CNI "with the goal of making it possible for the intelligence services to enter into contracts for technological renewal and infrastructure investment."[101] This was in addition to funding designed to facilitate the recruitment of five hundred more staff from 2016 to 2020. The government also increased the CNI's budget by 0.9 percent for 2021, reaching €300 million.[102] Accordingly, an emphasis was placed on the recruitment of university graduates in political science, international relations, history, and languages as well as "mathematicians, computer scientists, and telecoms engineers, precisely in order to modernize research systems, technology, analysis and management, and information search, as well as the cyber protection of critical infrastructures and information."[103] Moving forward, the latest director in charge of the CNI—Paz Esteban—has promised that the organization will once again be "transformed" with a "qualitative leap" which will make it more effective in "an increasingly complex security context."[104] "If we do not move," announced Esteban in early 2020, "we will be left behind and we will be irrelevant and those who threaten us will have won the game and we will not allow that."[105] It is interesting to see that willingness to evolve based on the new environment and threats comes from within the service that has made grand steps in terms of recruitment the past two decades. In short, the CNI remains a growing organization, continuing to offer a diverse number of roles all related to the challenges posed now and likely to be posed in the future.[106]

CONCLUSION

In evaluating each country's approach to recruitment of intelligence personnel from the early 1970s, we can see a marked variation in approach and progress over time. Indeed, all three have experienced some issues with recruitment. Portugal and Spain have addressed them and have seen improvements, and Greece has remained relatively stagnant. In this chapter, focus was put on the practices and procedures used to recruit intelligence personnel in Portugal, Greece, and Spain since their dictatorships fell. Emphasis was also put on their pathologies and the steps the countries have made to address them.

Military remnants and nepotism affected the intelligence services in Greece and Spain. Greece operated an intelligence service that recruited in multiple ways, all at the same time and for a long time. Of most note was the imposition of the divide between uniformed and civilian staff. This continued in the postauthoritarian environment, with only slight changes made by

Konstantinos Karamanlis and Andreas Papandreou. The former, while making the positive change of opening up the KYP to university graduates, did not discontinue military or police staffing, leaving the organization's hierarchal nature firmly entrenched. This did not change under Papandreou, who assigned hundreds of political appointees to the KYP—an opaque process that completely went against any notion of employing personnel based on merit and worthiness. A key point that needs to be highlighted here is that the requirements for civilians and uniformed officers completely varied, with minimum requirements for uniformed staff and a long list of high-level requirements for civilian staff. It was not just about who was being recruited—university graduates or uniformed officers—but also the varying grade of quality and skills between the two. Each iteration of laws passed into the 1990s altered but did not resolve these issues or disparities satisfactorily.

During its transition period and all the way to 1990s, Spain suffered from both of these elements: militarism and nepotism. Spain experienced several decades of having an overt military influence in intelligence affairs in addition to persistent cronyism, especially when it came to recruitment. Both continuing militarism and nepotism were enabled by the pact of forgetting but also the decision to recruit military officers, their close friends, and relatives into Spain's postauthoritarian intelligence organization, CESID. This highly discriminatory practice ensured that recruitment was based much less on merit and more on personal acquaintance. The organization thus quickly became completely unrepresentative of the Spanish society. Legal changes in 1995, however, addressed these shortcomings, with existing staff being reduced to provisional status pending performance review and new recruits being evaluated to a completely codified procedure. This was aided by the media's revelation of scandals, such as the GAL affair.

Quality and quantity of candidates and recruits increased after new threats emerged in Portugal and Spain. In Portugal, despite efforts to recruit based on merit, the overall pool of recruits and employed staff remained limited until the twenty-first century. This was due to the fact that after going through an intensive lustration process, Portugal had to start from zero. The 9/11 and the 11M attacks further boosted the public's perception of intelligence organizations and what role they could play in society. This subsequently facilitated a surge in candidates and those ultimately put forward for intelligence roles. For Portugal, the only difficulty—and this remains a constant for almost all intelligence organizations—was in matching ongoing recruitment against the wildly changing nature of the threats posed against the country. Although Portugal's process was for some time merit-based, roles did not always match overall requirements, something that hindered diversity at a time when Portugal desperately needed to attract candidates from specific backgrounds. This has been addressed proactively since 2015, when the rise of ISIS added pressure to trends that had begun with al-Qaeda in 2001 and new cyber threats encouraged the development of new technical profiles for recruitment that did not widely exist previously. Education and technical ability are therefore now the main criteria by which candidates are filtered and trained. Personal connections are not utilized, and candidates are not "picked from a crowd" by tutors, managers, or others.

Contrary to Portugal, Greece continued its nepotistic practices when it came to recruitment even after key critical junctures such as 9/11 occurred. Although the quantity of personnel was boosted, the quality was still questionable and the presence of uniformed staff persisted. Well into the twenty-first century, recruitment was still conducted in several ways, not all of them transparent. Cronyism in particular remained rampant, and uniformed personnel continued to be assigned under their own criteria despite the fact that the national organization was ostensibly under civilian control. The postponement of resolving this problem from 2010 onward as a result of a cessation of further public sector recruitment has finally offered Greece to review its process in order to make improvements. It is still too early to establish how these will develop, but, given Greece's past performance, a lot remains to be done to ensure that recruitment is conducted in ways that facilitate democratization.

The legal changes of 1995 served Spain well after 2001, when additional resources were made available to recruit a large number of new staff, many to fill gaps in the country's new effort against international terrorism. Some of them were appointed under opaque practices—with even those at the top guilty of employing family members and friends close to them—but the majority were recruited based on merit. As time has gone on and the resources allocated to intelligence have dramatically increased, this situation has only improved, with the 1995 regulations being used as the foundation upon which new role profiles are developed and candidates evaluated. Accordingly, though fraught with negatives historically, Spain has more recently done much to democratize the way it recruits intelligence staff as it continues to offer a diverse number of roles all related to the challenges posed now and likely to be posed in the future. Currently, and for the most part, Spain is recruiting personnel whose qualifications align with national threats.

Civil society's involvement and the willingness of policymakers emerge again as two key factors that supported or obstructed reform. For example, in Portugal, which faced minor limitations when it came to recruitment in comparison to Greece and Spain, media criticism of the intelligence recruitment process helped drive reform in most recent years. Equally, in Spain, revelations about the GAL affair meant that a renewed approach was established for recruitment in 1995. Although not able to completely resolve issues that had their roots in authoritarian legacies and truly reform the service, the media, as part of civil society, helped as a positive factor for some level of reform. The willingness of policymakers affected progress, as we saw in previous chapters too. Although the intentions to refocus public perception by changing recruitment practices was there, unfortunately the result was the politicization of the service. Greece is probably the most prominent example, with Papandreou's green guards swarming the Greek intelligence organization.

Authoritarian legacies emerge once again as a major barrier to intelligence democratization. Nondemocratic practices continued in the recruitment sphere even after transition with unqualified legacy and uniformed personnel still present within the intelligence services. When comparing the three case studies, it is evident that Portugal and Spain have moved closer to democratization, especially when looking at recruitment for the countries' intelligence services. Portugal established a meritocratic service from the start and was the only one that did not have to struggle with authoritarian legacies. Due to the purging process that it followed, the only issue that it faced was a low recruitment drive the first years of its foundation. Nepotism and militarism affected the Spanish intelligence service for a long time. Indeed, these elements affected the service not just in terms of who is recruited—military or civilian staff—but also the quality of personnel. This changed substantially after 9/11 and 11M. Spain has gone a long way from having to deal with a nepotistic and heavily militaristic service to a more meritocratic whose staff is qualified to tackle actual threats to national security. It is key to highlight here that Spain was the only country among the three that suffered a terrorist attack *internally*, a point that should have facilitated change to a greater extent. The country has also recently shown its commitment to continue to evolve its recruitment policies, given the changing environment. Greece has remained behind when compared to Portugal and Spain. Although it boosted its personnel numbers after 9/11, issues such as nepotism and the presence of uniformed staff in the EYP, as well as the hiring of unqualified personnel, have remained.

NOTES

1. Gill, *Intelligence Governance and Democratisation*, 45.
2. Gill, 45, 169.
3. Alexander Joffe, "Dismantling Intelligence Agencies," *Crime, Law and Social Change* 32 (1999): 340–41.
4. Vizela Cardoso, "As informações em Portugal resenha histórica" [Information in Portugal historical review], in *Estudos de Direito e Segurança* [Law and Security Studies], ed. Jorge Bacelar Gouveia and Rui Pereira (Lisbon: Almedina, 2015), 496.
5. *Government Gazette*, 131/1975, Series I of 1975-06-07.
6. Paula Serra, *DINFO: Histórias secretas do Serviço de Informações Militares* [DINFO: Secret Stories from the Military Intelligence Service] (Lisbon: Dom Quixote, 1998), 39.
7. Cardoso, "As informações em Portugal resenha histórica," 497.

8. Renato Marques Pinto, "As informações na idade da informação" [Information in the information age], *Revista Militar, II Século* 53, no. 4 (2001): 309.

9. Cardoso, "As Informações em Portugal resenha histórica," 497.

10. Marques Pinto, "As informações na idade da informação," 484.

11. Marques Pinto, 485.

12. Sónia Reis and Manuel Botelho da Silva, "O sistema de informações da República Portuguesa" [The information system of the Portuguese Republic], *Revista da Ordem dos Advogados* 67, no. 3 (2007): 3.

13. Law No. 29/82, *Diário da República*, no. 285/1982, Série I de 1982-12-11, Article 67: "The Information services of the Armed Forces shall be exclusively concerned with military information, within the scope of the missions assigned to them by the Constitution and by this law."

14. Eric Solsten, ed., *Portugal: A Country Study* (Washington, DC: Federal Research Division, Library of Congress, 1993), 266.

15. Pinto Arena, Portugal's Intelligence Evolution," 161.

16. António José Vilela, *Os códigos e as operações dos espiões Portugueses: O Recrutamento, os treinos, as técnicas, os informadores, os casos desconhecidos dos agentes que atuam na sombra* [The codes and operations of Portuguese spies: Recruitment, training, techniques, informants, unknown cases of agents who work in the shadows] (Lisbon: A Esfera dos Livros, 2015), 29.

17. José Vegar, "The Grey Threat: Presence of Jihadist Terrorism and Failings in the Portuguese National Security System," *Studies in Conflict and Terrorism* 31, no. 5 (2008): 466.

18. "Dezenas de espiões avaliam riscos de ameaças violentas em Portugal" [Dozens of spies assess risks of violent threats in Portugal], *Notícias ao Minuto*, December 10, 2012, www.noticiasaominuto.com/pais/27317/dezenas-de-espi%C3%B5es -avaliam-riscos-de-amea%C3%A7as-violentas-em-portugal%3E.

19. "Erro coloca a descoberto identidade de candidatos a espiões" [Error reveals identity of would-be spies], *Notícias ao Minuto*, June 24, 2015.

20. "Erro coloca a descoberto identidade."

21. "Falta pessoal nas secretas para fazer face à ameaça terrorista" [There is a lack of secret personnel to deal with the terrorist threat], *Notícias ao Minuto*, December 7, 2015, www.noticiasaominuto.com/pais/499503/falta-pessoal-nas-secretas-para -fazer-face-a-ameaca-terrorista>.

22. "Para ser espião tem de saber qual a carne que os muçulmanos não comem" [To be a spy you have to know what meat Muslims don't eat], *Notícias ao Minuto*, July 31, 2015, www.noticiasaominuto.com/pais/429823/para-ser-espiao-tem-de-saber -qual-a-carne-que-os-muculmanos-nao-comem>.

23. Vilela, *Os códigos e as operações dos espiões Portugueses*, 29.

24. "Recrutamento" [Recruitment], SIRP, www.sirp.pt/recrutamento.

25. Law 9/2007 and Law 30/84, 6. See https://www.pgdlisboa.pt/leis/lei_mostra _articulado.php?nid=1824&tabela=leis for more details.

26. "Director General's Curriculum Vitae—Former Director Generals," National Intelligence Service, www.nis.gr/portal/page/portal/NIS/Commanders.

27. "Greece Dismisses Chief of the Navy," *New York Times*, June 1, 1973, www.nytimes .com/1973/06/01/archives/greece-dismisses-chief-of-the-navy-government-said -to-speed-plans.html.

28. *Torture in Greece: The First Torturers' Trial 1975* (London: Amnesty International Publications, 1977).

29. Joseph Fitsanakis, "Τα τανκς της Μεταπολίτευσης" [The tanks of the Metapo-litefsi], *Eleftherotypia*, July 22, 2007, https://www.efsyn.gr/themata/fantasma-tis -istorias/60214_teleytaio-praxikopima.

30. Joseph Fitsanakis, *Ethniki asfalia ke sighrones ipiresies kataskopias stin Ellada* [National security and modern intelligence services in Greece] (Athens: Potamos, 2015), 18–22.

31. Fitsanakis, 24.

32. The DSE was the military wing of the KKE during the Greek Civil War. See Charles R. Shrader, *The Withered Vine: Logistics and the Communist Insurgency in Greece, 1945–1949* (Westport, CT: Praeger, 1999).

33. Papandreou's belief in the CIA's and KYP's collusion stemmed from finding, while in government, that the former was bankrolling KYP operations. He put a stop to the practice. In exile, he would also cite the allegation that several of the coup plotters were CIA agents as proof of American interference in Greek affairs. See "Andreas Papandreou Meets the Press," *Congressional Record*, April 22, 1968: "The present Prime Minister of Greece, Mr Papadopoulos, is probably the first CIA agent who has managed to become a Prime Minister."

34. Kevin Featherstone and Dimitris Papadimitriou, *Prime Ministers in Greece: The Paradox of Power* (Oxford: Oxford University Press, 2015), 90.

35. "Director General's Curriculum Vitae."

36. Law 1299/82, *Government Gazette*, October, 13, 1982.

37. Featherstone and Papadimitriou, *Prime Ministers in Greece*, 91.

38. Featherstone and Papadimitriou, 92.

39. The government sworn in after the June 3, 1985, election was declared to be "transitional" (it was also known as the "forty-five-day government") until a new operational blueprint was produced. See Featherstone and Papadimitriou, *Prime Ministers in Greece*, 95.

40. Lee Stokes, "Agents in Greek CIA Form New Union, Threaten Strike," *Miami Herald*, February 10, 1986.

41. Stokes.

42. Stokes.

43. "History: New Horizons," NIS, www.nis.gr/portal/page/portal/NIS/History/New Horizons. Directorate A is responsible for domestic intelligence. Directorate B is responsible for intelligence affairs abroad.

44. "History: New Horizons."

45. Apostolidis, *Mystiki Drasi*, 279.

46. Section 1, Article 3, Clause 1, ND 360/1992, 4–5.

47. Section 1, Article 3, Clause 4, Paragraphs b and d, ND 360/1992, 5.

48. Section 1, Article 5, Clause 2, Paragraph c, ND 360/1992, 8–9.

49. Section 1, Article 5, Clause 2, Paragraph c, ND 360/1992, 8–9.

50. Article 10, Branch PE1, Administrative Staff, ND 360/1992.

51. Articles 11–37, ND 360/1992.

52. Article 38, Paragraph 3, ND 360/1992.

53. Article 40, Paragraph 2, ND 360/1992.

54. Article 4, Nationality, Paragraphs 1–4, Law No. 2683 ΦΕΚ A 19 / 9.2.1999, Code of Status of Public Policy Administrative Employees and Employees N.P.D.D. general provisions.

55. Article 2, Presidential Decree No. 29, *Government Gazette*, A 26, 12.02.2001, Extension of Application of Specific Provisions of the Employee Code (Law

2683/99) to the Political Staff of the Secretary and Establishment of New Permanent Branches.

56. Articles 1–2, Presidential Decree No. 255, *Government Gazette*, A 225, 25.09.2002, Modification of Organism of the National Intelligence Service (EYP), PD 360/92, A 183.

57. Manolis Stavrakakis, "Seven Innovations for Modern Agents," *Ependitis*, October 28, 2001.

58. Pavlos Apostolidis, *Intelligence Services in the National Security System: The Case of EYP*, ELIAMEP Occasional Papers (Athens: ELIAMEP, 2007), 22.

59. Law No. 3649, National Intelligence Service and other provisions, March 2008.

60. Article 10, Categories of Personnel of Law No. 3649, National Intelligence Service and other provisions, March 2008.

61. Andrew Liaropoulos and Ioannis Konstantopoulos, "Reforming the Greek National Intelligence Service: Untying the Gordian Knot," *Journal of Mediterranean and Balkan Intelligence* 3, no. 1 (2014): 31–44. See also John Nomikos, "Intelligence Studies in Greece: The Development of an Academic Discipline," *Journal of Mediterranean and Balkan Intelligence* 5, no. 1 (2015); John Nomikos, "Reforming the Greek Intelligence-Security Community: New Challenges," *Journal of Romanian Intelligence Studies* 5 (2011); and Nomikos and Liaropoulos, "Truly Reforming or Just Responding to Failures?"

62. Alexandros Kalafatis, "'Ξεπαγώνουν' Οι Διαδικασίες Για 302 Προσλήψεις Στην ΕΥΠ" [The procedures for 302 recruitments in the EYP are "thawing"], HuffPost Greece, November 5, 2019, www.huffingtonpost.gr/entry/xepayonoen-oi -diadikasies-yia-302-proslepseis-sten-eep_gr_5dc12e40e4b03d0aacff848a.

63. Kalafatis.

64. Giorgos Bourdaras, "Clash in Parliament over New Intelligence Chief Criteria," *Kathimerini*, August 31, 2019, www.ekathimerini.com/244096/article/ekathimerini /news/clash-in-parliament-over-new-intelligence-chief-criteria.

65. Tasos Kokkinidis, "Greece Revamps Intelligence Services, Creates National Security Advisor Post," Greek Reporter, August 2, 2019, https://greekreporter.com/2019/08 /02/greece-revamps-intelligence-services-creates-national-security-advisor-post/.

66. "A 'New Area' in the Greek Cyber Army: EYP Is Staffed with 80 Hackers," *Ethnos*, June 13, 2020, www.ethnos.gr/politiki/110338_neo-aima-ston-elliniko-kyber nostrato-me-80-haker-stelehonetai-i-eyp.

67. Yiannis Souliotis, "Overhaul of EYP Includes Shift to Defense Ministry," *Kathimerini*, July 14, 2020, www.ekathimerini.com/254702/article/ekathimerini/news /overhaul-of-eyp-includes-shift-to-defense-ministry.

68. Sanz F. García, "Al servicio del estado: Inteligencia y contrainteligencia en España" [At the service of the state: Intelligence and counterintelligence in Spain], *Arbor* 180, no. 709 (2005): 100.

69. Madeline Davis, "Is Spain Recovering Its Memory? Breaking the 'Pacto del Olvido,'" *Human Rights Quarterly* 27, no. 3 (2005): 863.

70. Aguilar, *Justice, Politics and Memory in the Spanish Transition*, 102.

71. Bob de Graaff and James M. Nyce, eds., *Handbook of European Intelligence Cultures* (Lanham, MD: Rowman & Littlefield, 2016), 362.

72. De Graaff and Nyce, 362.

73. Article 2.5, Decree 1558/1977, July 4, 1977: "Under the direct dependence of the head of the Department [Ministry of Defense], the Higher Defense Information

Center [CESID] is created, which will incorporate the functions and Organisms of the Administration that are determined."

74. Díaz Fernández, "Spain: Intelligence in Context Today," in Bob de Graaff and James M. Nyce, eds., *Handbook of European Intelligence Cultures* (Lanham, MD: Rowman & Littlefield, 2016), 362–63.

75. Díaz Fernández, *Los servicios de intelligencia españoles*, 196.

76. Juan Antonio Martínez Sánchez, "Recruitment in the Spanish National Intelligence Center (CNI)," *Papeles del Psicólogo* 33, no. 3 (2012): 203.

77. José A. Olmeda, "Security Sector Reform in Spain: From Transition to Consolidation of Democracy," in *Beyond Settlement, Volume II: Making Peace Last after Civil Conflict*, ed. Vanessa Shields and Nicholas Baldwin (Madison, NJ: Fairleigh Dickinson University Press, 2005).

78. Díaz Fernández, "Halfway Down the Road," 441.

79. "Próxima Integración de Mujeres al CESID," *El País*, May 15, 1983, 1983, http:// elpais.com/diario/1983/05/16/espana/421884014_850215.html.

80. Eric Solsten and Sandra W. Meditz, eds., *Spain: A Country Study* (Washington, DC: Federal Research Division, Library of Congress, 1990), 330.

81. *Spain.*

82. Royal Decree 1324/1995 of July 28, 1995, which establishes the staff regulations of CESID, BOE no. 198, August 19, 1995.

83. Second transitory provision of Royal Decree 1324/1995 of July 28, 1995, which establishes the staff regulations of CESID, BOE no. 198, August 19, 1995.

84. Article 13, Temporary Staff Selection Process, Requirements, Tests, Royal Decree 1324/1995, July 28, 1995.

85. Article 16, Permanent Integration, Final Appointment, Royal Decree 1324/1995, July 28, 1995.

86. Martínez Sánchez, "Recruitment in Spanish National Intelligence Center," 203.

87. Fernando Reinares, "After the Madrid Bombings: Internal Security Reforms and Prevention of Global Terrorism in Spain," *Studies in Conflict and Terrorism* 32, no. 5 (2009): 2.

88. Reinares, 6.

89. Reinares, 6. Please note that for the National Police force, the percentage increase includes operational and support personnel, including translators. The percentage for the Guardia Civil only includes the former.

90. "El CNI contratará a 250 nuevos agentes contra el terrorismo" [The CNI will hire 250 new anti-terrorism agents], *El País*, October 12, 2004, https://elpais.com /diario/2004/10/13/espana/1097618403_850215.html.

91. Martínez Sánchez, "Recruitment in Spanish National Intelligence Center," 203.

92. Martínez Sánchez, 204.

93. Martínez Sánchez, 204.

94. J. Dezcallar, "Los servicios de intelligencia: Una herramienta indispensable" [The intelligence services: An indispensable tool], in *El terrorismo: Una amenaza del siglo XXI; XIV Seminario Internacional de Defensa* [Terrorism: A twenty-first-century threat; 14th International Seminar on Defense], ed. M. A. Aguilar and J. M. Ridao (Madrid: Asociación de Periodistas Europeos, 2002).

95. Cartas al Director, "Reforma urgente en el CNI" [Urgent reform in the CNI], *El País*, July 14, 2009, https://elpais.com/diario/2009/07/14/opinion/1247522408 _850215.html.

96. R. Jiménez, "El CNI: Al servicio de España y de los ciudadanos" [The CNI: At the service of Spain and its citizens], *Arbor* 180, no. 709 (2005): 153–81.

97. F. J. Palací and J. M. Peiró, *La incorporación a la empresa* [Joining a company] (Valencia: Promolibro, 1995).

98. Article 13, Temporary Staff Selection Process, Royal Decree 1324/1995 of July 28, 1995, which establishes the staff regulations of CESID, BOE no. 198, August 19, 1995.

99. Jiménez, "El CNI."

100. Martínez Sánchez, "Recruitment in Spanish National Intelligence Center," 208.

101. Quico Salles, "Acting Government Spends Further 60 Million Euros in National Intelligence Center," *La Vanguardia*, July 22, 2016. See also "Presupuesto 2021 aumentan un 0,9 % la partida del CNI hasta los 300 millones" [2021 budget increases for CNI by 0.9% to 300 million], *La Vanguardia*, October 28, 2020. https://www.lavanguardia.com/politica/20201028/4961152681/presupuesto-2021-aumentan-un-09--la-partida-del-cni-hasta-los-300-millones.html.

102. "Presupuesto 2021 aumentan un 0,9 %."

103. Salles, "Acting Government Spends."

104. Miguel González, "La nueva directora del CNI anuncia una profunda transformación del servicio secreto" [The new director of the CNI announces a profound transformation of the secret service], *El País*, February 11, 2020, https://elpais.com/politica/2020/02/10/actualidad/1581343192_163376.html.

105. González.

106. "Centro Nacional de Inteligencia: Perfiles" [National Intelligence Center: Profiles], CNI, www.cni.es/es/ingreso/perfiles/index.html?rutaGrupo=%2Fes%2Fingreso%2Fperfiles%2Fgrupo_001.html.

6

Targeting

In previous chapters, we examined lustration as a positive step for removing authoritarian elements from an intelligence service during their transition to democracy. This exclusion lays the groundwork for solid control and oversight, which in turn is the basis for fair recruitment procedures, a democratic collection process, and an open civil society. In this chapter, we will examine targeting as one of the SSR indicators to measure intelligence democratization in Portugal, Greece, and Spain and analyze why each case study had (or did not have) issues with following collection processes that are more aligned with democratic ideals.

Acquiring information is the foundation of intelligence. There are different ways to collect information, including open and secret. Agencies use open sources, such as newspapers, online sources, and magazines to compile information. When it comes to secret sources, agencies use different methods, including human intelligence (HUMINT) and imagery intelligence (IMINT). In a democratic regime, based on the SSR framework, collecting intelligence should align with the law and democratic principles. For example, unlike during authoritarian rule, emphasis should be put on targeting real and relevant threats to national security, not political enemies, while methods used to collect information should not violate human rights despite the fact that intelligence operations require a level of secrecy to be successful. Collection methods should also be proportionate to the threat. Targeting is a key indicator that helps us measure levels of intelligence democratization because it shows us who is the subject of intelligence collection and what the methods used by these intelligence services are (e.g., democratic, proportionate, or illegal). Looking at targeting is key because although there might be an endless amount of information concerning threats against national security, intelligence services have too limited an amount of resources to go after all of them. This means that there should be an organizational process that identifies and targets the most relevant threats to national security and allocates resources for information gathering. This chapter is important as it clearly showcases that authoritarian remnants, especially in Greece and Spain, did not sufficiently reform their targeting practices after the transition to democracy. Targeting also helps us pinpoint other interesting factors that can support or arrest reform.

It will become apparent that a persistent authoritarian mind-set in targeting and collection practices was the key barrier to reform in Greece and Spain. The focus on perceived threats as well as the use of illegal methods, such as wiretapping the king, were present in Greece and Spain well after the fall of their dictatorships. Substantive progress only came in Spain after later critical junctures occurred, such as the Madrid attacks on March 11, 2004. On the other hand, after a revolution that acted as a critical juncture and an intensive purging process, Portugal was the only country of the three that managed to create a strong control and oversight foundation, which was then followed by reformed targeting and collection practices.

As intelligence collection is a key component of a state's core task, which is to protect its citizens against threats, solid oversight structures are needed. This is to ensure that operations are not carried out illegally or in ways that threaten or abuse the safety and security of said citizens.[1] We examined control and oversight holistically in chapter 4. Indeed, it became evident that Portugal (at least on paper) has established a robust framework. Greece and Spain followed a different path, with both suffering from poor oversight systems. While it is key to understand initially if the legal foundation exists in law, it is also important to try to see whether what exists in law is practically applied. In this chapter, there will be references to key oversight parameters that fall under targeting, specifically to understand if the framework was there. If it was, did intelligence services in each case study follow it? In this chapter, therefore, we will also aim to observe the application of the control and oversight systems in relation to targeting, where possible. We will see that oversight was ineffective in Greece and Spain. This was evident by the several scandals and failures that entailed the focus of the intelligence organizations on irrelevant "threats" and the use of illegal collection methods. This was on top of the poor oversight basis that existed in Greece and the complete disregard of the one that roughly existed in Spain. However, it is harder to measure the applicability of the oversight structure in Portugal. On paper, Portugal has established a very strong basis for oversight. There is no substantive data that shows otherwise apart from a handful of isolated events, such as corruption issues. It is more difficult, therefore, to provide a clear causation relationship when we are looking at the applicability of oversight. On the contrary, we find that available, systematic reports produced by the Portuguese supervisory board, the CFSIRP, highlight the adherence of the intelligence services to democratic practices.[2] On the opposite side of the spectrum we find Spain, where a wealth of data highlights the innumerable systematic abuses by the intelligence services and their respective governments. Indicatively, we underline the GAL affair and the wiretapping of key figures, including the king. Although there is not a causation element here as the absence of scandals is not evidence in itself that Portugal's oversight has been effective, there is a correlation element because at the same time there is no available systematic data to demonstrate poor oversight.

Based on the above, we will aim to answer the following key questions: Do the intelligence services target actual threats to national security rather than threats to regime security, and if so, when did they start doing so? Do the intelligence services use any methods that are illegal under domestic law to collect information? Is there a legal basis for oversight when it comes to targeting? In the intelligence process, the first stage is "planning and direction" or "targeting," as highlighted by Peter Gill.

Before we dive into the analysis of the three case studies in terms of targeting, it is key to revisit a few additional factors that can support or obstruct progress in addition to the fundamental one: the legacies of the authoritarian past. Apart from the significance of critical junctures that we have also touched upon in several areas of this book, other important factors have emerged in the analysis as key trends across several indicators. The first is the relationship between the decision-makers and the intelligence services, which can act both as a barrier as well as a support lever. Indeed, the decision-makers' willingness for reform can aid the process. Equally, it can impede it if the policymakers use the intelligence services for their own benefit, something that is the case under authoritarian rule. The second is lack of public support of the intelligence services. This tends to be the case because the citizens of a state that just transitioned to democracy perceive its intelligence services as bêtes noires.[3] This negative sentiment due to memories of the painful past means that civil society distrusts the intelligence services, resulting in no public support. If the intelligence services adopt an open culture, however, they can positively influence civil society. In this way, levels of distrust are reduced. By the same logic, civil society can act as a positive element for reform, especially through the media. We will touch upon examples of this distrust with relevance to targeting in this chapter, but a detailed analysis on civil society will be provided in chapter 7. The third factor is cooperation across agencies within the intelligence community in order to be able to fight actual threats. This emerges in the analysis mainly during times of intelligence failures. Finally, there is the positive influence that foreign assistance might have through the passing on of professional expertise.[4]

PORTUGAL

Portugal took less time to make the collection of intelligence a civilian affair when compared to Greece and Spain. This was noteworthy, given the sheer amount of catching up that Portugal's authorities had to do and the ongoing primacy of the military in the democratization process. It was this that subsequently led some commentators to claim that Portugal was one of the best examples of a country that was only made a democracy by war.[5] While war was something that the Portuguese military understood, the intricacies of late twentieth century intelligence were not something that they fully comprehended, as we will see later on.

During the Estado Novo, defending Portugal's colonies against communism became the main focus in the government's political agenda and therefore the main subject of its intelligence.[6] After dismantling the DGS in 1974 and the PIM in 1975, the MFA and the Portuguese Armed Forces decided to take on complete responsibility for collecting intelligence themselves, instead of creating a new civilian intelligence organization. Their subsequent interest in military matters meant that collection resources were not generally allocated to other areas of growing importance, such as counterterrorism. As with other European countries at the time, Portugal continued to view this as a law-and-order activity rather than an essential responsibility of the state's intelligence actors. To this end, the PSP and the GNR were tasked with combating terrorist activity, with units such as the Grupo de Operações Especiais (GOE; Special Operations Group) being formed in 1978 to specifically respond to terrorism. This delegation of counterterrorism to police forces, while operationally sound, meant that Portugal was unable to proactively approach threats and instead found itself in a mostly reactive posture for the duration of the late 1970s and early 1980s. This was true of the authorities' responses to both domestic and international terrorism, the latter of which had become an issue of pressing concern in Europe since the 1972 Munich massacre.

Portugal was fortunate to initially experience only one major incident of Palestinian-related terrorism in 1979, when unknown assailants wounded the Israeli ambassador as he arrived at the Israeli embassy in Lisbon.[7] This event, however, marked the start of a period where Portugal became a battleground for a number of groups determined to showcase their credentials by staging violent acts on Portuguese soil. It also resulted in a struggle within the armed forces and police as they could not do much about the international terrorist groups operating in Portugal. First on the scene were Armenian terrorists who continued their campaign against Turkey by assassinating a diplomat outside his home in Lisbon in 1981.[8] This was followed in 1983 by a large-scale Armenian suicide assault on the Turkish embassy not long after the Abu Nidal Organization assassinated PLO representative Issam Sartawi in the coastal city of Albufeira.[9] Portugal responded to this terrorism threat by establishing Law No. 30 of September 5, 1984—the Framework Law of the Information System of the Portuguese Republic—which created the general basis for SIRP, a civilian intelligence service that had a main objective (by law) of combating this type of threat. In terms of oversight, the 1982 Penal Code acknowledged that terrorism was an issue that "needed to be combated severely by criminal law."[10]

Domestic terrorist groups also gave the Portuguese security forces their fair share of trouble in this time period. The Forças Populares 25 de Abril (FP-25; Popular Forces 25 April), for example, was a Far Left terrorist organization that had emerged in 1980 from the remains of the banned Partido Revolucionário do Proletariado–Brigadas Revolucionárias (Revolutionary Party of the Proletariat–Revolutionary Brigades). FP-25 was among the third wave of politically violent organizations that operated in Portugal from 1980 to 1987. The first wave of groups, such as the Liga de Unidade e Ação Revolucionária (League of Unity and Revolutionary Action) and the Brigadas Revolucionárias (Revolutionary Brigades), had attempted to bring down the Estado Novo but had been successfully contained by the DGS. In 1975 and 1976, right-wing groups such as Exército de Libertação de Portugal (Liberation Army of Portugal), which had been created by former PIDE deputy director Augustine Cardoso, similarly failed in their aim to reverse the actions the revolutionary government had taken.[11] Members of FP-25 aimed to succeed where the others failed, and many were "motivated by a belief that the principles espoused by the April [1974] revolution were starting to fade away, which was facilitating the re-emergence of the unjust society of the Salazar years. For some individuals, the situation could be resolved by nothing less than a socialist revolution."[12] To achieve this, they embarked on a widespread bombing campaign in 1980 that saw barracks, military bases, and army and police officers targeted by bombs announcing the group's claim to represent "the exploited Portuguese workers who had fought for the revolution."[13] To further their profile, they were soon robbing multiple banks to fund collaboration with other terrorist groups, including a rocket attack against the Royal British Club in Lisbon with the Provisional Irish Republican Army (PIRA).[14] By the start of 1984, the same year that legislation creating SIRP and the SIS was passed in the Portuguese parliament, they had blown up the offices of Air France and Lufthansa situated on Lisbon's Avenida da Liberdade, attacked the GNR's headquarters, and even "recovered" $800,000 from various banks.[15]

Over the course of the summer of 1984, using intelligence received from collaborators, Portuguese police arrested seventy-seven FP-25 members, including leading military officers, during Operation Orion.[16] The fact that the group's operational core had evaded capture, however, soon became clear after bombs were detonated outside major businesses on the same day that the detainees were arraigned in court.[17] Their continued attacks offered the SIS its first chance to handle an adversary that was causing concern both in Portugal and abroad.[18] Throughout the years leading to 1988, a gradual deterioration of the group's capabilities led to inactivity. This resulted in the group not posing a threat.[19] By achieving this aim, SIRP and the SIS fulfilled their purpose and displayed a remarkable ability to collect intelligence that ensured public safety. Of note is the fact that not a single major terrorist incident has occurred since the early 1980s in Portugal, whether from domestic or international groups.

Areas beyond military intelligence collection, such as counterterrorism, were not the military's strong suit. By the early 1980s, this weakness and its unfortunate outcomes had come to symbolize the overextension of the military's resources into areas that were inappropriate—not just in terms of intelligence collection but in civilian affairs in general. Thus, in 1982 Portugal's democratic politicians decided to draw a line on the recent past with major revisions to the country's constitution. Among the most important changes was the abolition of the MFA's Revolutionary Council and the restriction of DIFNO to military intelligence collection by a new defense law.[20] With these two actions, the way was clear in 1984 for the creation of a new intelligence organization that was to be staffed and controlled by civilians working for the benefit of Portuguese citizens rather than the state.

This created opportunities for experienced intelligence officers to join one of three potential new intelligence organizations: the SIS, responsible for counterterrorism; SIED, responsible for foreign intelligence; and the SIM, which would focus on military intelligence.[21] This division of responsibilities was important not only because it matched the model established by other Western democracies but also because it distinguished military intelligence collection that the armed forces had specialized in up to this point from the foreign and domestic intelligence collection that had been their Achilles' heel.

Due to critical junctures, such as 9/11 in the US and the attacks in Madrid, the Portuguese intelligence service continued to adjust in order to tackle this new threat. To ensure that this new threat is targeted properly, Portugal created the Unidade de Coordenação Antiterrorismo (UKAT: Counter-Terrorism Coordination Unit) in 2003 and also introduced a number of additional reforms.[22] UCAT brought together the services linked to antiterrorism, including the PCP, the SIS, the PSP, the GNR, the Borders and Foreigners Service, and the National Maritime Authority.[23] UCAT has indeed been the first step in "horizontal cooperation" with the UCAT's Joint Terrorism Analysis Center, collecting data and making risk assessments on a collective basis among "interested parties."[24]

Regardless, UCAT is limited because "it is neither a coordinating and centralising of information body on the phenomenon of terrorism, nor an actual agency of operational coordination."[25] Interestingly the findings outlined by the EU member countries provided by the peer review exercise of September 2005 underline the need for an intelligence and operational unit to be included as well as a decision-making entity.[26] In order to upgrade Portugal's security system, the country adopted a strategy that included strengthening preventive measures and combating crime and modernizing the services whose role is to protect its citizens. As a result, Portugal aligned its strategy with that of the EU, which included the incorporation of EU legal instruments into domestic law, the increase of resources (both material and human) for investigation purposes, and the establishment of coordination functions in order to tackle terrorist threats.[27] In 2020, on the SIS's website, threats to Portugal were defined as follows:

- Transnational Terrorism
- Classic Espionage
- Economic Espionage
- Organised Crime
- Ideological and Religious Extremism
- Money Laundering
- International Trafficking of Weapons of Mass Destruction (WMD)—Proliferation
- Trafficking of Human Beings and Illegal Migration
- Cybercrime
- New Types of Crime

The intelligence service highlights that the threats are "diverse, unpredictable and transnational," while it underlines that it is "strictly politically-neutral and ensures internal security through its exclusive mission of producing security intelligence, indispensable to maintaining the Rule of Law as set in the constitution."[28]

Equally, on SIED's official website, emphasis is put on the service's main objective, which is to "safeguard national independence, national interests and the external security of the Portuguese State," while always being in compliance with the Portuguese constitution. Based on that, the agency focuses on the following external threats that can harm internal security:

- International terrorist threats, international organized crime, including drug trafficking, illegal immigration and CBRN proliferation
- The security of the Portuguese communities abroad
- Early warning on events that could "compromise" the national interests
- The political, social, economic, energy and defense priorities of the Portuguese foreign policy[29]

SIED specifies its cooperation with internal counterparts within SIRP, as well as other Portuguese law enforcement agencies, to "protect the country, its people and its interests."[30] The adaptation of the legislative instruments in the declaration on terrorism of the European Council on March 25, 2004, and others emphasized by the United Nations in the fight against terrorism were incorporated in the Portuguese domestic law.[31] As an example, the offenses of terrorism, terrorism financing, and terrorism organization, which have been criminalized in Portugal since 1982, were revoked due to Law 52/2003 (Law on Combating Terrorism), which "transposed" into the Portuguese legal system the European Council's Framework Decision 2002/475/JHA. This new law, which resulted in Article 300 (about terrorist organizations) and Article 301 (about terrorism) of the Penal Code being revoked, underlines the punishment of terrorist acts, terrorist groups, and terrorist organizations. It also clearly defines what constitute offenses of terrorism, international terrorism, terrorist organizations, and terrorist groups.[32] One of the key elements in the Portuguese institutional structures as well as the law is the fact that there is a clear distinction among the activities that fall under the judiciary, the police, and intelligence organizations, respectively.[33] This means that there is not one organization only that controls the processes of collection and analysis through to prosecution.[34]

The law specifies that the SIS is prohibited from using covert means to collect evidence, including cautionary and police measures. This means that it cannot "conduct searches or undercover operations, nor enforce coercive measures or guarantee of patrimony, because it has no explicit legal coverage for this kind of work." Undercover operations can take place as part of a criminal investigation only and with the Judicial Police's direct or indirect intervention.[35] Despite that, as Rui Carlos Pereira notes, nothing prevents an intelligence agent from concealing his identity to collect information on a terrorist organization through contact with a member. The problem only arises if this agent is supposed to engage in preparatory or executive criminal acts for preventing a threat to internal security.[36] Intelligence officers, as Pereira writes, can engage in those acts if the democratic rule of law and security of the state are threatened. Therefore, an intelligence officer can justify actions such as providing a terrorist group with false documents to gain their trust by the right of necessity. This is linked to the notion of "proportionality" highlighted elsewhere in this book, whereby the interests that the officer serves are "more important than the ones which he overrules."[37]

Portugal focused on real, relevant threats from the start and with a robust control and oversight system in place managed to deal with those threats effectively. With this solid base from the foundation of SIRP in 1984, the intelligence organizations continued to upgrade and evolve with the new international and domestic environment and threats. Portugal's demilitarization and uprooting of authoritarian legacies through lustration helped establish a clear division between military and civilian intelligence organizations, allowing them to focus on real threats to national security, with no systematic abuses having been reported.

GREECE

If Portugal adopted a "revolutionary" approach to reform, Greece's approach was much more conservative. This was again a result of the conservative nature of Prime Minister Konstantinos Karamanlis, who returned to Greece to head a national unity government in 1974, as well as an authoritarian culture that persisted after the fall of the junta.[38] For while the MFA aimed to create a new order in Portugal by dismantling existing state institutions and implementing a progressive political program, Karamanlis limited himself to simply restoring what had been lost in 1967. This included the operational reputation of Greece's national intelligence organization, the KYP, which had declined somewhat under the junta regime due to the way in which major tasks had been granted to the ESA. Its subsequent subdued role in junta-sanctioned repressive activity made it easier for Karamanlis to try to reform the KYP rather than dissolve it altogether. Yet it also aided the notion that the KYP was not an organization in need of serious changes. Main "enemies of the state" continued to be Greek communists, while antijunta dissidents were also added to the agenda.[39]

Indeed, in the late 1970s, the governing ideology of the organization remained much unchanged from that which had occupied it in the 1960s and the 1950s. Communism remained the biggest threat in many minds, even in the face of evidence that the threats facing Greece were beginning to change substantially. This much became clear in 1975 when the CIA's chief of station in Athens, Richard Welch, was assassinated.[40] After having been identified as a member of the CIA by sections of the Greek media and East German press, Welch was targeted and killed by Revolutionary Organization 17 November. Taking its name from the date President Papadopoulos crushed the Athens Polytechnic uprising in 1973, the group chose "such a high-profile target for its first act in order to attract international publicity and to establish credibility as a revolutionary organisation" and was one of the most prominent groups of domestic terrorism.[41] Following this, the group went on to list its intentions to free Greece from "imperialist" American influence and to avenge the way "104 junta ministers, military commanders and police torturers had received nugatory sentences in the courts."[42] Welch's death marked the start of what would become a twenty-seven-year terrorist campaign.

Later that decade, however, the democratic rule entailed an appropriate response to the new threat. To facilitate this, Karamanlis put forward legislation for the 1978 Greek antiterrorism bill.[43] This clearly set out the legal parameters within which the KYP and the police could combat 17 November and any other groups like it, which at the beginning seemed like a step forward in terms of targeting and moving closer to democratic practices. In an illustration on how strongly the recent past had affected popular opinion, however, the bill was challenged by opposition politicians for the way in which it failed to define the "terrorism" it was meant to counter. Because of this, it was claimed that the bill would simply facilitate and legalize the kind of repressive intelligence activity that had occurred during the junta period.[44] This activity had resulted in "a negative surveillance culture and a popular mistrust of any state and police surveillance" and meant that Greeks were "afraid of any state and police filing, which can potentially classify them and their family members to exclude them from public benefits."[45] Accordingly, the bill was only passed in a watered-down form under the general designation of Special Penal Law. This came without the support of the main opposition party, namely Andreas Papandreou's newly formed left-wing party, PASOK. Consequently, the KYP was put in an unenviable position: tasked with neutralizing 17 November but without the legislative powers it needed to carry out activities effectively, without a majority of the Greek parliament's consent, and with the intense suspicion of the Greek population in general.

By choosing not to dissolve and replace the KYP when he was elected the first postjunta prime minister in late 1974, the conservative Karamanlis bequeathed his successor, the socialist Papandreou, an intelligence organization that was very similar to its original. At the top was a military officer and on all rungs of the management chain were other military officers on secondment. Karamanlis had previously sought to reduce the military's dominance by opening up the KYP's recruitment to university students and by giving civilian personnel more room for promotion. Despite this, however, the KYP remained a highly militarized organization at the start of the 1980s. The lack of civilians in key positions maintained its dangerous historical tendencies, which typically framed legitimate political opposition members as "enemies of the state." This remained difficult to overcome, given the tendency of military staff to honor tradition. Therefore, while on paper all members of the KYP answered to the prime minister, military staff were often unwilling to jeopardize their careers in the armed forces as a whole by going against the wishes of their military commanders.[46] This is particularly key as we can observe the inherent issues the service has faced when attempting to become a fairer, more democratic organization. To that end, a stickiness to an authoritarian-like culture is showcased. Indeed, in the 1950s the service was under the Geniko Epiteleio Ethinkis Aminas (GEETHA; Hellenic National Defense General Staff), and the perpetuation of the military's influence into the twenty-first century, as described by Pavlos Apostolidis, serves as an important reminder of the difficulties that Greek civilian authorities have had in ensuring effective democratic control over the national intelligence services, which has been obstructed by persistence of nondemocratic behavior.[47] The nepotism and favoritism that exist within the service come up as key factors that impede reform, one of the main issues being recruitment based on political affiliations with the party in office while the candidates' competencies are generally deemed irrelevant.[48]

The continued militarization of the service by legacy personnel affected the targeting process. Despite efforts by policymakers (in this instance Karamanlis) to establish a legal framework and redirect the KYP toward real threats, legacies of the past inhibited this process. Once again, therefore, we see how pernicious and sticky the legacies of nondemocratic regimes are. Factors that support progress, such as the policymaker's willingness to reform, cannot have a complete and true impact if the authoritarian legacies still exist within the intelligence institutions.

Additionally, surveillance operations against Greek socialists and communists continued until the middle of 1977.[49] This was several years after Karamanlis had legalized the KKE, so the legitimate need of the KYP to monitor its members and gather intelligence had evaporated. This unwarranted interference stemmed directly from Karamanlis's inheritance of an "overdeveloped, coercive security apparatus, which continued to restrict civil liberties and intrude into citizens' private lives, sorting them according to their political beliefs."[50] That they continued to pursue these kinds of activities was the result of a lingering official skepticism of citizens' rights as "autonomous individuals" and the idea of individual rights to privacy.[51] Thus, they were prepared to use the legal loopholes available to them to continue past practices that were questionable in the new political climate. This included exploiting the revised 1975 constitution, which stated that while "erroneously entering and searching a specific citizen's residence was unlawful," generally intercepting communications "on the grounds of national security" was still allowed.[52] The continuous pursuit of the KKE meant that real threats such as domestic terrorist groups were disregarded. Foremost among them, apart from the 17 November, was Epanastatikos Laikos Agonas (ELA; Revolutionary People's Struggle). As previously discussed, the KYP was admittedly hindered by flawed legislation that did not provide the service with credible powers in the fight against terrorism. It was also undermined by a lack of popular support, which is a testament to the lingering hatred caused by the junta, resulting in public sympathy for the terrorist groups. 17 November was able to exploit such sentiments by defining the KYP and Karamanlis as puppets of the United States, an easy win in a country then receptive to anti-Americanism. As one of their first communiqués stated, "Enough is enough. The American imperialists and their domestic agents [the KYP] must understand that the Greek people are not a flock of sheep."[53]

Public sympathy waned, though, as it became clear that 17 November was interested on waging a total war on all levels of Greek political society, even against the KKE. "Against all enemies," therefore, 17 November aimed to achieve its objectives through violence. The group consequently rejected charges from other left-wing groups that such violent tactics were counterproductive, arguing that its actions "shouldn't be seen as isolated acts of violence, but as parts of a long-term, multifaceted revolutionary process."[54]

Papandreou played a key role in focusing the KYP on the wrong "threat" during this crucial time as he believed himself to be a victim of state surveillance in the past. So, he set out to change the way the KYP behaved by staffing it with party loyalists, but this also had the effect of changing its operational focus. On one hand, there were positive changes, such as the passing of Law Decree 1415/84, which formally reoriented the KYP's operational aim away from targeting any number of Greek citizens associated with the political Left.[55] On the other, however, PASOK also curtailed the 1978 Special Penal Law, which the Karamanlis government had introduced specifically to counter terrorist groups like 17 November. This would not have been problematic had PASOK passed a new law, but instead nothing was done. As the group had secretly paused its terrorist campaign when PASOK took power, the authorities naively reasoned that "Greek terrorism was an ephemeral phenomenon attributed to a group of Far Left militants, which had auto-dissolved and did not pose any serious security threat."[56] Accordingly, the then minister of law, George Mangakis, felt comfortable enough to declare that "terrorism in Greece is nonexistent" before the antiterrorism law was eventually repealed in May 1983.[57] Indeed, when arguing in favor of this action, "PASOK made no modifications to its original argument that [Law] 774 was dangerous, unconstitutional, and 100 per cent unnecessary."[58] It was only five months later that 17 November began to encourage the opposite idea.

On the morning of November 15, 1983, US Navy captain George Tsantes and his driver were stopped at an intersection in the Athens suburb of Halandri when a motorcycle pulled alongside them. Its two riders shot the occupants of the car several times, leaving Captain Tsantes dead and his driver badly wounded.[59] Linking 17 November to the crime was the use of the same .45 caliber pistol that had killed Richard Welch in 1975. This was followed by the wounding of another US serviceman in April 1984 and a campaign of sporadic violence and crime from 1985 onward. Despite this violent resurgence, PASOK dismissed claims that 17 November posed any kind of threat worth pursuing. Instead, the government remained insistent that "the terrorist incidents were isolated occurrences of violence that were in no way central to the Greek political and social life, and in no way comparable to the terrorist problems of Italy, Germany, or Spain."[60]

Accordingly, the official response to the terrorism affecting Greece in the early 1980s was lethargic and inconsistent. As John M. Nomikos states, "neither an anti-terrorist strategy nor any strict measures were adopted in response," and most notably "the PASOK government did not examine the links between indigenous terrorism and the resistance groups, from which PASOK itself had risen."[61] This position was at odds with much of the rest of Europe's focus on developing intelligence capabilities specifically for counterterrorism, which had started gathering momentum since Black September's attack on the 1972 Munich Olympics. The KYP was, therefore, at a complete disadvantage when it began receiving pressure from American and European services to investigate the links between Greek terrorists and transnational terrorist groups such as the ELA and individuals such as "Carlos the Jackal" and Johannes Weinrich of the German urban guerrilla group Revolutionary Cells. Each of these had cooperated in an assassination attempt against the Saudi Arabian ambassador to Greece in 1983, and it was expected that other ELA members training in Lebanon would contribute to similar attacks in the future.

While ostensibly happy to help combat such violence, in reality PASOK displayed little appetite to empower the KYP or other elements of the state to do anything. This showed how prejudiced members of the then government remained against empowering the Greek security services. After having suffered "the dictatorship's wanton use of brutality," much suspicion and unenthusiasm remained for any initiative that promoted stricter security controls.[62] Instead, to the frustration of many other governments, PASOK preferred to receive and provide safe passage to some of the same groups and individuals that were perceived to be committing attacks on Greek soil. This was made more obvious after Israel drove Yasser Arafat and the PLO out of Lebanon in 1982. Despite losing their main base of operation, the PLO and its affiliates were able to continue making attacks against Israeli targets, a large number of which began occurring in Greece. Starting in 1982, Palestinian terrorists assassinated a Jordanian diplomat in Athens before following this up with an attack against the Jordanian embassy itself in 1983. The list of potential targets expanded again in 1984, when the British Council member Kenneth Whitty was also assassinated in Athens after being presumed to be a member of MI6.[63]

These attacks, which were coordinated by Abu Nidal and members of Black September, continued gathering pace throughout the 1980s with atrocities occurring in 1985. In that year, Abu Nidal's rogue splinter organization bombed the offices of the Royal Jordanian Airlines in Rome, Athens, and Cyprus.[64] Having had their reach curtailed by PASOK, the KYP and the Greek police services proved unable to stop these attacks or apprehend Nidal and his associates. After losing track of his whereabouts in 1984, it was not until 1987 that they became aware Nidal had arrived in Athens to liaise with Palestinian groups. Remarkably, he was not arrested at this time, as it was claimed by the United States that "the Greek government had made a deal with Abu Nidal which would exempt the country from terrorist activity."[65] Consequently Nidal was able to continue his campaign of terrorism against non-Greek targets, including three attacks in 1988 against the Israeli embassy in Cyprus, an attack against the ship *City of Poros* in Athens, and a bomb attack in Trokadero. An understanding of PASOK's inactivity against Palestinian terrorism on its soil can be drawn from its history of pro-Arab inclinations and pro-Palestinian sentiments in particular.[66] It was for this reason that Greece was the first member of the European Community to grant full diplomatic recognition to the PLO.[67] It is also why it gave Yasser Arafat a de facto state welcome when he visited Athens in 1982 and why the KYP could not act against the PLO's terrorist affiliates, even when they had intelligence that they might be plotting attacks within Greece.[68]

PASOK's politicization of the KYP in this regard also extended to the way the organization handled anti-Turkish militant groups. This included the Armenian Secret Army for the Liberation of Armenia (ASALA), and the Partiya Karkerên Kurdistanê (PKK; Kurdistan Workers' Party). Throughout the 1970s, ASALA conducted attacks against Turkish targets throughout Europe and the Middle East. Several occurred in Athens, and like Israel, Turkey soon accused Greece of facilitating terrorism against its interests.[69] This rhetoric only increased once the PKK began armed activity against the Turkish state in 1984. Like ASALA, the PKK distilled a large amount of its operational support from the diaspora community in Europe. Its members on the continent were instructed to either collect funds or to prepare attacks. The KYP was well aware of this and had the ability to disrupt the group's supply line from Europe to the Near East. However, PASOK instructed the KYP to not interfere with the PKK's operations because any member they arrested would have to be deported to Turkey. There they would likely be tortured and executed, and since Turkey was no friend of Greece, there was no harm in ignoring what the group was doing in Greece or simply "redirecting resources elsewhere."[70] This viewpoint was again habitual and based on many years of Greek antagonism against Turkey. Such engrained bias was not resolved by the KYP's transformation into the EYP in 1986.

From 1989 to 1993, the EYP benefited under the government led by the Nea Dimokratia (ND; New Democracy), a liberal-conservative political party, thanks to improved relations with Western intelligence services. As a result of their obsession with the historical involvement of the United States and Britain in Greek affairs, PASOK's ministers had actively spurned the two countries' efforts at cooperation. So disheartened by this were senior CIA and MI6 officials that after Panagiotis Bales became director of the EYP in 1990, he received formal complaints about the service's previous lack of cooperation.[71] They had little reason to complain, however, during the temporary time that New Democracy was in power. Indeed, having always criticized PASOK for the lethargic way in which it had responded to the different terrorist groups operating on Greek soil, New Democracy went out of its way to clamp down once in power. After having passed a new antiterrorist law—No. 1916/90—"which included a clause that banned the terrorist's proclamations from being published," the authorities went after the different Palestinian groups that still maintained a residual presence in Greece in the early 1990s.[72] Consequently, during raids throughout Athens on March 5, 1991, many Palestinians were arrested, and caches of weapons and explosives were uncovered. Several Greek terrorists were also picked up at the same time, including an individual who had been tried in Italy for the hijacking of the cruise ship *Achille Lauro*.[73] For the first time, the Greek government established laws that targeted real threats to national security and gave the intelligence service and the police the capability to pursue those targets.

Soon after this, the EYP focused its attentions on a Palestinian cell in Patras. On April 3, 1991, local police forces were advised to look out for the president of the Palestinian Student Union who had been identified as a member of Islamic Jihad. This was followed by warnings on April 16, 1991, that pointed to new information that a Palestinian, Abu al-Nubani, was planning to launch an attack against the British consulate in Patras.[74] Al-Nubani had been deported from Greece in February 1991 but managed to use a visa obtained in Algiers to get back into the country. According to EYP sources, Algeria at the time offered sanctuary to Palestinian bomb makers and terrorist trainers, and this is where the group received financial support.[75] Armed with this information, local security forces searched for al-Nubani and his associates but failed to apprehend them before a bomb one of them was carrying exploded and killed seven people.[76] The EYP knew that al-Nubani had communicated with someone in Algeria on April 15 and had received a green light to carry out his attack. His residence in Patras was not known, but rarely had the EYP generated such good intelligence on a potential terrorist attack. At the subsequent trial of al-Nubani and an associate, Ibrahim Bairat, it emerged that the Diéfthynsi Kratikís Asfáleias (DIKA; Directorate of State Security) had not informed the Patras police about what was going to happen. DIKA did not specify why this omission had occurred. Regardless, as a result of the link between the bombers and the PLO, five of the group's diplomats were expelled from the country as well as twenty other Palestinian civilians.[77] Although the EYP had been unable to prevent al-Nubani's bombing, his subsequent arrest and prosecution and the dismantling of his wider network ensured that no further Palestinian attacks occurred in Greece in the near term.

Despite these steps forward, though, more issues arose because of targeting the "wrong" threats, something that continued to bring up cooperation issues with foreign states. An example was the exposure of a US State Department employee who was spying for the EYP while employed at the US embassy in Athens. Steven Lalas was arrested by the Federal Bureau of Investigation (FBI) in 1993 and charged with providing classified information to the EYP.[78] The FBI's case against Lalas was an indictment of the strength of the EYP's agent-running capability. The EYP also made the mistake of transferring some of Lalas's material throughout the organization without redacting his personal details. This occurred due to the high volume of information that Lalas's was providing and the need to translate it rapidly.[79] According to one source, "Lalas was paid to pass information to a Greek official for most of the two years that he was posted in Athens." Altogether this amounted to roughly $20,000 for 240 documents.[80] The director of the EYP, Pavlos Apostolidis, worked hard to limit the damage of this incident while making sure that similar issues did not occur in the future. His efforts at damage control were made all the more difficult, however, due to the poor relations that the EYP had with the Greek Foreign Ministry. Indeed, many senior diplomats believed that the EYP was incompetent and that it delivered poor-quality information to policymakers. As Apostolidis found, this may have had something to do with the fact that all EYP officers that happened to interact with the Foreign Ministry were of "low quality." For their part, though, most EYP officers believed that diplomatic personnel were "inadequate" and "concessive" in patriotic matters.[81]

Additionally, more terrorist-related incidents occurred. On June 8, 2000, in an attack reminiscent of the murder of Richard Welch twenty-five years earlier, members of 17 November assassinated British defense attaché Stephen Saunders in Athens.[82] With each successive Greek government having failed to arrest or capture a single member of the group since it had begun its terrorist campaign, one of PASOK's stated priorities after winning the 1993 general election had been to dismantle this group.[83] This need was all the more pressing due to the way in which 17 November had evolved from 1985 onward, when it had begun its "second phase" of activity. From this time, the group expanded from conducting simple assassinations to "car bombings, rocket attacks, and Irish Republican Army (IRA) style improvised mortar bombardments."[84] A change in Greek strategy in 1989 had not altered this state of affairs even with the introduction of new counterterrorism measures and the transformation of the Greek police service.[85] PASOK's own post-1993 strategy was immediately undermined by the abolition of the 1916/90 antiterrorism law on the basis that it restricted freedom of expression.[86] With no replacement law brought in to make up for the legislative void the EYP faced, Greece's security environment declined to the point where NATO declared that Greece was the most dangerous place in Europe for US diplomats, businessmen, and tourists. By 1999 this culminated in Greece's own acknowledgment of the danger posed by groups such as 17 November, when MPS minister Michalis Chrisochoidis cited the threat and mentioned that the families of many victims had suffered silently after the 17 November attacks.[87] This is an interesting point because although bureaucracies tend to show resistance and reluctance to change, in the Greek case we observe that, for the second time, the service was experiencing a moment of truth (like during the Cyprus crisis) and raised the issue of terrorism as an actual threat.

Despite this declaration of intent, though, and incredibly after so many years, the EYP still lacked any solid information on the composition of 17 November, its intentions, and its capabilities, given that it was not a priority or targeted threat previously.[88] Even this information did not receive adequate analysis from Greek intelligence officers, who "appeared to have difficulties understanding what the terrorists wrote in their manifestos and communiqués."[89] This again illustrated the negative implications of the EYP's limited recruitment process, which favored those already in uniform and not likely to understand the more extreme fringes of Greek society. This is particularly interesting, as even when information was gathered on real threats, it could not be properly analyzed due to the inability of uniformed staff. Yet again, legacies of the authoritarian past obstructed the process. This cultural weakness paired with the EYP's relatively weak technical capabilities meant that it relied upon British investigators to help it begin tracking Saunders's killers. As Nomikos states, "the British were very systematic and brought good know-how, developing relevant wiretaps and other technical evidence. Additionally, the involvement of the Scotland Yard team was not received with the same suspicions and negatives as American participation."[90] It was this provision of expertise that ultimately led to the capture of 17 November's leadership rather than any independent breakthrough or development of expertise by the EYP, a cooperation that also helped to tackle illegal immigration via Turkey.[91] This aligns with what Florina Cristiana Matei and Thomas Bruneau classify as influence of foreign assistance whereby "visits, exchange of experts and advisors, education and training for intelligence personnel and outsiders, have resulted in . . . increased expertise of the intelligence agents."[92]

Presidential Decree 255/2002 gave the EYP more responsibilities in terms of targeting threats, which up to that point fell under the remit of the police. These included organized crime, illegal immigration, and drug trafficking, with emphasis being put on an annual report on the EYP's activities that has to be shared with the Greek parliament.[93] As explained in chapter 4, legislation regarding the EYP was not linked to the constitution's human rights and civil liberties. This only changed relatively recently with Law 3649/2008, which specifically underlined the following:

- The prevention and confrontation of activities that pose a threat to the democratic state, the fundamental human rights, the territorial integrity and the national security of the Greek State, as well as the national wealth of the Country.
- Preventing and dealing with the activities of terrorist organizations, as well as other organized crime groups.[94]

Indeed, several scandals (including the wiretapping of top-level government officials allegedly by the US), failures such as the Öcalan affair, and key events such as the 2004 Olympic Games in Athens have spurred the EYP to take steps forward in the past two decades, at least when it comes to a legal basis for targeting oversight, as well as a few practical measures.[95] For example, the EYP signed an agreement with the European Anti-Fraud Office (OLAF) in 2004. OLAF was interested in protecting the EU's financial interests by signing this agreement. In return, OLAF provided the EYP with financial resources for the purchase of technical equipment, something that would help with combating modern and relevant national threats.[96] More recently, it is only the aforementioned legal framework that provides a road map to the type of threats that the Greek intelligence service targets rather than any examples of the service's successes.

On the EYP's website in 2021, the following targets, among others, are specified as threats to national security:

- Terrorism
- Organized crime
- Financial crime
- Illegal migration
- Drug trafficking
- Cyber-crime[97]

SPAIN

In a reflection of both the Franco regime's paranoia and its extensive bureaucracy, Spain had a multitude of organizations all engaged in one form of intelligence collection or another when the king appointed Adolfo Suárez prime minister in 1976. This included the Ministry of Foreign Affairs, the Ministry of Information and Tourism, the Ministry of Trade Union Relations, as well as the Army, Navy, and Air Force Ministries, whose Second Sections advised on military intelligence matters.[98] The involvement of these organizations came on top of intelligence collection by Spain's primary intelligence organizations, which were ostensibly civilian. Among them were the BPS, whose paramilitary nature and repressive credentials had been nurtured over many years, including brief periods of training by both the Nazi Gestapo and SS.[99] Other civilian intelligence organizations had only slightly less reprehensible credentials. The SECED for example, had originally been tasked with monitoring subversion in 1972 when Spain's intelligence and security sector was already a crowded field. Its innovative tendencies stood out, however, when it "created the first computerised register of people and their activities, extending control, for the first time, to areas and activities not strictly political, but also related to trade union activity, student activism, and 'religious and intellectual' deviance."[100] Although he disagreed with their previous use, these were exactly the kind of capabilities that Suárez valued when he came to power. This was one of the reasons he relied on the SECED "to connect with President Tarradellas of Catalonia and *Lehendakari* (President) Leizola of the Basque region—both in exile—to ask them for their support in the transition process."[101] While reforming other elements of the Spanish intelligence community was quite straightforward, deciding what to do with the SECED was a more difficult matter.

Ironically, this was a problem that the previous Francoist government had also already struggled with. Although the SECED came under the control of the Ministry of Interior, its roots lead back to the Ministry of Defense and the army's High Command. Indeed, its immediate forerunner had been the OCN, a subsection of the Spanish military's SIAEM.[102] As discussed earlier, the OCN had infiltrated student subversive groups in the tumultuous year of 1968, and the SECED had taken over and expanded this work to include other areas from 1972 onward.[103] This had automatically put the SECED on a collision course with other components of the Franco regime. To prevent it from duplicating the work already being done by the paramilitary Guardia Civil, the Spanish military, and others, a high-level Commission of National Coordination of Information for State Security was created on September 26, 1973. This was chaired by the president and composed of the vice president, the interior minister, and other senior cabinet members. Its primary purpose was to centralize Spain's intelligence-collection processes and curtail the various inefficiencies and duplications of effort that pervaded the system.[104]

Despite such high-level representation, this commission failed in its efforts and left Suárez with the same problem to solve as when he came to power, albeit with the even more pressing consideration of how to democratize intelligence collection. Indeed, although Suárez and Manuel Gutiérrez Mellado's "provisional" reforms streamlined Spanish intelligence collection, they had the effect of militarizing it even further, with the presence of personnel from SIAEM's Third Section making CESID's internal composition very much like that of the KYP in Greece. Indeed, it was only five years later that CESID would begin recruiting civilians into its ranks.[105] As a result, Mellado's objective of creating "a new intelligence service that would break with the methods of espionage associated with the days of Franco and [that] would become a staunch ally in the difficult transition to democracy" was weakened from the outset.[106] These issues would not be fully resolved until as late as 2002—almost thirty years after the start of Spain's democratic transition.

Maj. José Luís Cortina, the leader of CESID's elite AOME, cherished all power and acted completely autonomously. The only cosmetic control feature was Javier Calderón, CESID'S director, who simply asked the organization to do his bidding. The major would then carry out missions, collecting information "without answering to anybody about his manner of obtaining it."[107] There was no oversight of the way information was collected. Such an arrangement defied the earlier legislative framework that Spanish deputies had created and ignored the increases in oversight that they were meant to entail. The fact that the Prime Minister, Adolfo Suárez, had previously had to intervene directly to stop CESID from pursuing illegal intelligence collection spoke volumes about just how effective these measures had been. He had to force CESID to dismantle the system of telephone tapping installed in Telefónica, the national telephone company.[108] Consequently, with such a wide gap between the amount of oversight that was in place on paper and what was applicable in reality, Spain's government was left vulnerable to threats emanating from some of the same individuals who had sworn to protect it. With the protection that el pacto del olvido had given them, they were free to take up positions in CESID and elsewhere and propagate the ideology and methodology of the Franco-era intelligence services.

It was perhaps inevitable that this would enable some kind of confrontation between the Francoists and the democratic government, especially given the growing sense of impatience that developed in official circles over Prime Minister Suárez's handling of the war against the ETA. This is not to say that Suárez was entirely unaware of the danger his government was in. It is certainly claimed that by 1981 he knew a coup was in the making and planned to forestall it by stepping down. The coup was not forestalled, however, since Leopoldo Calvo-Sotelo (Suárez's planned successor) appeared to have no program of his own and would continue the dead-end policies of Suárez.[109] At this time, the ETA also looked to actively contribute to the destabilization of the country by trying to showcase how inadequate the government was in responding to their threats and actions. To this end, its attacks on police and army officers from the late 1970s onward aimed to "incite the armed forces to a possible rebellion against the government."[110] This happened on February 23, 1981, when approximately two hundred members of the Guardia Civil under Lt. Col. Antonio Tejero stormed the Congress of Deputies while it was in session and took the entire lower parliament hostage.[111] Authoritarian elements and a nondemocratic culture were maintained within CESID from the outset. Not only was the service heavily militarized, but it was also targeting perceived enemies rather than real threats to national security.

After 1982 CESID was neither a civilian intelligence organization nor a de facto extension of the Spanish military. Instead, it was a hybrid organization tasked with collecting foreign intelligence, conducting counterespionage activities, securing classified NATO information, and conducting counterterrorism activities. It was to do so both for the minister of defense and the president—a new development that entailed CESID acting as both a collector and collator of intelligence, similar to the original specified function of the American CIA.[112]

In 1984 the Spanish Anti-Terrorism Law was established. It was then that it was possible to see for the first time—beyond the criteria already included in the constitution—the legal foundation upon which intelligence collection was being carried out. Court Judgment No. 199, which followed in 1987, further narrowed things by legally defining a terrorist group as one that stimulates a strong feeling of insecurity in members of the population so that "citizens are unable to exercise the fundamental rights inherent in their ordinary and habitual coexistence as members of society," which is particularly caused "by the use of the weapons in their possession and by the type of crimes they commit" and, finally, by the methodical commission of serious offenses using weapons and explosives.[113] On paper, such definitions and rulings again helped keep CESID on track by limiting its ability to legally pursue individuals that did not fit such a profile or come close to it but against whom intelligence officers may have borne a historical grievance—domestic communists, for example. CESID would operate in this manner against the ETA in concert with Spanish police forces up until 2002, when the exogenous shock of 9/11 encouraged the creation of the CNI.

For the period leading to 1995, the key issues pertaining to the Spanish intelligence community included the overlapping responsibilities across agencies as well as the constant shift in the intelligence services' objectives. The main focus was on "military involution" and terrorism, and it was only in the mid-1980s that the Spanish government instructed CESID to also focus outside Spain and establish a "foreign structure."[114] In 1995 Spanish media reported that the intelligence service had spied on several key individuals across the country, including journalists, businessmen, and even the king. This resulted in the vice president, the minister of defense and the director of CESID losing their jobs. The scandal was known as "the Perote case" due to documents appropriated by Juan Alberto Perote, a former intelligence services chief.[115] In addition, during the Partido Popular government in 1998, it was revealed that the CESID was spying on the political arm of the ETA, which at the time was a legal political party.[116] Authoritarian methods for collecting information continued while, as in Greece, perceived enemies or rivals were targeted. Once again, we can see that authoritarian remnants impeded progress.

As Antonio M. Díaz Fernández claims, throughout the years intelligence communities have proved to be "ineffective" in terms of providing early warnings to decision-makers. Diaz Fernández cites several attacks to underpin his claim, including those in New York, Bali, Madrid, London, Bombay, and just outside Washington. He highlights that the "roots" of these failures lie in the Cold War and include (a) the focus by the services on the wrong threat, (b) the disconnect between the decision-makers and the intelligence services, and

(c) the "inadequate" organization of the intelligence community.[117] All of the above points are evident in Spain's case. Following the 9/11 attacks, the CNI was created as the heir to CESID in 2002. The CNI's objective is to fight against "all the serious threats that menace Spain."[118] The most serious threat Spain had to tackle was international terrorism and its hit on Spanish soil on March 11, 2004.

11M is a great example that showcases Fernandez's argument. Indeed, when the attacks happened, Prime Minister José Maria Aznar quickly drove the conversation toward accusing the ETA of the bombings. However, the government's credibility started to diminish, with a lot of Spaniards believing that the former deliberately tried to blame the ETA. This was because its popularity would grow due to the broad public support for its hard-line stance against the ETA and reinforce its potential win in the upcoming general elections, which were to take place three days after the bombings.[119] A parliamentary commission was set up in June 2004 to investigate the attacks as well as the way the government responded. In the inquiry, several key issues were discussed, a few pertaining to the intelligence role and capabilities to fight the new threat of international terrorism. The inquiry highlighted the relevance of the threat and the need to be able to fight it: "The services, strategies and procedures regarding antiterrorism should, from then on, be suitable to the new circumstances." It also stated that Spain's security forces, including the CNI, had provided warnings with regard to the "growing threats of Islamist terrorism" and pointed out that this risk increased and became more visible as a consequence of Spain's participation in the Iraq War.[120] However, the report continues, saying that the policymakers did not adopt the "necessary measures to control this threat" despite the information provided to them by the security forces, while they also "distorted" the data provided and tried to "bias" the public on the entity responsible for the attacks.[121]

When it came to reevaluating the way Spain would be in a position to deal with international terrorism, José Antonio Alonso (interior minister from 2004 to 2006) said in October 2005 that the government began to make decisions "as soon as we took power or as soon as we possibly could make them. For this reason, the great majority of them naturally preceded the Commission's recommendations for action in this area."[122] It is key to note that as international terrorism had become priority, over three hundred people were arrested for being involved in related activities, and plans to carry out new attacks were stopped in time.[123] The commission underlined key steps within the report and with regard specifically to the security forces' activities against Islamist terrorism, including cooperation across institutions domestically and abroad, and legal measures for the collection and analysis of information and the control of sources that finance terrorism.

Indeed, very soon after the 2004 Madrid bombings, the decision was made to strengthen central police units of information and intelligence as well as their branches deployed on a local level.[124] The CNI received a significant boost in human as well as material resources after the Madrid attacks, while the creation of new units was established.[125] The CCN was to boost the government's defensive posture through training staff, certifying products, and acquiring security technology.[126] Another great initiative included the creation of the Centro Nacional de Coordinación Terrorista (CNCA: National Center for Antiterrorist Coordination). Part of the Plan to Combat Terrorism, which aims to combat all forms of terrorism, the CNCA is "a complementary and auxiliary organ of the State Security Forces, which will not itself take charge of their individual missions." Based on the law, it is clear that the CNI and its director are responsible for the day-to-day activities, while the direction of the whole of the Spanish intelligence community falls under the deputy prime minister.[127] The reforms that followed the Madrid attacks, though, brought to light other issues, such as intelligence coordination among agencies.[128]

As with Portugal, it took a critical juncture for Spain to start truly reforming. The Madrid attacks were indeed the key catalyst that facilitated reform, which had been impeded for decades due to authoritarian legacies. These included the militarization of the service as well as the targeting of perceived threats and the use of illegal means and methods to collect information. Additional limitations throughout the years contributed to the resistance of reform and are part of a continuous trend from previous chapters. These came up even during the turmoil of the 11M attacks and included the problematic relationship between decision-makers and the intelligence organizations. Indeed, as with a few examples in the Greek case, the Spanish intelligence organization provided timely warning and adequate intelligence on real threats that were not received well by the decision-makers. On the contrary, the latter tried to distort the intelligence and use it for political purposes. Of course, we have seen this happen in more mature democracies—the American case of alleged weapons of mass destruction in Iraq is the most prominent example. The point, though, remains that irrelevant threats were targeted for a long time, while illegal collection methods were systematically used.

CONCLUSION

Intelligence collection is a fundamental area of the intelligence cycle and indeed a key one when it comes to comparing an authoritarian with a democratic regime. In this chapter, emphasis was put on intelligence collection for Portugal, Greece, and Spain after their dictatorships fell in the 1970s. It asked whether real threats were targeted as opposed to perceived enemies and whether the methods used to collect information on these threats were lawful. Reference was also made to the rules and laws within the legal framework of each country, to see if there were proper oversight structures regarding targeting. In regard to targeting, Portugal seems to be ahead of the other two countries for several reasons.

Greece and Spain targeted perceived rather than real threats for a long time. Portugal focused on real threats right from the start, whereas Greece and Spain continued to focus on perceived threats. Indeed, the several terrorist attacks by the likes of FP-25 urged for the creation of a civilian intelligence service in Portugal. Terrorism was at the top of the agenda from the beginning, as it represented a real national threat to the country. Unlike Greece and Spain, Portugal recognized the significance of the terrorist threats in the early 1980s and quickly created a civilian intelligence service to deal with them. Although Greece and Spain faced similar threats, they disregarded them. Key to this approach were legacies of the past that impeded the services from focusing on real, relevant threats. The intelligence services were indeed politicized, with directors using them for their own benefit in Spain and policymakers militarizing them in Greece. This resulted in the pursuit of perceived threats. The EYP continued to focus on communism while ignoring terrorist activities coming from 17 November. Spain put an emphasis on student subversive groups in the early 1970s and the collection of intelligence that was useful for the armed forces the years after that. It was not until the critical junctures of 9/11 and 11M emerged in the early 2000s that Spain took important steps to reform and made counterterrorism a priority.

Portugal established a civilian intelligence service with clear responsibilities early on. Based on targeting, a clear set of specific responsibilities was established in Portugal. Not only did Portugal create a civilian intelligence service to deal with new threats at the time, but it also ensured that there was a division of responsibilities so each agency was aware of what fell under its remit. This included not only the country's intelligence services but also the police and the judiciary. Contrary to Portugal, the Greek intelligence service suffered from an unclear set of responsibilities and a high volume of seconded uniformed personnel who were not adequately qualified. This created issues regarding the types of tasks that fell to civilians and those that fell to uniformed staff. In Spain, on the other hand, there were far too many services involved in intelligence collection, again creating a blurry division of responsibilities across the different agencies. The legal framework was not clear enough, and the existence of multiple intelligence divisions created cooperation issues, an issue that was very prominent during the 11M inquiry.

Intelligence-collection methods used in Greece and Spain were illegal for a long time. Greece targeted communists as well as socialists in the 1970s and 1980s by using surveillance methods. Spain faced a series of scandals as it became public that the intelligence service was using illegal practices to collect information. This included the wiretapping of several high-ranking state officials, including the king. Contrary to Greece and Spain, Portugal, while focusing on real threats, also ensured that there was a robust legal framework with regard to any covert methods used. Under law, the notion of proportionality was clear, something that was completely absent both from a legal as well as a practical perspective in the other two.

The legal frameworks for targeting in Greece and Spain have been poor. Portugal managed to establish a strong legal framework with incorporating EU's strategy, with EU legal instruments embedded into domestic law and terrorism being at the top of the agenda when it came to national threats. Conversely, Greece struggled to provide the EYP with the necessary resources as well as clear objectives based on a robust legal framework when it came to real threats, such as terrorism. Poor antiterrorism laws were passed and removed several times. This correlates with the fact that Greece continued to suffer from 17 November's terrorist activity for twenty-five years. Inadequate legal framework for oversight of targeting, politicization of the intelligence services, with their directors using them as they saw fit, and weak recruitment and staffing issues contributed to another twenty-five years of 17 November terrorist attacks on Greek soil. The above meant that although Greece had started in the 1990s to face terrorism, it did not have the proper legal framework to support the Greek intelligence service to tackle it. Spain's strong efforts to tackle terrorism, a real threat, came into force only after the exogenous 9/11 attacks as well as the Madrid attacks. During the years following these critical junctures, Spain indeed made substantive progress in the intelligence-collection sphere, including the boost in resources as well as intelligence cooperation.

We can see a correlation between the poor control and oversight framework that existed in Greece and Spain, which resulted in intelligence failures and scandals, with policymakers and intelligence directors acting as they pleased when it came to intelligence matters. Indeed, evidence seems to suggest that oversight was ineffective in Spain and Greece—scandals including the GAL affair in Spain and the Vodafone case in Greece demonstrated this quite clearly. On the other hand, Portugal is a harder case to measure. Its absence of scandals does not constitute evidence of effective oversight, but at the same time there are no systematic examples or data to showcase the opposite. Lack of scandals might correlate with effective oversight, but it would be impossible to demonstrate causation in the absence of some form of evidence that would allow us to process-trace oversight action through to some change in behavior from Portuguese intelligence. The main point that available data suggests, based mainly on the CFSIRP's reports, is that the Portuguese intelligence service abides by democratic rules, principles, and behavior.

Politicization of intelligence collection as well as civil society sentiment were key catalysts that emerged in the available literature. During authoritarian regimes, intelligence agencies become politicized "as politicians use them to deter and remove potential political adversaries, aggressive investigative journalists, and other possible opponents."[129] Politicization is "often alleged to be a defining characteristic of autocratic and totalitarian regimes" and, as analyzed in previous chapters, civil society plays a key role in holding intelligence services to account.[130] At times, though, civil society can act as a barrier to reform rather than support it. Greek society demonstrated distrust toward the KYP in the 1980s due to negative sentiment from the junta period. This resulted in an effort to establish a legal framework to fight terrorism with no support from civil society. Additionally, this leftover negative sentiment toward the junta and its practices meant that Andreas Papandreou politicized intelligence collection as well as recruitment. Similarly, in Spain, civil society was disengaged from CECID. This took place until scandals, such as the GAL affair, started to emerge. At the same time, Manuel Gutiérrez Mellado, along with other individuals in charge of CESID, used the service the way they desired. There was no knowledge of the methods they used until the Perote case came to light. Spain has taken more steps to foster the involvement of civil society in intelligence affairs in the past two decades, as will be analyzed in chapter 7.

With regard to targeting, both Greece and Spain have taken steps to focus on actual threats in more recent decades. However, it should be remembered that there always exists an interlinked relationship between the intelligence services and the policymakers. As it became apparent in chapter 3 with regard to each country's purging approach and in this chapter with regard to politicization, policymakers can be at fault when intelligence services suffer from a failure. Policymakers can ignore good intelligence, as evidenced by the 11M case, and they can use the intelligence service and the data provided to them for their own political agenda. It is therefore key to understand that it is not just about intelligence services not getting it right—it is also about ensuring that policymakers use intelligence for the citizens' safety and security and not for their own political gain. Additionally, it is important to also focus on educating policymakers on what intelligence means and how intelligence services work.

Interagency cooperation was another issue that came up when looking at intelligence targeting. Indeed, Portugal established UCAT, which focused on terrorism. Its purpose was interagency cooperation. Although this agency had its shortcomings, in this regard Portugal was still miles ahead of Greece and Spain. No incidents have been documented or reported in the available literature as to any interagency issues within the Portuguese intelligence community. Greece suffered several intelligence failures due to the lack of interagency cooperation, particularly with the police. A key example was the case of Abu al-Nubani. More cases like that of Steven Lalas also showcased poor cooperation between the Greek and foreign intelligence services, such as the MI6 and CIA. To this day, Greece suffers from turf wars among its agencies, an element that creates issues when it comes to intelligence collection. At the same time, in Spain, because of the increased number of agencies, there was a duplication of efforts, evidenced by the lack of interagency cooperation. However, Spain has taken bigger steps to establish a solid interagency cooperation framework since the Madrid attacks.

As analyzed in previous chapters, democratization is a process and not an end destination. When comparing Portugal, Greece, and Spain with regard to intelligence collection, it is evident that Portugal has made more steps. It indeed targeted real threats with the establishment of its first civilian intelligence service, while it also focused on founding a proper legal framework that ensures illegal practices that can violate human rights are not allowed within a democratic rule of government. Nonetheless, Greece and Spain have made some positive steps toward democratization in terms of intelligence targeting the past two decades. After 9/11 and 11M, both countries focused on targeting relevant and real threats while slowly trying to set out a legal framework for targeting specifically. Despite these steps, a long way remains for Greece (and Spain) to reach Portugal.

All the above outlined limitations have their roots in authoritarian legacies that persisted after the fall of the Greek and Spanish dictatorships and hence acted as a barrier to reform. Portugal's approach, to go through intensive lustration, correlates with its ability to establish strong oversight mechanisms and subsequently target real threats without having to deal with authoritarian-like collection methods, such as wiretapping. Contrary to Portugal, Greece and Spain, having not uprooted nondemocratic components from their intelligence institutions, continued to suffer from a poor oversight structure that resulted in abuses of power and the use of intelligence organizations for political purposes. The services' use of illegal methods to collect information while they focused on the "wrong" threats rendered them ineffective for a long time. This only started to change after critical junctures took place, predominantly in Spain, which experienced on Spanish soil key events such as 11M. Authoritarian legacies are one of the most insidious obstacles to reform, which is showcased within the targeting aspects of intelligence too. These can only be "broken" by a key event or critical juncture, as demonstrated so far in this book, and an intensive purging process, which can aid change and set the basis for a vigorous control and oversight setup. Consequently, this can open the road to targeting real threats, the exclusion of illegal activities, a fair recruitment process, and an open civil society that trusts intelligence organizations.

NOTES

1. Gill and Phythian, *Intelligence in an Insecure World*, 148–49; Robert M. Clark, *Intelligence Collection* (Los Angeles: SAGE, 2014); Ross Bellaby, "What's the Harm? The Ethics of Intelligence Collection," *Intelligence and National Security* 27, no. 1 (2012).
2. See chapter 4 for more detail on the CFSIRP, its objectives, and work.
3. Matei and Bruneau, "Intelligence Reform in New Democracies," 613.
4. Matei and Bruneau, 613.
5. Nancy Bermeo, "War and Democratization: Lessons from the Portuguese Experience," *Democratization* 14, no. 3 (2007): 388–406.
6. Teresa Rodrigues and José Duarte de Jesus, "Portugal: Particulars of the Portuguese Intelligence Services," n.d., https://www.academia.edu/31529723/Portugal _Particulars_of_the_Portuguese_Intelligence_Services.
7. "Israeli Envoy in Lisbon Is Wounded and Guard Slain in Embassy Raid; Arafat's Visit Cited," *New York Times*, November 14, 1979, www.nytimes.com/1979/11/14 /archives/israeli-envoy-in-lisbon-is-wounded-and-guard-slain-in-embassy-raid .html.
8. "Turkish Envoy in Lisbon Is Killed by Gunman," *New York Times*, June 8, 1982, www.nytimes.com/1982/06/08/world/around-the-world-turkish-envoy-in-lisbon -is-killed-by-gunman.html.
9. Milt Freudenheim and Henry Giniger, "A New Armenian Death Mission," *New York Times*, July 31, 1983, www.nytimes.com/1983/07/31/weekinreview/the-world -a-new-armenian-death-mission.html.
10. Section 32 of Part III (Special Part) of the Portuguese Criminal Code Decree-Law No. 400/82, *Diário da República*, no. 221/1982, 1st supplement, Series I of 1982-09-23. See also Section I, Article 1, "Definição e fins de segurança interna" [Definition and purposes of homeland security] of Law No. 20/1987 of June 12, 1987—"Lei de Segurança Interna" (Homeland Security Law).
11. Ronald H. Chilcote, *The Portuguese Revolution: State and Class in the Transition to Democracy* (Plymouth, UK: Rowman & Littlefield Publishers, 2012), 153. Many of the FP-25 members once belonged to the Revolutionary Party of the Proletariat, a violent faction active in the months after the revolution.
12. Raquel da Silva, *Narratives of Political Violence: Life Stories of Former Militants* (New York: Routledge, 2019), 48.
13. CIA, Directorate of Intelligence, "Portugal: FP-25 at a Crossroads," *Terrorism Review*, 1985, 9.
14. Barry Hatton, *Queen of the Sea: A History of Lisbon* (London: C. Hurst, 2018), 274.
15. Hatton, 274.
16. CIA, "Portugal," 10.
17. CIA, 10.
18. CIA, 10.
19. Director of National Intelligence, "April Warning and Forecast Report," National Intelligence Council, April 28, 1988, 2, https://www.cia.gov/readingroom/print /1984261.
20. Law No. 29/82, *Diário da República*, no. 285/1982, Série I de 1982-12-11, Article 67: "The Information services of the Armed Forces shall be exclusively concerned with military information, within the scope of the missions assigned to them by the Constitution and by this law."

21. Law No. 29/82, *Diário da República*, no. 285/1982, Série I de 1982-12-11, Articles 19.1 and 20.1: "The Strategic Defense Information Service is the agency responsible for producing the information necessary to guarantee the national independence and the external security of the Portuguese State," and "The Military Intelligence Service is made up of the departments responsible for producing military information necessary for the accomplishment of the missions of the Armed Forces, including the guarantee of military security."

22. Júlio Pereira (deputy general-prosecutor, current secretary-general of SIRP), "Segurança interna: O mesmo conceito, novas exigências" [Internal security: The same concept, new requirements], *Segurança e Defesa*, no. 3 (2007): 97.

23. Pinto Arena, "Portugal's Intelligence Evolution," 160–77.

24. Pinto Arena, 160–77.

25. Pinto Arena, 160–77.

26. Manuel Carlos Freire, "Coordenador das 'secretas' quer reestruturar luta antiterrorista," ['Secret' coordinator wants to restructure anti-terrorism fight], *Diário de Notícias*, October 31, 2008, https://www.dn.pt/arquivo/2008/coordenador-das-secretas-quer-reestruturar-luta-antiterrorista-1133897.html.

27. Pinto Arena, "Portugal's Intelligence Evolution."

28. SIS, accessed February 5, 2021, https://www.sis.pt/. See also Rodrigues and Duarte de Jesus, "Portugal."

29. SIED, accessed on February 5, 2021, https://www.sied.pt/.

30. SIED.

31. Council of the European Union, EU Counter-Terrorism Coordinator, "EU Action Plan on Combating Terrorism," 15358=09 ADD 1 REV 1, Brussels, November 27, 2009.

32. Pinto Arena, "Portugal's Intelligence Evolution."

33. Portugal's internal national security system is based on two subsystems: the Sistema de Segurança Interna (SSI; System of Internal Security) and the Sistema de Informações da República Portuguesa (SIRP; Portuguese Republic Intelligence System). The SSI coordinates the security forces and services (Foreigners and Borders Service [SEF], the Judicial Police [PJ], the Public Security Police [PSP], and the National Republican Guard [GNR]). It is led by a secretary-general who reports directly to the prime minister. The second branch, SIRP, covers the intelligence apparatus, with "jurisdiction" over the two intelligence agencies, the SIS and SIED, and their respective secretary-generals, under the guidance of the government. Pinto Arena, "Portugal's Intelligence Evolution."

34. Rui Carlos Pereira, "A produção de informação na democracia de direito" [The production of information in democracy under the rule of law], 1998, https://www.macaudata.mo/macaubook/book103/html/01601.htm.

35. Pinto Arena, "Portugal's Intelligence Evolution," 160–77.

36. Rui Carlos Pereira, "O consumo e o tráfico de droga na lei penal portuguesa" [Consumption and drug trafficking in Portuguese criminal law], *Revista do Ministério Público*, no. 65 (1996): 74–76. See also Pereira, "A produção de informação na democracia de direito."

37. Pereira, "A produção de informação na democracia de direito," 19.

38. Sotiropoulos, "Authoritarian Past and Contemporary Greek Democracy," 451.

39. Martin Douglas, "Dimitrios Ioannidis, Greek Coup Leader, Dies at 87," *New York Times*, August 17, 2010, www.nytimes.com/2010/08/17/world/europe/17ioannidis.html.

40. Apostolidis, *Intelligence Services in National Security System.*

41. John M. Nomikos, "Terrorism, Media, and Intelligence in Greece: Capturing the 17 November Group," *International Journal of Intelligence and CounterIntelligence* 20, no. 1 (2007): 67.

42. Kassimeris, *Europe's Last Red Terrorists,* 69.

43. The antiterrorist law, 774/78, was introduced in 1978 by the party New Democracy. See Parliamentary Proceedings, April 3, 1978–May 12, 1978.

44. Parliament Proceedings, Plenary Sessions, April 3, 1978–May 12, 1978.

45. Kees Boersma et al., eds. *Histories of State Surveillance in Europe and Beyond* (New York: Routledge, 2014), 59.

46. Apostolidis, *Mystiki Drasi,* 264.

47. Apostolidis, 264–67.

48. Apostolidis, 264–67.

49. Boersma et al., *Histories of State Surveillance,* 59.

50. Minas Samatas, *Surveillance in Greece: From Anti-Communism to Consumer Surveillance* (New York: Pella Publishing, 2004), 39.

51. Samatas, 39.

52. Samatas, 40.

53. George Kassimeris, "For a Place in History: Explaining Greece's Revolutionary Organization 17 November," *Journal of Conflict Studies* 27, no. 2 (2007), 131. https://journals.lib.unb.ca/index.php/JCS/article/download/10547/11864?inline=1.

54. "Apantisi sta kommata kai tis organoseis" [Answers to parties and political groups], *Eleftherotipia,* April 1977.

55. Fitsanakis, *Ethniki asfalia ke sighrones ipiresies kataskopias stin Ellada,* 130.

56. Nomikos, "Terrorism, Media, and Intelligence in Greece," 65–78.

57. Aleksis Papachelas and Tasos Telloglou, *17: Φάκελος 17 Νοέμβρη* [17: The 17 November dossier] (Athens: Estia Publications, 2002).

58. Kassimeris, *Europe's Last Red Terrorists,* 169–70.

59. Kassimeris, 70.

60. Kassimeris, 170.

61. Nomikos, "Terrorism, Media, and Intelligence in Greece," 68.

62. Nomikos, 68.

63. Richard Norton-Taylor, "Diplomatic Mission," *Guardian,* June 9, 2000, www.theguardian.com/world/2000/jun/09/richardnortontaylor1.

64. Apostolidis, *Mystiki Drasi,* 269.

65. Kassimeris, *Europe's Last Red Terrorists,* 82.

66. David John Allen and Alfred Pijpers, *European Foreign Policy-Making and the Arab-Israeli Conflict* (The Hague: Martinus Nijhoff, 1984), 112.

67. "Arafat in Greece in Snub to Arabs" *New York Times,* September 2, 1982, www.nytimes.com/1982/09/02/world/arafat-in-greece-in-snub-to-arabs.html.

68. "Papandreou Puts out Greek Welcome Mat for PLO's Arafat," *Christian Science Monitor,* September 3, 1982, www.csmonitor.com/1982/0903/090371.html.

69. Apostolidis, *Mystiki Drasi,* 270.

70. Apostolidis, 271.

71. Apostolidis, 311.

72. Nomikos, "Terrorism, Media, and Intelligence in Greece," 69.

73. Apostolidis, *Mystiki Drasi,* 238.

74. Edward Mickolus and Susan L. F. Simmons, *Terrorism, 1992–1995: A Chronology of Events and a Selectively Annotated Bibliography* (Westport, CT: Greenwood, 1997), 98.
75. Apostolidis, *Mystiki Drasi*, 284.
76. Mickolus and Simmons, *Terrorism, 1992–1995*, 98.
77. "Greek Court Gives Palestinians Stiff Sentences for 1991 Bombing," Jewish Telegraphic Agency, July 20, 1992, http://www.jta.org/1992/07/20/archive/greek -court-gives-palestinians-stiff-sentences-for-1991-bombing.
78. Steve Bates, "VA. Arrest Made in a Spy Case from Greece," *Washington Post*, May 4, 1993, https://www.washingtonpost.com/archive/local/1993/05/04/va-arrest-made -in-a-spy-case-from-greece/f99601ca-9080-4696-a878-5a30a9aa26d9/.
79. Apostolidis, *Mystiki Drasi*, 280–81.
80. Bates, "VA. Arrest Made."
81. Apostolidis, *Mystiki Drasi*, 290.
82. Apostolidis, 290.
83. Kassimeris, *Europe's Last Red Terrorists*, 81.
84. George Karyotis, "Greek Terrorism: The Demystification of the 'Phantom Organization, 17 November'" (conference paper, LSE Symposium on Modern Greece, London School of Economics, June 21, 2003), 7.
85. Nomikos, "Terrorism, Media, and Intelligence in Greece," 69.
86. Nomikos, 69.
87 "Dikees dikes, dimokratikes nikes kai plhges pou paramenoun anihtes" [Fair trials, democratic victories and wounds that remain open], June 25, 2022, https:// www.chrisochoidis.gr/12191/dikaies-dikes-dimokratikes-nikes-kai-pliges-poy -paramenoyn-anoichtes/.
88. For more information on 17 November, see Kassimeris, *Europe's Last Red Terrorists*.
89. Kassimeris, 81.
90. Nomikos, "Terrorism, Media, and Intelligence in Greece," 71
91. Apostolidis, *Mystiki Drasi*, 305.
92. Matei and Bruneau, "Intelligence Reform in New Democracies," 618.
93. Presidential Decree N.D. 255/2002 (Athens: Greek Parliament, 2002).
94. Article 2, Mission of Law 3649/2008, National Intelligence Service and other provisions, *Government Gazette*, A 39, 3.3.2008.
95. In 2006 the Greek newspaper the *News* revealed the illegal tapping of more than one hundred mobile phones in the Vodafone Hellas network. The phones included those of high-ranking government officials and civil servants, such as the mayor of Athens and the prime minister and members of his family. Top-level businessmen's phones were also tapped. The media reported at the time that US intelligence services were the alleged suspects. The Öcalan affair: PKK founder Abdullah Öcalan was taken captive in Kenya on February 15, 1999, on his way from the Greek embassy to the international airport in Nairobi, in an operation by the Millî İstihbarat Teşkilatı (MIT: Turkish National Intelligence Organization).
96. Apostolidis, *Mystiki Drasi*, 304–5.
97. National Intelligence Agency, www.nis.gr.
98. F. García Sanz, "Al servicio del estado: Inteligencia y contrainteligencia en España" [At the service of the state: Intelligence and counterintelligence in Spain], *Arbor* 180, no. 709 (2005): 100.

99. Stanley G. Payne, *Franco and Hitler: Spain, Germany, and World War II* (New Haven, CT: Yale University Press, 2009), 119.

100. Boersma et al., *Histories of State Surveillance.*

101. Bob de Graaff and James M. Nyce, eds., *Handbook of European Intelligence Cultures* (Lanham, MD: Rowman & Littlefield, 2018), 362.

102. Juan Muría Peñaranda y Algar, "*Los servicios de intelligencia en la transición*" [The intelligence sevices in the transition], *Arbor* 180, no. 709 (2005): 99.

103. Peñaranda y Algar, 101.

104. Ignacio José San Martín, *Servicio especial: A las órdenes de Carrero Blanco; De Castellana a El Aaiun* [Special service: At the orders of Carrero Blanco; From Castellana to El Aaiun] (Barcelona: Planeta, 1984), 49–50.

105. "Próxima Integración de Mujeres al CESID," *El País,* May 15, 1983, http://elpais .com/diario/1983/05/16/espana/421884014_850215.html.

106. Florina Cristiana Matei, Andrés de Castro García, and Carolyn C. Halladay, "On Balance: Intelligence Democratization in Post-Franco Spain," *International Journal of Intelligence and CounterIntelligence* 31, no. 4 (2018): 777. See also Andrea Gimenez-Salinas, "The Spanish Intelligence Services," in *Democracy, Law and Security: Internal Security Services in Contemporary Europe,* ed. Jean-Paul Brodeur, Peter Gill, and Dennis Tollborg (London: Ashgate, 2003).

107. Cercas, *Anatomy of a Moment,* 199.

108. Díaz Fernández, "Halfway Down the Road."

109. George E. Glos, "Danger Signals for Spain," *Royal Institute of International Affairs* 38, no. 1 (1982): 28.

110. Glos, 27.

111. Bill Cemlyn-Jones, "King Orders Army to Crush Coup," *Guardian,* February 23, 1981, https://www.theguardian.com/world/1981/feb/23/spain.fromthearchive.

112. Cemlyn-Jones.

113. Appeals of unconstitutionality numbers 285 and 292/1985, sentence number 199/1987 of December 16, BOE no. 7, January 8, 1988. See also paragraph 1 of Article 18, Guarantee and Control of Measures, Organic Law 9/1984 of December 26 against the action of armed gangs and terrorist elements and the development of article 55.2 of the Constitution, BOE no. 3, January 3, 1985, 70–72, and appeals of unconstitutionality numbers 285 and 292/1985, sentence number 199/1987 of December 16, BOE no. 7, January 8, 1988, 12–27. Please refer to chapter 4 for more detail.

114. Antonio M. Díaz Fernández, "The Spanish Intelligence Community: A Diffuse Reality," *Intelligence and National Security* 25, no. 2 (2010), 223–44.

115. Díaz Fernández, "Halfway down the Road." The publication of the documents on the Perote case showed how the service tapped mobile phone conversations. It is unknown if the figures who were targeted were done so at random or whether the electronic surveillance of those figures had been "premeditated."

116. Díaz Fernández.

117. Díaz Fernández.

118. Article 2 of Royal Decree 421/2004 of March 12, which regulates the National Cryptological Center.

119. Fernando Reinares, "After the Madrid Bombings: Internal Security Reforms and the Prevention of Global Terrorism in Spain," Real Instituto, October 14, 2008, http://www.realinstitutoelcano.org/wps/portal/rielcano_en/contenido?WCM

_GLOBAL_CONTEXT=/elcano/elcano_in/zonas_in/international+terrorism /dt40-2008. See also Jorge Dezcallar, *Valió la pena: Una vida entre diplomáticos y espías* [It was worth it: A life among diplomats and spies] (Barcelona : Ediciones Península, 2015).

120. Cortes Generales, Diario de Sesiones del Congreso de los Diputados, Comisiones de Investigación Sobre el 11 de Marzo de 2004, VIII Legislatura, 2005, 24.

121. Cortes Generales, 24.

122. Cortes Generales, nr 407, 2.

123. Fernando Reinares, "Cuál es la amenaza que el terrorismo yihadista supone actualmente para España" [What is the threat that jihadist terrorism currently poses to Spain?], ARI nr 33/2007, Elcano Royal Institute, Madrid, www.realinstitutoelcano .org; Javier Jordán, "Las redes yihadistas en España: Evolución desde el 11-M" [Jihadist networks in Spain: Evolution since 11-M], Athena Intelligence Occasional Paper no. 17, 2007, www.athenaintelligence.org.

124. Fernando Reinares, *Terrorismo Global* [Global terrorism] (Madrid: Taurus, 2003); Fernando Reinares, "Conceptualizando el terrorismo internacional" [Conceptualizing international terrorism], Elcano Royal Institute, no. 82 (2005); Fernando Reinares, "El terrorismo global: Un fenómeno polimorfo" [Global terrorism: A polymorphous phenomenon], ARI nr 84/2008, Elcano Royal Institute, www.real institutoelcano.org.

125. Díaz Fernández, "Spanish Intelligence Community," 223–44.

126. Article 2 of Royal Decree 421/2004 of March 12, which regulates the National Cryptological Center, BOE, no. 68, March 19, 2004, https://www.boe.es/eli/es/rd /2004/03/12/421.

127. Díaz Fernández, "Spanish Intelligence in the Mediterranean Context," 159–60.

128. Ruben Arcos, "Intelligence Design: Restructuring the Spanish Security Apparatus," *IHS Jane's* 24, no. 8 (2012): 36. See also Florina Cristiana Matei and Thomas C. Bruneau, "Policymakers and Intelligence Reform in New Democracies," *International Journal of Intelligence and CounterIntelligence* 24, no. 4 (2011).

129. Matei and Bruneau, "Intelligence Reform in New Democracies," 609.

130. Len Scott and Peter Jackson, "The Study of Intelligence in Theory and Practice," *Intelligence and National Security* 19, no. 2 (2004): 150.

7

Civil Society

We could not conclude this book's discussion of intelligence democratization without putting emphasis on civil society and the components that associate with it. Indeed, civil society is one of the most important factors that can both drive reform and be used as an SSR indicator to help measure intelligence democratization. Civil society encompasses groups that can drive the conversation on intelligence; the media, which can be a watchdog and urge institutions to change; access-to-information laws, which bring a degree of transparency; and partnerships between intelligence organizations and universities, which can farm knowledge and establish an intelligence discipline. All three case studies were affected by the strength or weakness of their civil societies. Portuguese civil society aided the Carnation Revolution, which operated as a critical juncture. Since then, it continues to be engaged and was keen to know what the Portuguese intelligence services do. Civil society groups, the media, and partnerships with universities all have helped in maintaining a robust and open civil society in Portugal that facilitates reform and drives democratization. This, in addition to the complete uprooting of authoritarian elements that took place early on during the transition period, helped push Portugal ahead of the other two case studies.

On the other hand, both Greece and Spain suffered from authoritarian legacies within the civil society spectrum. Greece's civil society was highly politicized, with a closed intelligence culture and a poor media presence. Spain experienced the deep roots of the authoritarian past due to the "pact of forgetting." Civil society started to be more involved, with the media playing a major role for reform as it brought several scandals to light in the 1990s. Indeed, the Spanish media was a key catalyst that facilitated a more open culture, including partnerships with universities and an established intelligence discipline. In this chapter, therefore, focus will be put on answering questions such as: Are there civil society groups and a robust media presence that drive informal oversight? Are there established partnerships between universities and the intelligence services? Is there an open culture of intelligence? Is there a legal basis for oversight through, for instance, transparency laws? The answers to those questions will argue that Portugal has made the most progress in civil society when compared to the other two cases, while it will be seen that authoritarian legacies were the main barrier for reform in Greece and Spain. The media acted as a positive lever for reform in recent years in Spain, and hence it is an area that needs closer attention within the SSR wider framework.

A BRIEF OVERVIEW OF CIVIL SOCIETY

In addition to managing the affairs of the country, almost every democratic government also finds itself waging a nonstop battle for the approval of the governed in order to achieve a sense of legitimacy beyond the occasional election. This, in turn, leads to constant interactions with civil society, including think tanks, activists, and NGOs, which routinely focus on issues of public interest.[1] As Philippe Schmitter contends, this interface is essential for both the stability and growth of a democratic-regime type as "the long-term viability of a given democratic regime may come to depend on the configuration and behaviour of such groups."[2] According to Kerstin Hamann and Paul Christopher Manuel, both their strength and efficacy can be determined through consideration of three sets of criteria. First of all, there is density, or "how many organisations exist and how many citizens are incorporated into them." Second, what is their role and function? Finally, what linkages exist between them, and are they consensual or conflictual?[3] Each of them is subject to constant change. Thus, while civil society may appear weak at the beginning of a democratic transition period, this can quickly change as democratic rule consolidates.[4] The result is typically a wide variety of entities that may not focus on intelligence organizations specifically but have a close interest in the underlying effect of their activities and the laws that empower them. This can include civil and human rights groups, privacy advocates, net neutrality activists, and others. When looking at intelligence specifically in a democratic state, we see that civil society is active and uses the "limited" transparency to drive the debate on intelligence issues.[5]

The media can enhance the effect of these organizations by both offering a platform to their messages and providing the public with a greater understanding of the effect that government policies have. In short, the media provides the society with the information it needs to debate key issues, including "current policies, public issues, societal threats, the potential failings of its institutions as well as necessary reforms." In this way, the media "fulfils major democratic responsibility, the duty to make issues transparent and therefore to help citizens to gain information about and exert oversight of the state's executive bodies."[6]

Certainly, although it is argued that there are in fact different types of media systems, some of which enhance democracy less than others, the normative idea has always been that the news media provides "a sufficient supply of meaningful public affairs information to catch the eye of relatively inattentive citizens."[7] In this way, it "serves" the public by bringing it information that it otherwise would not know about—and, in some cases, information that governments would rather the public did not. In this way, the media can form the last line of defense after all the traditional oversight methods have failed. Claudia Hillebrand, for example, argues that were it not for the news media, it is likely that the world would not have known of the abuses that occurred at Abu Ghraib, the extraordinary rendition program managed by the CIA, or the NSA's unparalleled collection of the public's electronic data.[8] The outrage generated by the subsequent negative headlines inevitably led to some introspection about how to prevent further revelations, particularly in the NSA case, but also a reining in of the behavior that had been displayed in the first place. In other words, once they became the source of enormous amounts of attention, the organizations themselves changed in order to better fit with the public's view of how they should be, at least until something else came to light.

In the background, assisting these entitles or making their lives harder, is the presence or absence of freedom of information laws and other associated data-access rights. By default, most intelligence organizations are exempt from public information requests, but some aspects of their work are occasionally open to public scrutiny. This can come in addition to outreach initiatives conducted by organizations themselves, which can be used to educate the public about the nature of their work. Universities are often the main recipients of this outreach, due to the recruitment opportunities that such interactions help offer, but the additional effect is greater oversight from academia and the individual. Overall, in each of the case studies, civil society and within it the media can be seen to have played an important role in offering oversight of intelligence organizations. They have highlighted failures, questioned methods, and offered the public the chance to voice its thoughts on matters that may have been "buried" in order to facilitate the overall transition process. The effect of this has differed from country to country, but the overarching momentum as a result has been toward greater openness and transparency on the part of intelligence organizations, with more efforts being directed into working with civil society rather than against it, at least in recent years.

Portugal

Historically, Portugal has always had a rather weak civil society, with elites in Lisbon maintaining a close control over society at the expense of the urban and rural poor.[9] This was the case from the formation of the First Republic all the way until the later years of the Estado Novo, when the populace began to tire of the Overseas War and the political restrictions maintained by Marcelo

Caetano. Although the Carnation Revolution itself was a military enterprise, it led to a level of mass mobilization not seen previously in Portugal, with all areas of society suddenly free to speak their minds and make their voices heard. It is for this reason that Schmitter noted that "Portugal experienced one of the most intense and widespread mobilization experiences of any of the neo-democracies."[10] Across the country, a wide range of associations and movements developed: political, parents', youth, women's, environmental, neighborhood, unions and workers', cooperatives, farmers', and professional.[11] The energy of the people, however, refused to dissipate, and it was something that the newly empowered authorities were unable to ignore. Indeed, they even embraced it, as the testimony of Mario Murteira, a Left-oriented economist and government minister in revolutionary Portugal states: "Several times when I was in important conversations with [Prime Minister] General Vasco Gonçalves, . . . we were more spectators in a great popular movement than actors" when looking at the demonstrations from the prime minister's office window.[12]

Eventually, the MFA even attempted to co-opt this mass mobilization through a Program for Cultural Activism and Political Enlightenment. This aimed to achieve "ample participation of the people in the life of the nation" through the national coordination of schools, local communities, squatter movements, and "all cultural associations of the country."[13] The result was a symbiosis between the MFA and wider society, with the organization evolving from a military group to a "revolutionary movement" under the banner of the Alianca Povo–MFA (MFA–People's Alliance).[14] One of the greatest impacts this had was stymying the formal creation of a new Portuguese intelligence organization. Although plans were drawn up that envisaged a civilian Departamento Nacional de Informações (DNI; National Information Department), they were never enacted. After years of antipathy toward the state's intelligence services, the majority of Portugal's citizens were unwilling to endorse the creation of a new organization.[15] Instead of advocating the creation of something new, therefore, activists demanded the destruction of what had existed, with one of the most popular demands being the prosecution of former regime insiders. This applied in particular to members of PIDE and the DGS who had actively resisted the revolution.[16] The destruction of PIDE, therefore, was massively reinforced by the Portuguese civil society. To this end, civil society contributed to the sentiment of the necessity of the uprooting authoritarian elements, opening the road toward democratization.

Inevitably the sudden mass mobilization of the population led to divisions and conflict, with society polarizing along ideological lines. In the north, landowners and Salazarists formed an antirevolutionary movement, and peasant unions formed in the south, while communists worked to activate the working classes in the cities.[17] All of this came to a head during the "hot summer of 1975," when the moderate forces of the MFA finally won out against both rightists and those on the far left. This ultimately enabled the MFA to develop and pass a new constitution whose purpose was to "ensure the transition to socialism by creating conditions for the democratic exercise of power by the working classes."[18] To this end, it contained many protections and rights not previously afforded to citizens under past regimes. For example, there was Article 268, which granted citizens "the right to be informed by the Administration, whenever they so request, of the progress of the processes in which they are directly interested . . . , as well as to know the definitive resolutions that are taken on them."[19] If citizens believed that such actions and administrative acts were illegal, they were subsequently guaranteed the ability to litigate against them.[20]

Such arrangements, in addition to Article 38—which enshrined freedom of the press and media—benefited the country's media outlets, which underwent radical change during the transition period.[21] Central administrative and managerial bodies, which had long stifled freedom of the press, were effectively abolished, censorship services were purged and dissolved, and the official state newspaper—which had been maintained by artificial subscriptions—was wound up.[22] This was a period of great upheaval in the Portuguese media environment, and as nationalization efforts later gathered pace, many of the newspapers that remained initially fell under the control of the state. Fortunately, greater freedom meant that additional independent ones could be opened with foreign financial support. This gave others the ability to start their own papers and hire journalists purged by communists and other extremists. The relative stability that Portugal witnessed from 1975 onward soon facilitated a surge in media entities. This had a profound effect when it came to the rolling back of the initial purges that had occurred following the Carnation Revolution, with the victims organizing themselves into the Movimento Pro-reintegração dos Despedidos sem Justa Causa (MPDJC; Movement for the Reintegration of the Unfairly Dismissed). Although opposed by the trade unions and the Far Left, the MPDJC was supported by political moderates and several of the new private newspapers, from the *Jornal Novo* to the Socialist Party's own newspaper, *A Luta*. The culmination of its campaign was the reintegration of former members of PIDE and the DGS into society, with their rights as former public employees restored, providing they had not taken part in "illegal activities."[23] This not only marked a huge victory for the MPDJC but also showcased the strength that newly empowered civil society entities and the media could bring to bear in postauthoritarian Portugal. Although those individuals were reintegrated into society, they were completely excluded from occupying positions in the newly established intelligence services.[24]

In 1984 the legal framework was laid for the creation of SIRP, the SIS, SIED, and the SIM. What was notable in the framework was how visible the influence of popular sentiment was on the rules and laws underpinning the creation of SIRP and eventually the SIS. Certainly, the restrictions placed on the two organizations and the oversight mechanisms put in place were themselves indicative of the legacy left both by PIDE and the citizens who had called for purges from 1974 onward. Thanks to the protections enshrined in the 1976 constitution and maintained during the 1982 amendments, citizens could also still request information relating to SIRP's activities and litigate against them.[25] The government took a few steps to amend this in 1989 when "the right of access to administrative files and records" became enforceable only when it was "without prejudice to the provisions of the law in matters relating to internal and external security, criminal investigation and the privacy of individuals."[26] This stipulation remained the case in 1993, when a formal mechanism was established for citizens to access administrative documents—the 1993 Law of Access to Administrative Documents. This told citizens in no uncertain terms that documents containing information "whose knowledge is assessed as being at risk or causing damage to the internal and external security of the State shall be subject to an interdiction of access or access under authorization."[27] Indeed, such documents were only to be available for consultation when they had been deemed appropriate for declassification.

Given this stricter approach to accessing documents, from 1993 onward the task of informal oversight was widened to specialized interest groups and the wider media. The latter saw a period of intense privatization in the 1990s as public assets were sold off and restrictions on private media, particularly broadcast media, were lifted.[28] This served to enhance the media's independence and boost its role as a conduit of informal oversight. The media, and therefore the populace, only naturally wanted to know what links, if any, existed between Portuguese intelligence and the Spanish GAL affair when revelations reached their peak in 1995.[29] With an engaged civil society, therefore, that drove the Carnation Revolution and the subsequent uprooting of the authoritarian elements through lustration, Portugal had a strong media presence, ready to challenge the country's intelligence services early on.

Although Portugal did not have to deal with authoritarian elements after lustration, it did have to deal with a corruption scandal. As Florina Cristiana Matei and Thomas Bruneau argue, corruption is one of the key factors that can obstruct reform in a newly transitioned state.[30] The most prominent example centered on the rise and fall of SIED director Jorge Silva Carvalho, who, after leaving SIED in 2010, joined a company called Ongoing Strategy Investments. What the media later revealed was that Carvalho had utilized his privileged position to gather information that his new employer could benefit from, which included using SIED and SIS resources to bug the phone of a journalist. Carvalho consequently was arrested for abuse of power and for breaching state secrecy laws in order to profit commercially.[31] Portugal had to deal with only isolated incidents, and the media aided further reform when it came to them.

With regard to further developments on the access-of-information front, more developments took place in more recent years. In 2014 a letter from the president of the Commission for Access to Administrative Documents stated that while this state of affairs should be improved due to the way in which it constituted "a systemic exception to the principles of transparency, publication and open administration," any new mechanism would need to match those of other EU and NATO member states.[32] Consequently, the cap on transparency was slightly amended in 2016 as a result of EU-level influence, with third parties being granted access to information only if the applicant had specific written authorization and could demonstrate that they have a direct, personal, legitimate, and constitutionally protected interest sufficiently relevant to justify access.[33] This facilitated a public campaign against the SIS's collection of electronic metadata, something that the president of the Association of Portuguese Judges argued should "only be legally accessible by the judicial authorities, within the framework of a criminal case, when a crime is suspected. Not by administrative authorities, as is the case with SIS."[34] As a result, Law No. 4/2017, which enabled such data collection to go ahead, was created.[35]

SIRP has attempted in recent years to establish an even more open service by establishing various educational initiatives with the Information Management School of the New University of Lisbon (NOVA IMS), the Institute of Social and Political Sciences (ISCSP) of University of Lisbon, the Naval School, and the Portuguese National Defense Institute (IDN).[36] This has included the copromotion of courses such as Intelligence in Democracy (by SIRP and IDN) and postgraduate programs such as Intelligence Management and Security (by NOVA IMS, SIRP, and IDN).[37] SIRP has also taken the time to invest in a high-quality website, which informs users on the purpose and history of SIRP, the SIS, and SIED, how they are organized, and under which laws they operate. This marks an attempt to connect with citizens directly and offer messages that otherwise can only reach them via the media.

SIRP's secretary-general proclaimed in 2019 that these and other measures had been successful in helping the organization "open up to society," with "very positive steps" being made in achieving transparency from 2009 to 2019.[38] The mass mobilization of society that began in 1974 has left a legacy of a public keen to maintain the protections afforded to them in the postauthoritarian environment and willing to hold their government and official organizations to account. This, combined with a free press, has helped ensure that even when other checks and balances fail, there is, eventually, accountability.

Greece

A general historical consensus exists that Greece has typically had a weak civil society.[39] This was the result of a large and dominant state structure that did not facilitate the growth of strong political parties and that discouraged horizontal links within the populace. The Greek Orthodox Church, for example, far from being a source of independent opinion, had instead developed deep ties with the state. The same was the case for many local authorities, which over time had become very dependent on the central administration to fulfill their wants and needs. It is to this end that Nicos P. Mouzelis describes the relationship between the state and the masses in the twentieth century as being a series of "patron-client" relationships.[40] Kevin Featherstone, meanwhile, says that Greek political culture was unfortunately dominated by "suffocating bureaucracies, clientelism, strong attachment to a single church and net outward migration of labour."[41] This was one of the main reasons why the junta was not overthrown "from below" but instead dissolved from within. Through the aggressive use of repressive measures and the crushing of any large-scale demonstration of opposition, the junta had kept shut any "windows of opportunity" that might have enabled the growth of civil society.[42] When democracy returned to Greece from 1974 onward, therefore, there were few organizations that citizens could join even if they wanted to. There was, however, a host of parties to choose from, and these wasted no time in establishing their own volunteer groups to capture the public's enthusiasm. Politicization, therefore, was present in Greece not only in terms of recruitment but also civil society.

Parties on the left and right were soon building their own labor organizations, professional associations, student groups, women's associations, and more. These in turn then fought over seats in the governing bodies of leading associations, further politicizing different aspects of society and the economy and making it so that when these groups voiced opposition to government policy, it was likely because it was simply the policy of "the opposition" more than anything else.[43] Indeed, one common policy of Greek governments in the 1970s and 1980s was to staff the most important civil society entities with progovernment insiders so as to undermine any potential opposition to their policies. This "monitoring from above" "was accomplished with the help of a docile judiciary which produced court decisions changing the composition of the governing boards of peak labour associations. 'Monitoring from above' was also affected by the Ministry of Labour which controlled the finances of peak associations."[44] Such arrangements seriously disrupted the ability of Greek civil society to develop along organic lines and achieve meaningful oversight thereafter.

Accordingly, those groups that did develop independently remained a minority and often continued to bear the same kind of "resistance orientation" that they held from 1967 to 1974. This included those students, intellectuals, and left-wing activists who had vehemently opposed the military junta and often borne the brunt of its antagonism and repressive activities. Following democracy's revival, they continued to pursue their previous activities, denouncing what they perceived as maliciousness behind government decision-making and calling for social justice. This included painting the KYP as a tool of government repression that had worked against the people from its inception and continued to do the bidding of the CIA.[45] As if to confirm this notion, surveillance operations against Greek socialists and communists continued until the middle of 1977, as explained in chapter 6.[46] This was several years after Konstantinos Karamanlis legalized the Greek Communist Party and ended the KYP's requirement to monitor party members. That unwarranted operations continued was a testament to how Greece had an "overdeveloped, coercive security apparatus, which continued to restrict civil liberties and intrude into citizens' private lives, sorting them according to their political beliefs."[47] Officially, therefore, there remained a lingering skepticism of citizens' rights as "autonomous individuals" and the idea of individual rights to privacy.[48]

With no formal way of requesting information on what the KYP or the government was doing, citizens had little ability to gain an understanding of how the organization was behaving. They were simply expected to "have faith" that the KYP was not carrying out illegal activities. This, however, was easier said than done in an environment where the public could not verify what was going on and there existed a closed intelligence culture. Even the media struggled to offer a meaningful independent oversight role due to the fact that up until the 1980s "the state had the monopoly over radio and television, and the public broadcasting organizations were directly subordinate to the respective departments of press and information."[49] More than half of the national newspaper market, meanwhile, was controlled by just four families, each of whom had close relationships with the main political parties.[50] Such a close connection between the media and political class inevitably led to a lack of objectivity and balance when it came to press coverage. Instead, media outlets and newspapers often promoted party practices and discourse that had little relevance to social issues. The result was "apolitical overpoliticization" of politics and government affairs and passionate, yet uncritical, coverage.[51] Because of this, government explanations for policies or incidents, when they were presented, were often met with intense skepticism, an issue John Nomikos attributes to the intense trauma that the dictatorship period had wrought on the Greek public.[52]

This was reinforced by the inability of citizens to effectively engage with government departments as well as the state intelligence service. Indeed, even when the EYP was created in 1986, the system was still set up to make it as hard as possible for individuals to find out about the new intelligence organization. Law 1599/1986, for example, was designed to boost government transparency and granted every citizen "the right to have access to administrative documents other than those relating to the private or family life of third parties."[53] The majority of government departments, however—not just those involved in national security and intelligence work—had the broad ability to block the disclosure of information if they felt it breached confidentiality regulations or would impede the investigation of a crime or administrative offense.[54] As a result, the individual citizen was very much reliant on other actors to gather information for them. With the number of new voluntary associations declining, a greater emphasis was placed on the media, which at this time was changing rapidly thanks to a rise in new broadcast channels and new methods of corporate organization. Having dominated the media landscape for so long, the former ruling families sold out to or were replaced by a rising class of entrepreneurs who had already made money elsewhere.

These individuals were keen to establish their own conglomerates and take advantage of advertising revenue and a burgeoning consumer culture.[55] Such changes did not automatically overturn the traditions of defense and partisanship that had long been the norm, however, increasing cynicism not just with party politics itself but the media covering it as well. This became clear after 1989 when an embezzlement scandal engulfed Andreas Papandreou's government and the prosocialist press alternated between condemning and defending the mess.[56] The resultant "formation of a new socio-political consensus, the fatigue of the electorate and gradual disillusionment with party politics all aggravated the crisis of credibility of the Greek press."[57] Accordingly, survey numbers in the 1990s showed that Greeks had become quite disengaged from state affairs and the accompanying media coverage. In 1996, for example, the number of daily newspaper copies sold per one thousand inhabitants was 590 in Norway, 445 in Sweden, and 331 in Britain, while only 153 in Greece.[58]

Consequently, those overseas were likely to know just as much, if not more, about Greek intelligence affairs than Greek citizens themselves. This was particularly true when it came to the EYP and the PKK, as analyzed in chapter 6. They were joined at this time by the Far Left group Dev-Sol, later renamed Devrimci Halk Kurtuluş Partisi-Cephesi (DHKR-C; Revolutionary People's Liberation Party/Front). Like the PKK, Dev-Sol had found shelter in Greece under the PASOK government after having assassinated a number of Turkish security and military officials.[59] Inevitably the Turkish reaction to this was negative. This was especially the case when in August 1991 the Turkish media published information explaining in detail how PKK guerrillas moved between Greece and Syria. This was followed by more stories in January 1992 about how Turkey's armed forces felt about being unable to stop the group, which by then had spread across all of Europe.[60] As Greek journalists could not make contact with intelligence officers who had firsthand knowledge of or who had participated in such operations, they were reliant on substitutes, such as elected or appointed officials. These usually had little knowledge on the matters at hand and promoted policy agendas over meaningful dialogue.[61]

Greek journalists were also prone to dismissing problems. 17 November is certainly one such terrorist group that benefited from several Greek administrations not acknowledging that it was a serious threat, as analyzed in chapter 6. Rather than challenging the assertion of isolated incidents of violence, the sympathetic press repeated claims made by the EYP that 17 November was either an externally controlled group or one that did not exist at all.[62] This allowed enthusiasts of 17 November to fill the information void by propagating reports on the group's behalf, something that eventually granted it the image of Robin Hood vigilantes who only hurt villains from the dictatorship period or rich industrialists who could afford to pay ransoms.[63] This only changed after the popular MP Pavlos Bakoyannis was murdered on September 26, 1989, and the New Democracy government passed a new antiterrorism law, 1916/90. It included a clause that prevented the media from publishing anything that could be seen to aid terrorist groups, including their proclamations or communiqués. Adherence with this clause was brief, however, with the PASOK government quickly abolishing it on the grounds of freedom of speech. Accordingly, political squabbling over 17 November continued, with the media now literally in the firing line—the offices of the TV station Mega Channel being hit by two rocket-propelled grenades on March 15, 1995, which killed twelve.[64]

Anxious citizens could only watch all this with concern. This was because revisions made in 1999 to the law governing public access to administrative documents did not grant the government as broad a power to reject requests for information as the original text. Yet the revisions still allowed "the competent administrative authority" the ability to deny requests if satisfaction would "complicate the investigation of judicial, administrative, police or military authorities in relation to the commission of a crime or administrative breach."[65] This impasse ended only after the murder of the British military attaché, Stephen Saunders, in Athens on June 8, 2000. Following this, the Greek government amended its communication policy and undertook various initiatives designed to indicate the seriousness with which it now treated terrorism. Among them was the broadcast of "One Minute of Silence," a text outlining the government's counterterrorism strategy. This was accompanied by media coverage of an appeal made by Saunders's widow, in addition to the elevation of a civil society group comprising relatives of those who had fallen victim to terrorism.[66] Then a degree of oversight was made possible through the creation of the ADAE under Law 3115/2003. The purpose of this independent authority was recorded as being to ensure the confidentiality of mail and all other forms of free correspondence or communication as highlighted in previous chapters.[67] Remarkably, it was empowered to do so through issuing regulations and performing audits on communications network service providers and public entities, including the

EYP. It could hold hearings that such providers and entities would be obliged to attend and respond to complaints raised by the public and to evidence gathered by special investigative powers.[68] Any findings would subsequently be forwarded to the minister of justice, the speaker of parliament and the leaders of the parties represented in the parliament.[69]

In addition to this real-time monitoring, the EYP also opened itself up to scrutiny of its past by establishing a mechanism by which it would declassify its records, starting with the period 1953 to 1958. Indeed, under Article 3 of Law 3649/2008, the EYP was to establish a Historical Archive Service. This was to report "directly to the Commander of the Ministry of Defense, with the main task of classifying and utilizing documents and audio-visual material. These documents and material are declassified after the lapse of 50 years, by decision of the Commander of the EYP, after the opinion of a three-member Declassification Committee, formed by employees of the EYP."[70] The only materials that would not be released to the public were those that were "being computerized, those that are worn out and in need of maintenance, as well as those whose disclosure could harm national interests or personality rights."[71] This came as a boon to Greek academics and intelligence enthusiasts long stifled by arbitrary classification rulings and regulations that preventing information sharing. For example, there is the Athens-based Research Institute for European and American Studies (RIEAS), which has published articles on intelligence studies and terrorism alongside a host of other academic disciplines since 2006.[72] It has come alongside a growth in media attention, with more outlets covering intelligence issues. Regrettably, much of this coverage continues to remain brief and insubstantial. Rather than presenting analysis or diverging viewpoints, most outlets continue to report "the facts" as they are presented by government officials, who, as mentioned earlier, often have no specialist expertise. Often little context is given for whatever latest event is occurring, and as a result the public is not left well-informed of either the immediate situation or how it fits into a wider perspective.[73] A few years ago, John Nomikos, the director of RIEAS, suggested the creation of an intelligence academy that would collaborate with foreign intelligence academics and Greek universities. He also underlined the need for academics and think tanks to cooperate with the EYP in order to "make an opening to society."[74] Unfortunately, no steps have been taken to work toward such a suggestion.

Based on these factors, Greece's authoritarian culture has not really changed. Nondemocratic elements persist, with politicized civil society groups, a closed intelligence culture, and a weak media presence. The absence, even in recent years, of strong academic work contrary to Portugal and Spain has also meant that Greece has made very little progress toward intelligence democratization when it comes to civil society.

Spain

Spain is unique among the three case studies due to the way in which political society and civil society diverged early in the democratic transition process. Indeed, unlike in Portugal where initial political developments were heavily influenced by mass mobilization and in Greece where mass mobilization was heavily influenced by political parties, there was little symbiosis in Spain. The root cause was, of course, the decision by political elites to proceed with democratic rule as quickly and quietly as possible, with various compromises being made to ensure overall stability. This quickly eliminated the possibility of radical change and killed any momentum that activist groups had received following the death of Carrero Blanco in 1973 and Franco himself in 1975. As Tiago Fernandes puts it, "Elites simply had no plan for altering the basic social and economic structures of society," and because the country's democratic transition was being controlled from above, "nor was there any opportunity to be taken by popular-sector civil society organizations."[75] Certainly, by approving the Amnesty Act of July 30, 1976, the new democratic government quickly satisfied the demands of a large number of citizens, specifically the 150,000 who had signed a petition for its implementation.[76] Miguel Herrero de Miñón, one of the bill's main drafters reflected, "The first major issue which I found on my desk when I took office as Principal Secretary was the amnesty for politically motivated crimes." He continued: "This was not a demand of the opposition but, more importantly, of public opinion, and one which only a few weeks earlier I myself had described in the press as the 'collateral' for the great pact of national reconciliation."[77]

Although described in this manner by Miñón, the act itself quickly became known as the pact of forgetting—not only because it forgave crimes conducted against the state but crimes conducted by the state itself. In this way, former Francoists were able to maintain their positions of power in local authorities, public administrations, state schools, the military, the police, and the judiciary as analyzed in previous chapters.[78] On paper, they and the opposition were equals, but the reality was that only one side was genuinely invested in democracy, while the other did it out of convenience and loyalty to the king. To ensure balance, it was the opposition that often had to give up their ideals, none more so than the Left. Having been left out in the political cold for so long, the two major left-wing parties, the Partido Socialista Obrero Españo (PSOE; Spanish Socialist Workers Party) and the Spanish Communist Party, dropped those policies that had generated the most interest within their political base—for example, economic nationalization and agrarian reform—in order to appease the ruling classes.[79]

Such moves in the interest of "political legitimacy" soon led to the decline of civil society groups who suddenly found themselves abandoned by their former patrons. Among them were the urban neighborhood movements, which during the 1960s and early 1970s had become among the largest in Western Europe.[80] Also affected, however, were the country's major unions and other entities such as the Federation of Rural Workers that saw their roles reduced as government decision-making prioritized technocratic interests over consultations. Incredibly, what little power they had was reduced even further by the maintenance of Francoist legal restrictions on freedom of association. The 1978 constitution, for example, continued the practice of requiring new associations to receive a *declaración de utilidad publica* (declaration of public utility) before they could be considered legitimate. To do so, they had to endure a highly discretionary process dependent on the council of ministers and often only granted to entities that promoted welfare, education, culture, or sports. Following this, if the authorities believed that *individual members* had conducted a criminal offense, then the entire organization could be held responsible and dissolved.[81] Such power was often used to curtail organized dissent and prevent the establishment of any meaningful informal oversight on the part of civil organizations. This was further reinforced by the de facto granting of an exemption to CESID under Article 105, which otherwise allowed citizens to challenge administrative provisions that affected them and request access to administrative files and records.[82]

Informal oversight, therefore, was poor and "controlled" as during the Franco era. True informal oversight soon only came from the Spanish media, which after forty years of enduring authoritarian rule and vast sets of restrictions began to experience a liberation of sorts. While the state-controlled television and radio outlets continued to promote the government's interpretation of events, "new newspapers such as *El País* and *Diario 16* marked a dramatic change from newspapers controlled by the state or linked to religious or ideological groups."[83] Thus, from 1978, with groups such as the ETA and Grupos de Resistencia Antifascista Primero de Octubre (GRAPO; First of October Antifascist Resistance Groups) waging war against the state, journalists began to cover issues such as intelligence, which had previously been off-limits. Antonio M. Díaz Fernández identifies those covering them as soon falling into three camps: those who endorsed CESID's perspectives and attitudes, namely Pilar Urbano; those who were critical of CESID, such as Fernando Rueda; and those who sought to "combine historical rigour with solid journalistic style."[84] However, given how limited their knowledge of intelligence matters initially was and how limited society's knowledge initially was, coverage was not exactly in-depth. There was simply not the incentive to pursue investigations that were difficult to carry out and frustrated by official censors, particularly when the public did not necessarily recognize what was pertinent information. Consequently, the bulk of intelligence-themed news focused on what the CIA, the KGB, or the Cubans were up to, with the reporting style resembling "the style of fiction literature, in which espionage was displayed as a game. Emphasis was laid upon covert actions, the Cold War, and cloak-and-dagger operations."[85] This theme of entertaining pieces over substantive items continued until 1981, when Col. Antonio Tejero and other military personnel attempted to overthrow the democratic government.

What followed was a period of intense public and legislative interest in the "hidden elements" of Spanish power, particularly the country's intelligence services. Tejero and his followers encouraged this previously unheard of self-examination by claiming in court that CESID had masterminded their attempt to bring down the government and had given it their full support when it was in motion.[86] These statements subsequently unleashed an avalanche of media stories that focused on claims made by several political leaders, trade unionists, and professionals that their offices had been raided and wiretapped, presumably by CESID.[87] From 1979 to 1982, for example, *El País* published 167 articles on intelligence matters, indicating a growing interest in the state's war against the ETA and other terrorist groups.[88] As authoritarian legacies continued in Spain, the media provided an informal way of oversight when the formal oversight mechanisms, which were not robust enough, had failed. After this, however, news and press coverage became more routine, and aside from the odd rumor of a politically motivated wiretapping, "most news reports dealt with unspectacular issues such as pending reform of the intelligence services, the replacement of the director of CESID . . . and the mechanisms that should be used to coordinate all security forces."[89] What they and their audience did not necessarily know was that they were perhaps just as well informed on intelligence matters as many of their own members of parliament. This was particularly the case when it came to the Grupo Mixto, which, as mentioned earlier, struggled to gain access to the information it was supposed to be receiving. Indeed, the inability to receive meaningful insight from official sessions meant that the deputies and the Spanish public in general were henceforth almost entirely reliant on external media sources to form an understanding of what CESID was doing.[90] This was especially the case when another law restricting the public's right to access government information was passed in 1992 and the media received an even greater informal oversight role than it had previously.[91]

This became very clear in 1994 when *El Mundo* began publishing articles based on interviews with two Spanish policemen who were being prosecuted for alleged connections with the GAL. GAL death squads had primarily operated in the Basque region of Spain until 1987. Its victims were targeted based on their perceived membership of either the ETA itself or the wider Basque nationalist movement, but the organization was also prone to making mistakes, as when it kidnapped a man believing him to be someone else.[92] What *El Mundo's* readers did not know was that the GAL had in fact been created by elements of the Spanish government in October 1983, though the idea of using such groups to fight the ETA was not new. In fact, the Francoist prime minister Luis Carrero Blanco had previously planned to bring Spain's various Far Right groups under government control for this exact reason. The objective was to "use them to fight a dirty war—outside the law but protected by the state—against the opposition, and especially against ETA."[93] Carrero's subsequent assassination by the ETA on December 20, 1973, had prevented him from putting his plan into practice, but it is a testament to the ingrained ways of thinking wrought by Francoist rule that others did so anyway when Spain became a democracy. By 1975, therefore, when much of wider Spain was occupied with the country's democratization following the death of Franco, groups of government officials independently established the GAL's forerunner, the Batallón Vasco Español (BVE; Basque Spanish Battalion).[94]

The BVE established a template that GAL members would subsequently emulate, targeting "ETA members and many ordinary Basque citizens as well. Its death squads were mainly made up of mercenaries, directed by members of the security forces."[95] The BVE operated for six years in total, until it ceased operations after Tejero's unsuccessful coup attempt in 1981. The fact that the GAL was so able to so readily pick up where the BVE left off was indicative of not only the weak oversight structures on Spanish intelligence at this time but also the willingness of intelligence officers and government officials to still behave in a Francoist manner. What is all the more surprising is that it was the PSOE that facilitated this behavior. Much has been said about how this was a result of the PSOE's perceived weakness vis-à-vis the Spanish establishment and its desire to prove its strength. This was because when the socialists took office at the end of 1982, "they were caught between the fear of losing the support of the armed forces and the renewed killings by the Basque separatist organisation."[96] The latter problem had been one of the key reasons that Tejero had found support among elements of the Spanish Armed Forces and CESID when he tried to overthrow the government. There was no guarantee that another attempt would not find more support among these disgruntled institutions that were still staffed by Francoists. Among socialists in Spain, this was no idle threat since they "were painfully aware of the terrible price exacted from Spain's last left-of-centre government, the 1936 Popular Front, for failing to maintain 'public order.'"[97] Consequently, a decision was taken to seek a quick solution to the problem posed by the terrorist group. As Paddy Woodworth characterizes it, "Someone in the state apparatus accepted the offer from the GAL who said: 'Give us the money and cover, and we will clean things up for you. If you give us a free hand, we will finish off ETA in a very short space of time. . . . We want to do it with the security of knowing that we have the support of a left-wing and democratic party.'"[98]

Originally arrested in 1991 for helping to arrange two GAL attacks that occurred in 1985, the two officers interviewed by *El Mundo* had initially pled not guilty and refused to share any details about their case. Their expectation was that this would earn them the gratitude of the government and a quick pardon.[99] When this did not happen, they decided instead to reveal what they knew to the magistrate in charge of their prosecution in an attempt to receive lesser sentences. The information they provided soon implicated several senior officers in Spain's antiterrorist high command and led to a series of outlandish claims in the media. Among them it was said that "CESID agents kidnapped a beggar and two drug-addicts as medical guinea-pigs in preparation for the kidnapping of a leading Basque terrorist, and dubbed their kidnap plan Operation Mengele."[100] Nevertheless, the magistrate's case received further unexpected aid in the summer of 1995 when *El Mundo* began receiving and publishing highly classified CESID files covering all kinds of illegal activity. Although he denied any involvement, it is highly likely that the documents came from a collection of 1,245 microfilms that Colo. Juan Alberto Perote—a former head of AOME— illegally took from CESID when he left the organization in 1991.[101]

As documents showed, CESID—and presumably, therefore, the minister of defense and the foreign minister—were entirely aware of the arrangements that had been made to coordinate the GAL's activities against the ETA. CESID had even gone so far as to conduct a cost-benefit analysis in the event that the arrangements became public. This analysis showing "a keen appreciation that such actions [support of the GAL], if traced to the security forces, would be counter-productive and boost popular support for ETA."[102] In other words, the rewards to be gained through using the GAL outweighed any risk that might emerge. *El Mundo*'s subsequent reporting triggered a scandal unprecedented in Spanish politics and resulted in parallels with the coverage that the *Washington Post* had previously generated in the United States during the infamous Watergate scandal. The climax came on June 12, 1995, when the newspaper released a report detailing how CESID had illegally wiretapped "top representatives of the state, including King Juan Carlos I, several ministers, businessmen, journalists, and political leaders" since 1992.[103] After initial attempts at weathering the political storm by denying the various allegations failed, the minister of defense agreed to submit to parliamentary questioning on CESID's operations and conduct. When even this proved insufficient to quell public outrage, the minister, the vice president, and the director-general of CESID all agreed to resign.[104]

Questions remained, however, as to who in the government had been responsible for sanctioning support for the GAL. Of most interest was the identity of so-called Señor X, who was listed in the leaked CESID documents as the highest authority to approve the group's actions. At the time, many claimed that this individual was the prime minister himself, Felipe González. Yet although he went out of his way to frustrate the various investigations into the GAL and his government, González never formally admitted to supporting the GAL's activities. The closest he came was in arguing that groups like the GAL were arguably necessary since "democracy is defended in the sewers as well as the salons."[105] Accordingly, although widely believed to have been instrumental in allowing official support for the GAL during the 1980s and trying to cover up this support thereafter, González was not prosecuted, due to a perceived lack of evidence.[106] This was not the case for other high level individuals, such as the former interior minister, the former secretary of state for security, two former governors, and members of the Guardia Civil and CESID. All of them were eventually prosecuted and imprisoned for crimes linked to the GAL.[107]

El Mundo followed this success in March 1998 by publishing a report on CESID's illegal wiretapping of the Basque party Herri Batasuna, the ETA's political branch. The newspaper's revelations not only blew this specific operation but also led to the dismantling of an entire network of undercover operatives and informants. The scandal came as another blow against CESID and the Spanish government, with the minister of defense having to go to great lengths to explain to the parliament why the organization had been spying on a legitimate political party.[108] Incredibly, CESID spent a great deal of time attempting to find out who had leaked information to the press in the first place, illegally spying on two journalists and two individuals at the Ministry of Defense.[109] Their efforts to curtail further press coverage was stymied, however, by other newspapers, such as *El País, La Vanguardia*, and *El Periódico*.

The negative coverage that such informal oversight led to was one of the underlying reasons that CESID was ultimately dismantled and replaced with the CNI in 2002, with 9/11 accelerating the process. Since then, the Spanish media and press have been seen to have assumed the role of "watchdog" or "fire alarm" when it comes to Spanish intelligence, fulfilling extensively their fourth-estate obligations to inform the public.[110] *El Mundo* again showcased its investigatory credentials by revealing the misappropriation of public funds by CNI director Alberto Saiz so that he could go on hunting and fishing trips. This in turn "triggered further stories on illegal activities by the Director of the Intelligence Service, including charges of nepotism, misappropriation of public monies, and a lack of oversight."[111] The final outcome was Saiz's dismissal and an acknowledgment that the CNI still had room for improvement when it came to oversight.

Another positive outcome of the media's coverage and informal oversight of Spanish intelligence was that it provided inspiration for the development of intelligence studies as an academic pursuit. In 2001 the CNI started a project called Spanish Intelligence Culture, which aimed to link intelligence services and economic, social, academic, and cultural entities. This initiative has helped create "intelligence reserves," meaning groups of experts in different areas who "assist the intelligence community in its missions."[112] This field began gaining momentum in 2004 and 2005 when the CNI began signing outreach agreements with universities. As a result, research teams focused on intelligence began to grow at the Rey Juan Carlos University of Madrid, Carlos III University of Madrid, the University of Barcelona, the Autonomous University of Barcelona, the University of Valencia, the University of Zaragoza, the University of Granada, the University of Alicante, the University of Santiago de Compostela, and the University of Malaga.[113] The CNI has stated that the purpose of such outreach is transactional. So, while on one hand the universities and students can learn from their experience and research, the CNI can on the other benefit from the knowledge and experience of scholars on relevant issues and matters of interest to intelligence services.[114] For a long time after transition, Spain suffered tremendously from legacies of its authoritarian past, which had resulted in a closed civil society on top of a weak oversight structure and a focus on perceived threats. However, the Spanish service has gone a long way the past few years, with critical junctures, such as 9/11 and 11M, and the media aiding the route toward reform and democratization.

CONCLUSION

In this chapter, emphasis has been put on civil society in Portugal, Greece, and Spain, both as an indicator that helps measure intelligence democratization and as a factor that supported or impeded reform. When looking at civil society, a key area that emerges in SSR literature, we looked into the following key pointers: solid media coverage over intelligence affairs, the existence or not of robust legal frameworks for public access to documents, and partnerships between the intelligence services with universities. The public sentiment toward intelligence was also highlighted because it is an element that facilitated but at times also hindered progress. It is evident that all three countries at various points faced limitations when it came to civil society. Portugal, having removed its authoritarian past, managed to establish a strong and engaged civil society early on. Except for a few minor hiccups, existent in even mature democracies, it continues to work toward a more open service. Spain appears to have made real progress in civil society matters over intelligence in recent years. Greece remains far behind them.

Portugal and Spain are ahead of Greece regarding partnerships between universities and the intelligence services. When it comes to working closely with universities, Spain appears to have made good progress over the past two decades to establish an intelligence discipline there. This has helped both sides learn from each other. Portugal has also done very well in introducing and establishing a strong intelligence discipline with universities and high-profile schools and institutes around the country. There has been a copromotion of courses as well as a postgraduate program on intelligence. Greece on the other hand, has fallen way behind compared to the other two, with no established intelligence discipline. RIEAS is the only research institute that has tried the past decade to drive the conversation on intelligence, with some success mainly within academic circles.

Sentiment toward intelligence services during the authoritarian regimes of the case studies persisted during transition and acted both to support and obstruct intelligence democratization. Civil society in Portugal was very suspicious of the new intelligence service in the early 1980s due to the legacy sentiment toward Salazar's PIDE. This is a reason why the purging process was pushed mainly by the people rather than the government. In the 1990s Portuguese suspicion grew, given the Spanish GAL affair—this is when media played a key role. The government's effort to reach its citizens by opening up the service more throughout the years has helped make further progress. Additionally, civil society groups and associations started to form quickly during the transition period in Portugal. This boosted informal oversight. In Greece, the citizens equated the KYP with the junta and were extremely suspicious of it being used as a government tool again. Later on, and until today, due to the absence of real media oversight and no study of the discipline of intelligence, Greek citizens do not have a proper understanding of what the EYP is, what its objectives are, and whether (and how) they can interact with it. There is, therefore, a general disengagement on their part. In Spain, the pact of forgetting acted as a barrier to intelligence democratization not only in terms of recruitment but also in civil society matters. As civil society wanted to forget the past, it pushed for the implementation of the pact of forgetting, and, like in Greece, it was disengaged from CESID until scandals started to emerge. At this point it was the media rather than civil society groups or associations that tried to hold the Spanish government to account.

The revelation of scandals in Spain (and Portugal) acted as a positive catalyst for informal oversight and, eventually, reform. In Portugal a new, independent press was established relatively quickly during the transition period. It has driven conversations about intelligence matters and has also facilitated change due to its revelation of scandals and issues. Portugal's handful of incidents were dealt with quickly and effectively, to which the media contributed. As part of the change, the result has been the launch of a strong intelligence discipline as well as a high-quality website where the services' objectives are clearly stated. This provides a direct channel to the public, an alternative to the media. Contrary to Portugal, the presence of the media in Greece is of low quality and most of the time linked to political parties, as are the majority of any civil society groups or associations. Although this "apolitical overpoliticization" decreased in the late 1980s when entrepreneurs founded new press outlets, any informal oversight from the media remained limited. This is because even though direct partisanship by media stations was mitigated, the quality of the press was extremely low. The closed culture that came from the service contributed to that. Unfortunately, media sources upon which any coverage was based was very poor. This situation has persisted since the 1990s. Indeed, there is no special expertise in the Greek media. Spain moved closer to intelligence democratization due to the media. New independent presses, such as *El País*, came in relatively quickly. Although coverage was not as in-depth initially (one of the reasons being that the public did not exactly know what was pertinent information), over time it focused on key issues, including scandals such as the GAL affair and the wiretapping of the king, the need for reform, and interagency cooperation. The result of this high-quality press that emerged due to CESID's illegal activities helped push to establish the CNI, a new civilian intelligence service in 2002. The media in Spain continues to drive informal oversight over the CNI. In recent years, it has been reporting on issues and challenges facing the service as well as the government as a whole. Due to this coverage, the latter has admitted that there is still room for improvement.

All cases faced some level of limitation when it came to the legal basis for internal oversight. As with every other indicator, the existence of a robust legal framework and oversight is key for that indicator to work effectively. Indeed, all three countries experienced shortcomings when it came to a legal framework for informal oversight. This usually means that there are no adequately solid laws to guarantee a free press, the creation of civil society associations, and the citizens' rights to access information.

Starting with Portugal, there are a few positive elements within the law that offer a basis for informal oversight. For example, at the beginning of the transition, the law and constitution dictated that Portuguese civil society has the right to litigate against any administrative acts that were illegal and request information from SIRP. Freedom of the press and the media was also added to the constitution. This slightly changed later. In the past decade, for instance, the legal framework included caveats that made it difficult for the public to access information as easily as before.[115] However, a more open structure in comparison to the other two countries has been established through the open access of, for instance, historical archives to the public.

The presence of caveats within the law has been prominent in Greece. Although based on the existing legal framework Greek citizens have access to administrative documents, individual departments have the right to block it. Despite an effort for the EYP to be more open and transparent with the creation in 2008 of a Historical Archive Service, any documentation becomes accessible only after fifty years. There exists a closed, authoritarian-like culture of intelligence that does not create a solid basis for an active civil society or a close relationship between the public and the intelligence organizations. This is opposite to Portugal's PIDE and DGS archives, which are accessible to everyone. Spain, on the other hand, continued to experience Francoist practices after its transition. For instance, any potential civil society organization needed to have a "declaration of public utility" for it to be legitimate. This past decade, transparency laws have come into force, but as in Greece these include caveats. For example, the 2013 transparency law included limitations to the right of access for any information that related to national security, defense, foreign relations, public safety, and other subject areas within the domain of the CNI, while sources confirm that historians struggle with the declassification process in Spain.[116]

The mass mobilization that took place in Portugal before the Carnation Revolution showed that change came from within Portuguese society itself. This laid the basis for an open civil society during and after the transition period. With the need for change coming from the people, leading to a critical juncture and the uprooting of authoritarianism, Portugal created an open intelligence-service culture. In Greece, the subsequent politicization culture of all aspects of society, including the media, meant that authoritarian legacies persisted and resulted in a closed intelligence system. In Spain, "ways of doing things" were stuck in the Francoist era, with the pact of forgetting being pushed forward by Spanish society. It was only after the revelation of high-profile scandals that one saw reform being pursued. The above shows that Portugal has made the most steps toward democratization when looking at civil society, compared to Greece and Spain.

In this chapter, it has become clear that the media plays a key role in holding a government and state institutions to account when other, more formal actors fail to do so. The media can encourage intelligence reform and "increased transparency."[117] This, of course, applies to mature democracies too. Media played a key role in Spain, as it was one of the factors that supported change and pushed for reform on numerous occasions. An interesting finding is that more attention should be placed on the media as a factor that can facilitate reform and on its need to be included in the SSR framework. As Marina Caparini argues, "the security sector community and wider peacebuilding community have in general been slow to appreciate the vital role of the news media in sustaining and strengthening democratic processes, and thus the need to incorporate the news media in SSR efforts."[118] Based on the evidence, this chapter supports Caparini's argument and encourages further research on the media within the SSR framework.

NOTES

1. Robert Putnam, "Bowling Alone: America's Declining Social Capital," *Journal of Democracy* 6, no. 1 (1995): 65–78.

2. Philippe Schmitter, "Alternatives for the Future European Polity: Is Federalism the Only Answer?," in *Démocratie et construction européenne* [Democracy and European construction], ed. Mario Telò (Brussels: Éditions de l'Université de Bruxelles, 1995), 285.

3. Kerstin Hamann and Paul Christopher Manuel, "Regime Changes and Civil Society in Twentieth-Century Portugal," *South European Society and Politics* 4, no. 1 (1999): 72.

4. Hamann and Manuel, 73.

5. Gill, *Intelligence Governance and Democratisation*, table 2.1.

6. Antje Fritz, *Watching the Watchdogs: The Role of the Media in Intelligence Oversight in Germany*, Working Paper no. 138 (Geneva: Geneva Centre for Security Sector Governance, 2004), 1.

7. James Curran, Shanto Iyengar, Anker Brink Lund, and Inka Salovaara-Moring, "Media System, Public Knowledge and Democracy: A Comparative Study," *European Journal of Communication* 24, no. 1 (2009): 47.

8. Hillebrand, "Role of News Media in Intelligence Oversight," 690–91.

9. David S. Landes, ed., *Western Europe: The Trials of Partnership*, Critical Choices for Americans (Lexington, MA: Lexington Books, 1977), 241. See also Juan J. Linz, "From Great Hopes to Civil War: The Breakdown of Democracy in Spain," in *The Breakdown of Democratic Regimes*, ed. Juan J. Linz and Alfred Stepan (Baltimore: Johns Hopkins University Press, 1979). See also Juan J. Linz, ed., *Informe sociologico sobre el cambio politico en España, 1975–1981* [Sociological information on political changes in Spain, 1975–1981] (Madrid: Fundación Foessa, 1981), and Juan J. Linz and Alfred Stepan, *Problems of Democratic Transition and Consolidation* (Baltimore: Johns Hopkins University Press, 1998).

10. Philippe C. Schmitter, "The Democratization of Portugal in Its Comparative Perspective," in *Portugal e a transição para a democracia (1974–1976)* [Portugal and the transition to democracy (1974–1976)], ed. Fernando Rosas (Lisbon: Colibri, 1999), 360.

11. Tiago Fernandes, "Rethinking Pathways to Democracy: Civil Society in Portugal and Spain, 1960s–2000s," *Democratization* 22, no. 6 (2015): 1083.

12. Robert Fishman, "How Civil Society Matters in Democratization: Setting the Boundaries of Post-Transition Political Inclusion," *Comparative Politics* 49, 3 (2017): 399.

13. Charles Downs, "Residents' Commissions and Urban Struggles in Revolutionary Portugal," in *In Search of Modern Portugal: The Revolution and Its Consequences*, ed. Lawrence S. Graham and Douglas S. Wheeler (Madison: University of Wisconsin Press, 1983), 10.

14. Fernandes, "Rethinking Pathways to Democracy," 1084.

15. "História das Informações" [Information history], SIRP, www.sirpt/quem-somos/historia.

16. Costa Pinto, "Authoritarian Legacies," 177.

17. Costa Pinto, 178.

18. Article 2, Democratic State and Transition to Socialism, Constitution of the Portuguese Republic (Decree of 10/04 1976).

19. Article 269, Rights and Guarantees of the Administered, paragraph 1, 1976 Portuguese constitution, https://www.parlamento.pt/Parlamento/Documents/CRP1976.pdf.

20. Article 268, Rights and Guarantees of the Administered, paragraph 2, 1976 Portuguese constitution, https://www.parlamento.pt/Parlamento/Documents/CRP1976.pdf.

21. Paragraph 3 being particularly notable: "Freedom of the press implies the right of journalists, under the terms of the law, to access sources of information and to the protection of professional independence and secrecy, as well as the right to elect editorial boards." See Article 38, Decree of April 10, 1976, Constitution of the Portuguese Republic.

22. Costa Pinto, "Authoritarian Legacies," 187.

23. Costa Pinto, 193.

24. Solsten, *Portugal*. See also Sónia Reis and Manuel Botelho da Silva, "O sistema de informações da República Portuguesa," *Revista da Ordem dos Advogados* 67, no. 3 (2007).

25. Article 268, Rights and Guarantees of the Administered, 1982 Portuguese constitution, https://dre.pt/web/guest/pesquisa/-/search/375254/details/normal?l=1.

26. Article 268, Right and Guarantees of the Administered, 1989 Portuguese constitution, https://dre.pt/home/-/dre/496551/details/maximized.

27. Article 5, Internal and External Security, paragraph 1, Law No. 65/93 of August 26, Access to Administration Documents, https://dre.pt/pesquisa/-/search/632408/details/maximized.

28. Francisco Rui Cádima, "The Media and Democracy in Portugal," *Verso e Reverso* 24, no. 55 (2010): 15–16.

29. "Nome de Cavaco Silva invocado em processo dos grupos antiterroristas de libertação" [Cavaco Silva's name invoked in the process of anti-terrorist liberation groups], *Jornal de Notícias*, April 5, 2011, www.jn.pt/mundo/nome-de-cavaco-silva-invocado-em-processo-dos-grupos-antiterroristas-de-libertacao-1823278.html.

30. Matei and Bruneau, "Intelligence Reform in New Democracies," 614–15.

31. "PS quer saber se ex-espião manteve vínculo com estado após 2010" [PS wants to know if former spy maintained links with the state after 2010], *Notícias ao Minuto*, March 27, 2013, www.noticiasaominuto.com/politica/57941/ps-quer-saber-se-ex-espi%C3%A3o-manteve-v%C3%ADnculo-com-estado-ap%C3%B3s-2010?utm_medium=social&utm_source=twitter.com&utm_campaign=buffer&utm_content=geral.

32. Article 2, General Appreciation, paragraph 1 of a letter dated 13-02-2014 between António José Pimpão, president of CADA, and Dr. Fernando Negrão, chairman of the Constitutional Affairs, Rights, Freedoms and Guarantees Committee, Lisbon.

33. Article 6, Restrictions and Right of Access, paragraphs 1–9, Law No. 26/2016, August 22, 2016, https://dre.pt/web/guest/pesquisa/-/search/75177807/details/maximized.

34. "O SIS não pode ter acesso a dados Pessoais" [SIS cannot have access to Personal data], *Notícias ao Minuto*, July 4, 2015, www.noticiasaominuto.com/pais/415872/o-sis-nao-pode-ter-acesso-a-dados-pessoais.

35. Organic Law No. 4/2017, *Diário da República*, no. 164/2017, series I, 2017-08-25.

36. João Estevens and Teresa Ferreira Rodrigues, "Democracy and Intelligence Culture in Portugal (1974–2019): A Complex Relationship," *International Journal of Intelligence, Security, and Public Affairs* 22, no. 1 (2020): 36.

37. Estevens and Ferreira Rodrigues, 36.
38. "SIRP faz avaliação 'claramente positiva' da abertura à sociedade" [SIRP makes a 'clearly positive' assessment of openness to society], *Notícias ao Minuto*, January 29, 2019, www.noticiasaominuto.com/pais/1188414/sirp-faz-avaliacao-claramente-positiva-da-abertura-a-sociedade.
39. Phillipe C. Schmitter, "An Introduction to South European Transitions from Authoritarian Rule: Greece, Portugal, Spain, and Turkey," in *Transition from Authoritarian Rule: Southern Europe*, ed. Philippe C. Schmitter, Guillermo O' Donnel, and Lawrence C. Whitehead (Baltimore: Johns Hopkins University Press, 1986), 6–8.
40. Nicos P. Mouzelis, *Politics in the Semi-Periphery: Early Parliamentarism and Late Industrialisation in the Balkans and Latin America* (London: Macmillan, 1987).
41. Kevin Featherstone, "Socialist Parties in Southern Europe and the Enlarged European Community" (paper, UACES/Centre of Mediterranean Studies Conference, Bristol, UK, October 23, 1987), as referenced in Fotini Papatheodrou and David Machin, "The Umbilical Cord That Was Never Cut: The Post-Dictatorial Intimacy between the Political Elite and the Mass Media in Greece and Spain," *European Journal of Communication* 18, no. 1 (2003): 33–34.
42. See, for example, the crushing of the Athens Polytechnic uprising.
43. Dimitri A. Sotiropoulos, *Formal Weakness and Informal Strength: Civil Society in Contemporary Greece*, Discussion Paper no. 16 (London: Hellenic Observatory, London School of Economics, 2004), 17–18.
44. Sotiropoulos, 17–18.
45. The CIA has always denied that it sponsored the 1967 coup in any way or controlled KYP's activities. For many on the Greek left, however, CIA manipulation of Greek affairs has been treated as a fact and supported by many different sources. See, for example, "London Paper Asserts C.I.A. Engineered the Coup in Greece," *New York Times*, July 1, 1973, www.nytimes.com/1973/07/01/archives/london-paper-asserts-c-i-a-engineered-the-coup-in-greece-sent-to.html.
46. Boersma et al., *Histories of State Surveillance*, 59.
47. Minas Samatas, *Surveillance in Greece*, 39.
48. Samatas, 39.
49. Papatheodrou and Machin, "Umbilical Cord," 32.
50. Nikos Leandros, *The Print Mass Media of Communication in Greece* (Athens: Delphini, 1992).
51. Papatheodrou and Machin, "Umbilical Cord," 35.
52. Nomikos, "Terrorism, Media, and Intelligence in Greece," 66.
53. Paragraph 1, Article 16, Right to Know of Administrative Documents, Law 1599/1986, State-Citizen Relations, Introduction of a New Type of Identity Card and other provisions.
54. Paragraph 1, Article 16, Law 1599/1986.
55. Papatheodrou and Machin, "Umbilical Cord," 38.
56. "Grave Scandal for Greece," *New York Times*, June 18, 1989, www.nytimes.com/1989/06/18/world/grave-scandal-for-greece.html.
57. Papatheodrou and Machin, "Umbilical Cord," 40.
58. UNESCO, *Statistical Yearbook* (Paris: UNESCO, 1999).
59. Apostolidis, *Mystiki Drasi*, 288.
60. Apostolidis, 288.

61. Nomikos, "Terrorism, Media, and Intelligence in Greece," 66.
62. Karyotis, "Greek Terrorism," 7. A 1982 report of the Greek National Intelligence Service (NIS/EYP) pointed out that 17 November was a "phantom organization" that possibly does not exist but is a loosely organized group of isolated anarchists that share a common belief in armed struggle.
63. Helena Smith, "Terrorists Hold Greece Hostage," *Guardian*, May 27, 1999 https://www.theguardian.com/world/1999/may/27/helenasmith.
64. Christos Demetis, "Όταν η 17 Νοέμβρη Χτύπησε Το MEGA—Τι Έλεγε ο Κουφοντίνας Στη Δίκη" [When N17 hit Mega—what Koufontinas said at the trial], *News 24/7*, October 28, 2018, www.news247.gr/media/otan-i-17-noemvri-chtypise-to-mega-ti-elege-o-koyfontinas-sti-diki.6662185.html.
65. Paragraph 5, Article 3, Law No. 2690, *Government Gazette*, A 45, 9.3.1999, Ratification of the Code of Administrative Procedure and other provisions.
66. Nomikos, "Terrorism, Media, and Intelligence in Greece," 72.
67. Paragraph 1, Article 1, Law No. 3115, *Government Gazette*, A 47, 27.2.2003.
68. Paragraph 2, Article 1, Law No. 3115, *Government Gazette*, A 47, 27.2.2003.
69. Article 9, Law No. 3115, *Government Gazette*, A 47, 27.2.2003.
70. Article 3, Composition and Structure, Law No. 3649, *Government Gazette*, A 39, 3.3.2008, National Intelligence Service and other provisions.
71. Article 3, Composition and Structure, Law No. 3649, *Government Gazette*, A 39, 3.3.2008, National Intelligence Service and other provisions.
72. RIEAS, https://www.rieas.gr/about-us.
73. See, for example, two major news stories that received only minor coverage: "Public Order Minister Assures Intelligence Service Not Bugging Political Parties," *Kathimerini*, October 9, 2013, www.ekathimerini.com/news/154471/public-order-minister-assures-intelligence-service-not-bugging-political-parties/, and "Βαρουφάκης: Επί Κυβέρνησης Τσίπρα η ΕΥΠ Παρακολουθούσε Και Υπουργούς" [Varoufakis: During the Tsipras Government, the EYP Wiretapped Ministers too], *Ethnos*, August 5, 2019, www.ethnos.gr/politiki/54171_baroyfakis-epi-kybernisis-tsipra-i-eyp-parakoloythoyse-kai-ypoyrgoys.
74. Nomikos, "Intelligence Studies in Greece."
75. Fernandes, "Rethinking Pathways to Democracy," 1087.
76. Paloma Aguilar, "Collective Memory of the Spanish Civil War: The Case of the Political Amnesty in the Spanish Transition to Democracy," *Democratization* 4, no. 4 (1997): 92.
77. Aguilar, 92. See also Edward Malefakis, "Spain and Its Francoist Heritage," in *From Dictatorship to Democracy: Copying with the Legacies of Authoritarianism and Totalitarianism*, ed. J. H. Herz (Westport, CT: Greenwood, 1982).
78. Malefakis, "Spain and Its Francoist Heritage, 216.
79. J. M. Maravall and J. Santamaria, "Political Change in Spain and the Prospects for Democracy," in *Transitions from Authoritarian Rule: Tentative Conclusions about Uncertain Democracies*, ed. Guillermo O'Donnell and Philippe C. Schmitter (Baltimore: Johns Hopkins University Press, 1986), 80–84.
80. Patricia L. Hipsher, "Democratization and the Decline of Urban Social Movements in Chile and Spain," *Comparative Politics* 28, no. 3 (1996): 291.
81. Fernandes, "Rethinking Pathways to Democracy," 1090–91.
82. Article 105, Spanish constitution, BOE no. 311, December 29, 1978.
83. Papatheodorou and Machin, "Umbilical Cord," 35–36.

84. Díaz Fernández, "Intelligence Services and Mass Media," 91.

85. Díaz Fernández, 93.

86. Díaz Fernández, 93.

87. Díaz Fernández, 93.

88. Díaz Fernández, 94.

89. Díaz Fernández, 95.

90. Díaz Fernández, *Los servicios de intelligencia españoles*, 295.

91. This law stated that the public's "right to access" was not allowed to be exercised when it came to files containing information on national defense, state security, or the prosecution of crimes. See Paragraph 5b, Article 37, Right of Access to Files and Records, Law 30/1992 of November 26, on the Legal Regime of Public Administrations and Common Administrative Procedure, BOE no. 285, November 27, 1992.

92. William Chislett, *Spain: What Everyone Needs to Know* (New York: Oxford University Press, 2013), 126.

93. Chislett, 67.

94. Javier García, "Del Batallón Vasco Español a los GAL" [From the Spanish Basque Battalion to the GAL], *El País*, April 7, 1985, https://elpais.com/diario/1985/04/08/espana/481759208_850215.html.

95. Sebastian Balfour, *The Politics of Contemporary Spain: Reader in Contemporary Spanish Studies* (Abingdon, UK: Routledge, 2005), 67.

96. Chislett, *Spain*, 125.

97. Balfour, *Politics of Contemporary Spain*, 69.

98. Balfour, 70.

99. Balfour, 64.

100. "Spain's State-Sponsored Death Squads," BBC News, July 29, 1998, http://news.bbc.co.uk/2/hi/europe/141720.stm.

101. Díaz Fernández, "Intelligence Services and Mass Media in Spain," 96.

102. Díaz Fernández, 96.

103. Díaz Fernández, 96.

104. Díaz Fernández, 97.

105. Richard Jackson and D. Pisoiu, *Contemporary Debates on Terrorism* (London: Routledge, 2018), chap. 4.

106. Fernando Jiménez, "Political Scandals and Political Responsibility in Democratic Spain," *West European Politics* 21, no. 4 (1998): 84.

107. Angel Smith, *Historical Dictionary of Spain* (Lanham, MD: Rowan & Littlefield, 2017), 321.

108. Díaz Fernández, "Intelligence Services and Mass Media in Spain," 98.

109. Díaz Fernández, 98.

110. Matei, de Castro García, and Halladay, "On Balance," 777.

111. Díaz Fernández, "Intelligence Services and Mass Media in Spain," 101.

112. CNI official website, http://www.cni.es/es/culturainteligencia/intoduction. See also Díaz Fernández, "Spanish Intelligence in the Mediterranean Context," 160.

113. Rubén Arcos, "Academics as Strategic Stakeholders of Intelligence Organizations: A View from Spain," *International Journal of Intelligence and CounterIntelligence* 26, no. 2 (2013): 340.

114. CNI official website, http:/www.cni.es.

115. Article 6, Restrictions and Right of Access, paragraphs 1–9, Law No. 26/2016, August 22, 2016, https://dre.pt/web/guest/pesquisa/-/search/75177807/details/maximized.

116. Article 14, Law 19/2013, December 9, on transparency, access to public information, and good governance, BOE no. 295, 12/10/2013.

117. Matei and Bruneau, "Intelligence Reform in New Democracies," 621.

118. Marina Caparini, ed., *News Media and Security Sector Reform: Reporters on Telling the Story* (Münster: LIT Verlag, 2010).

Conclusion

On April 25, 1974, the streets of Lisbon were filled with soldiers, tanks, and assorted armored vehicles. Cheering them on were thousands of civilians, some of whom distributed red carnations among the crowd. There was no parade scheduled that day but instead a military coup that saw the forty-two-year regime of António de Oliveira Salazar and his heir, Marcello Caetano, consigned to the dustbin of history. In the two years that followed, the Greek junta was also replaced, and the government of Francoist Spain dissolved. Such was the beginning of the so-called third wave of democratization, a process of change that affected every aspect of the countries involved, from the structure of their societies to the organization of their national institutions.[1] No part of the state escaped the touch of democratization, even in the intelligence sphere, but this is not to say that all of the intelligence organizations democratized at the same pace or depth. We need to remember that democratization is a process rather than an end destination. As highlighted earlier in the book, even mature democracies face issues when it comes to intelligence democratization, as evidenced by the scandals that have come to light in the United States in recent years. The question, therefore, is not which case study has reached a full intelligence democratization status, if that is ever possible, but rather which has taken more steps toward it.

The analysis compared the levels of intelligence democratization in the Portuguese, Greek, and Spanish intelligence services from the fall of their dictatorships to 2021. To do so, the analysis used five SSR indicators that emerged from the available literature on intelligence democratization, SSR, and the countries in question: lustration, control and oversight, recruitment, targeting, and civil society. Based on these indicators, key questions for each of them were examined:

- **Lustration:** Did each state go through a robust lustration process, and, if so, when? What was the (positive) effect of lustration for each country?
- **Control and oversight:** Is there a legal basis for oversight? Is there sufficient control? Is there proper parliamentary oversight? Are there any

other established forms and levels of (external) oversight, such as judiciary? Can we make observations around their applicability?

- **Recruitment:** Do the intelligence services hire based on merit and qualifications or loyalty to the regime/government? If yes to the former, when did they start doing so? Are there police and/or military personnel present in the civilian intelligence services?
- **Targeting:** Do the intelligence services target actual threats to national security, and, if so, when did they start doing so? Do the intelligence services use methods that violate domestic law to collect information? Is there a legal basis for oversight when it comes to targeting?
- **Civil society:** Are there civil society groups and a robust media presence that drive informal oversight? Are there established partnerships between universities and the intelligence services? Is there an open culture of intelligence? Is there a legal basis for informal oversight through, for instance, transparency laws?

The SSR indicators examined in the book are somewhat interlinked. For example, there cannot be a solid control and oversight system without a process of lustration preceding its establishment. Equally, there cannot be a robust recruitment process or targeting without a strong control and oversight structure. The SSR indicators help measure the intelligence democratization levels in each country. *Based on the analysis through the SSR lens, we can posit that there is indeed a difference across the three cases.* The analysis shows that the Portuguese intelligence service is the most democratized when compared to the Greek and the Spanish ones because it uprooted authoritarian elements early on. Critical junctures facilitated progress across all three case studies but at different times. When authoritarian roots are so well established, only by an intensive process of lustration and/or a critical juncture can substantial reform take place. Civil society is key in driving reform as well as participating in critical junctures, as evidenced in the case of Portugal. Portugal is the most democratized across the three based on the findings of the comparison that follow.

The case studies that did not apply a proper *lustration* process faced more resistance when they tried to apply reform and move closer to democratizing. When looking at lustration as one of the indicators examined in this book, it becomes evident that each country applied a different approach. Portugal followed a more intensive lustration process, with an established committee dedicated to purge any authoritarian elements. This led to a smoother transition process whereby solid control and oversight mechanisms were launched and applied quickly. Contrary to Portugal, Greece decided to apply a "decapitating" lustration strategy, with only the top-level junta officials being punished. In the medium and long run, this resulted in legacy personnel taking on high-ranking

TABLE C.1. SSR indicators in Portugal, Greece, and Spain

	Portugal	Greece	Spain
Lustration: Did each case study go through a robust lustration process, and if so, when? Did case studies that did not apply a solid lustration process meet resistance later?	**Yes.** Complete uprooting of authoritarian elements early on.	**No.** A "decapitating" approach to lustration was followed, resulting in authoritarian legacies within the Greek intelligence service.	**No.** A "pact of forgetting" established a business-as-usual status quo, with Francoist components persisting after the fall of the dictatorship.
Control and oversight: Is there a legal basis for oversight? Is there sufficient control? Is there proper parliamentary oversight? Are there any other established forms and levels of external oversight, such as judiciary? Are they cosmetic or real?	**Yes.** Fom the establishment of SIRP, strong internal and external oversight, including judiciary and solid legal framework. Key examples: the assembly's supervisory board, which runs mandatory inspections, and the SIRP framework law.	**No.** Executive oversight along with parliamentary questions are main elements. Cosmetic external oversight with EYP being able to bypass the authority of the Greek Ombudsman. Executive control is the most prominent type of oversight.	**No, but some progress has been made.** Symbolic legal framework, with key deputies not allowed to have access to classified information. Some progress after the GAL affair, with deputies gaining the authority to influence how much money is assigned to CESID and what it was used for. Progress after 9/11 with better judiciary oversight.
Recruitment: Do the intelligence services hire based on merit and qualifications or loyalty to the regime/government? If yes to the former, when did they start doing so? What exactly were the staff recruited to do? And how were they approached—through open and transparent means? Or was it through opaque practices, such as personal contacts, direct appointments, or "friendly recommendations"? Are police and/or military personnel part of the civilian intelligence democratization?	**Yes.** Initially limited personnel due to lustration process that the service had gone through and legacy of PIDE suspicion from the public. Since 9/11 and 11M, as well as more recently, increase of more relevant and qualified staff for current threats.	**No.** Highly militarized and nepotistic even to the present day, with limited qualified nonuniformed personnel. Stagnant since 2010 due to financial crisis, but opportunity for improvement in the future.	**No, but progress has been made.** Initially highly militarized and nepotistic. Some nepotism remains, but mainly recruitment is based on merit, with a diverse number of roles all related to relevant threats.

	Portugal	Greece	Spain
Targeting: Do the intelligence services target actual threats to national security, and if so, when did they start doing so? Do the intelligence services use any illegal methods to collect information? Is there a legal basis for oversight when it comes to targeting?	**Yes.** Focus on real threats from the beginning, with a robust legal framework that highlighted clear responsibilities. The notion of "proportionality" was also embedded in the law.	**No, but limited progress has been made.** Focus on communism using surveillance methods for a very long time, with terrorism being characterized as a "non-threat." Unclear set of responsibilities, given the high volume of military personnel in secondment. After 9/11, more focus on real, relevant threats.	**No, but progress has been made.** Emphasis on perceived threats such as student subversive groups. Initially, and for a long time, too many services involved in collection, creating a blurry division of responsibilities. Illegal methods with massive scandals emerging (e.g., GAL affair and the wiretapping of key figures). 9/11 and the Madrid attacks pushed Spain to focus on real threats while resources increased.

office positions in Greece's security institutions and a poor oversight structure. Similarly, Spain took things one step further, with the "pact of forgetting" effectively amnestying illegal activities that had taken place during the authoritarian rule. Because of this, Spain also struggled for a long time and came across deep resistance features when it tried to democratize. Of key importance was the fact that any legal framework was mostly cosmetic, while the country kept experiencing high levels of undemocratic intelligence behavior. The GAL affair and the wiretapping of key figures, such as the king, are two key examples that demonstrate such legacy culture. These kinds of activities continued until key critical junctures, such as 9/11 and 11M, emerged and acted as catalysts for reform in Spain.

Control and oversight **varied significantly across the three case studies, from absence of mechanisms to the presence of ineffective ones. This affected targeting, recruitment, and civil society groups.** Regarding control and oversight, Portugal seems to have been ahead of Greece and Spain from early on. This was not only because of the presence of internal and external oversight but also because of its robustness. A key example includes the CFSIRP, which runs *mandatory* inspections, as well as the fact that the opposition is involved in the control and oversight process. Up to this day, "opinions" generated by CFSIRP, which has access to a wealth of information, confirms that intelligence services have abided by democratic principles. This contrasts with Spain, where for a very long time representatives of areas such as Catalonia and the Basque region had no say in any of the control and oversight proceedings. At the opposite end, one finds Greece, whose main oversight structure relies upon executive control and parliamentary questions to which answers can be avoided based on the excuse of "national security." Comparably, Spain currently lies somewhere in between. Although it started with a cosmetic legal framework, it has made rapid steps forward the past two decades. Indeed, at present, there are better oversight mechanisms, including the judiciary, which was lacking significantly previously.

Recruitment is a key indicator that is linked to lustration as well as civil society. Legacies of the authoritarian past severely affected Greece and Spain. After a robust purging process, Portugal was able to build a new intelligence service without any authoritarian remnants. This presented a few limitations in the short run. For instance, it was difficult to recruit from scratch due to civil society's suspicion of PIDE. Up until the 1990s and early 2000s, therefore, recruitment was thin. Since then the Portuguese intelligence service has focused on recruiting staff able to fight real threats to Portuguese national security. On the opposite side, we observe Greece, whose service was and still is suffering from nepotistic practices, something that started with Papandreou"s "green guards." This has affected the quality of staff, while a strong presence of uniformed personnel still exists. This is a result mainly of authoritarian legacies as well as the effort of the policymakers to distance themselves from them. Although in theory the logic of distancing themselves from authoritarian elements was sound, in practice it resulted in the service becoming extremely politicized. The service has remained stagnant as it stopped recruiting in 2010 due to the financial crisis. There exists, however, an opportunity for the service to now revise its practices and move toward more democratic ones. Spain had highly militarized and nepotistic services for a long time, a result that emerged due to the Francoist legacies that persisted. It is interesting to note, however, that despite these issues, Spain has made significant progress in recent years. Again, critical junctures, such as 9/11 and 11M, played a key role in supporting this change. Spain is now recruiting mainly on the basis of merit and focuses on candidates who have the academic and technical skills that are relevant to current and real threats. A very small number of candidates is reported to still be recruited based on connections rather than merit. Big steps have been made in Spain, with more progress needed.

Targeting **actual rather than perceived threats came late for most of the case studies' countries, with illegal, authoritarian-like collection methods persisting for a long time.** Portugal was indeed the only among the three that focused on real, relevant threats from early on. After going through an intensive purging process that gave it the ability to uproot nondemocratic elements, which resulted in a vigorous control and oversight system, Portugal was able to target relevant threats to national security. Portugal responded to terrorist activities quickly in the 1980s. Since then and especially after 9/11 and the Madrid attacks, it has only built onto its solid framework to continue combating relevant threats. On the other hand, both Greece and Spain focused on perceived enemies for a long time, namely communism and student subversive groups. Spain suffered from a long series of systematic scandals that revealed the unconstitutional and illegal practices CESID was involved in, including the GAL affair. Spain indeed made significant steps after 9/11 and 11M, with more emphasis on terrorism, a strong boost in resources, and a better legal framework and oversight system to target those threats (although a few shortcomings persist). Critical junctures, such as 9/11, had a limited effect on Greece, which increased the personnel of the service after the attacks and started to target real threats, although authoritarian legacies remained in the recruitment process.

Portugal and Spain have established more active and open civil societies when it comes to intelligence, compared to Greece. As civil society was a key force that facilitated the fall of the dictatorship in Portugal and pushed for lustration during the transition period, it helped establish an open culture and a general sentiment to always check the country's institutions. Today Portugal has an open civil society that engages with the intelligence services, a strong media presence, and partnerships with universities. Portugal has also established a website with clear objectives as well as a national archive where PIDE documentation is accessible to the general public. Although Spain has made significant progress in the past two decades, it did not have a strong start like Portugal. Indeed, for decades after the end of the Franco era, Spanish civil society was disengaged from intelligence affairs as a result of the pact of forgetting. After the revelation of massive scandals, 9/11, and 11M, Spanish civil society's interest in intelligence matters changed. The media played a fundamental role in this as it revealed the authoritarian-like and illegal activities CESID was involved in. During the past two decades, the Spanish intelligence service has established partnerships with universities and founded a solid intelligence discipline, while the media continues to play a key role in providing informal oversight. Unfortunately, Greece has remained behind the other two countries as it continues to lack university partnerships, a robust media presence, and a clear legal framework for public access to information.

In this conclusion, up until now, we have mainly examined the "how." Indeed, it is evident that there are different levels of intelligence democratization across the three case studies based on the chosen indicators of the SSR lens. The Portuguese intelligence service emerges as the most democratized when compared to the other two. We will now focus on the "why." Why do the three intelligence services therefore experience different levels of intelligence democratization? A few elements emerged in the analysis as factors that can support or impede reform. We have observed them throughout the book, but it is key to sum them up here.

***Authoritarian legacies* emerge as the main reason why reform has been resisted and democratization has been slower in Greece and Spain.** Portugal has been the only country in the three case studies that did not suffer from authoritarian remnants that obstructed reform. This was because it managed to uproot those elements early on through a process of lustration. Civil society played a key role in this process, as it was the Portuguese populace that helped drive the fall of the dictatorship and the Carnation Revolution as well as the purging process that followed. Greece, on the other hand, continued to experience the deep roots of authoritarianism that continued after the fall of the junta. This resulted in a poor control and oversight system, with the intelligence service focusing on perceived threats for a long time, a politicized organization with nepotistic recruitment process, and a closed civil society. The Francoist culture persisted in Spain in all areas of society and its institutions, including the Spanish intelligence services. This meant that with the pact of forgetting, control and oversight mechanisms, where existent, were purely cosmetic. Their poor applicability was obvious in the several high-profile scandals that emerged in the media which revealed that CEDID's collection practices were vastly illegal, while the service targeted perceived rather than actual threats. Civil society was disengaged for a long time until those scandals came to light in the mid-1990s. Since then and with the two critical junctures of 9/11 and 11M, one of which took place on Spanish soil, Spain has made tremendous progress across the four analyzed indicators, something that has resulted in authoritarian practices no longer being standard practice and significant steps being made toward intelligence democratization.

***Civil society* pushed for or arrested change throughout all case studies and across several indicators, including lustration.** Civil society has been a key indicator to help measure intelligence democratization in each case study. When it comes to civil society, though, it is not only the indicator on its own that matters but also the fact that it can act as a factor that can support or arrest change. In Portugal, although the Carnation Revolution was mainly a military affair, it was the mass mobilization that pushed for the fall of the authoritarian regime. The change, therefore, came from within. Following that and when looking at lustration, it became evident that civil society played a fundamental role in the way the Portuguese purging process took place. Given the civil society's extremely negative sentiment toward PIDE, a more "radical" method to lustration was needed. In Spain, on the other hand, the citizens' urge to forget the past led to a completely different "method"—that of the pact of forgetting.

In Greece, the faction-based result of the fall of the junta across the Greek populace meant that Konstantinos Karamanlis needed to get rid of any junta elements while keeping the military and security sector onside. This resulted in a moderate decapitating strategy, with authoritarian legacies remaining. Civil society is, therefore, a strong catalyst that can support as well as arrest reform.

The willingness of the decision-makers emerged as another interesting factor that can push for reform. Apart from the very prominent existence of authoritarian elements within the supposedly transitioned intelligence services, the relationship between the latter and the decision-makers of each country repeatedly came up as a factor that facilitated or obstructed intelligence democratization. This factor, however, can be linked to authoritarian legacies. As Florina Cristiana Matei and Thomas Bruneau argue, due to nondemocratic legacies intelligence gets "politicized, as politicians use them to deter and remove potential political adversaries."[2] We shared several examples where this happened, both in Greece and Spain. At times, though, despite the secretive nature of intelligence, decision-makers can make a difference and push for reform if they are willing. Matei and Bruneau bring up the examples of Brazil and Romania. They claim that "lack of experience, limited knowledge on intelligence, and the secretive nature of bureaucratic intelligence agencies, did not ultimately discourage decision-makers in Brazil and Romania from embarking upon reforming the new intelligence services."[3] Earlier on, we saw Karamanlis being eager to drive reform with a few interesting legal rules on terrorism being put in place. This was irrespective of the fact that PASOK, which came to power after Karamanlis, revised and removed them. Therefore, it is not always the intelligence services that act as barriers to reform. Indeed, the relationship between producers and consumers of intelligence is equally important. Policymakers should be willing to educate themselves about what intelligence is and how to use it based on democratic principles, while intelligence services should try to be open and transparent as well as willing to work with the former.

Critical junctures have operated as a key spark for reform. Another key element that came up in the analysis as supporting institutional change across all three cases was critical junctures.[4] These included the 9/11 and 11M attacks, shocks that resulted in several reforms, particularly in Spain, which experienced attacks on its own soil. These reforms positively affected the control and oversight structure, recruitment, collection, and targeting in Spain. Although some authoritarian elements remain, Spain has made great progress in the intelligence sphere after those critical junctures took place. Portugal adapted quickly to the new environment and the emergence of new threats with no real impediments due to authoritarian legacies because those had been uprooted early on. On the other hand, although Greece made a few positive steps, it failed to achieve substantial progress. Indeed, authoritarian legacies persist to this day despite those key events that pushed for reform in Spain. More discussion, therefore, is needed to explore whether critical junctures can "overrule" authoritarian elements or if their uprooting is necessary so that when key events occur, the adaptation to the new status quo is smoother, as we saw happening in Portugal.

From the above, it becomes clear that the intelligence democratization levels in Portugal, Greece, and Spain are different mainly because authoritarian legacies obstructed reform in Greece and Spain. Portugal managed to uproot those legacies early on, which resulted in a robust control and oversight system, an intelligence service that targeted real, relevant threats, a fair recruitment process, and an intelligence culture open to civil society. The authoritarian legacies as a factor that consistently impeded change, although absolutely key, should not take away from other factors that supported (or obstructed) reform. These included civil society itself, the willingness of policymakers, and the importance of critical junctures, which usually are paired with the emergence of new threats. We touched upon those in the indicator-focused chapters.

Today, as authoritarianism resurges in countries around the globe, it is more important than ever to track the policies of such regimes and push back against those that violate basic human rights. The international community and democratic governments can play a vital role in ensuring that steps toward democratization continues in government institutions, including intelligence services. SSR indicators, including a push for lustration and different forms of oversight, including informal oversight such as by the media, can help keep these resurging authoritarian actors in check and avoid their consolidation.

This book has broken new ground as it looked at three understudied cases outside the Anglosphere through the SSR framework and in a comparative way. The analysis showed that the SSR framework, although traditionally criticized for its applicability in the intelligence domain, can be used as a measurement that demonstrates the different levels of intelligence democratization. It is hoped that this book will act as an inspiration for other authors to pursue applying the SSR framework to other intelligence democratization case studies. Authoritarian legacies along with other catalysts came up as factors that can arrest or foster reform. The application of a robust lustration process aided Portugal to start from scratch without any authoritarian remnants within its intelligence services. Although lustration has historically been an understudied and disregarded area within the intelligence spectrum, this analysis showed that there is a correlation between intelligence democratization and lustration. To this end, lustration is perhaps an area for which more research is needed, and it is encouraged by this author. Finally, the media has acted as a key factor that can aid reform. Indeed, along with lustration, the importance of the media within intelligence democratization and the SSR framework is another area that begs for further research.

NOTES

1. Huntington, *Third Wave.*
2. Matei and Bruneau, "Intelligence Reform in New Democracies," 616.
3. Matei and Bruneau, 616.
4. Estevez, "Intelligence Community Reforms."

SELECTED BIBLIOGRAPHY

PRIMARY SOURCES

Agencia Estatal Boletín Oficial del Estado [Official Government Bulletin]. https://www .boe.es/.

Centro Nacional de Inteligencia [National Intelligence Centre]. https://www.cni.es/.

Conselho de Fiscalização do Sistema de Informações da República Portuguesa [Council for the Oversight of the Intelligence System of the Portuguese Republic]. https:// cfsirp.pt/.

Constitution of Greece. http://www.hri.org/docs/syntagma/artcl25.html#A6.

Diário da República. https://dre.pt/dre/home.

Greek Parliament. Official website. https://www.hellenicparliament.gr/.

National Intelligence Centre. http://www.cni.es.

National Intelligence Service. "History: A Brief Chronicle of the Greek Intelligence Services before EYP." www.nis.gr/portal/page/portal/NIS/History/BeforeEYP.

Portuguese Parliament. Official website. https://www.parlamento.pt/.

Procuradoria-Geral Distrital Lisboa [District Attorney General's Office Lisbon]. https:// www.pgdlisboa.pt/leis/lei_mostra_articulado.php?nid=764&tabela=leis.

Serviço de Informações de Segurança [Security Information Service]. Official website. https://www.sis.pt.

Serviço de Informações Estratégicas de Defesa [Strategic Defence Information Service]. Official website. https://www.sied.pt.

Sistema de Informações da República Portuguesa [Information System of the Portuguese Republic]. "Historia." www.sirp.pt/quem-somos/historia.

SECONDARY SOURCES

Born, Hans, and Marina Caparini, eds. *Democratic Control of Intelligence Services: Containing Rogue Elephants.* Abingdon, UK: Routledge, 2007.

Born, Hans, and Ian Leigh. *Making Intelligence Accountable: Legal Standards and Best Practice for Oversight of Intelligence Agencies.* DCAF Handbook Series. Oslo: Publishing House of the Parliament of Norway, 2005.

Bruneau, Thomas C., and Steven C. Boraz, eds. *Reforming Intelligence: Obstacles to Democratic Control and Effectiveness.* Austin: University of Texas Press, 2011.

Caparini, Marina. "Controlling and Overseeing Intelligence Services in Democratic States." In Born and Caparini, eds., *Democratic Control of Intelligence Services,* 3–24. Abingdon, UK: Routledge, 2007.

Cercas, Javier. *The Anatomy of a Moment*. London: Bloomsbury, 2011.

Costa Pinto, António. "Authoritarian Legacies, Transitional Justice and State Crisis in Portugal's Democratization." *Democratization* 13, no. 2 (2006): 173–204.

———. "Coping with the Double Legacy of Authoritarianism and Revolution in Portuguese Democracy." *South European Society and Politics* 15, no. 3 (2010): 395–412.

Costa Pinto, António, and Leonardo Morlino, eds. *Dealing with the Legacy of Authoritarianism: The "Politics of the Past" in Southern European Democracies*. Abingdon, UK: Routledge, 2013.

Díaz Fernández, Antonio M. "Halfway Down the Road to Supervision of the Spanish Intelligence Services." *Intelligence and National Security* 21, no. 3 (2006): 440–56.

———. *Los servicios de intelligencia españoles: De la guerra civil hasta el 11-M* [The Spanish intelligence services: From the civil war to 11-M]. Madrid: Alianzia Editorial, 2006.

Fitsanakis, Joseph. *Ethniki asfalia ke sighrones ipiresies kataskopias stin Ellada* [National security and modern intelligence services in Greece]. Athens: Potamos, 2015.

Gallagher, Tom. "Controlled Repression in Salazar's Portugal." *Journal of Contemporary History* 14, no. 3 (1979): 385–402.

Gill, Peter. *Intelligence Governance and Democratisation: A Comparative Analysis of the Limits of Reform*. Abingdon, UK: Routledge, 2016.

Gill, Peter, and Michael Andregg, eds. *Democratization of Intelligence*. Abingdon, UK: Routledge, 2017.

Gill, Peter, and Mark Phythian. *Intelligence in an Insecure World*. Cambridge: Polity, 2006.

Leigh, Ian. "National Courts and International Intelligence Cooperation." In *International Intelligence Cooperation and Accountability*, edited by Hans Born, Ian Leigh, and Aidan Wills, 231–51, Abingdon, UK: Routledge, 2011.

Letki, Natalia. "Lustration and Democratisation in East-Central Europe." *Europe-Asia Studies* 54, no. 4 (2002): 529–52.

Linz, Juan J., and Alfred Stepan. *Problems of Democratic Transition and Consolidation: Southern Europe, South America, and Post-Communist Europe*. Baltimore: Johns Hopkins University Press, 1998.

Matei, Florina Cristiana, and Thomas Bruneau. "Intelligence Reform in New Democracies: Factors Supporting or Arresting Progress." *Democratization* 18, no. 3 (2011): 602–30.

Matei, Florina Cristiana, and Andrés de Castro García. "Transitional Justice and Intelligence Democratization." *International Journal of Intelligence and CounterIntelligence* 32, no. 4 (2019): 717–36.

Matei, Florina Cristiana, Andrés de Castro García, and Carolyn C. Halladay. "On Balance: Intelligence Democratization in Post-Franco Spain." *International Journal of Intelligence and CounterIntelligence* 31, no. 4 (2018): 769–804.

Pinto Arena, Maria do Céu. "Portugal's Intelligence Evolution in the Post-9/11 World." *International Journal of Intelligence and CounterIntelligence* 25, no. 1 (2012): 160–77.

Reinares, Fernando. "After the Madrid Bombings: Internal Security Reforms and Prevention of Global Terrorism in Spain." *Studies in Conflict and Terrorism* 32, no. 5 (2009): 367–88.

Schreier, Fred. "The Need for Efficient and Legitimate Intelligence." In Born and Caparini, eds., *Democratic Control of Intelligence Services*, 25–46.

Wheeler, Douglas L. "In the Service of Order: The Portuguese Political Police and the British, German and Spanish Intelligence, 1932–1945." *Journal of Contemporary History* 18, no. 1 (1983): 1–25.

INDEX

Note: Figures and tables are indicated by page number in *italics.*

ABOUT THE AUTHOR

SOFIA TZAMARELOU is a senior consultant for the media measurement industry at Commetric in London. Throughout her career in the research and analysis sectors, she has worked as an analyst, senior manager, and director. She holds a doctorate in intelligence studies from Brunel University and master's degrees in intelligence studies and security studies from Brunel University and Aberystwyth University, respectively. Dr. Tzamarelou leads workshops that focus on data analysis, including data storytelling and how to mitigate cognitive bias. Her profile can be found at https://www.linkedin.com/in/sofia-tzamarelou-phd/.